You're Reading the
WRONG WAY!

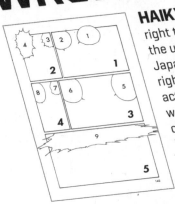

HAIKYU!! reads from right to left, starting in the upper-right corner. Japanese is read from right to left, meaning that action, sound effects and word-balloon order are completely reversed from English order.

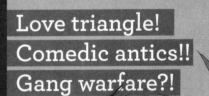

Thank you for picking up *Haikyu!!* volume 36! By the way, did you know that there are *Haikyu!! kokeshi* dolls? The picture to the right is of some of those dolls made into acrylic stands. I spotted them in Sendai and just had to buy them. Tanaka looks way too good as a kokeshi doll. Is his Ultimate Form a kokeshi doll?!

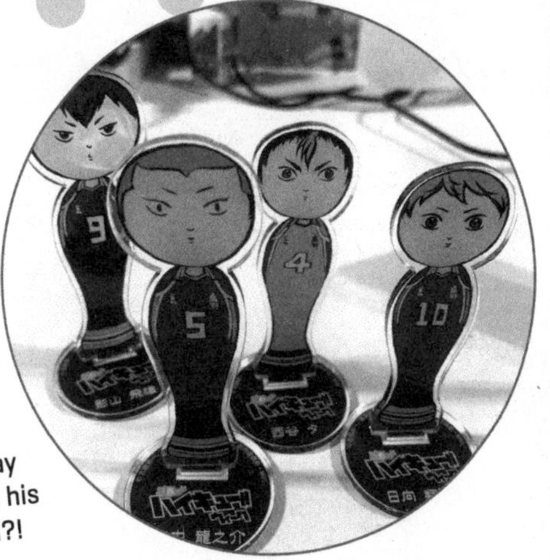
9
5
4
10
龍之介

HARUICHI FURUDATE began his manga career when he was 25 years old with the one-shot *Ousama Kid* [King Kid], which won an honorable mention for the 14th Jump Treasure Newcomer Manga Prize. His first series, *Kiben Gakuha, Yotsuya Sensei no Kaidan* [Philosophy School, Yotsuya Sensei's Ghost Stories], was serialized in *Weekly Shonen Jump* in 2010. In 2012, he began serializing *Haikyu!!* in *Weekly Shonen Jump*, where it became his most popular work to date.

HAIKYU!!

VOLUME 36
SHONEN JUMP Manga Edition

Story and Art by
HARUICHI FURUDATE

Translation **1** **ADRIENNE BECK**
Touch-Up Art & Lettering **2** **ERIKA TERRIQUEZ**
Design **3** **JULIAN [JR] ROBINSON**
Editor **4** **MARLENE FIRST**

HAIKYU!! © 2012 by Haruichi Furudate
All rights reserved.
First published in Japan in 2012 by SHUEISHA Inc., Tokyo.
English translation rights arranged by SHUEISHA Inc.

The stories, characters and incidents mentioned
in this publication are entirely fictional.

Printed in the U.S.A.

Published by VIZ Media, LLC
P.O. Box 77010
San Francisco, CA 94107

10 9 8 7 6 5 4 3 2 1
First printing, January 2020

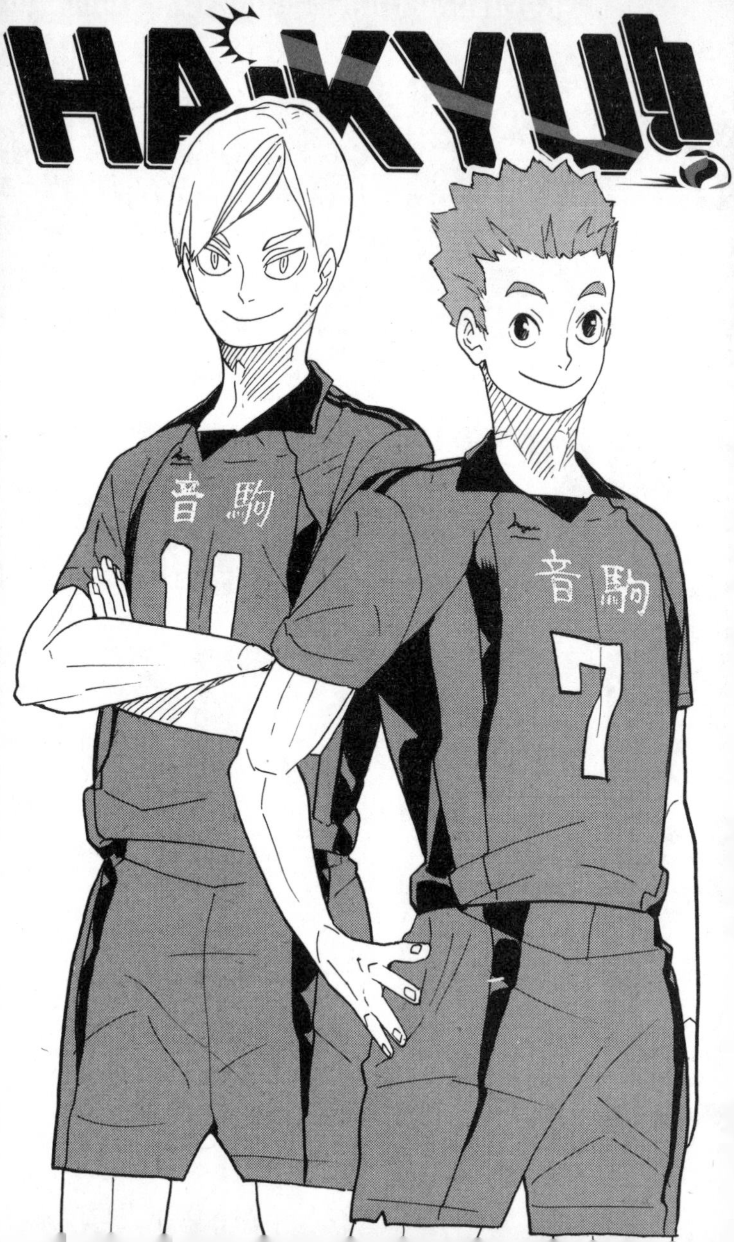
HAIKYU!!
音駒
11
音駒
7

Karasuno High School Volleyball Club

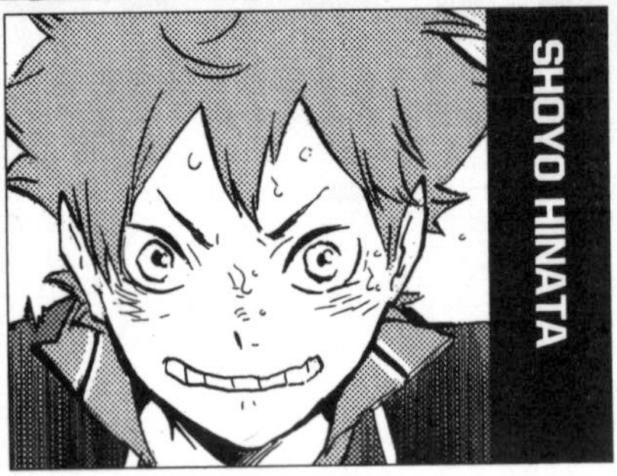
SHOYO HINATA

1ST YEAR / MIDDLE BLOCKER
Even though he doesn't have the best body type for volleyball, he is super athletic. Gets nervous easily.

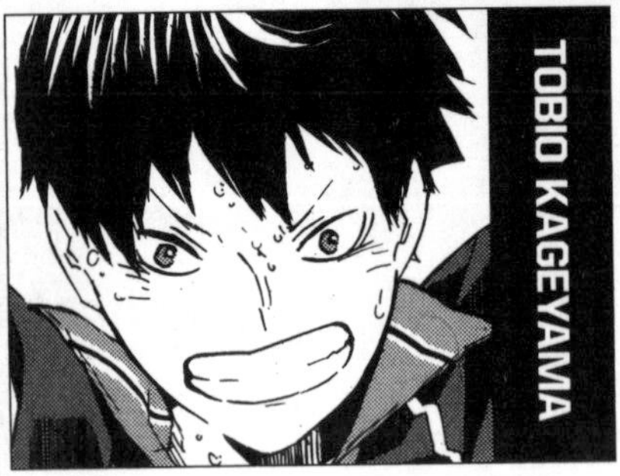
TOBIO KAGEYAMA

1ST YEAR / SETTER
His instincts and athletic talent are so good that he's like a "king" who rules the court. Demanding and egocentric.

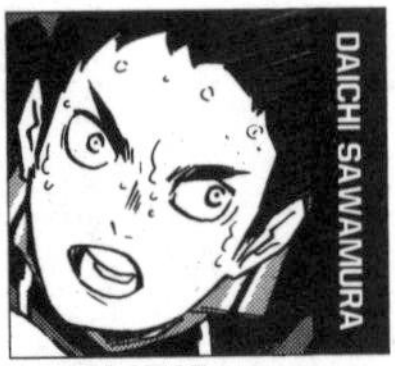
DAICHI SAWAMURA

3RD YEAR (CAPTAIN)
WING SPIKER

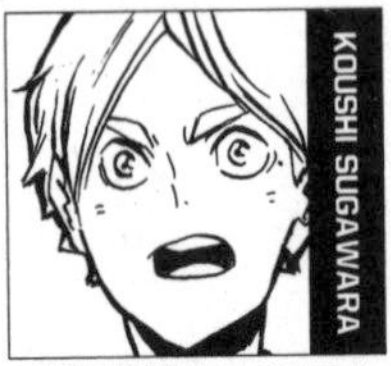
KOUSHI SUGAWARA

3RD YEAR (VICE CAPTAIN)
SETTER

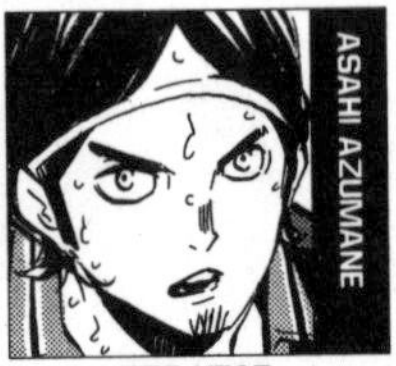
ASAHI AZUMANE

3RD YEAR
WING SPIKER

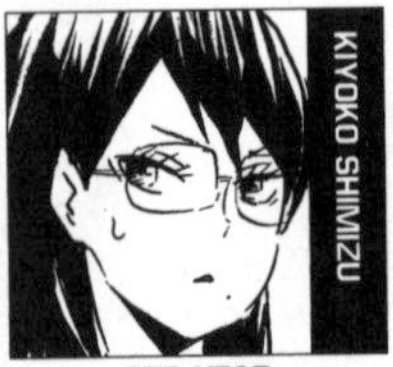
KIYOKO SHIMIZU

3RD YEAR
MANAGER

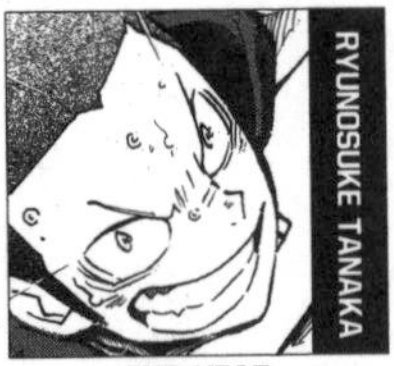
RYUNOSUKE TANAKA

2ND YEAR
WING SPIKER

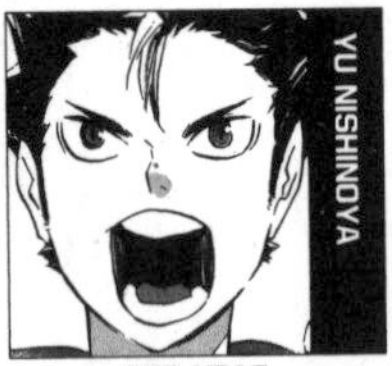
YU NISHINOYA

2ND YEAR
LIBERO

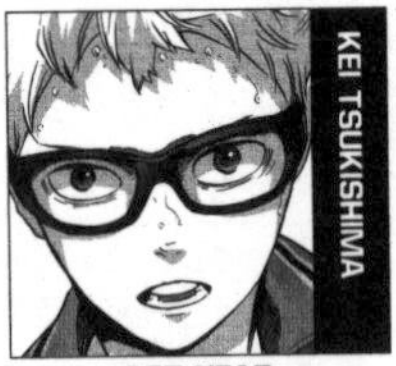
KEI TSUKISHIMA

1ST YEAR
MIDDLE BLOCKER

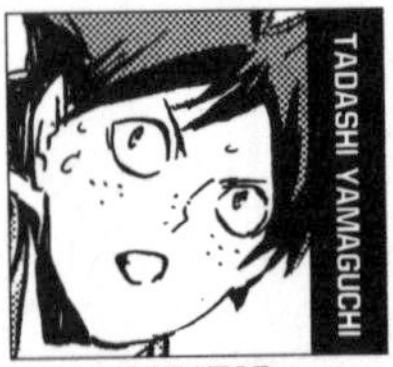
TADASHI YAMAGUCHI

1ST YEAR
MIDDLE BLOCKER

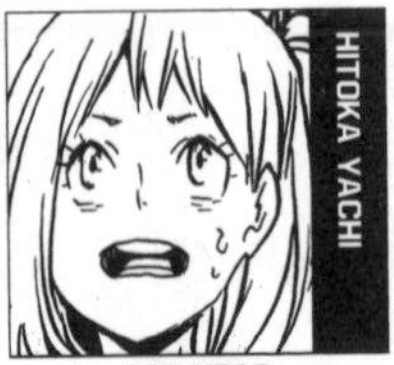
HITOKA YACHI

1ST YEAR
MANAGER

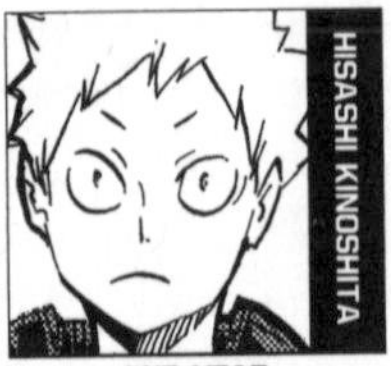
HISASHI KINOSHITA

2ND YEAR
WING SPIKER

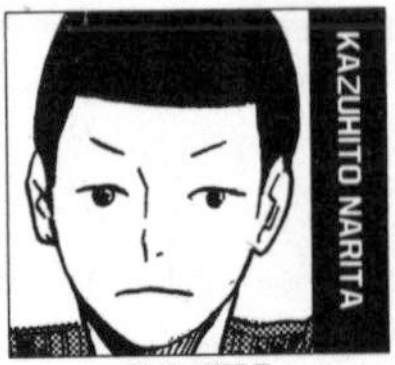
KAZUHITO NARITA

2ND YEAR
MIDDLE BLOCKER

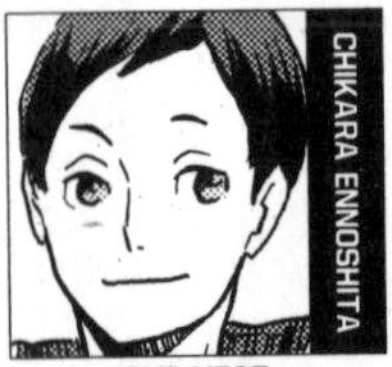
CHIKARA ENNOSHITA

2ND YEAR
WING SPIKER

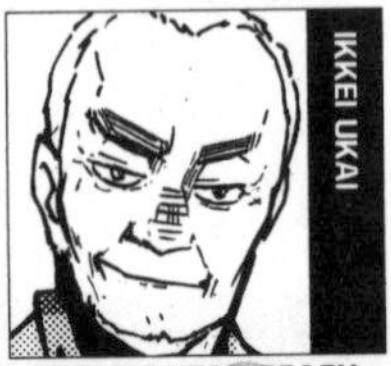
IKKEI UKAI

FORMER HEAD COACH

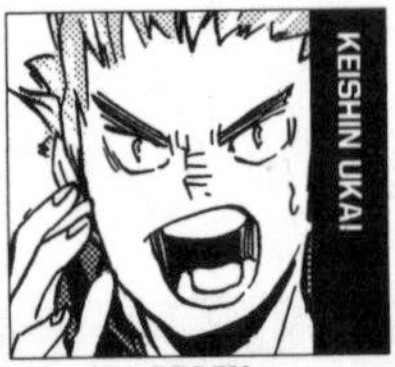
KEISHIN UKAI

COACH

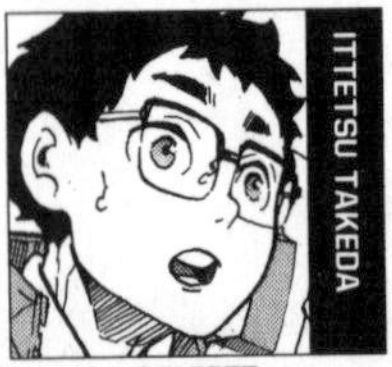
ITTETSU TAKEDA

ADVISER

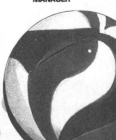

CHARACTERS

NATIONAL SPRING TOURNAMENT ARC

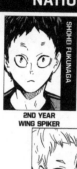

Nekoma Team

SHOHEI FUKUNAGA
TAKETORA YAMAMOTO
NOBUYUKI KAI
TETSURO KUROO

2ND YEAR WING SPIKER

2ND YEAR WING SPIKER

3RD YEAR (VICE CAPTAIN) WING SPIKER

3RD YEAR (CAPTAIN) MIDDLE BLOCKER

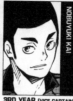

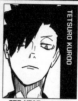

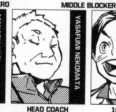

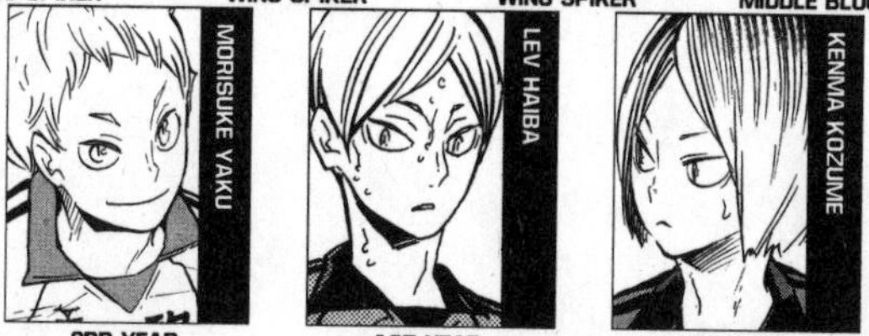

MORISUKE YAKU
LEV HAIBA
KENMA KOZUME

3RD YEAR LIBERO

1ST YEAR MIDDLE BLOCKER

2ND YEAR SETTER

MANABU NAOI
YASAFUMI NEKOMATA
YUKI SHIBAYAMA
SOU INUOKA

COACH

HEAD COACH

1ST YEAR LIBERO

1ST YEAR MIDDLE BLOCKER

Fukurodani Academy Volleyball Club

KEIJI AKAASHI
KOTARO BOKUTO

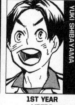

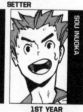

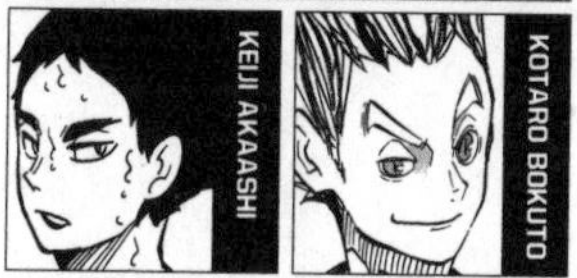

2ND YEAR SETTER

3RD YEAR (CAPTAIN) WING SPIKER

Nohebi Academy Volleyball Club

MIKA YAMAKA
SUGURU DAISHO

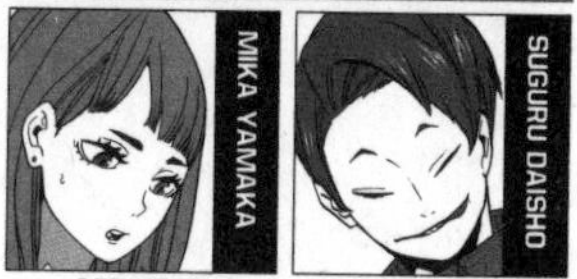

1ST YEAR LIBERO

3RD YEAR (CAPTAIN) WING SPIKER

Ever since he saw the legendary player known as "the Little Giant" compete at the national volleyball finals, Shoyo Hinata has been aiming to be the best volleyball player ever! He decides to join the volleyball club at his middle school and gets to play in an official tournament during his third year. His team is crushed by a team led by volleyball prodigy Tobio Kageyama, also known as "the King of the Court." Swearing revenge on Kageyama, Hinata graduates middle school and enters Karasuno High School, the school where the Little Giant played. However, upon joining the club, he finds out that Kageyama is there too! The two of them bicker constantly, but they bring out the best in each other's talents and become a powerful combo. It's day 3 of the Spring Tournament, and the Dumpster Battle is in full swing! Nekoma has taken set 1, and the battle for set 2 is turning into a grueling endurance test of long rallies. Karasuno manages to rack up some points with its serving, but Kozume's clever planning takes advantage of Karasuno's defense to effectively trap Hinata! With Hinata's approach lanes blocked, Kageyama makes a daring move to pry open a path for him, sending the ball high up in an arcing four set! Hinata sees the ball, and his eyes shine as he gives the ground a hard push...

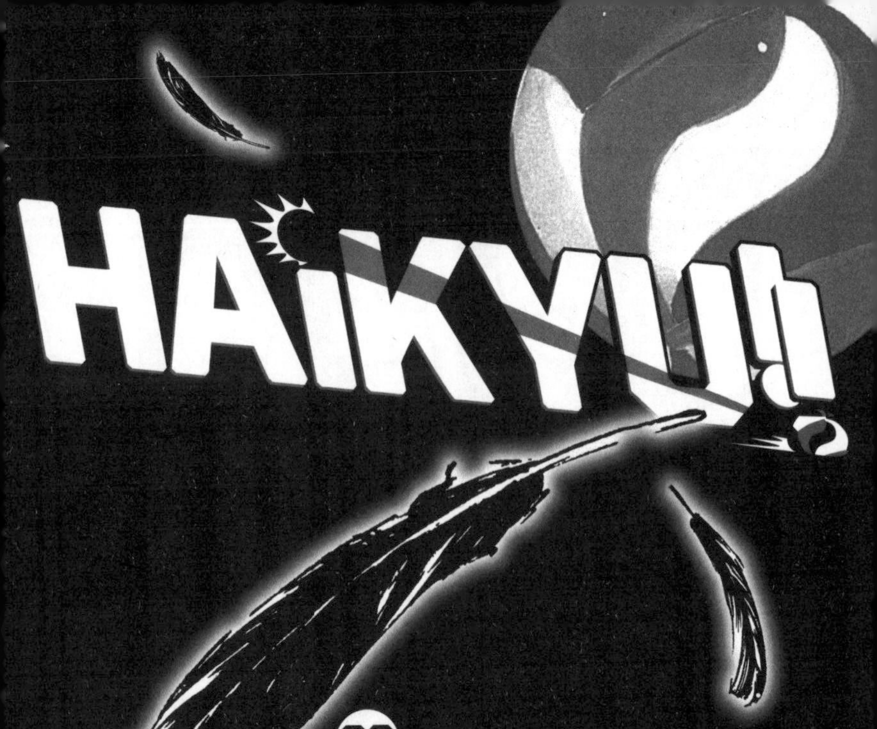

HAIKYU!!

36 I WIN

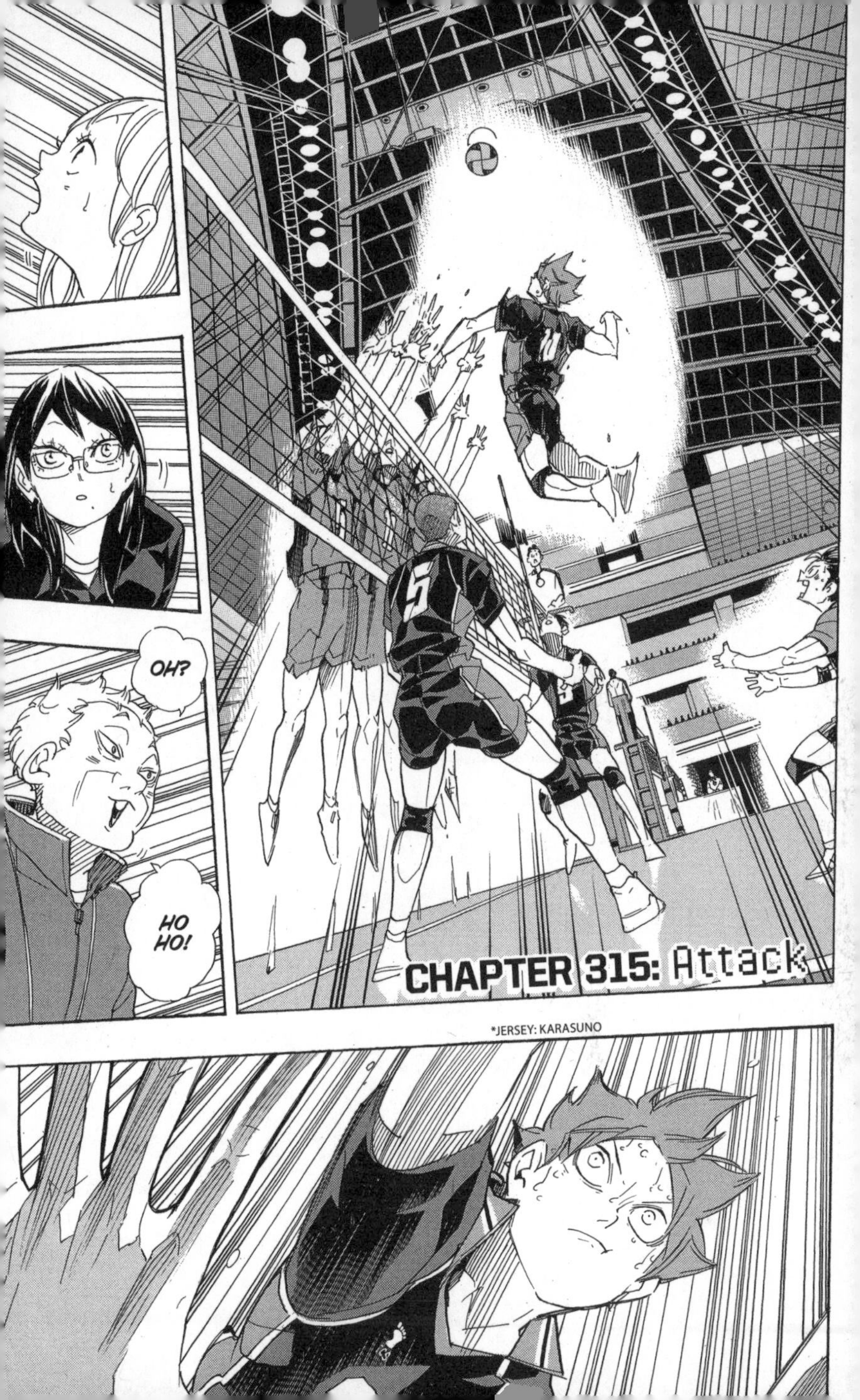
CHAPTER 315: Attack
OH?
HO HO!
*JERSEY: KARASUNO

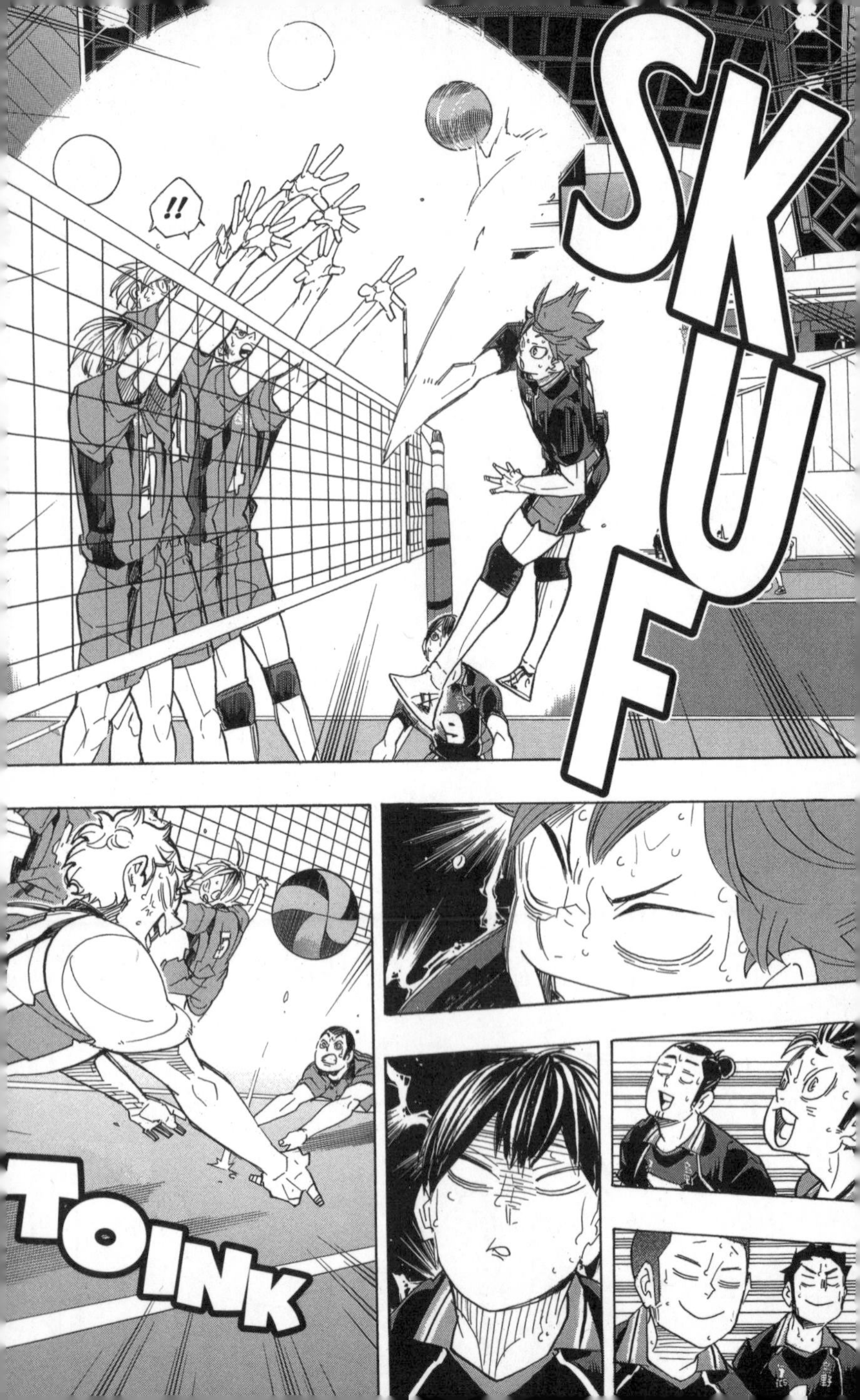
SKUUF
!!
TOINK

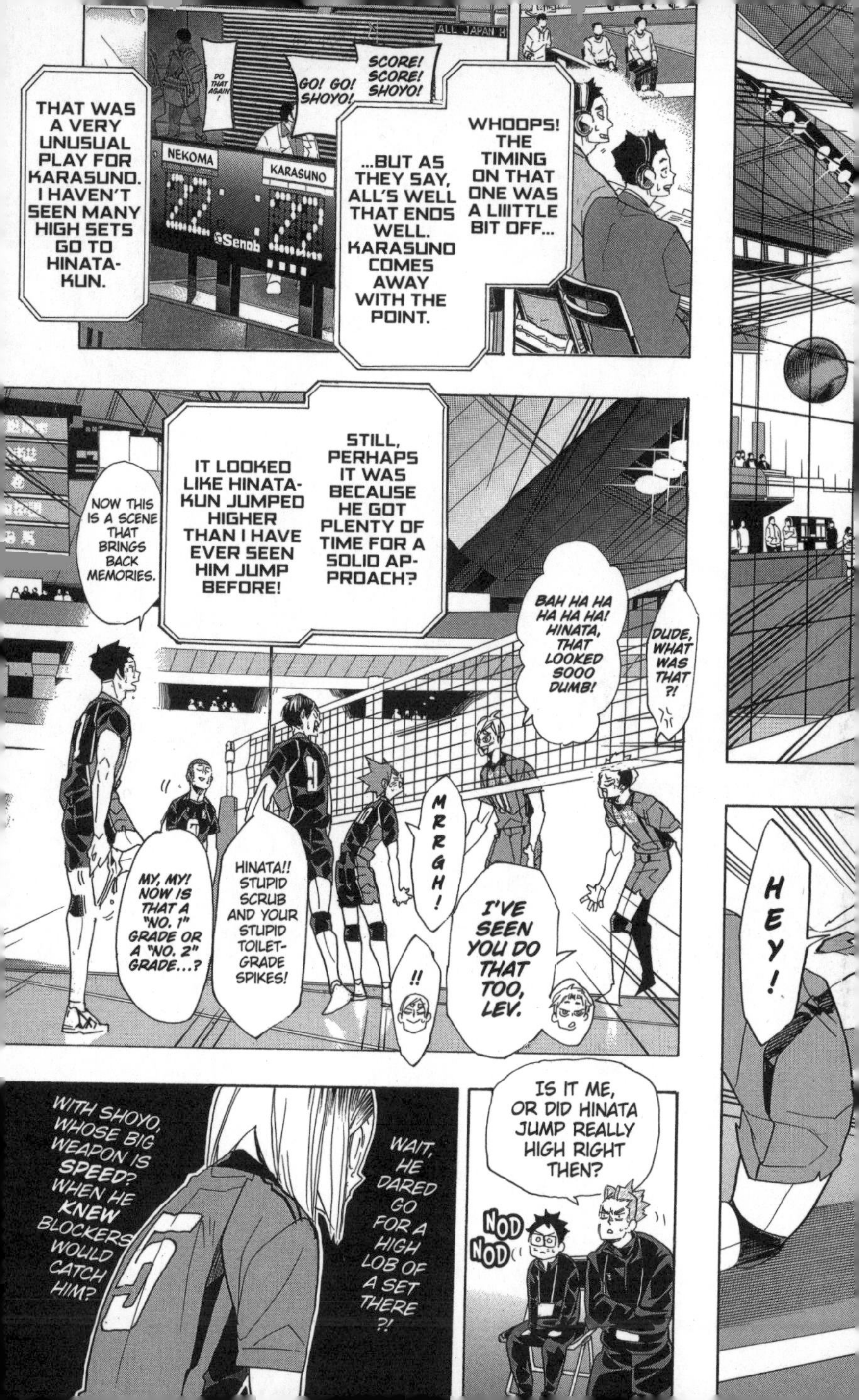
WHOOPS! THE TIMING ON THAT ONE WAS A LIIITTLE BIT OFF...
...BUT AS THEY SAY, ALL'S WELL THAT ENDS WELL. KARASUNO COMES AWAY WITH THE POINT.
SCORE! SCORE! SHOYO!
GO! GO! SHOYO!
DO THAT AGAIN!
NEKOMA
KARASUNO
Senob
THAT WAS A VERY UNUSUAL PLAY FOR KARASUNO. I HAVEN'T SEEN MANY HIGH SETS GO TO HINATA-KUN.
STILL, PERHAPS IT WAS BECAUSE HE GOT PLENTY OF TIME FOR A SOLID AP-PROACH?
IT LOOKED LIKE HINATA-KUN JUMPED HIGHER THAN I HAVE EVER SEEN HIM JUMP BEFORE!
NOW THIS IS A SCENE THAT BRINGS BACK MEMORIES.
DUDE, WHAT WAS THAT?!
BAH HA HA HA HA HA! HINATA, THAT LOOKED SOOO DUMB!
MRRGH!
I'VE SEEN YOU DO THAT TOO, LEV.
!!
HINATA!! STUPID SCRUB AND YOUR STUPID TOILET-GRADE SPIKES!
MY, MY! NOW IS THAT A "NO. 1" GRADE OR A "NO. 2" GRADE...?
HEY!
IS IT ME, OR DID HINATA JUMP REALLY HIGH RIGHT THEN?
NOD NOD
WAIT, HE DARED GO FOR A HIGH LOB OF A SET THERE?!
WITH SHOYO, WHOSE BIG WEAPON IS SPEED? WHEN HE KNEW BLOCKERS WOULD CATCH HIM?

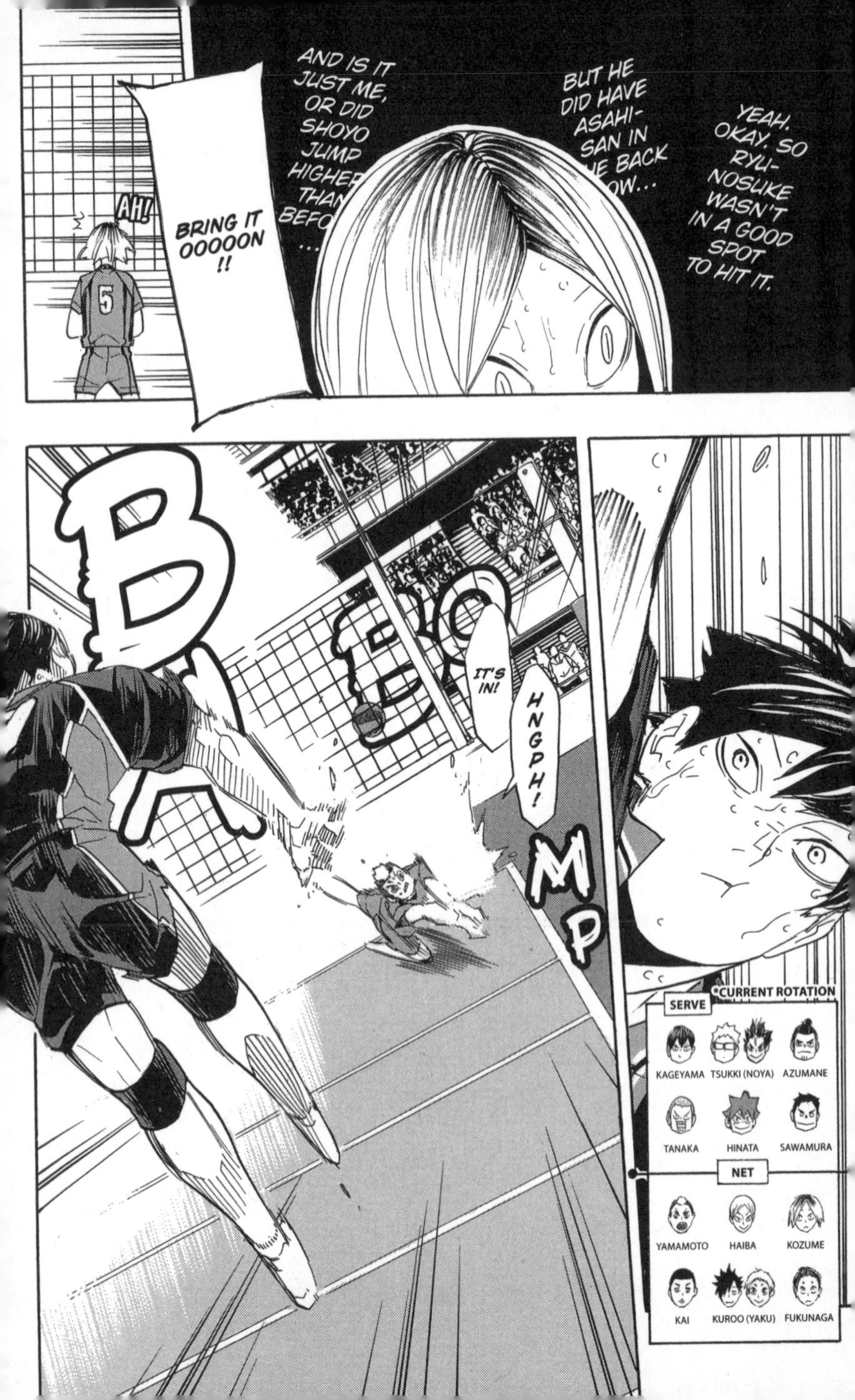

YEAH. OKAY, SO RYUNOSUKE WASN'T IN A GOOD SPOT TO HIT IT.
BUT HE DID HAVE ASAHI-SAN IN HE BACK OW...
AND IS IT JUST ME, OR DID SHOYO JUMP HIGHER THAN BEFO ...
AH!
BRING IT OOOOON!!
*CURRENT ROTATION
SERVE
KAGEYAMA
TSUKKI (NOYA)
AZUMANE
TANAKA
HINATA
SAWAMURA
NET
YAMAMOTO
HAIBA
KOZUME
KAI
KUROO (YAKU)
FUKUNAGA
BAMP
IT'S IN!
HNGPH!

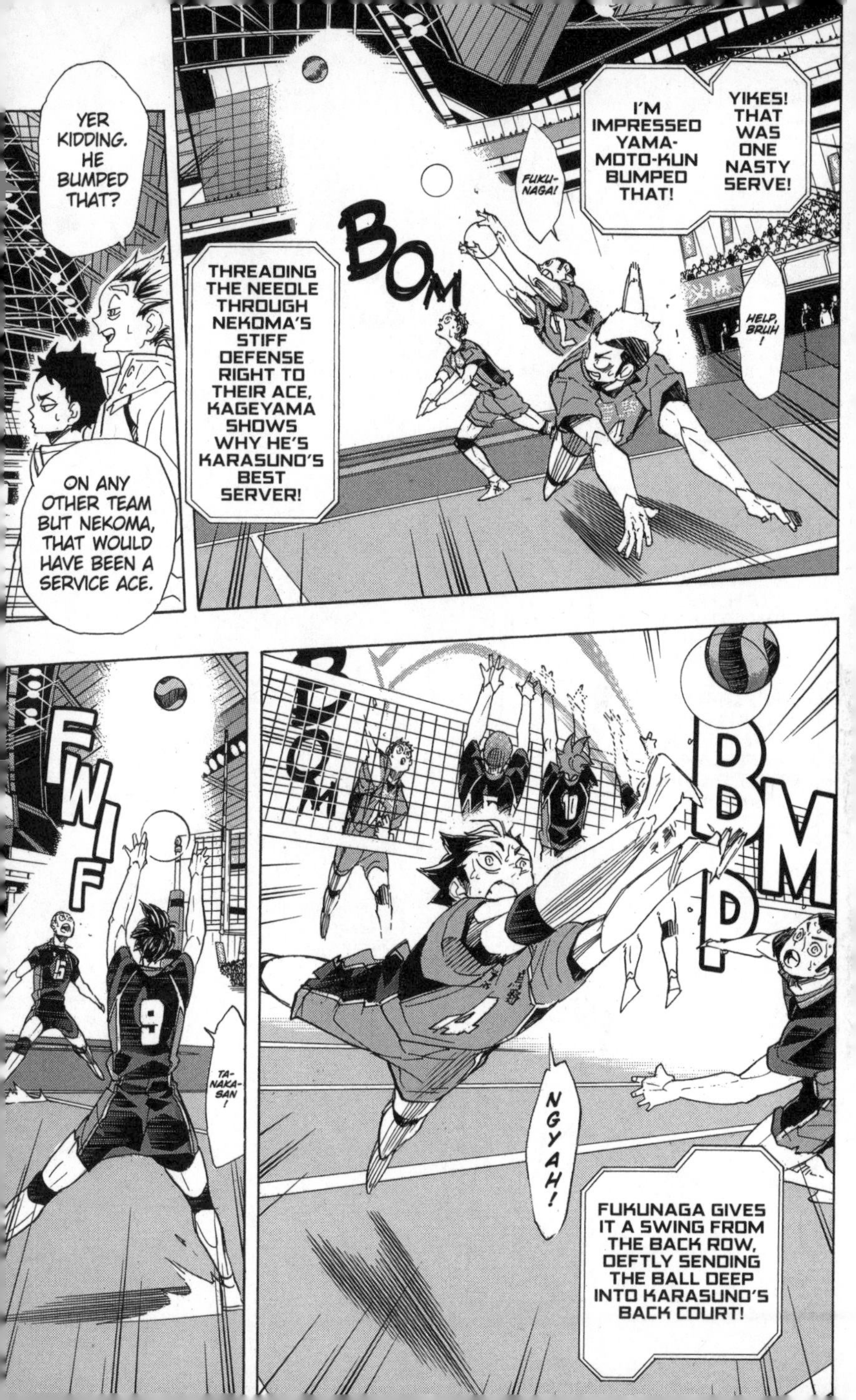
YIKES! THAT WAS ONE NASTY SERVE!
I'M IMPRESSED YAMAMOTO-KUN BUMPED THAT!
FUKUNAGA!
BOM
HELP, BRUH!
THREADING THE NEEDLE THROUGH NEKOMA'S STIFF DEFENSE RIGHT TO THEIR ACE, KAGEYAMA SHOWS WHY HE'S KARASUNO'S BEST SERVER!
YER KIDDING. HE BUMPED THAT?
ON ANY OTHER TEAM BUT NEKOMA, THAT WOULD HAVE BEEN A SERVICE ACE.
BOM
NGYAH!
FUKUNAGA GIVES IT A SWING FROM THE BACK ROW, DEFTLY SENDING THE BALL DEEP INTO KARASUNO'S BACK COURT!
FWIF
TANAKA-SAN!

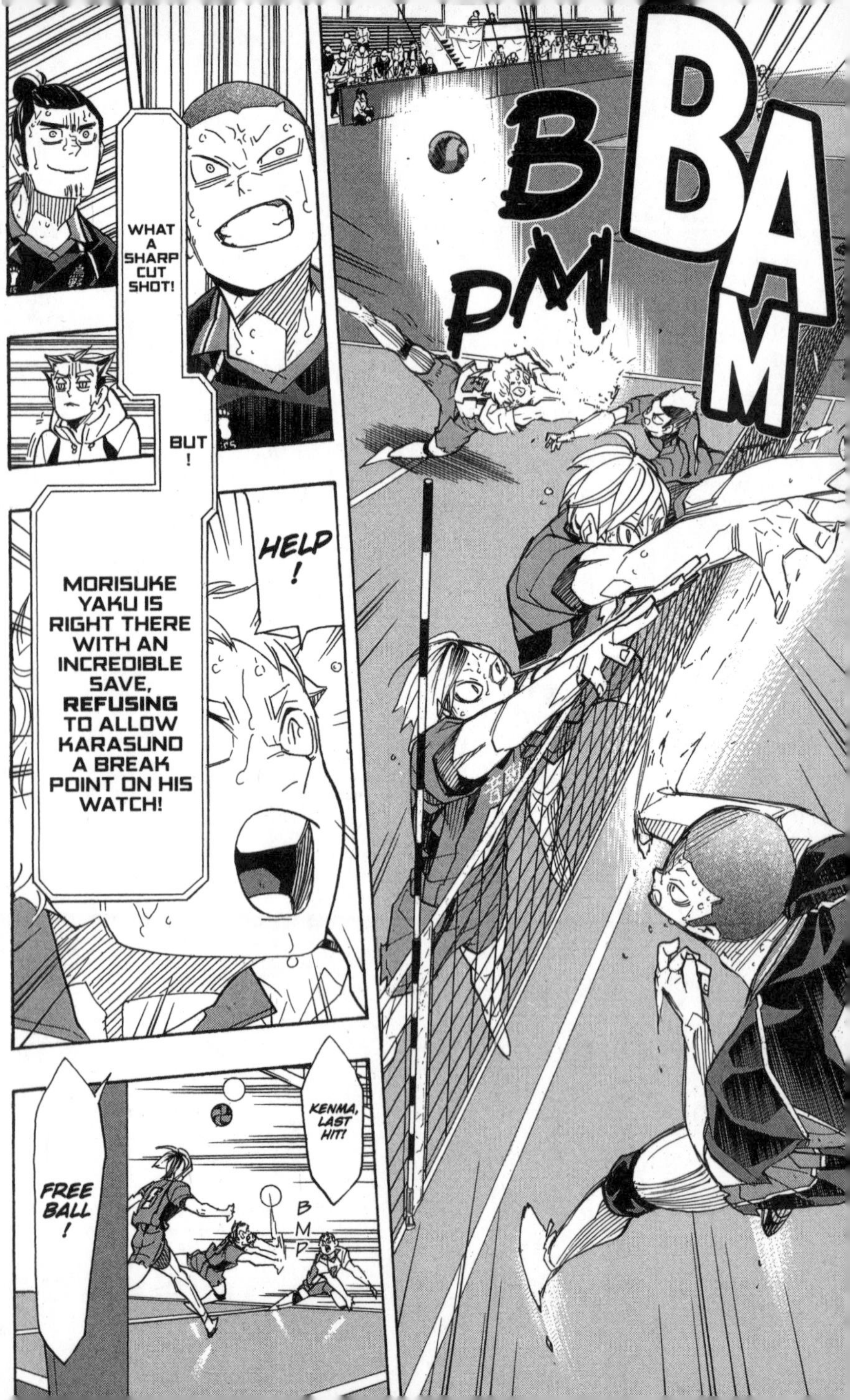
BAM
BPM
WHAT A SHARP CUT SHOT!
BUT!
MORISUKE YAKU IS RIGHT THERE WITH AN INCREDIBLE SAVE, REFUSING TO ALLOW KARASUNO A BREAK POINT ON HIS WATCH!
HELP!
KENMA, LAST HIT!
FREE BALL!
BMP

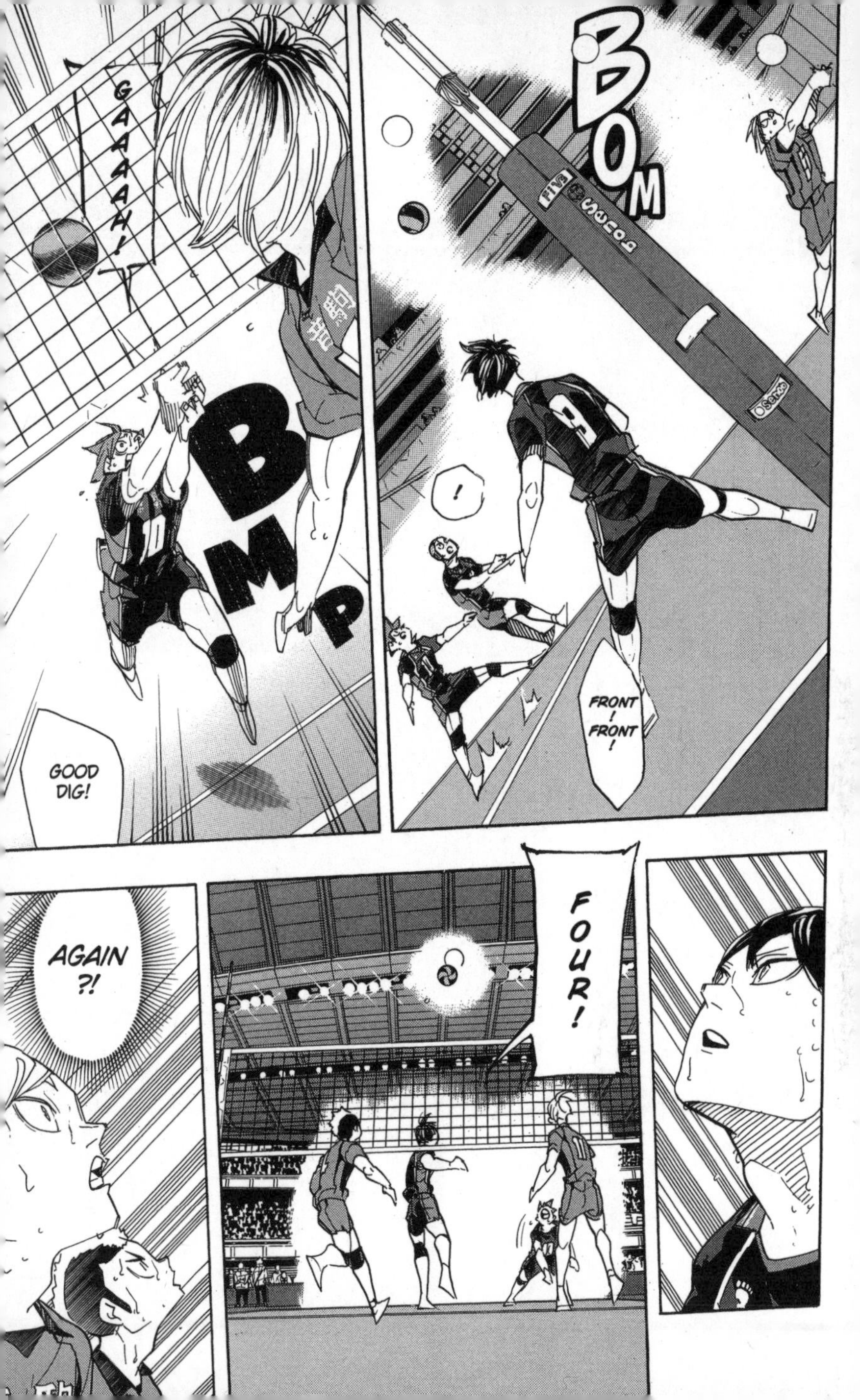

BOM
!
FRONT! FRONT!
GAAAAAH!
BMP
GOOD DIG!
FOUR!
AGAIN ?!

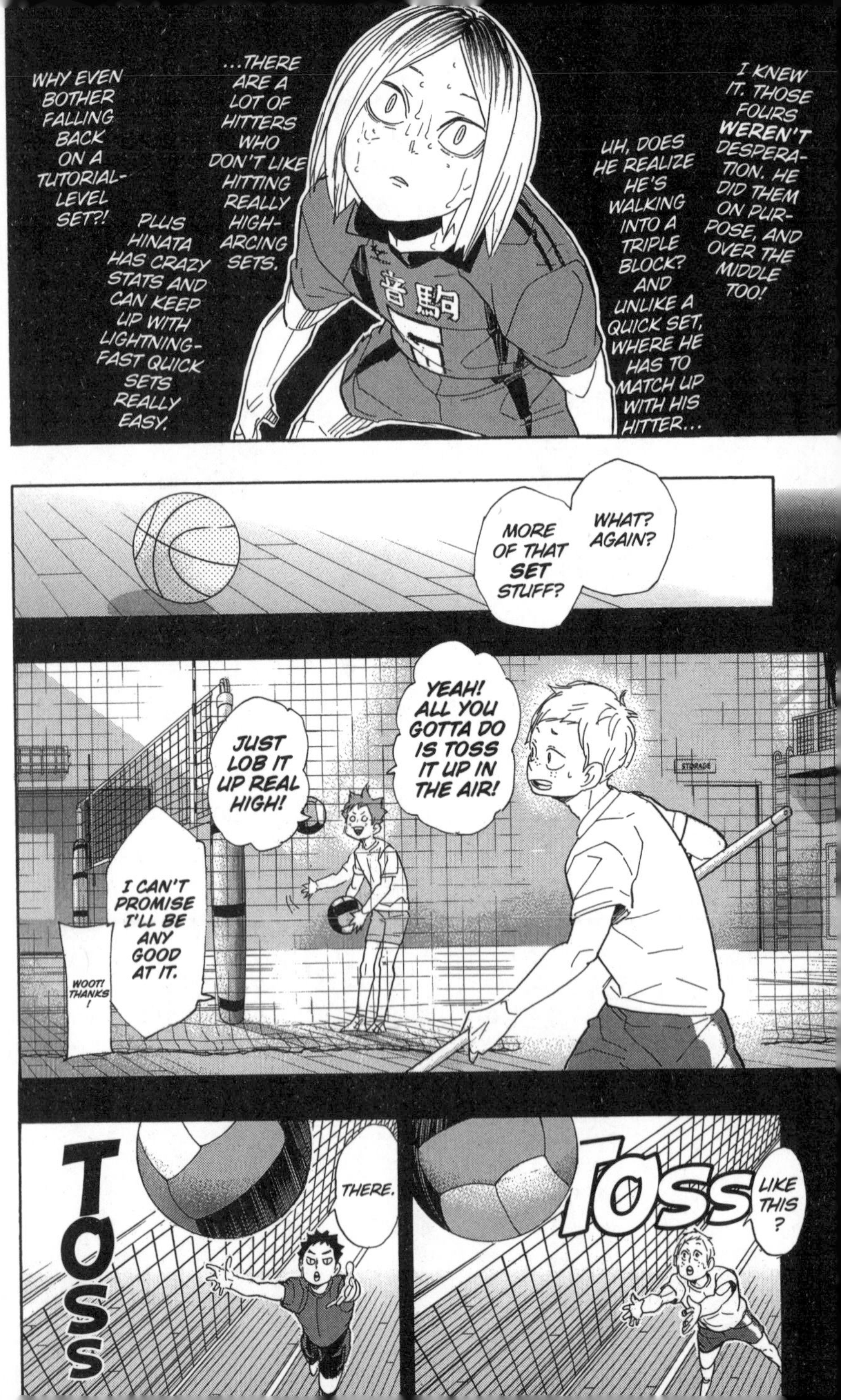
I KNEW IT. THOSE FOURS WEREN'T DESPERATION. HE DID THEM ON PURPOSE, AND OVER THE MIDDLE TOO!
UH, DOES HE REALIZE HE'S WALKING INTO A TRIPLE BLOCK? AND UNLIKE A QUICK SET, WHERE HE HAS TO MATCH UP WITH HIS HITTER...
...THERE ARE A LOT OF HITTERS WHO DON'T LIKE HITTING REALLY HIGH-ARCING SETS.
WHY EVEN BOTHER FALLING BACK ON A TUTORIAL-LEVEL SET?!
PLUS HINATA HAS CRAZY STATS AND CAN KEEP UP WITH LIGHTNING-FAST QUICK SETS REALLY EASY.
WHAT? AGAIN?
MORE OF THAT SET STUFF?
YEAH! ALL YOU GOTTA DO IS TOSS IT UP IN THE AIR!
JUST LOB IT UP REAL HIGH!
I CAN'T PROMISE I'LL BE ANY GOOD AT IT.
WOOT! THANKS!
TOSS
LIKE THIS?
TOSS
THERE.

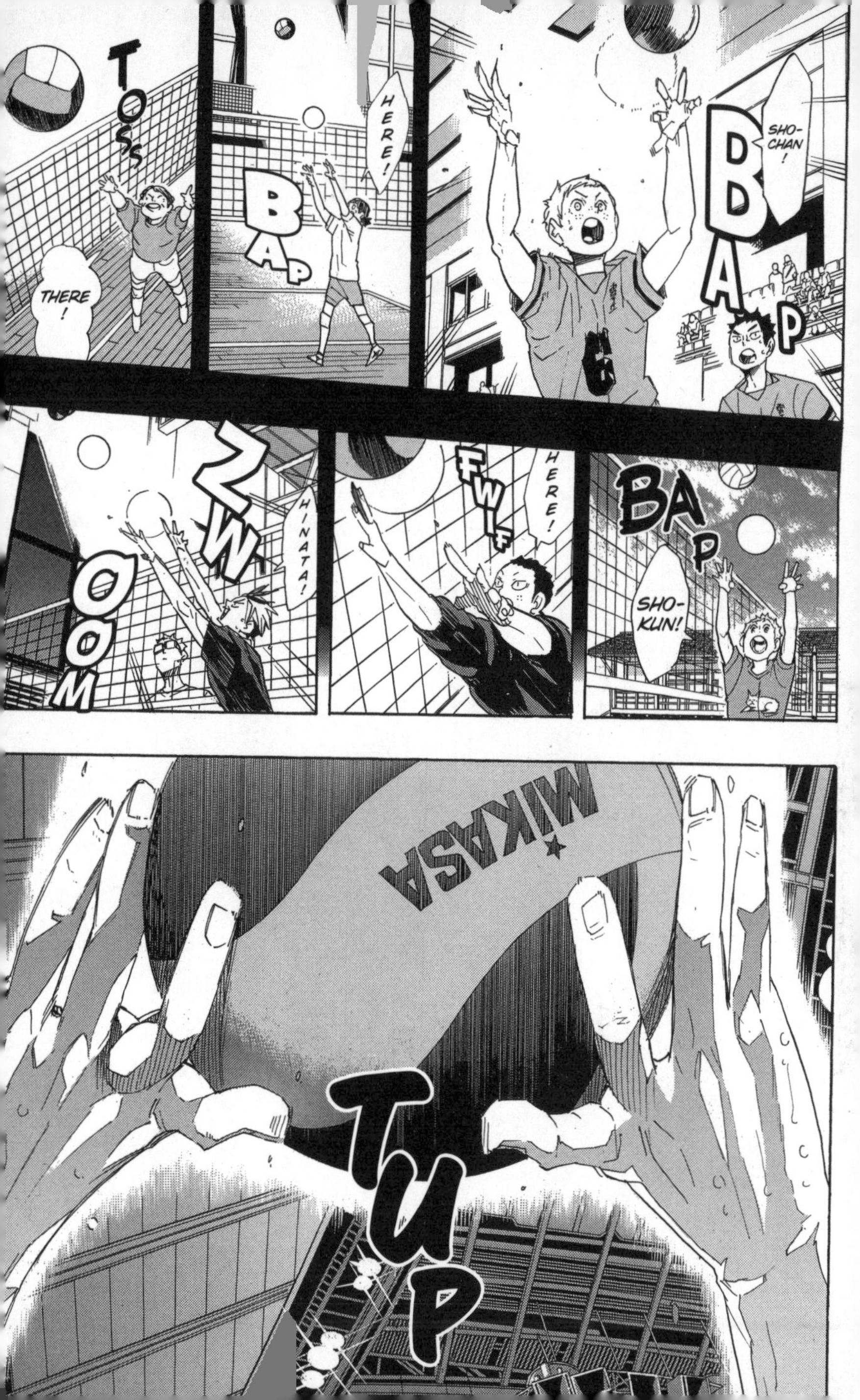
SHO-CHAN!
BAP
HERE!
BAP
TOSS
THERE!
BAP
SHO-KUN!
HERE!
FWIF
HINATA!
ZWOOM
MIKASA
TUP

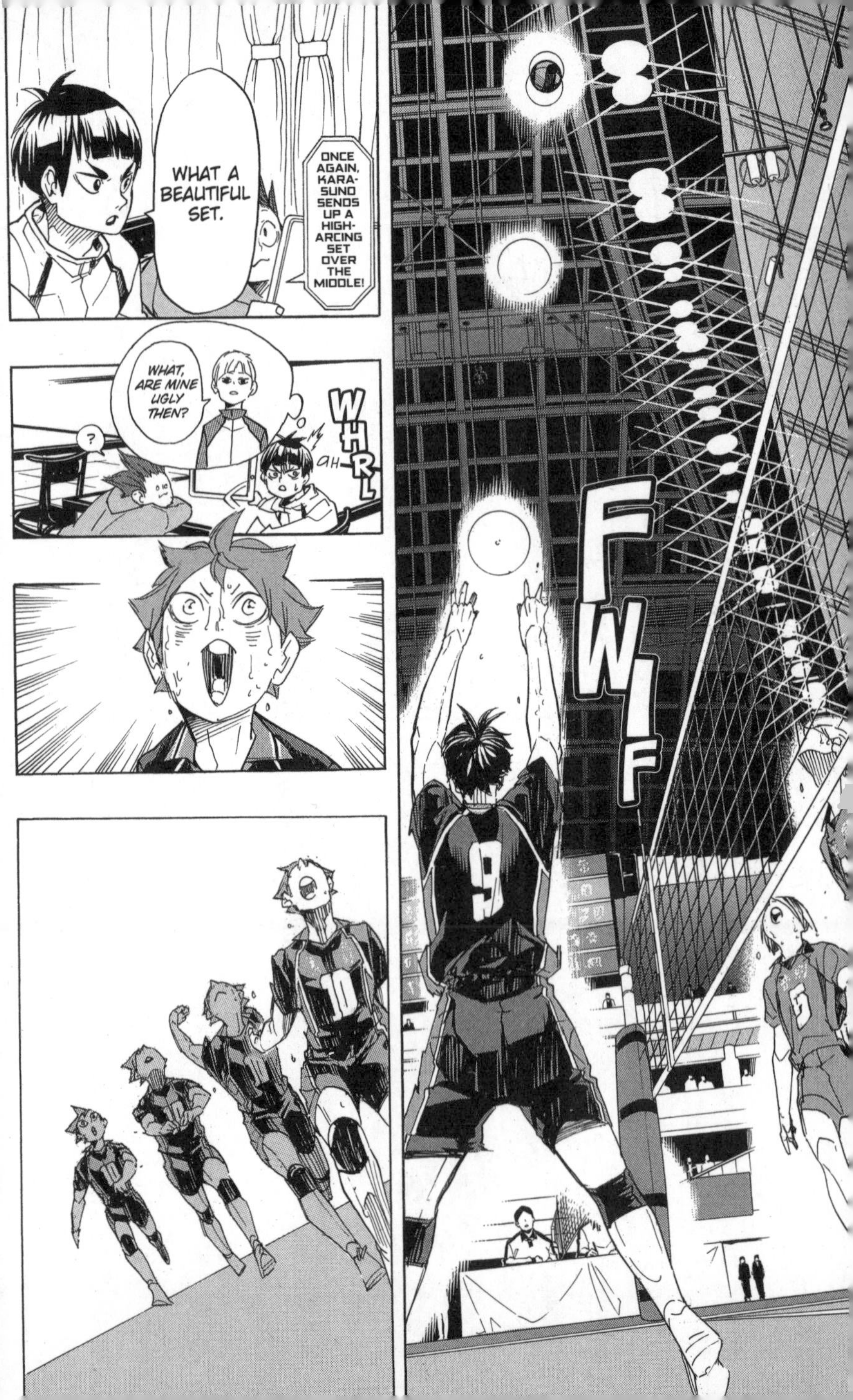
FWIF
ONCE AGAIN, KARA-SUNO SENDS UP A HIGH-ARCING SET OVER THE MIDDLE!
WHAT A BEAUTIFUL SET.
WHRL
AH-
WHAT, ARE MINE UGLY THEN?
?

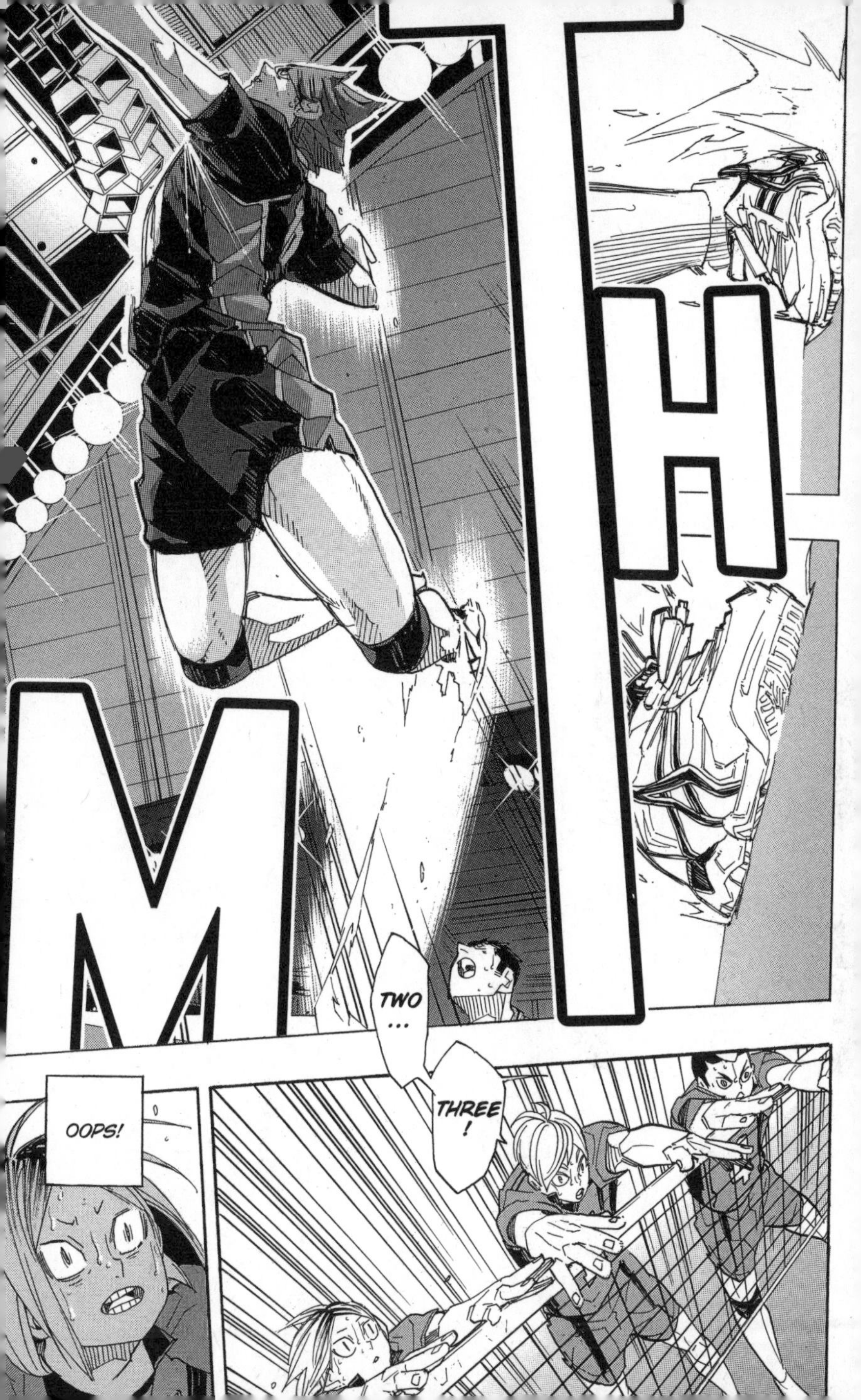

TWO ...
THREE !
OOPS!

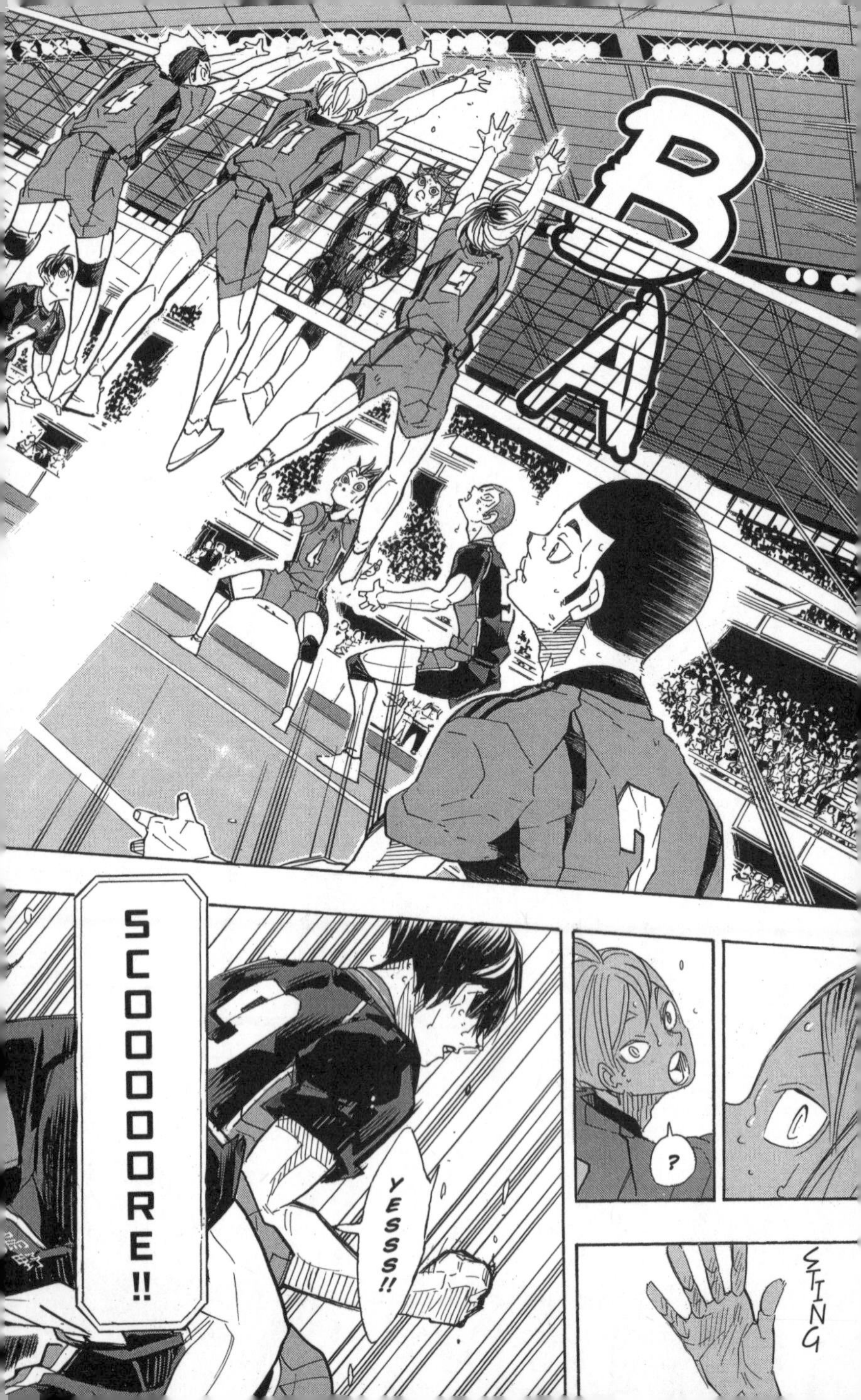
BA
?
STING
SCOOOOOOORE!!
YESSS!!

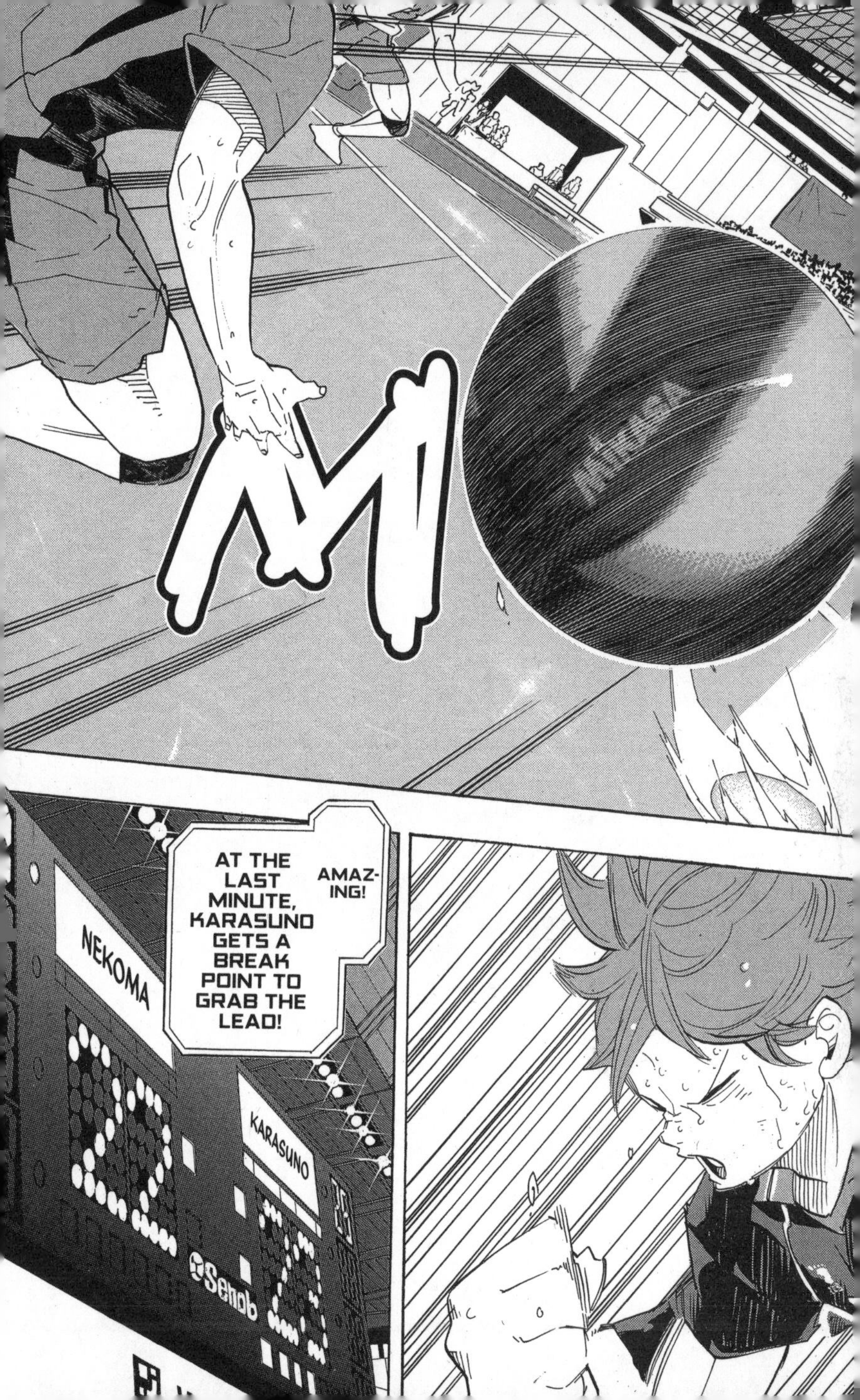
AMAZ-ING!
AT THE LAST MINUTE, KARASUNO GETS A BREAK POINT TO GRAB THE LEAD!
NEKOMA
KARASUNO

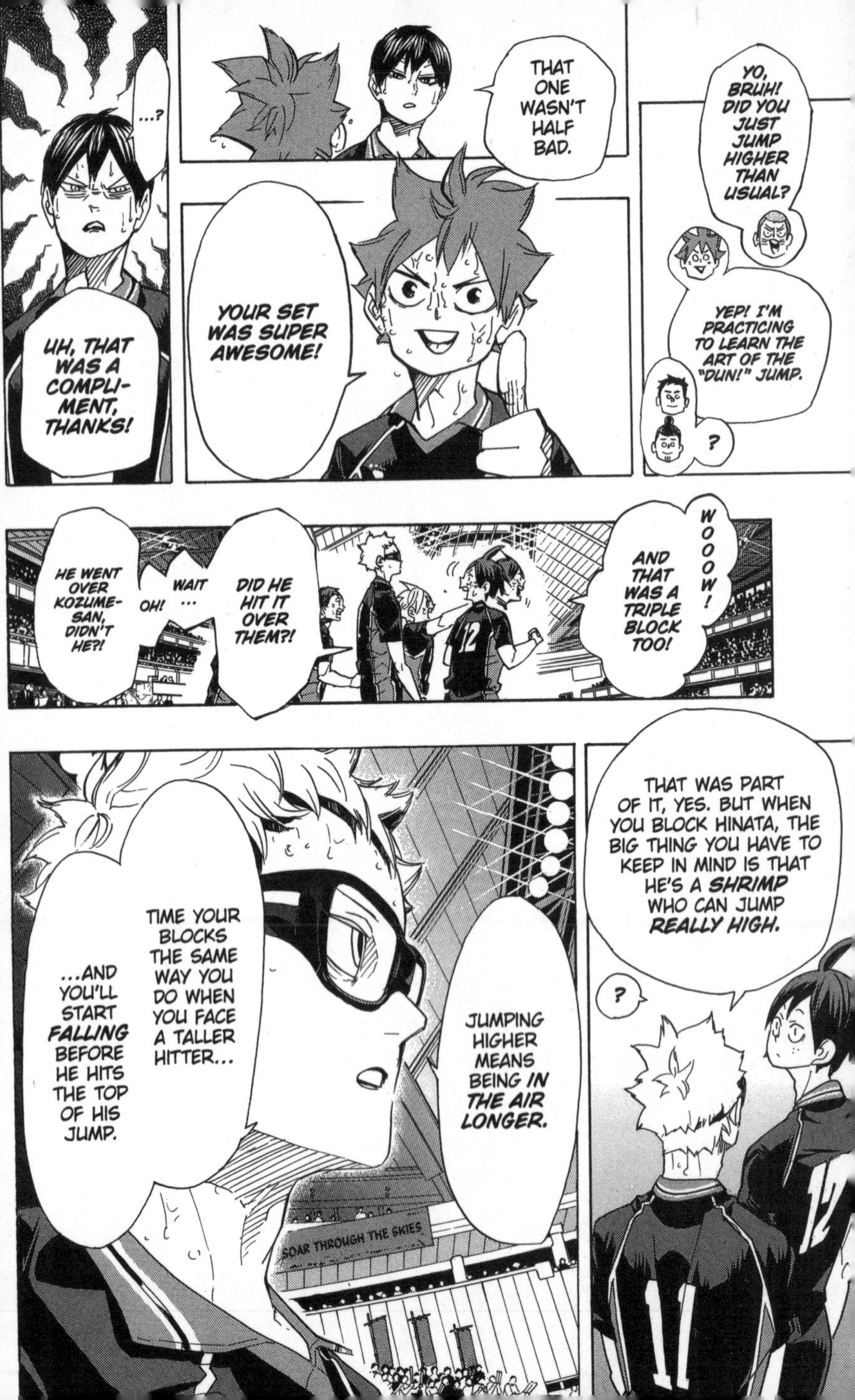
YO, BRUH! DID YOU JUST JUMP HIGHER THAN USUAL?
YEP! I'M PRACTICING TO LEARN THE ART OF THE "DUN!" JUMP.
?
THAT ONE WASN'T HALF BAD.
YOUR SET WAS SUPER AWESOME!
...?
UH, THAT WAS A COMPLIMENT, THANKS!
WOOOOW!
AND THAT WAS A TRIPLE BLOCK TOO!
DID HE HIT IT OVER THEM?!
WAIT...
OH!
HE WENT OVER KOZUME-SAN, DIDN'T HE?!
THAT WAS PART OF IT, YES. BUT WHEN YOU BLOCK HINATA, THE BIG THING YOU HAVE TO KEEP IN MIND IS THAT HE'S A SHRIMP WHO CAN JUMP REALLY HIGH.
?
JUMPING HIGHER MEANS BEING IN THE AIR LONGER.
TIME YOUR BLOCKS THE SAME WAY YOU DO WHEN YOU FACE A TALLER HITTER...
...AND YOU'LL START FALLING BEFORE HE HITS THE TOP OF HIS JUMP.
SOAR THROUGH THE SKIES

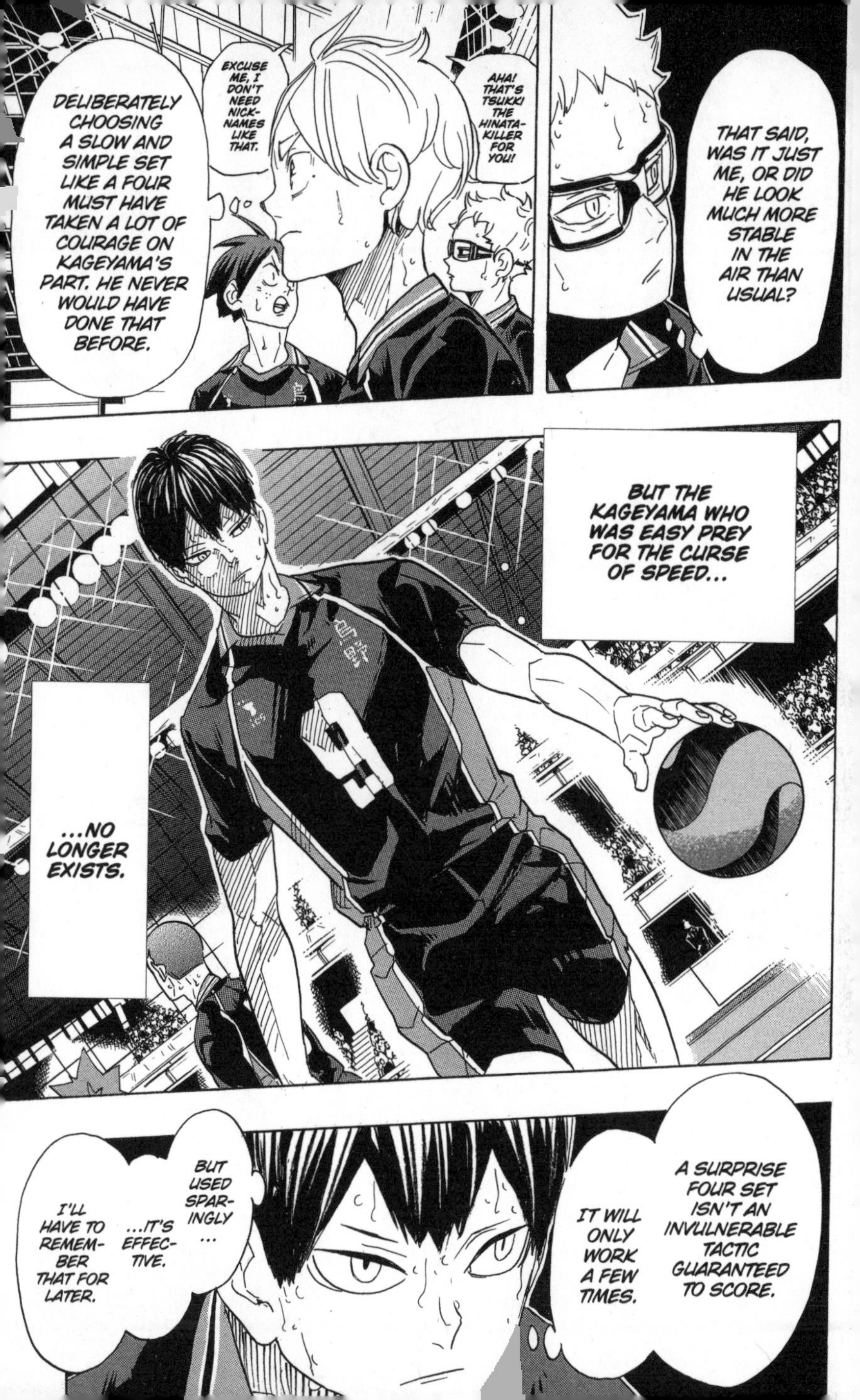
THAT SAID, WAS IT JUST ME, OR DID HE LOOK MUCH MORE STABLE IN THE AIR THAN USUAL?
AHA! THAT'S TSUKKI THE HINATA-KILLER FOR YOU!
EXCUSE ME, I DON'T NEED NICK-NAMES LIKE THAT.
DELIBERATELY CHOOSING A SLOW AND SIMPLE SET LIKE A FOUR MUST HAVE TAKEN A LOT OF COURAGE ON KAGEYAMA'S PART. HE NEVER WOULD HAVE DONE THAT BEFORE.
BUT THE KAGEYAMA WHO WAS EASY PREY FOR THE CURSE OF SPEED...
...NO LONGER EXISTS.
A SURPRISE FOUR SET ISN'T AN INVULNERABLE TACTIC GUARANTEED TO SCORE.
IT WILL ONLY WORK A FEW TIMES.
BUT USED SPAR-INGLY...
...IT'S EFFEC-TIVE.
I'LL HAVE TO REMEM-BER THAT FOR LATER.

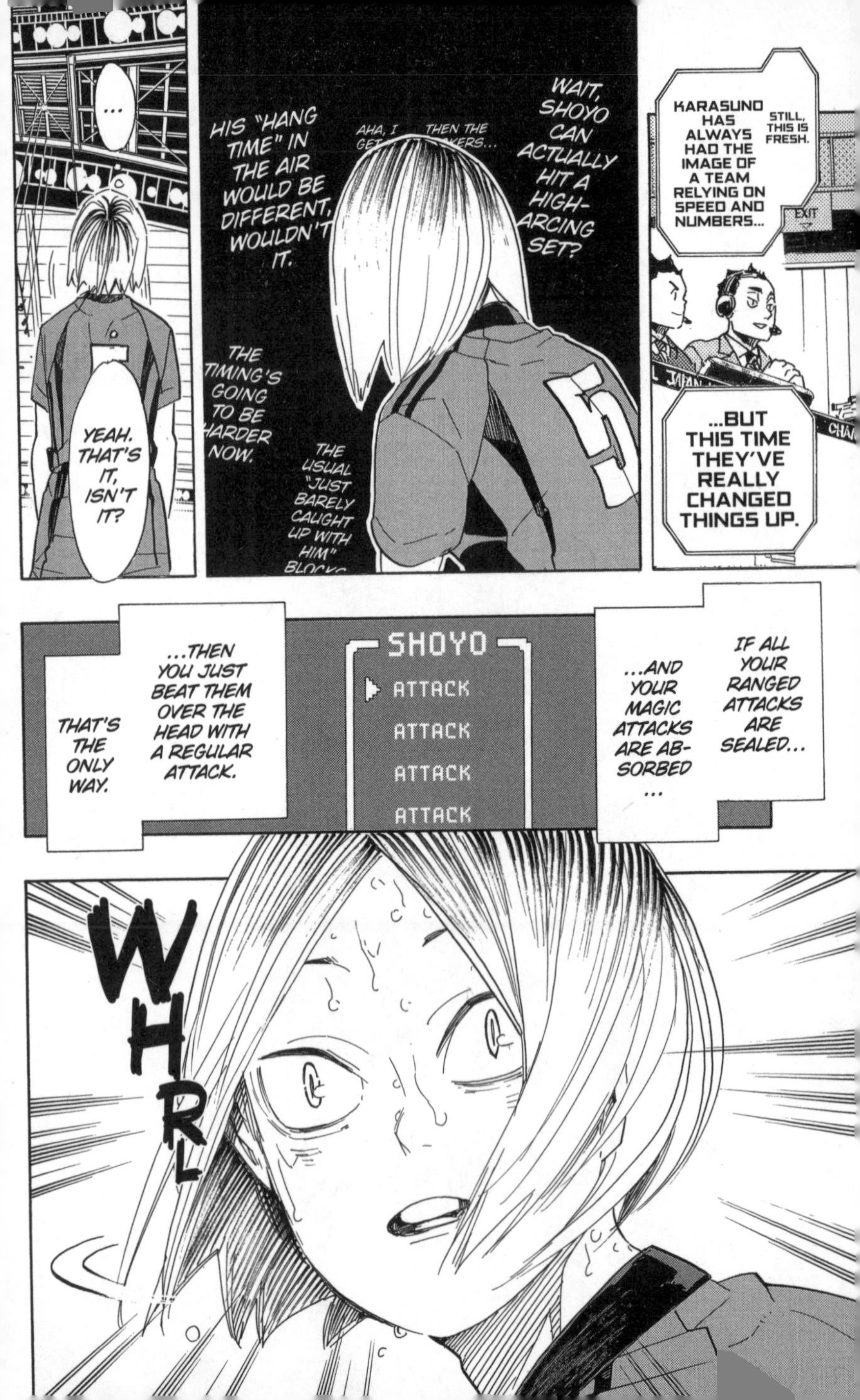
KARASUNO HAS ALWAYS HAD THE IMAGE OF A TEAM RELYING ON SPEED AND NUMBERS...
STILL, THIS IS FRESH.
...BUT THIS TIME THEY'VE REALLY CHANGED THINGS UP.
WAIT, SHOYO CAN ACTUALLY HIT A HIGH-ARCING SET?
HIS "HANG TIME" IN THE AIR WOULD BE DIFFERENT, WOULDN'T IT.
THE TIMING'S GOING TO BE HARDER NOW.
THE USUAL "JUST BARELY CAUGHT UP WITH HIM" BLOCKS
...
YEAH. THAT'S IT, ISN'T IT?
IF ALL YOUR RANGED ATTACKS ARE SEALED...
...AND YOUR MAGIC ATTACKS ARE ABSORBED...
SHOYO
ATTACK
ATTACK
ATTACK
ATTACK
...THEN YOU JUST BEAT THEM OVER THE HEAD WITH A REGULAR ATTACK.
THAT'S THE ONLY WAY.
WHRL

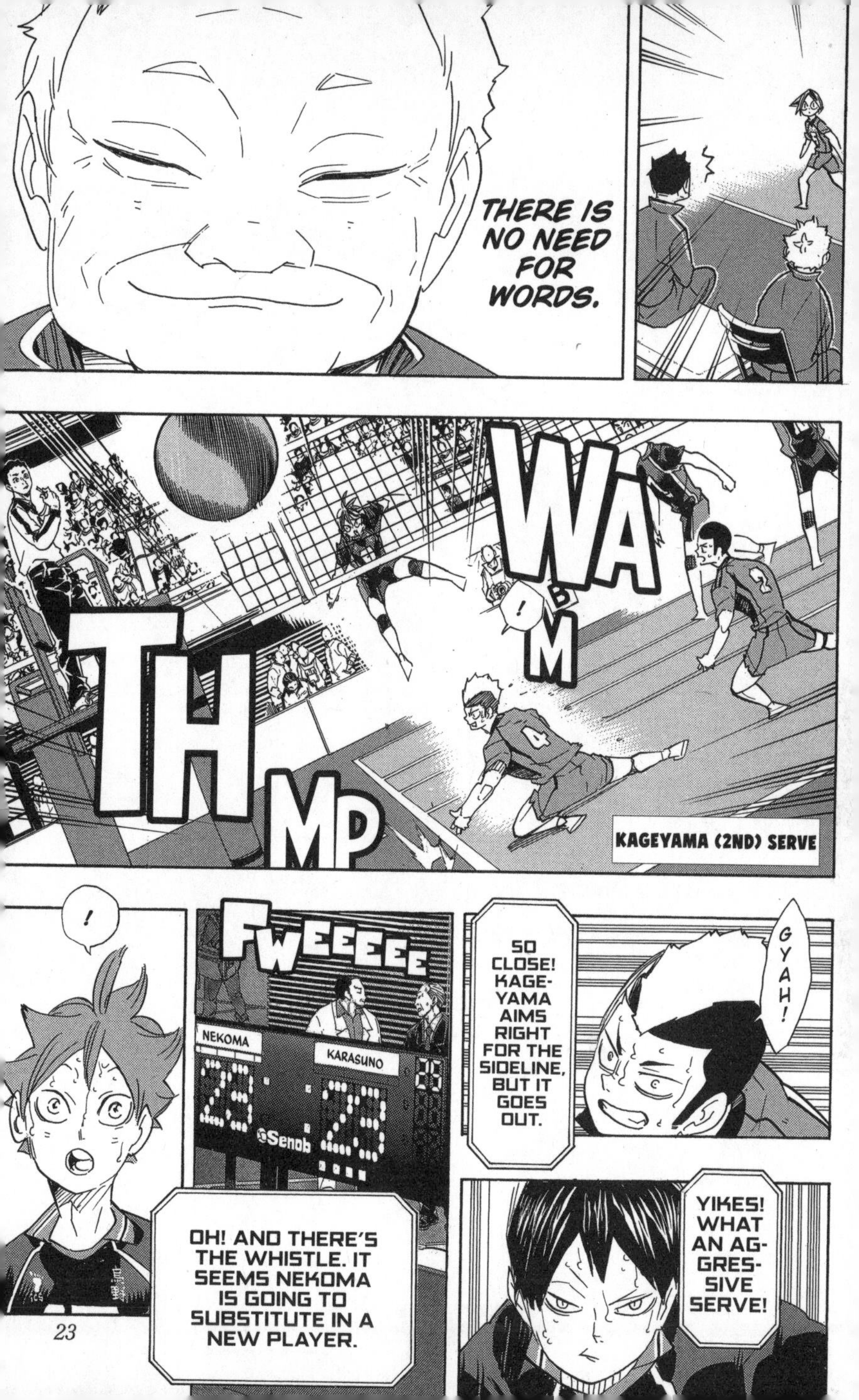
THERE IS NO NEED FOR WORDS.
WA
!
BM
TH
MP
KAGEYAMA (2ND) SERVE
GYAH!
SO CLOSE! KAGE-YAMA AIMS RIGHT FOR THE SIDELINE, BUT IT GOES OUT.
YIKES! WHAT AN AG-GRES-SIVE SERVE!
FWEEEEE
NEKOMA
KARASUNO
Senob
OH! AND THERE'S THE WHISTLE. IT SEEMS NEKOMA IS GOING TO SUBSTITUTE IN A NEW PLAYER.
!

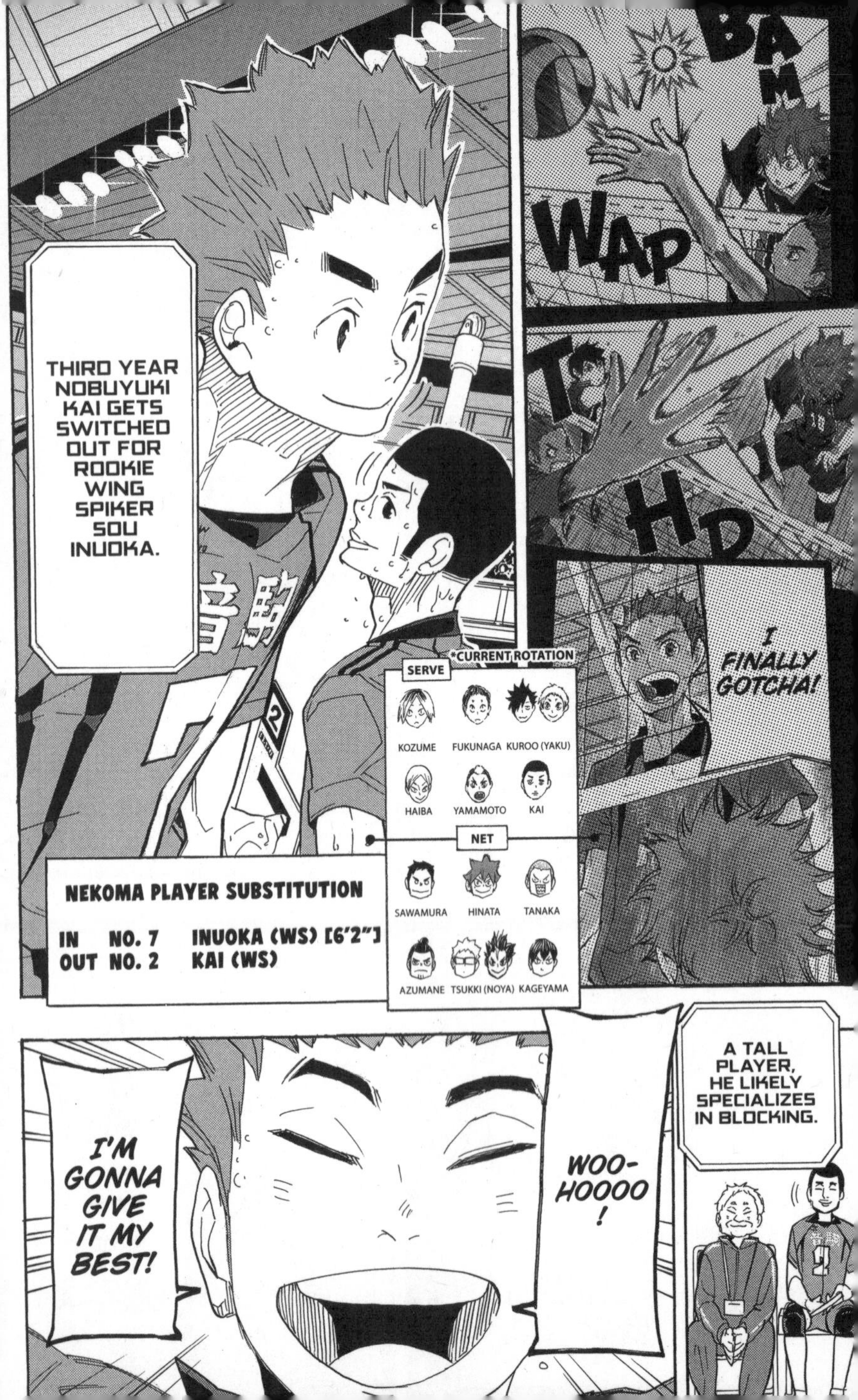
BAM
WAP
THD
I FINALLY GOTCHA!
THIRD YEAR NOBUYUKI KAI GETS SWITCHED OUT FOR ROOKIE WING SPIKER SOU INUOKA.
*CURRENT ROTATION
SERVE
KOZUME
FUKUNAGA
KUROO (YAKU)
HAIBA
YAMAMOTO
KAI
NET
SAWAMURA
HINATA
TANAKA
AZUMANE
TSUKKI (NOYA)
KAGEYAMA
NEKOMA PLAYER SUBSTITUTION
IN NO. 7 INUOKA (WS) [6'2"]
OUT NO. 2 KAI (WS)
A TALL PLAYER, HE LIKELY SPECIALIZES IN BLOCKING.
WOO-HOOOO!
I'M GONNA GIVE IT MY BEST!

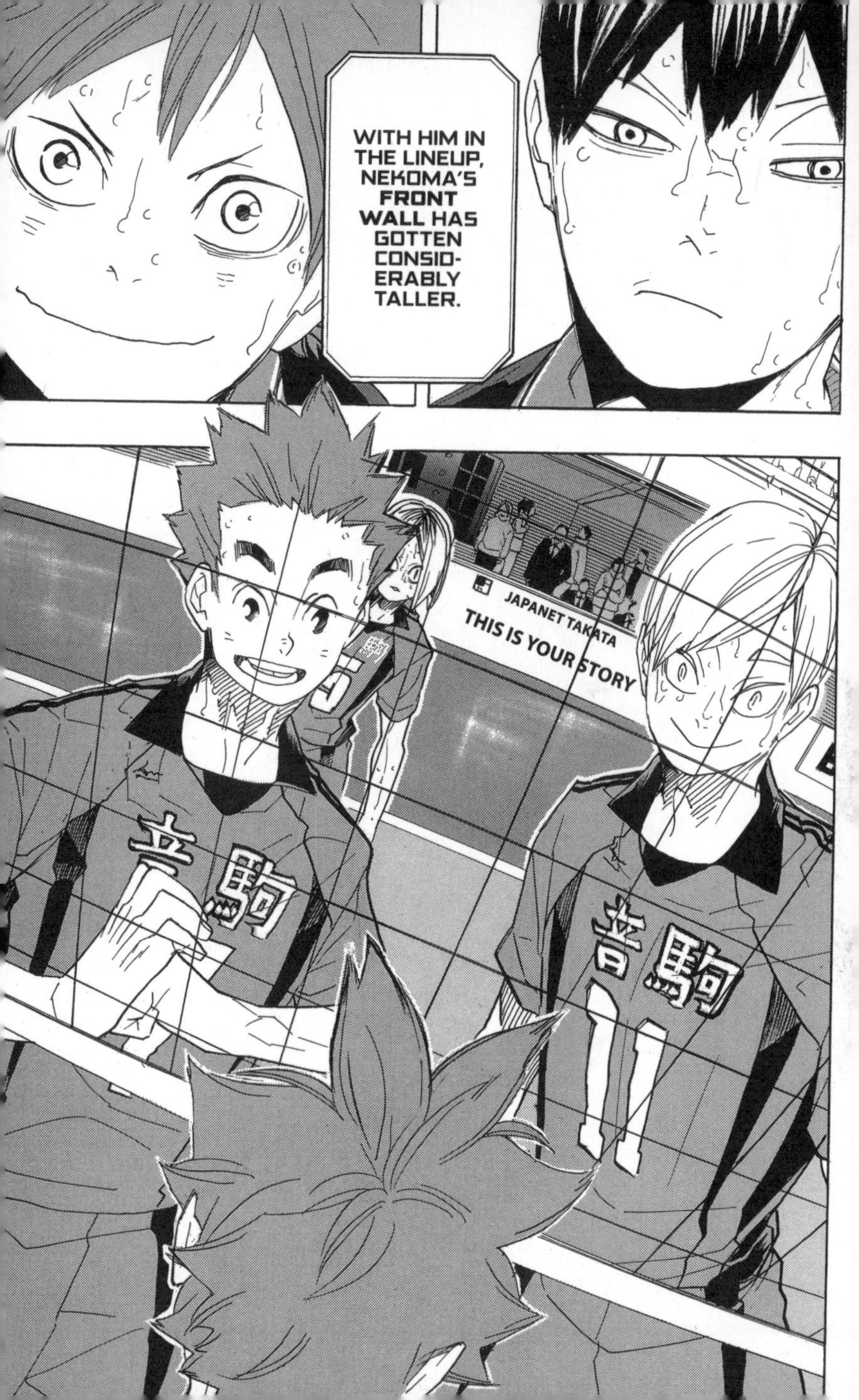
WITH HIM IN THE LINEUP, NEKOMA'S FRONT WALL HAS GOTTEN CONSIDERABLY TALLER.
JAPANET TAKATA
THIS IS YOUR STORY

WHEN CHAPTER 315 FIRST RAN IN THE WEEKLY MAGAZINE IN JAPAN, THE FLAVOR COMMENT IN THE LAST PANEL SAID, "NEKOMA EQUIPS TWO SHIELDS!" NOW, IT'S USUALLY THE EDITORS WHO THINK UP THOSE LITTLE COMMENTS AND ADD THEM IN. WHEN I SAW THAT ONE, I WAS LIKE, "CRAP! THEY GOT ME! I WANTED TO SAY THAT!" I'VE HAD NO TIME AT ALL TO PLAY VIDEO GAMES LATELY, AND I'M REALLY STARTING TO FEEL HOW OUT OF TOUCH I AM WITH THEM. IT'S FRUSTRATING.

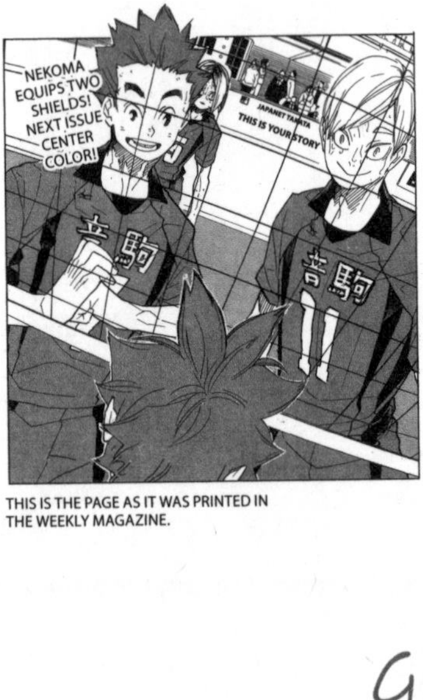
NEKOMA EQUIPS TWO SHIELDS! NEXT ISSUE CENTER COLOR!
THIS IS YOUR STORY
音駒
音駒

THIS IS THE PAGE AS IT WAS PRINTED IN THE WEEKLY MAGAZINE.

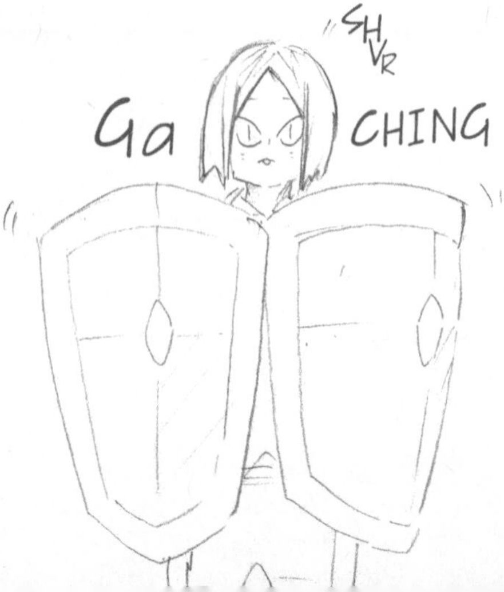
SHVR
Ga CHING

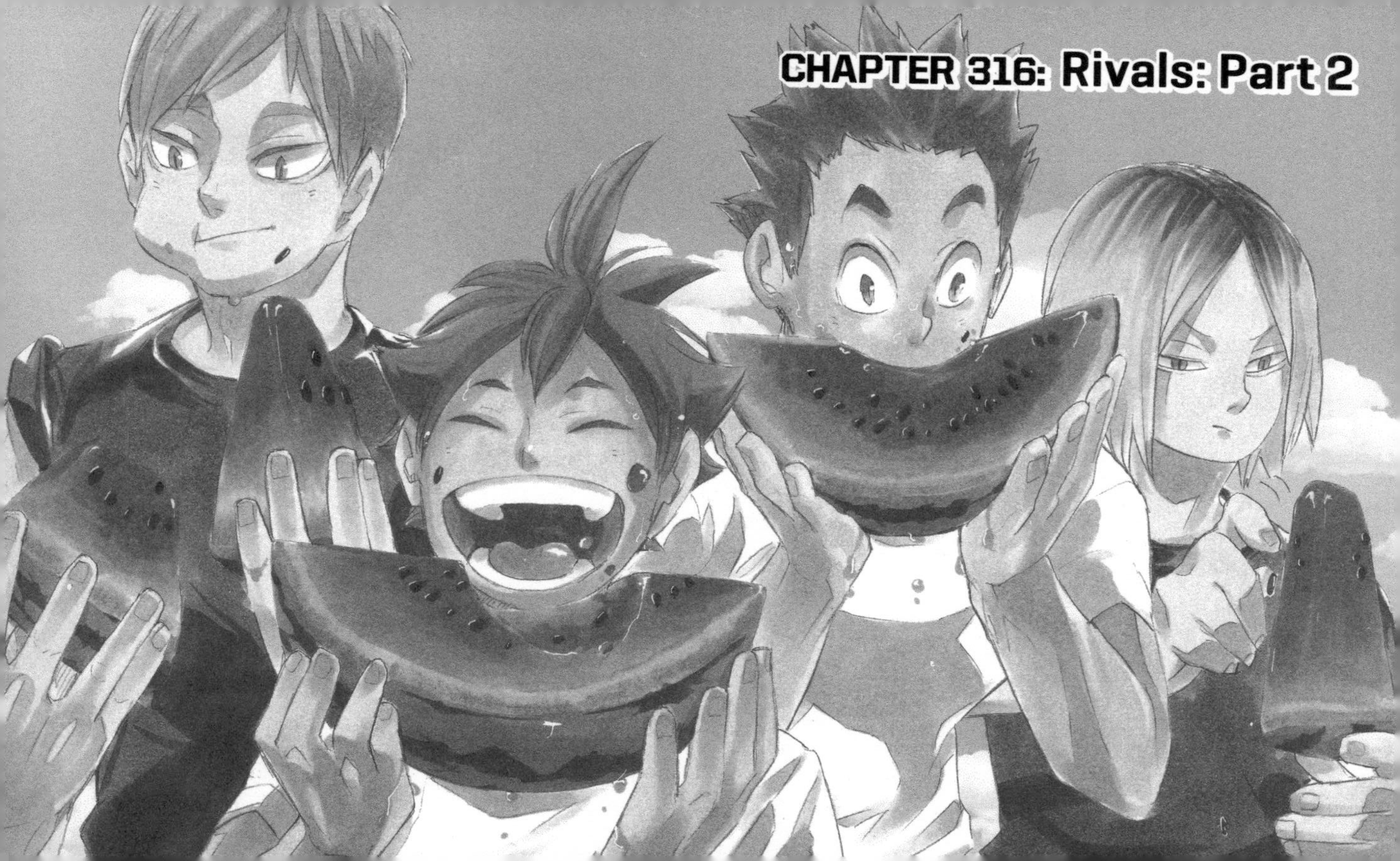
CHAPTER 316: Rivals: Part 2

HAIKYU!!

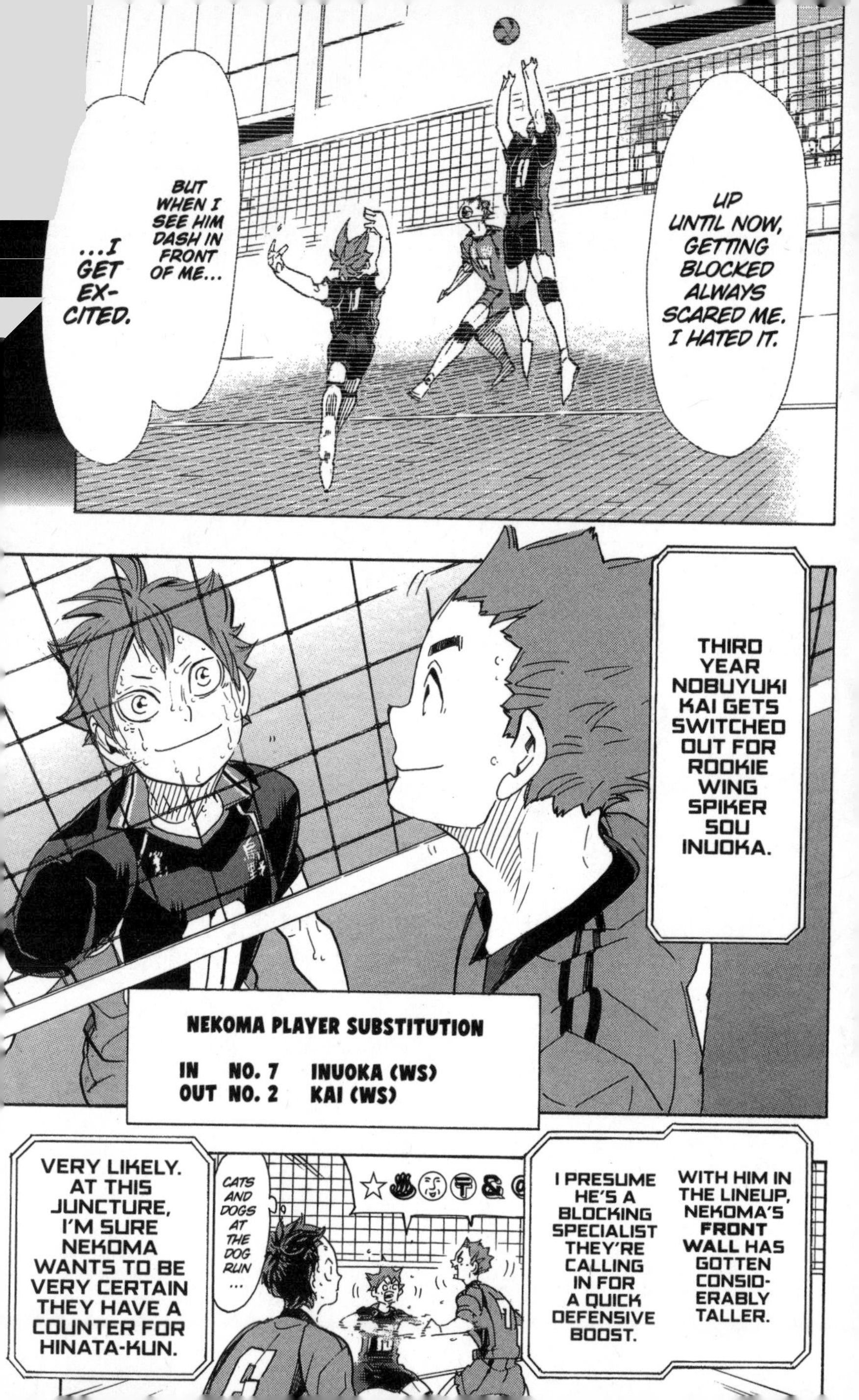
UP UNTIL NOW, GETTING BLOCKED ALWAYS SCARED ME. I HATED IT.
BUT WHEN I SEE HIM DASH IN FRONT OF ME...
...I GET EX-CITED.
THIRD YEAR NOBUYUKI KAI GETS SWITCHED OUT FOR ROOKIE WING SPIKER SOU INUOKA.
NEKOMA PLAYER SUBSTITUTION
IN NO. 7 INUOKA (WS)
OUT NO. 2 KAI (WS)
WITH HIM IN THE LINEUP, NEKOMA'S FRONT WALL HAS GOTTEN CONSID-ERABLY TALLER.
I PRESUME HE'S A BLOCKING SPECIALIST THEY'RE CALLING IN FOR A QUICK DEFENSIVE BOOST.
CATS AND DOGS AT THE DOG RUN...
VERY LIKELY. AT THIS JUNCTURE, I'M SURE NEKOMA WANTS TO BE VERY CERTAIN THEY HAVE A COUNTER FOR HINATA-KUN.

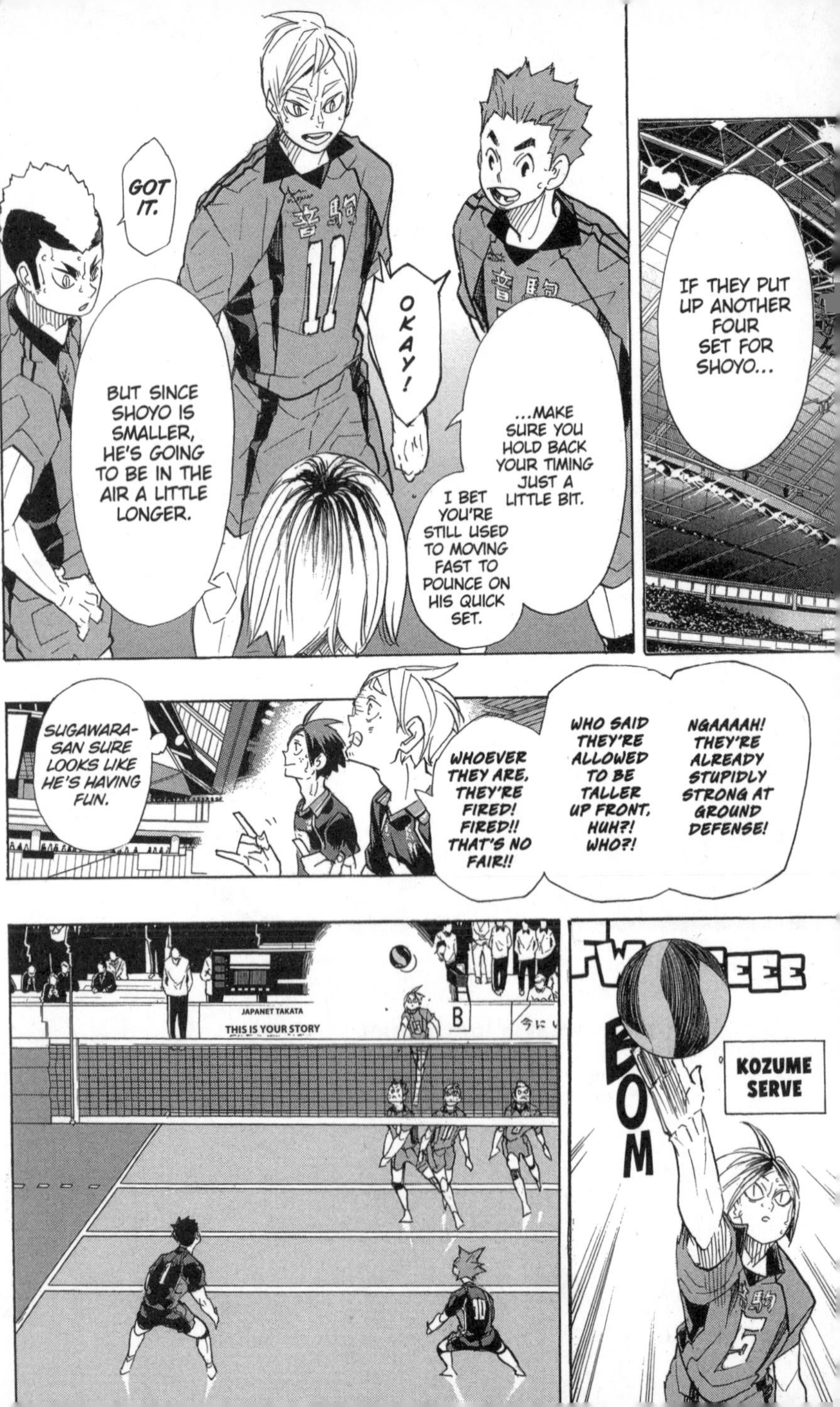
IF THEY PUT UP ANOTHER FOUR SET FOR SHOYO...
...MAKE SURE YOU HOLD BACK YOUR TIMING JUST A LITTLE BIT.
I BET YOU'RE STILL USED TO MOVING FAST TO POUNCE ON HIS QUICK SET.
BUT SINCE SHOYO IS SMALLER, HE'S GOING TO BE IN THE AIR A LITTLE LONGER.
OKAY!
GOT IT.
NGAAAAH! THEY'RE ALREADY STUPIDLY STRONG AT GROUND DEFENSE!
WHO SAID THEY'RE ALLOWED TO BE TALLER UP FRONT, HUH?! WHO?!
WHOEVER THEY ARE, THEY'RE FIRED! FIRED!! THAT'S NO FAIR!!
SUGAWARA-SAN SURE LOOKS LIKE HE'S HAVING FUN.
FW EEE
BOM
KOZUME SERVE
JAPANET TAKATA
THIS IS YOUR STORY
B

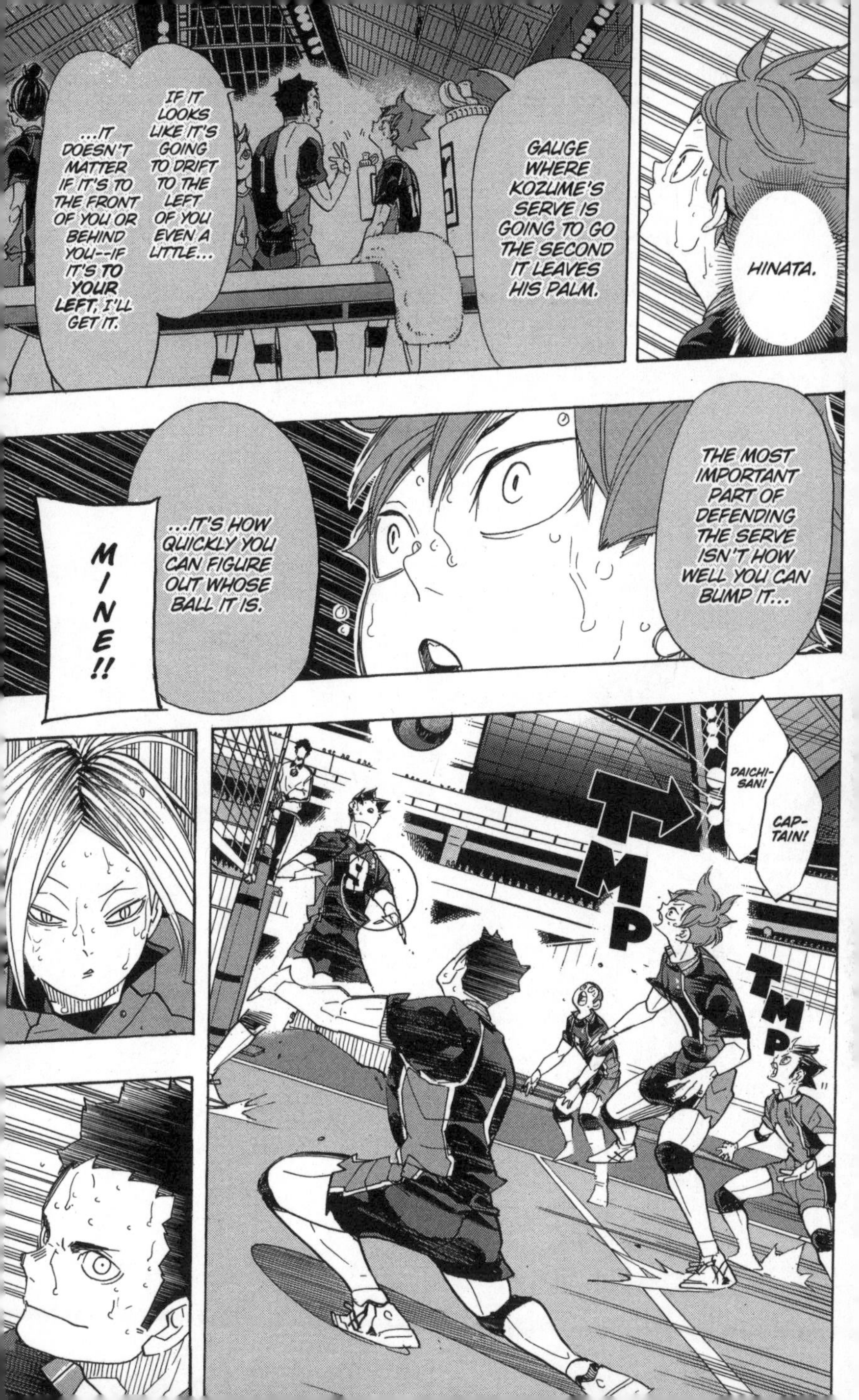
HINATA.
GAUGE WHERE KOZUME'S SERVE IS GOING TO GO THE SECOND IT LEAVES HIS PALM.
IF IT LOOKS LIKE IT'S GOING TO DRIFT TO THE LEFT OF YOU EVEN A LITTLE...
...IT DOESN'T MATTER IF IT'S TO THE FRONT OF YOU OR BEHIND YOU--IF IT'S TO YOUR LEFT, I'LL GET IT.
THE MOST IMPORTANT PART OF DEFENDING THE SERVE ISN'T HOW WELL YOU CAN BUMP IT...
...IT'S HOW QUICKLY YOU CAN FIGURE OUT WHOSE BALL IT IS.
MINE!!
DAICHI-SAN!
CAP-TAIN!
TMP
TMP

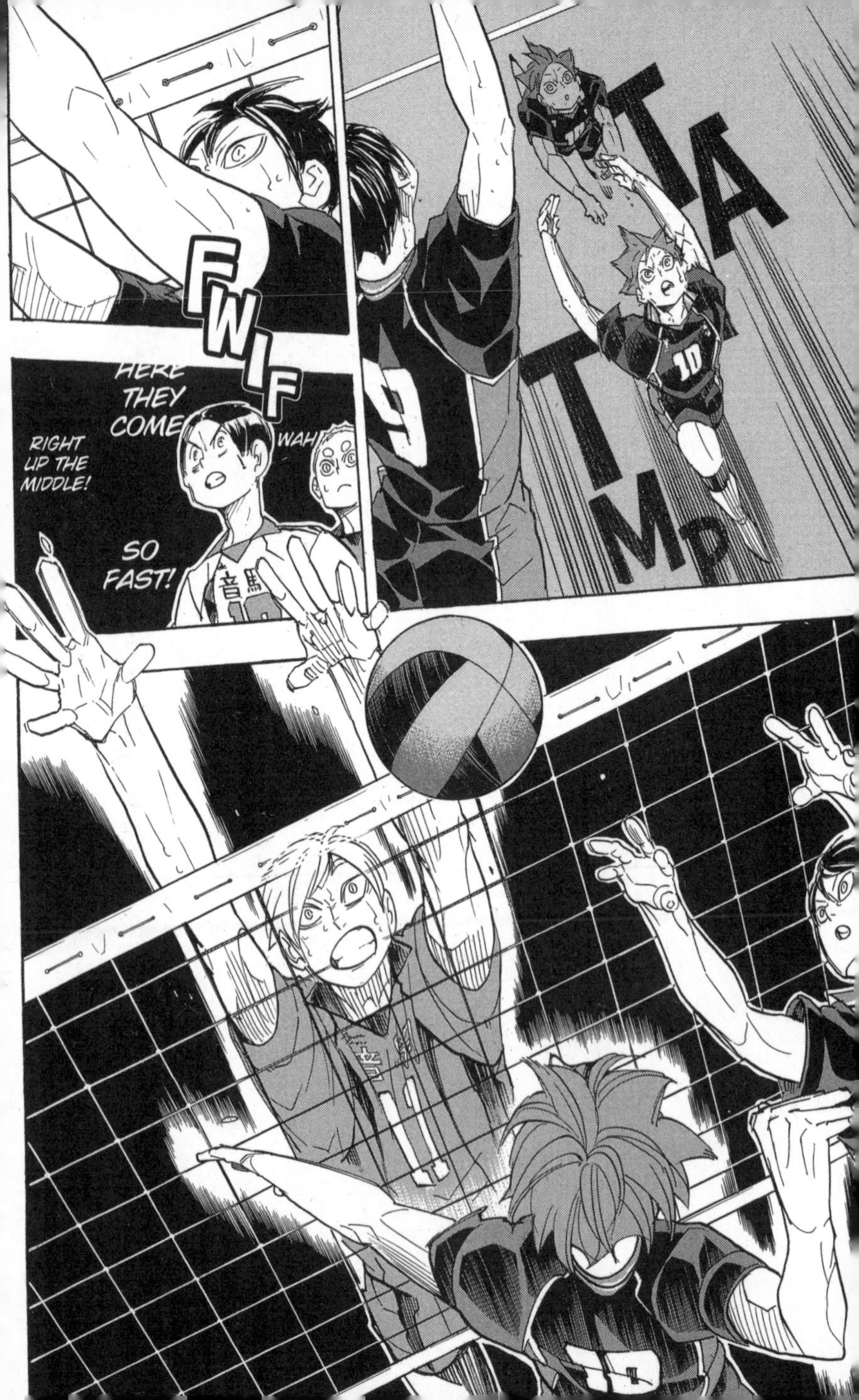
TA
TMP
FWIF
HERE THEY COME
WAH
RIGHT UP THE MIDDLE!
SO FAST!

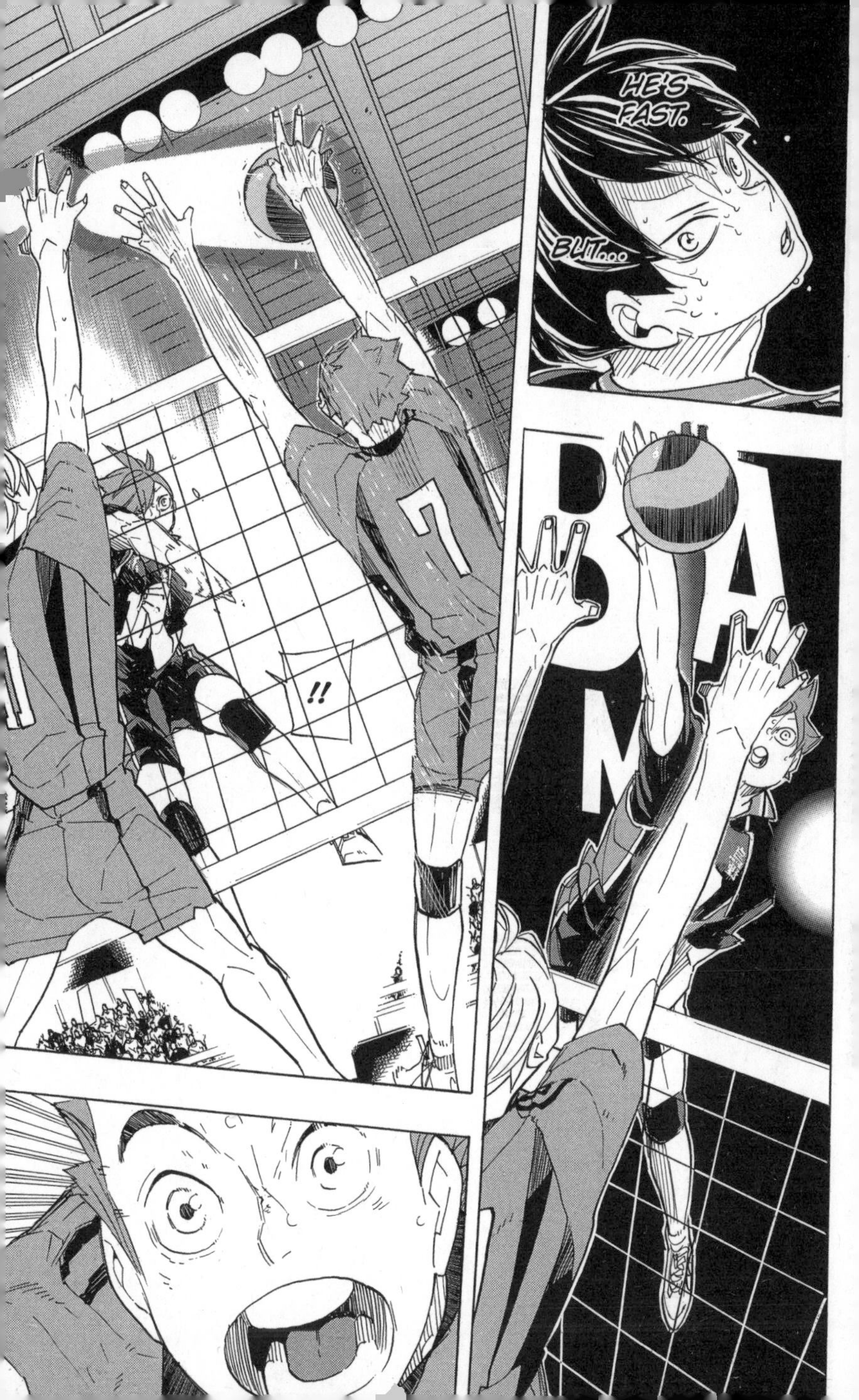
HE'S FAST.
BUT...
BAM
!!

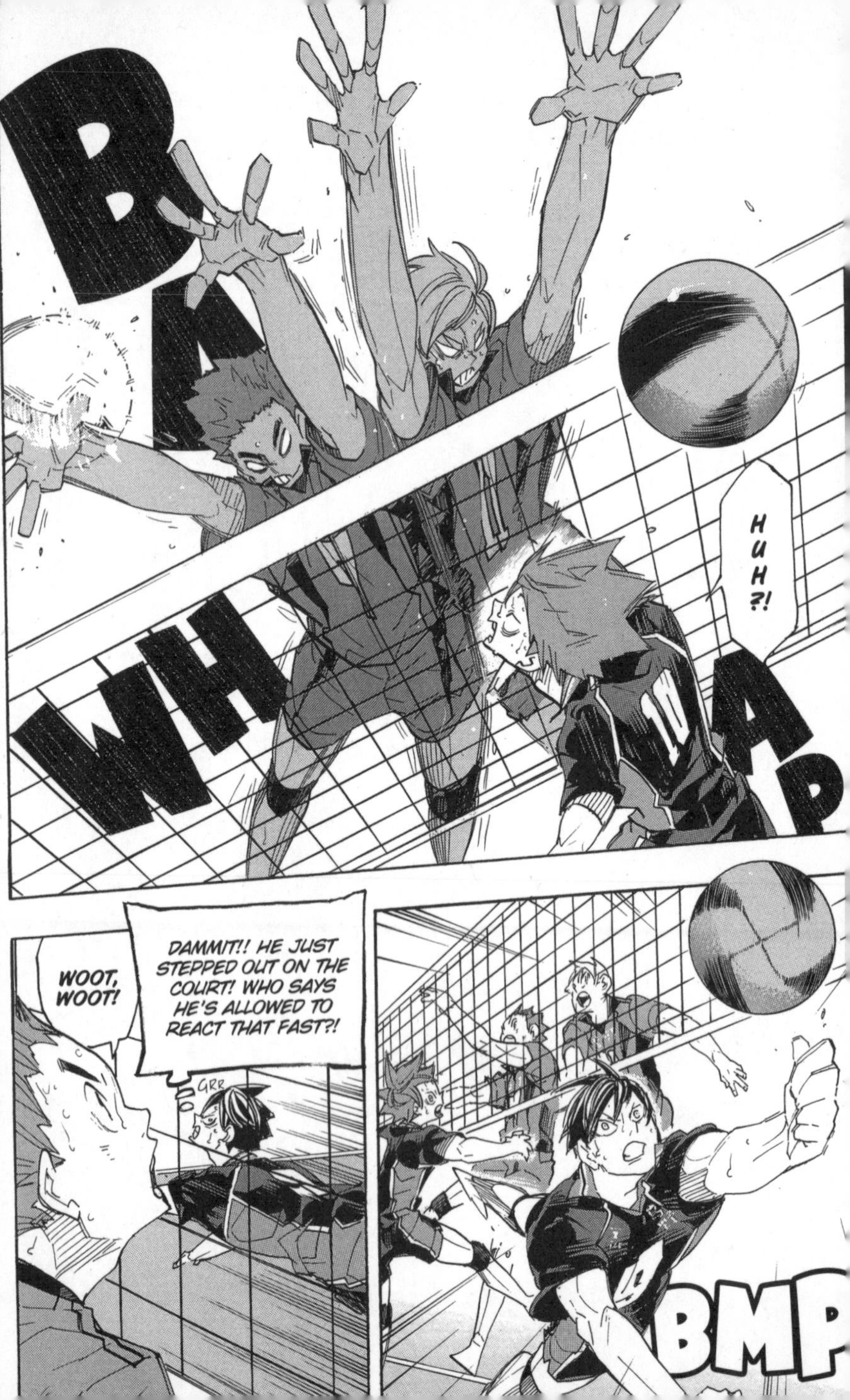
BA
HUH?!
WHAP
BMP
DAMMIT!! HE JUST STEPPED OUT ON THE COURT! WHO SAYS HE'S ALLOWED TO REACT THAT FAST?!
WOOT, WOOT!
GRR

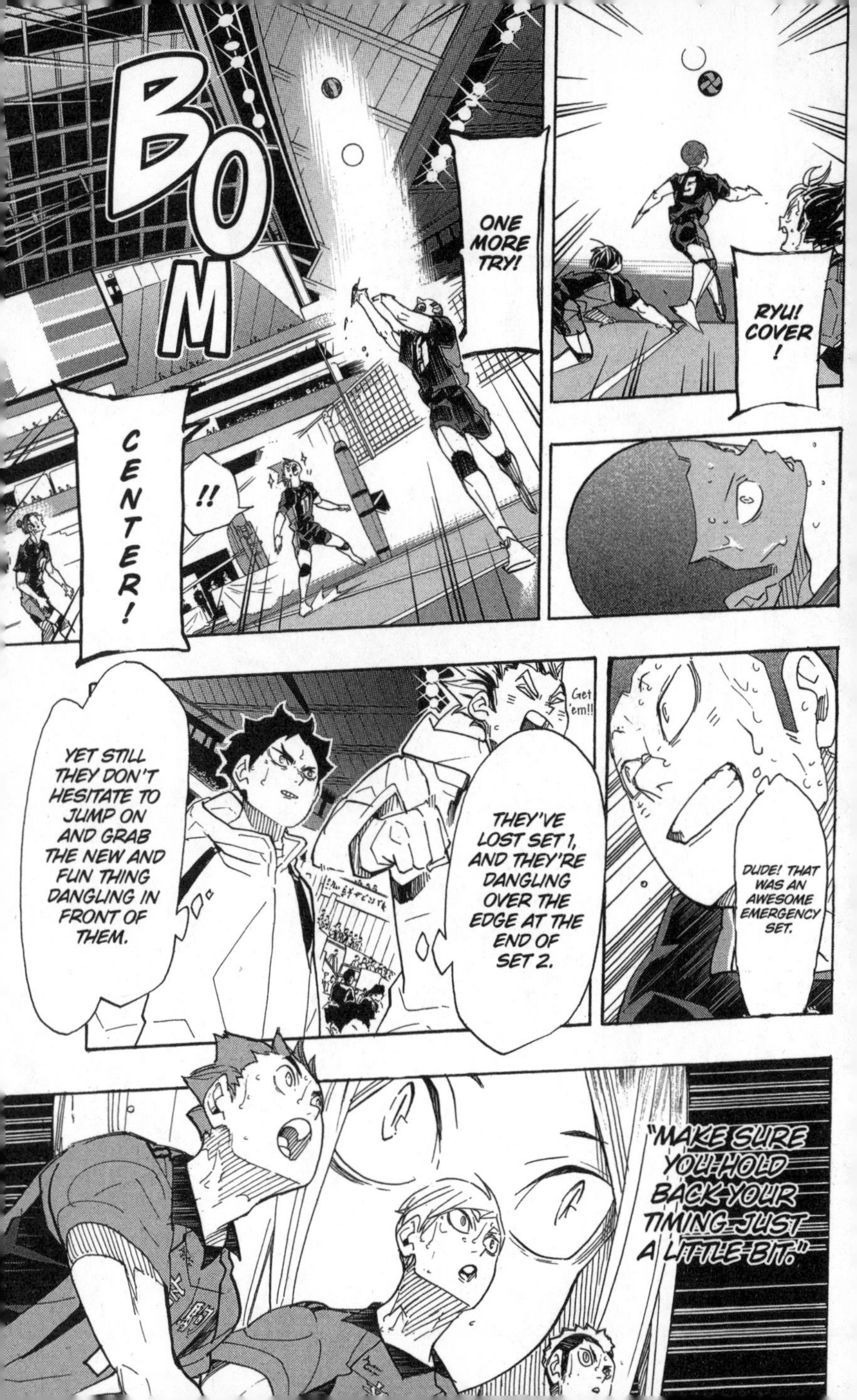
RYU! COVER!
ONE MORE TRY!
BOMM
!!
CENTER!
DUDE! THAT WAS AN AWESOME EMERGENCY SET.
Get 'em!!
THEY'VE LOST SET 1, AND THEY'RE DANGLING OVER THE EDGE AT THE END OF SET 2.
YET STILL THEY DON'T HESITATE TO JUMP ON AND GRAB THE NEW AND FUN THING DANGLING IN FRONT OF THEM.
"MAKE SURE YOU HOLD BACK YOUR TIMING JUST A LITTLE BIT."

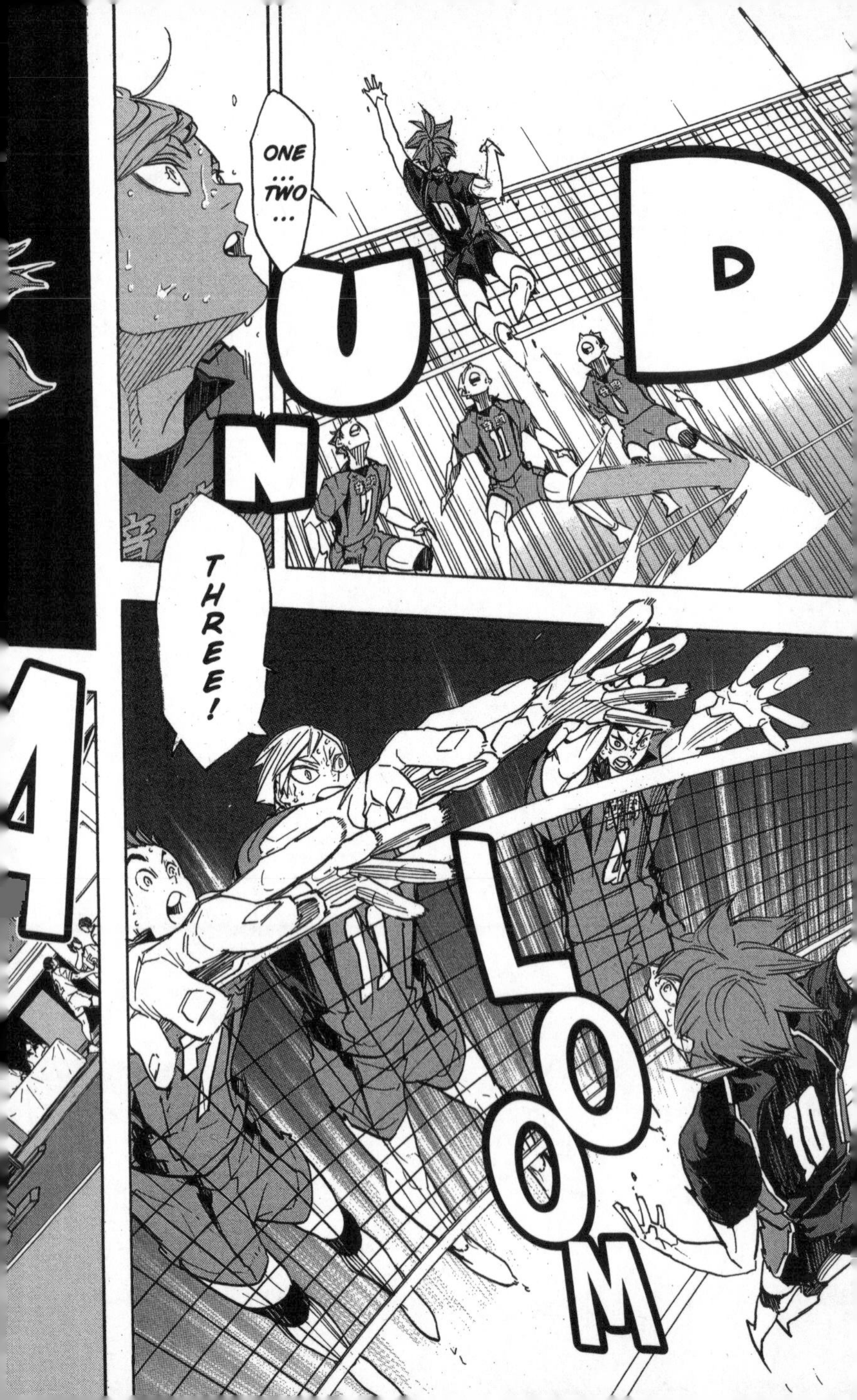
ONE ... TWO ...
D
U
N
THREE!
A
L
O
O
M

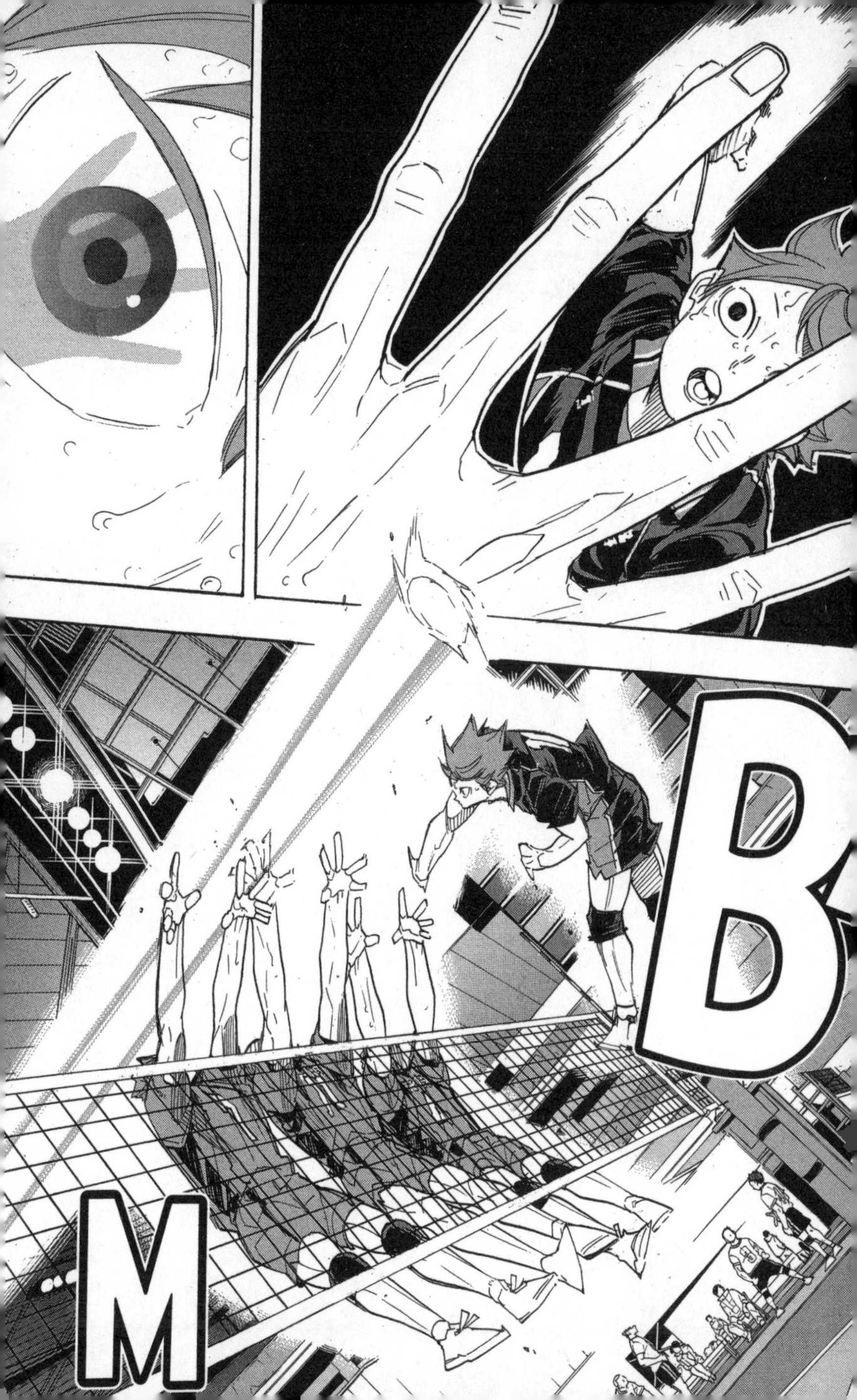
B
M

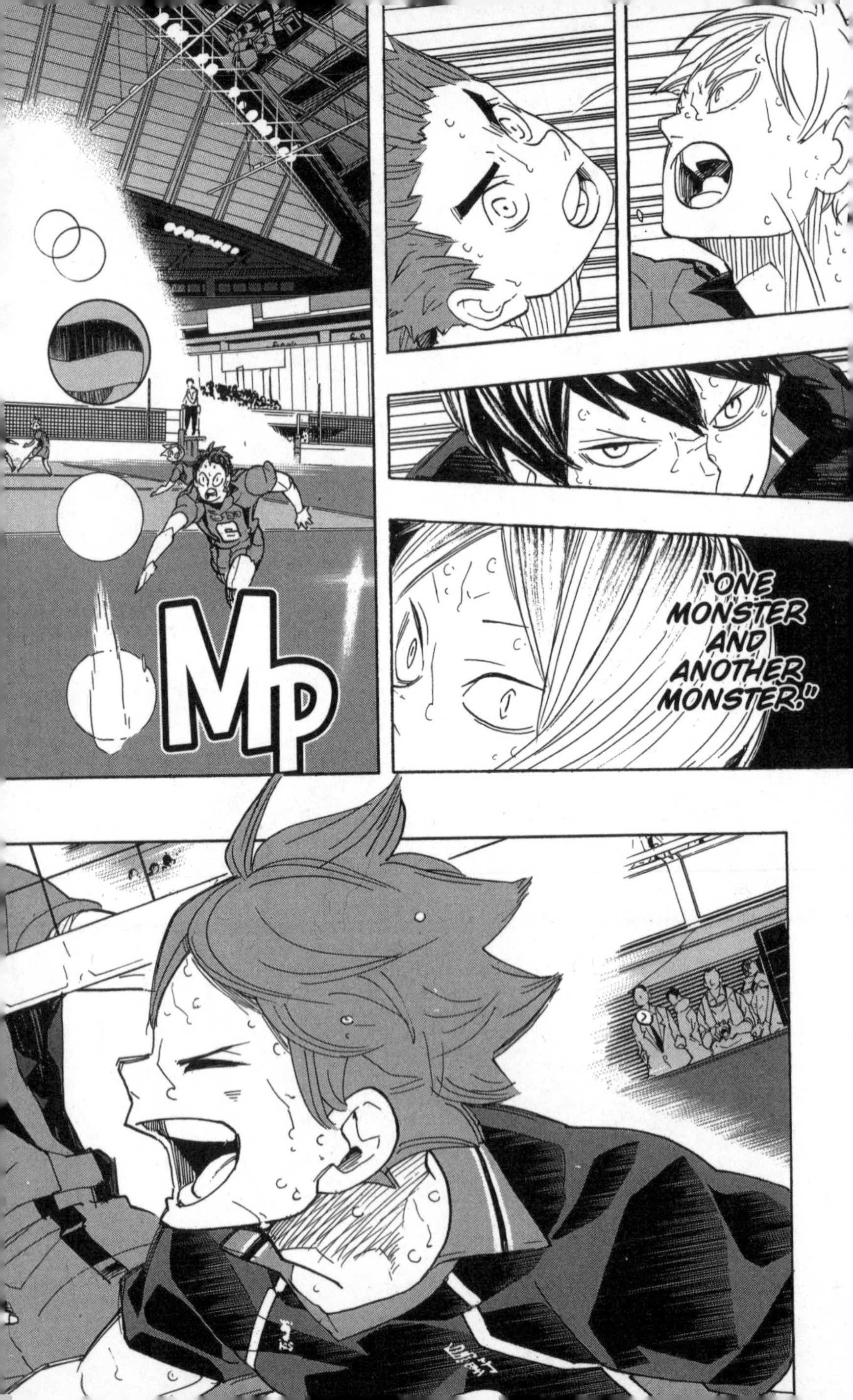
"ONE MONSTER AND ANOTHER MONSTER."
MP

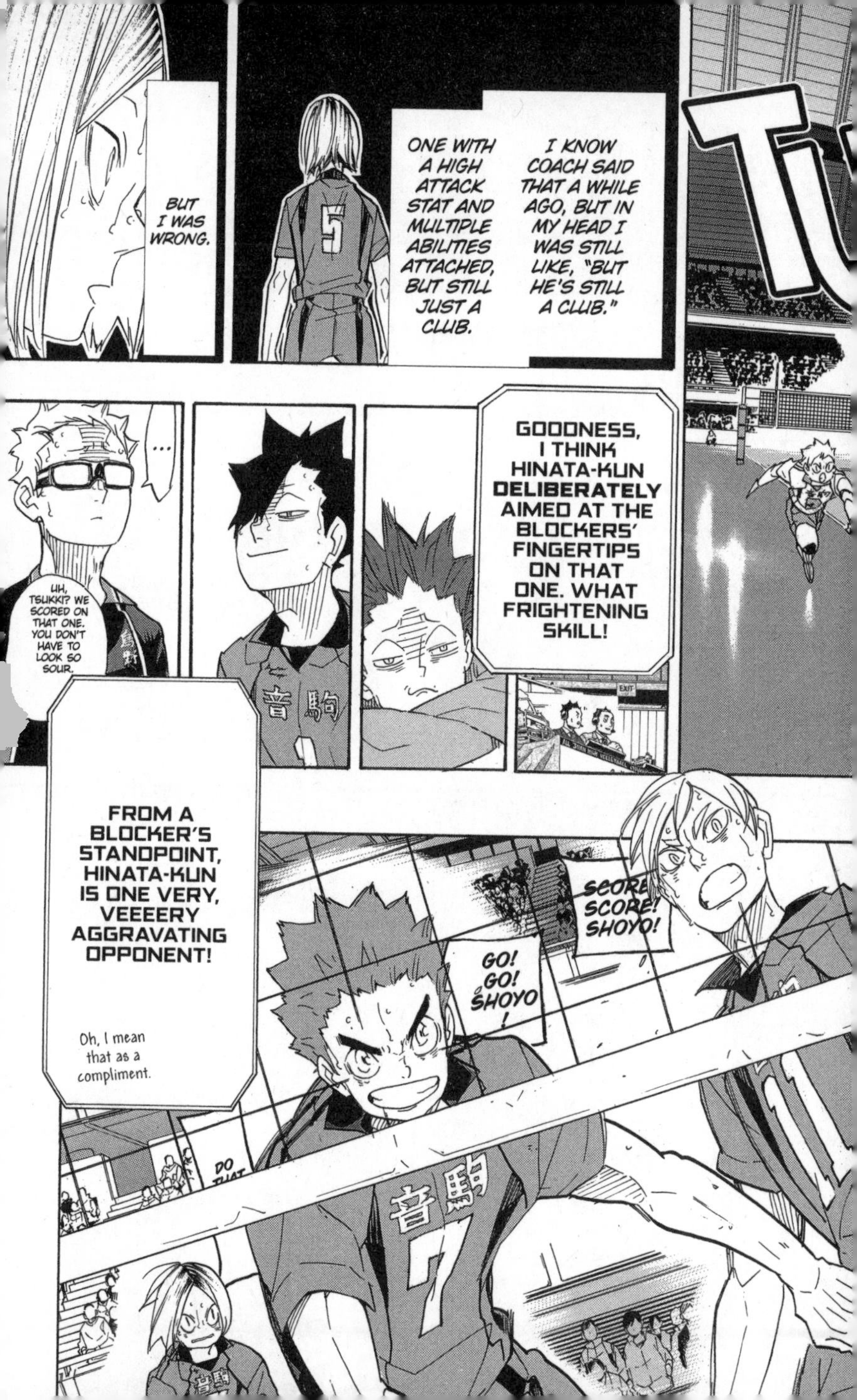
I KNOW COACH SAID THAT A WHILE AGO, BUT IN MY HEAD I WAS STILL LIKE, "BUT HE'S STILL A CLUB."
ONE WITH A HIGH ATTACK STAT AND MULTIPLE ABILITIES ATTACHED, BUT STILL JUST A CLUB.
BUT I WAS WRONG.
GOODNESS, I THINK HINATA-KUN DELIBERATELY AIMED AT THE BLOCKERS' FINGERTIPS ON THAT ONE. WHAT FRIGHTENING SKILL!
...
UH, TSUKKI? WE SCORED ON THAT ONE. YOU DON'T HAVE TO LOOK SO SOUR.
SCORE SCORE! SHOYO!
GO! GO! SHOYO!
FROM A BLOCKER'S STANDPOINT, HINATA-KUN IS ONE VERY, VEEEERY AGGRAVATING OPPONENT!
Oh, I mean that as a compliment.
DO THAT

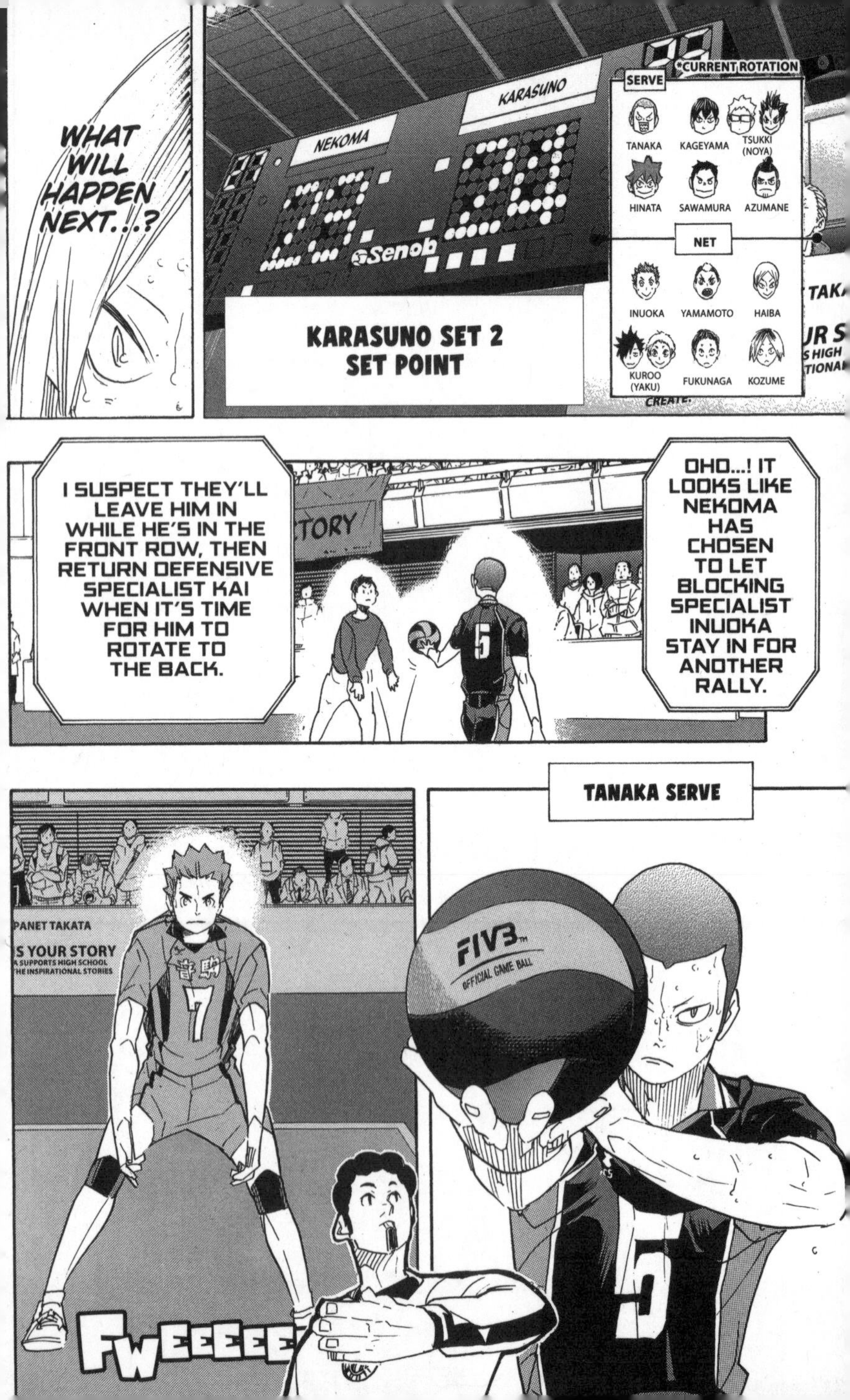
*CURRENT ROTATION
SERVE
TANAKA
KAGEYAMA
TSUKKI (NOYA)
HINATA
SAWAMURA
AZUMANE
NET
INUOKA
YAMAMOTO
HAIBA
KUROO (YAKU)
FUKUNAGA
KOZUME
KARASUNO
NEKOMA
KARASUNO SET 2 SET POINT
WHAT WILL HAPPEN NEXT...?
OHO...! IT LOOKS LIKE NEKOMA HAS CHOSEN TO LET BLOCKING SPECIALIST INUOKA STAY IN FOR ANOTHER RALLY.
I SUSPECT THEY'LL LEAVE HIM IN WHILE HE'S IN THE FRONT ROW, THEN RETURN DEFENSIVE SPECIALIST KAI WHEN IT'S TIME FOR HIM TO ROTATE TO THE BACK.
TANAKA SERVE
FIVB
OFFICIAL GAME BALL
FWEEEEE

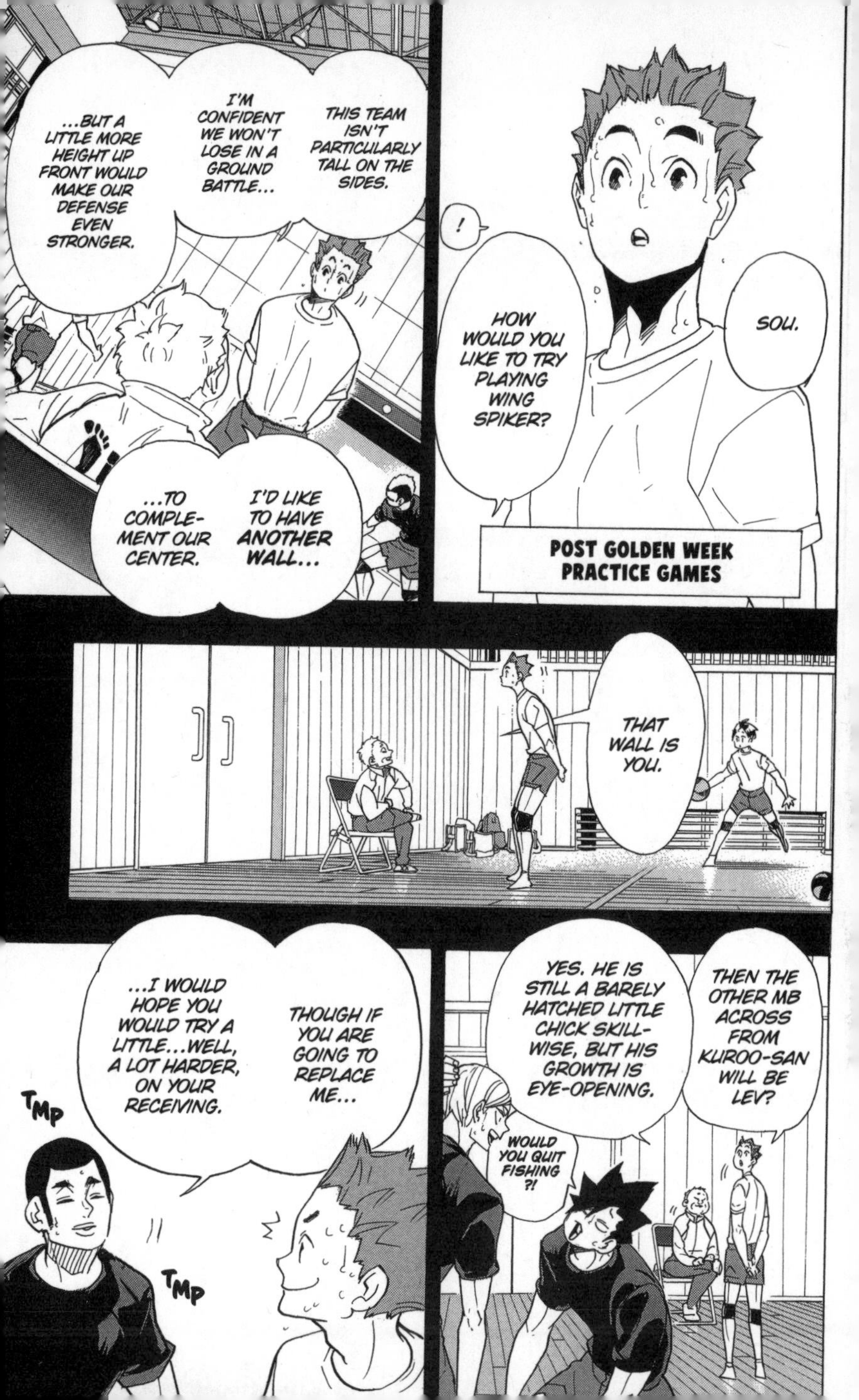
SOU.
!
HOW WOULD YOU LIKE TO TRY PLAYING WING SPIKER?
POST GOLDEN WEEK PRACTICE GAMES
THIS TEAM ISN'T PARTICULARLY TALL ON THE SIDES.
I'M CONFIDENT WE WON'T LOSE IN A GROUND BATTLE...
...BUT A LITTLE MORE HEIGHT UP FRONT WOULD MAKE OUR DEFENSE EVEN STRONGER.
I'D LIKE TO HAVE ANOTHER WALL...
...TO COMPLEMENT OUR CENTER.
THAT WALL IS YOU.
THEN THE OTHER MB ACROSS FROM KUROO-SAN WILL BE LEV?
YES. HE IS STILL A BARELY HATCHED LITTLE CHICK SKILL-WISE, BUT HIS GROWTH IS EYE-OPENING.
WOULD YOU QUIT FISHING?!
THOUGH IF YOU ARE GOING TO REPLACE ME...
...I WOULD HOPE YOU WOULD TRY A LITTLE...WELL, A LOT HARDER, ON YOUR RECEIVING.
TMP
TMP

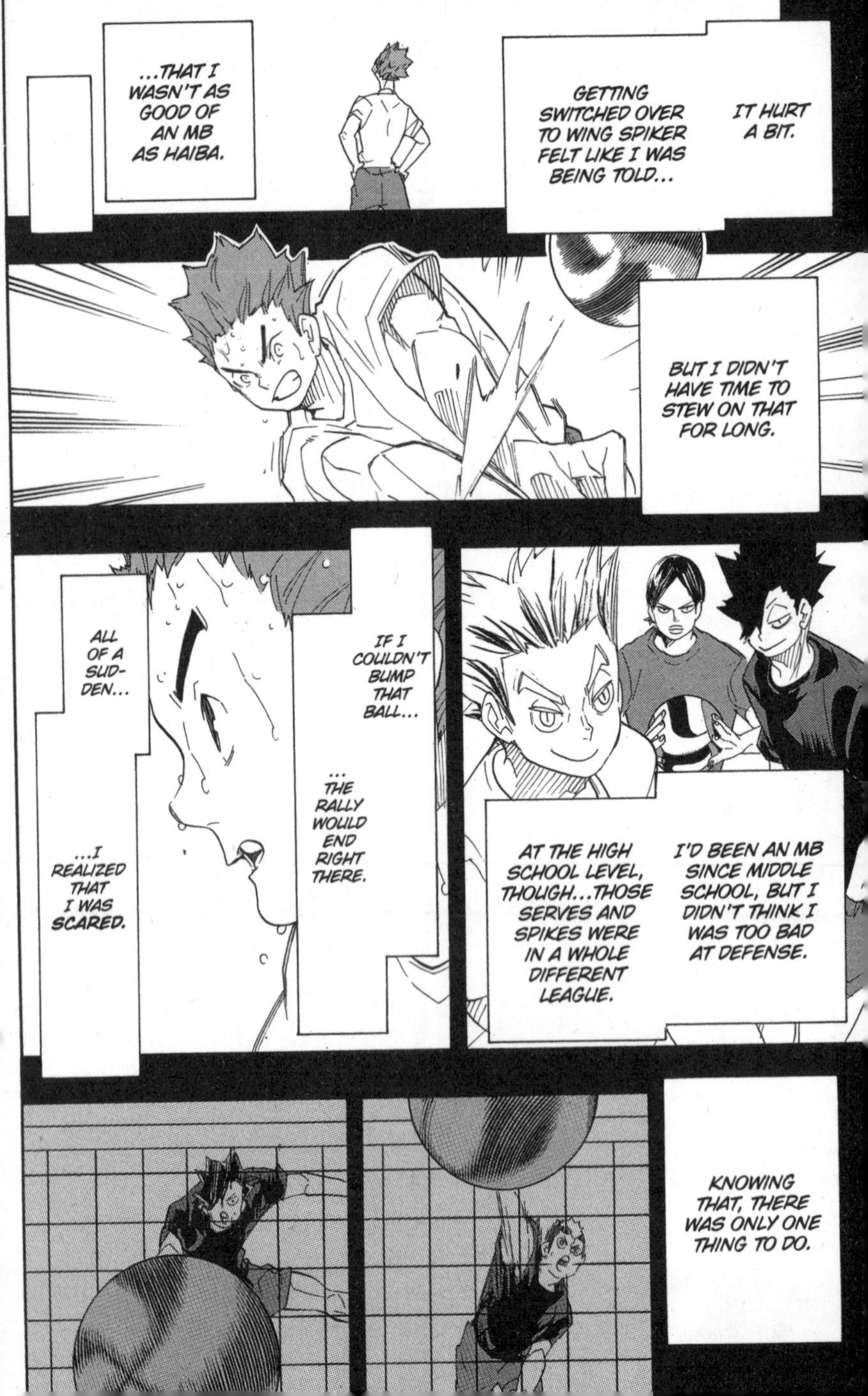
IT HURT A BIT.
GETTING SWITCHED OVER TO WING SPIKER FELT LIKE I WAS BEING TOLD...
...THAT I WASN'T AS GOOD OF AN MB AS HAIBA.
BUT I DIDN'T HAVE TIME TO STEW ON THAT FOR LONG.
I'D BEEN AN MB SINCE MIDDLE SCHOOL, BUT I DIDN'T THINK I WAS TOO BAD AT DEFENSE.
AT THE HIGH SCHOOL LEVEL, THOUGH...THOSE SERVES AND SPIKES WERE IN A WHOLE DIFFERENT LEAGUE.
IF I COULDN'T BUMP THAT BALL...
...THE RALLY WOULD END RIGHT THERE.
ALL OF A SUD-DEN...
...I REALIZED THAT I WAS SCARED.
KNOWING THAT, THERE WAS ONLY ONE THING TO DO.

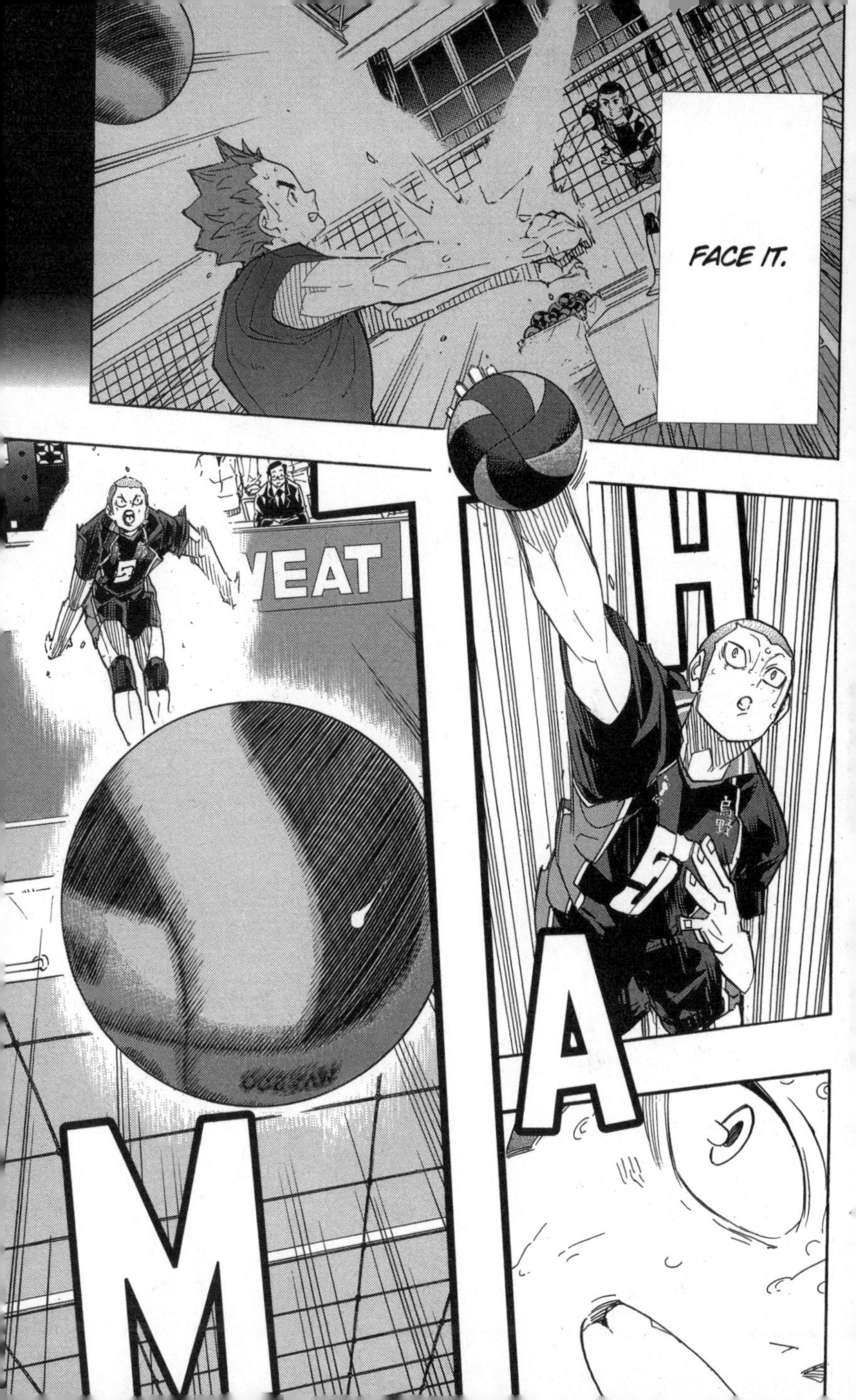
FACE IT.
VEAT
H
A
M

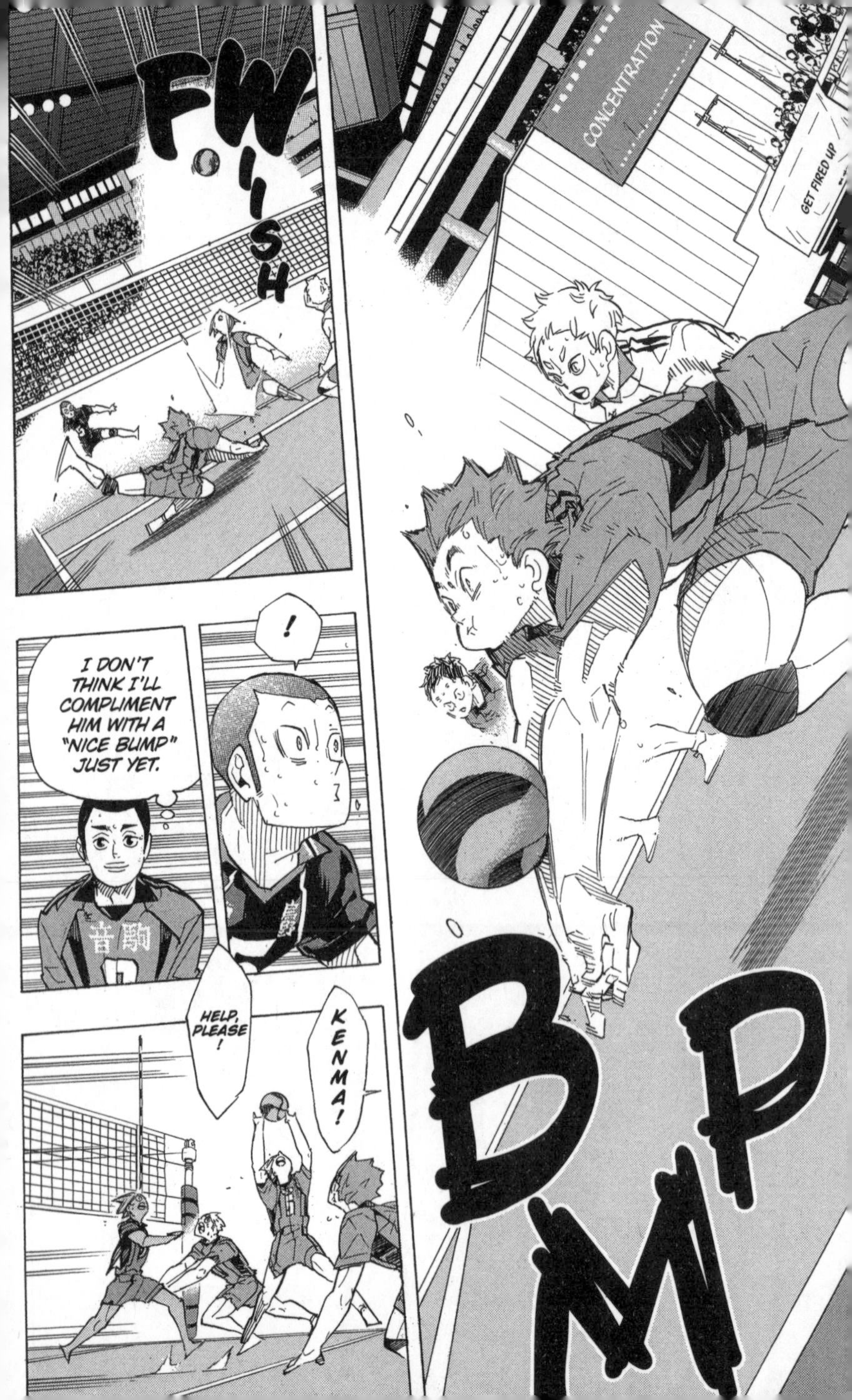
CONCENTRATION
GET FIRED UP
BUMP
FWISH
!
I DON'T THINK I'LL COMPLIMENT HIM WITH A "NICE BUMP" JUST YET.
音駒
KENMA!
HELP, PLEASE!

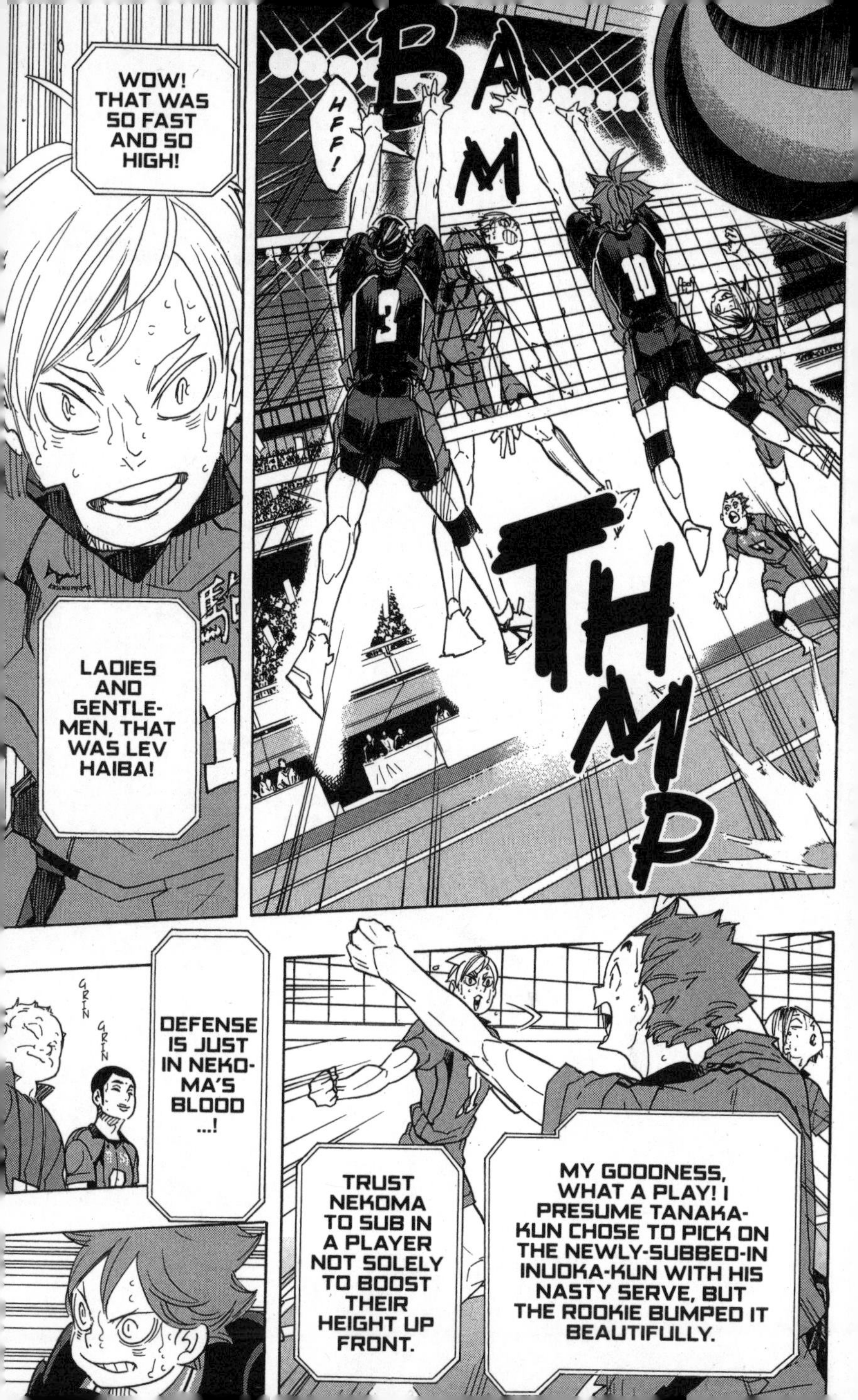
HFF!
BAM
THUMP
WOW! THAT WAS SO FAST AND SO HIGH!
LADIES AND GENTLEMEN, THAT WAS LEV HAIBA!
MY GOOODNESS, WHAT A PLAY! I PRESUME TANAKA-KUN CHOSE TO PICK ON THE NEWLY-SUBBED-IN INUOKA-KUN WITH HIS NASTY SERVE, BUT THE ROOKIE BUMPED IT BEAUTIFULLY.
TRUST NEKOMA TO SUB IN A PLAYER NOT SOLELY TO BOOST THEIR HEIGHT UP FRONT.
DEFENSE IS JUST IN NEKOMA'S BLOOD ...!
GRIN
GRIN

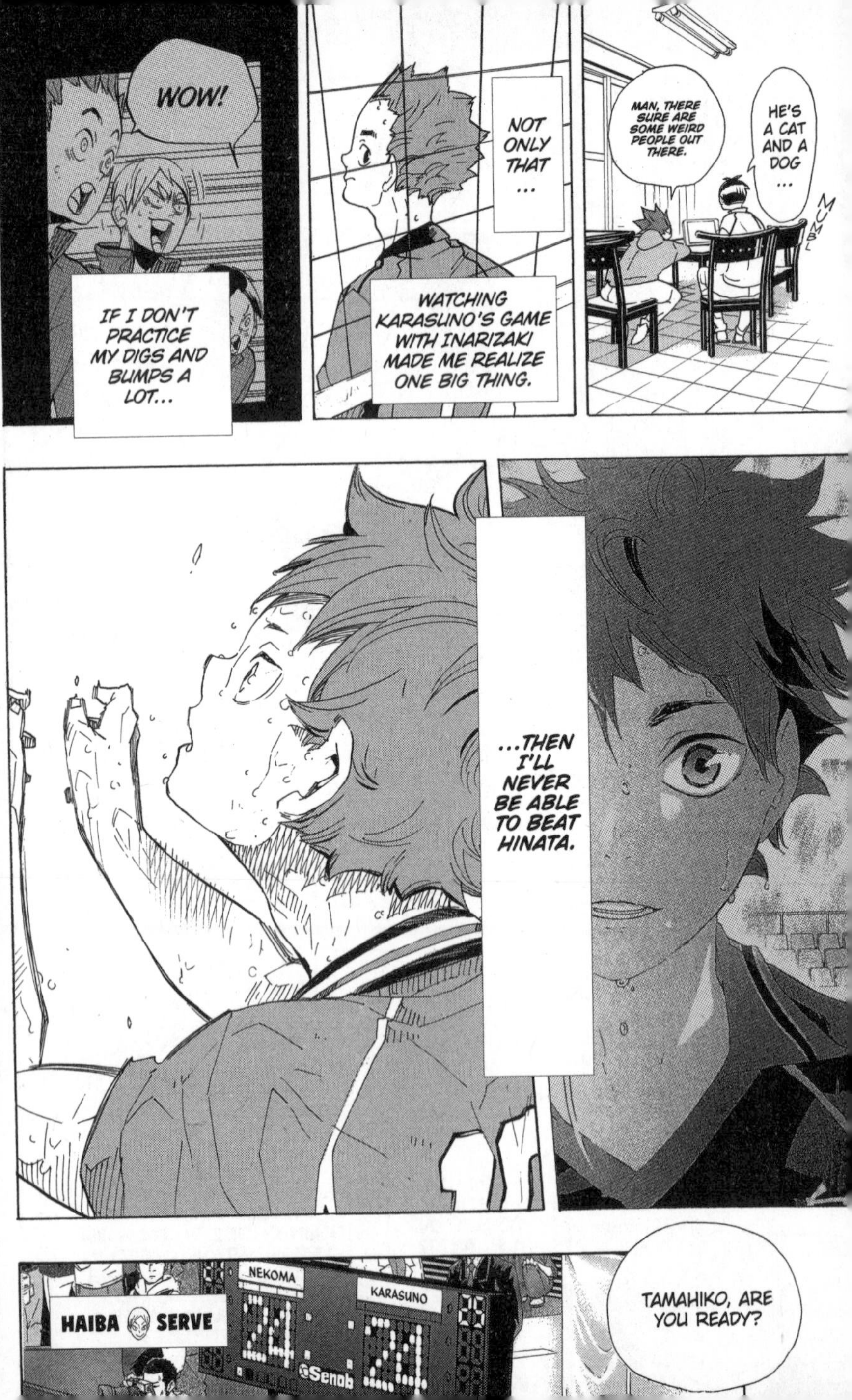
HE'S A CAT AND A DOG ...
MUMBL
MAN, THERE SURE ARE SOME WEIRD PEOPLE OUT THERE.
NOT ONLY THAT ...
WATCHING KARASUNO'S GAME WITH INARIZAKI MADE ME REALIZE ONE BIG THING.
WOW!
IF I DON'T PRACTICE MY DIGS AND BUMPS A LOT...
...THEN I'LL NEVER BE ABLE TO BEAT HINATA.
TAMAHIKO, ARE YOU READY?
NEKOMA
KARASUNO
HAIBA SERVE

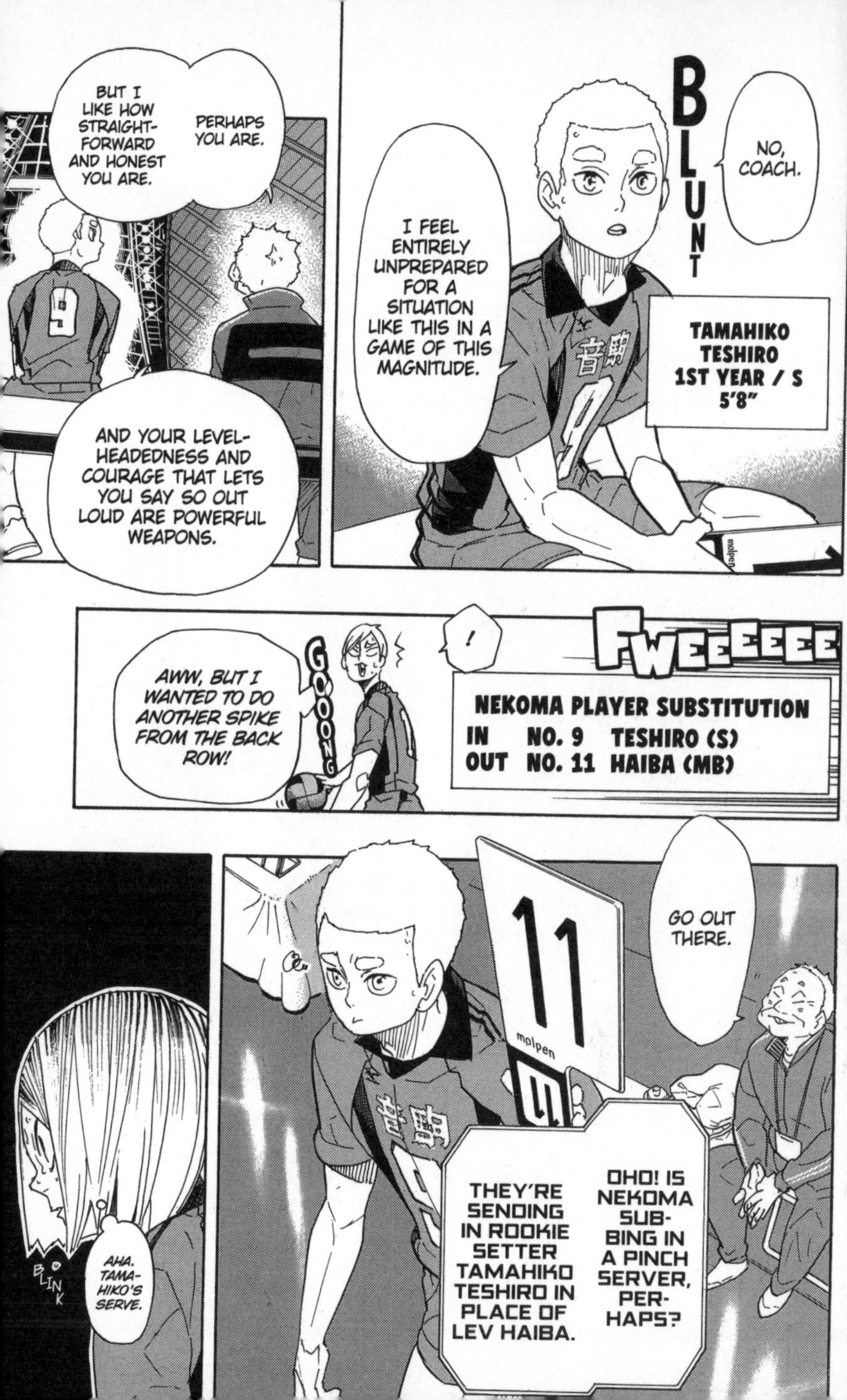

NO, COACH.
BLUNT
I FEEL ENTIRELY UNPREPARED FOR A SITUATION LIKE THIS IN A GAME OF THIS MAGNITUDE.
TAMAHIKO TESHIRO
1ST YEAR / S
5'8"
PERHAPS YOU ARE.
BUT I LIKE HOW STRAIGHT-FORWARD AND HONEST YOU ARE.
AND YOUR LEVEL-HEADEDNESS AND COURAGE THAT LETS YOU SAY SO OUT LOUD ARE POWERFUL WEAPONS.
FWEEEEEE
NEKOMA PLAYER SUBSTITUTION
IN NO. 9 TESHIRO (S)
OUT NO. 11 HAIBA (MB)
!
GOOONG
AWW, BUT I WANTED TO DO ANOTHER SPIKE FROM THE BACK ROW!
GO OUT THERE.
11
OHO! IS NEKOMA SUB-BING IN A PINCH SERVER, PER-HAPS?
THEY'RE SENDING IN ROOKIE SETTER TAMAHIKO TESHIRO IN PLACE OF LEV HAIBA.
BLINK
AHA. TAMA-HIKO'S SERVE.

HELLO FROM BEYOND THE (PAGE) EDGE!! GUESS WHICH PANEL THIS IS!!

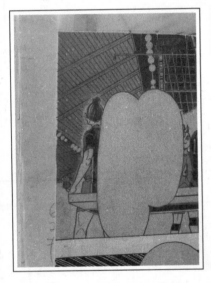

FROM CHAPTER 316

I THINK I'D LIKE TO SHOW OFF SOME OF THE LITTLE SCRIBBLES THAT SOMETIMES APPEAR IN PLACES THAT DON'T GET PRINTED.

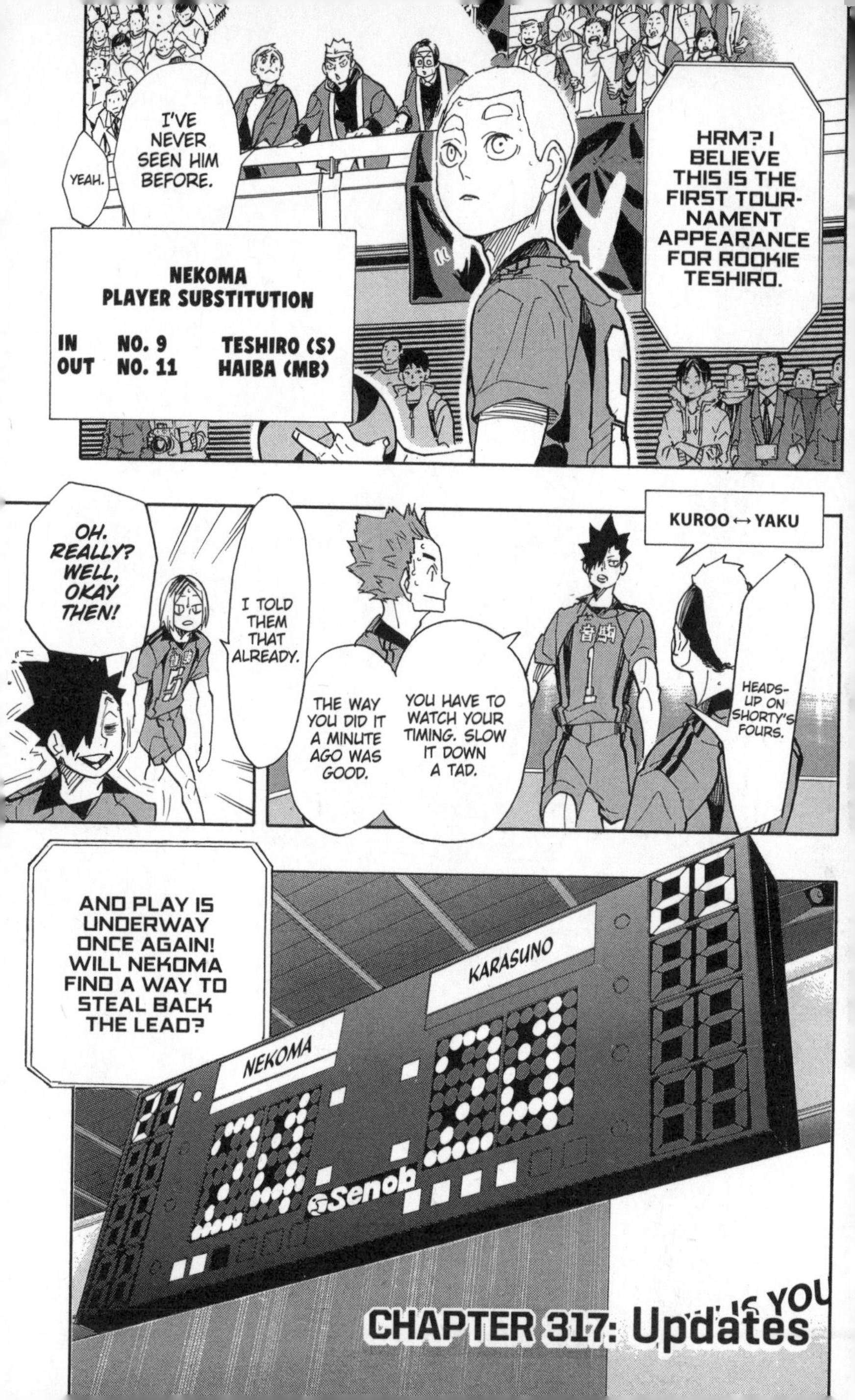
HRM? I BELIEVE THIS IS THE FIRST TOUR-NAMENT APPEARANCE FOR ROOKIE TESHIRO.
I'VE NEVER SEEN HIM BEFORE.
YEAH.
NEKOMA PLAYER SUBSTITUTION
IN NO. 9 TESHIRO (S)
OUT NO. 11 HAIBA (MB)
KUROO ↔ YAKU
HEADS-UP ON SHORTY'S FOURS.
YOU HAVE TO WATCH YOUR TIMING. SLOW IT DOWN A TAD.
THE WAY YOU DID IT A MINUTE AGO WAS GOOD.
I TOLD THEM THAT ALREADY.
OH. REALLY? WELL, OKAY THEN!
AND PLAY IS UNDERWAY ONCE AGAIN! WILL NEKOMA FIND A WAY TO STEAL BACK THE LEAD?
KARASUNO
NEKOMA
Senob

CHAPTER 317: Updates

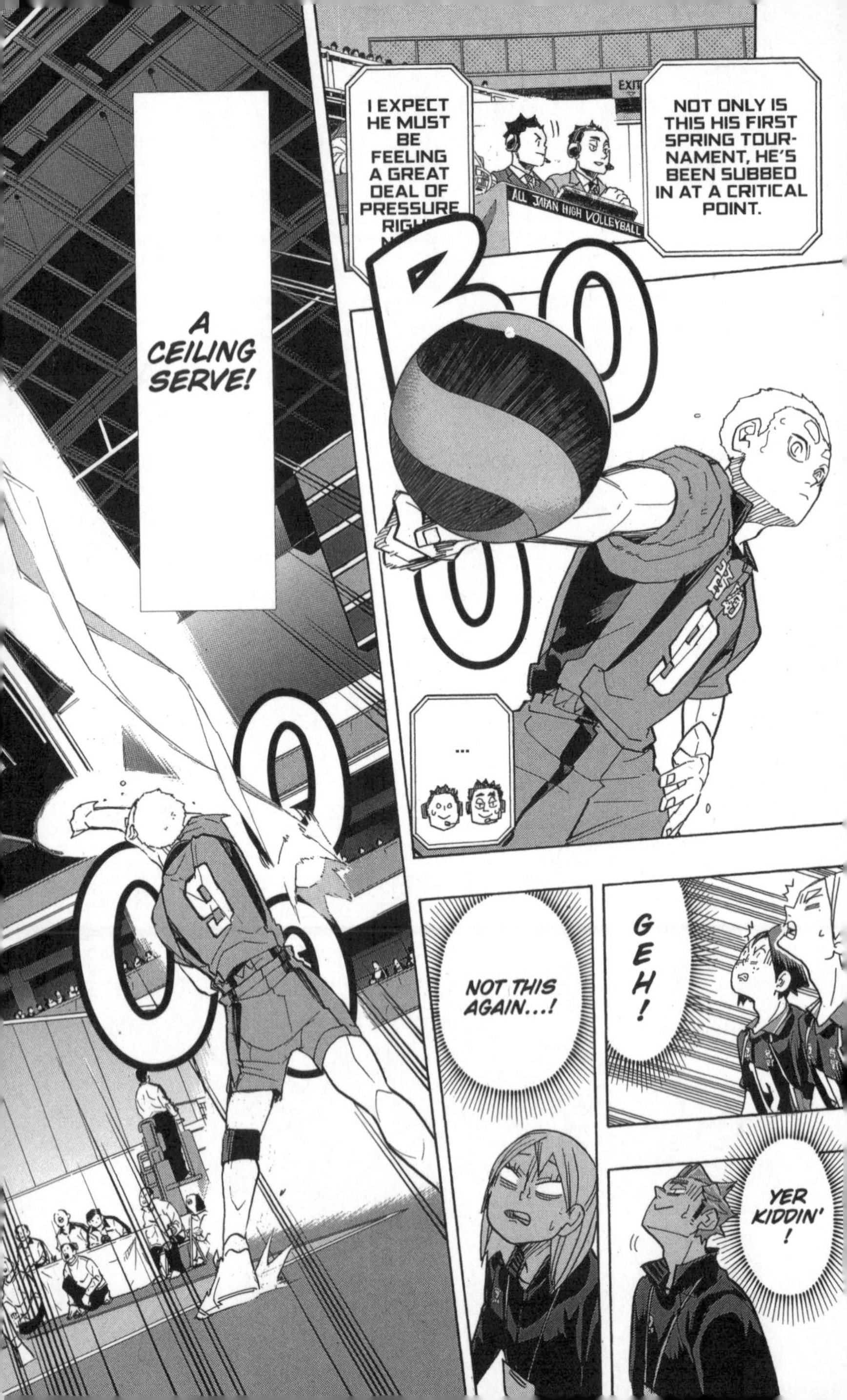
NOT ONLY IS THIS HIS FIRST SPRING TOURNAMENT, HE'S BEEN SUBBED IN AT A CRITICAL POINT.
I EXPECT HE MUST BE FEELING A GREAT DEAL OF PRESSURE RIGH
EXIT
ALL JAPAN HIGH VOLLEYBALL
...
GEH!
NOT THIS AGAIN...!
YER KIDDIN'!
A CEILING SERVE!

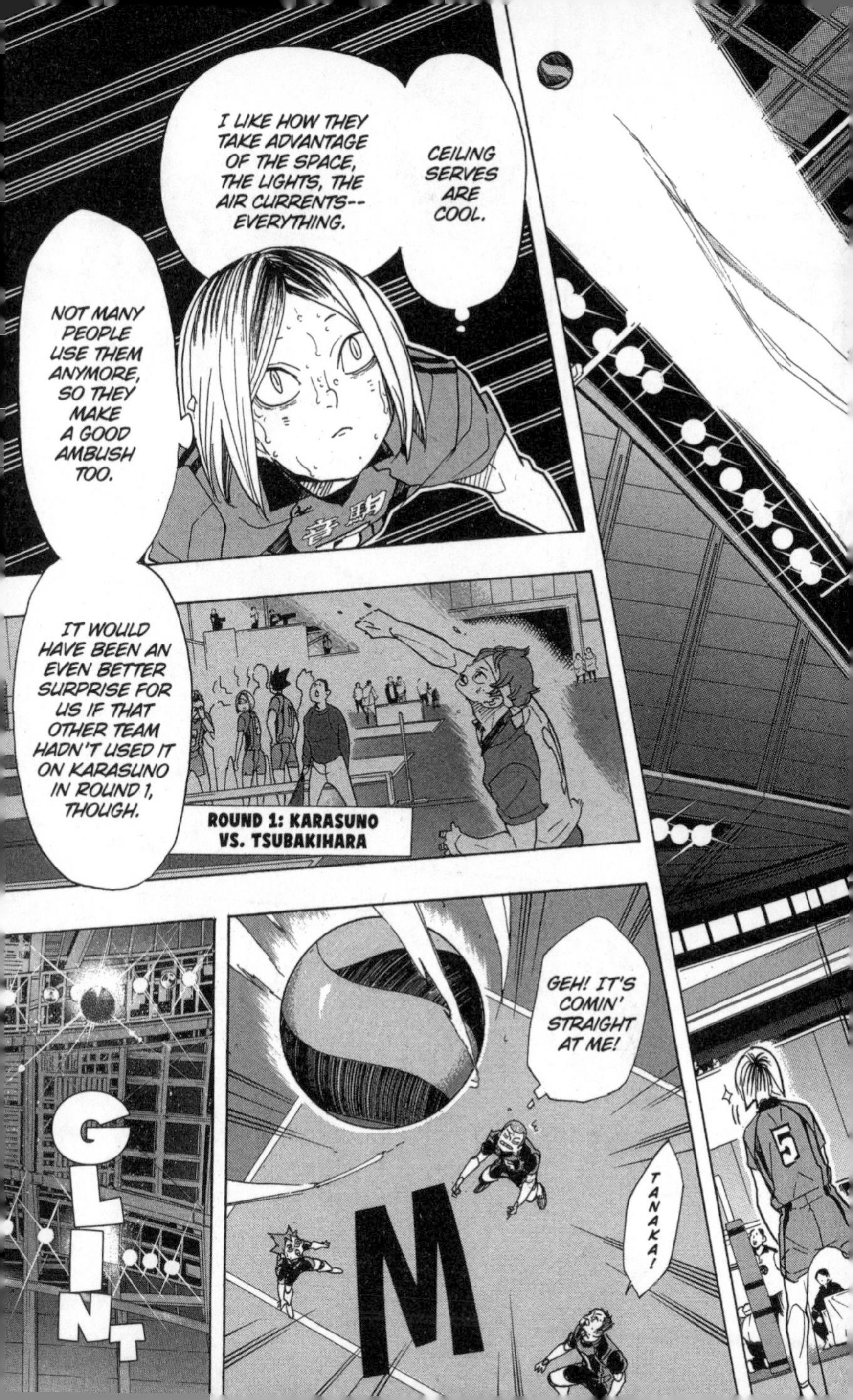
CEILING SERVES ARE COOL.
I LIKE HOW THEY TAKE ADVANTAGE OF THE SPACE, THE LIGHTS, THE AIR CURRENTS-- EVERYTHING.
NOT MANY PEOPLE USE THEM ANYMORE, SO THEY MAKE A GOOD AMBUSH TOO.
IT WOULD HAVE BEEN AN EVEN BETTER SURPRISE FOR US IF THAT OTHER TEAM HADN'T USED IT ON KARASUNO IN ROUND 1, THOUGH.
ROUND 1: KARASUNO VS. TSUBAKIHARA
TANAKA!
GEH! IT'S COMIN' STRAIGHT AT ME!
M
GLINT

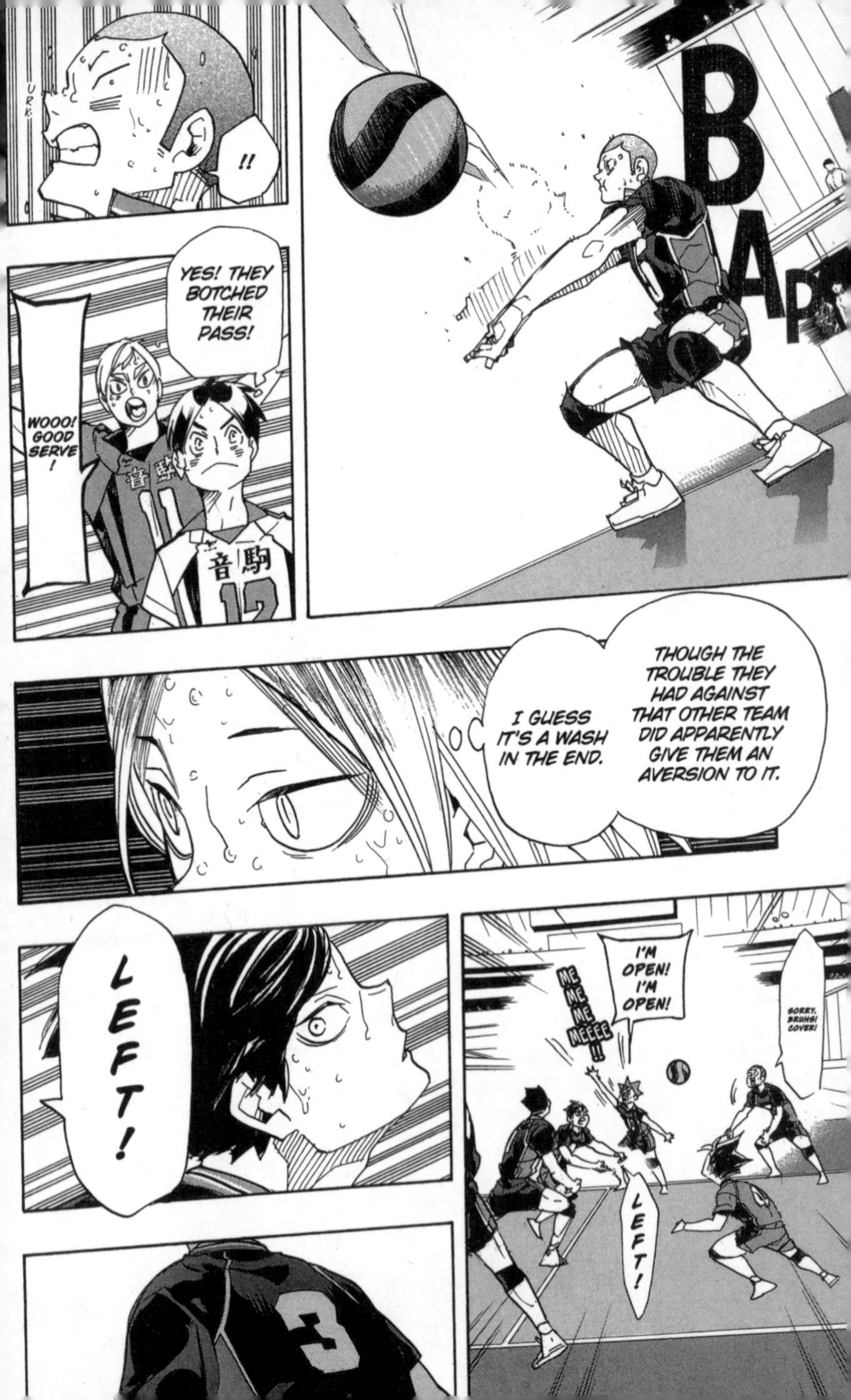
BAP
URK
!!
YES! THEY BOTCHED THEIR PASS!
WOOO! GOOD SERVE!
THOUGH THE TROUBLE THEY HAD AGAINST THAT OTHER TEAM DID APPARENTLY GIVE THEM AN AVERSION TO IT.
I GUESS IT'S A WASH IN THE END.
SORRY, BRUHS! COVER!
I'M OPEN! I'M OPEN!
ME ME ME MEEEE!!
LEFT!
LEFT!

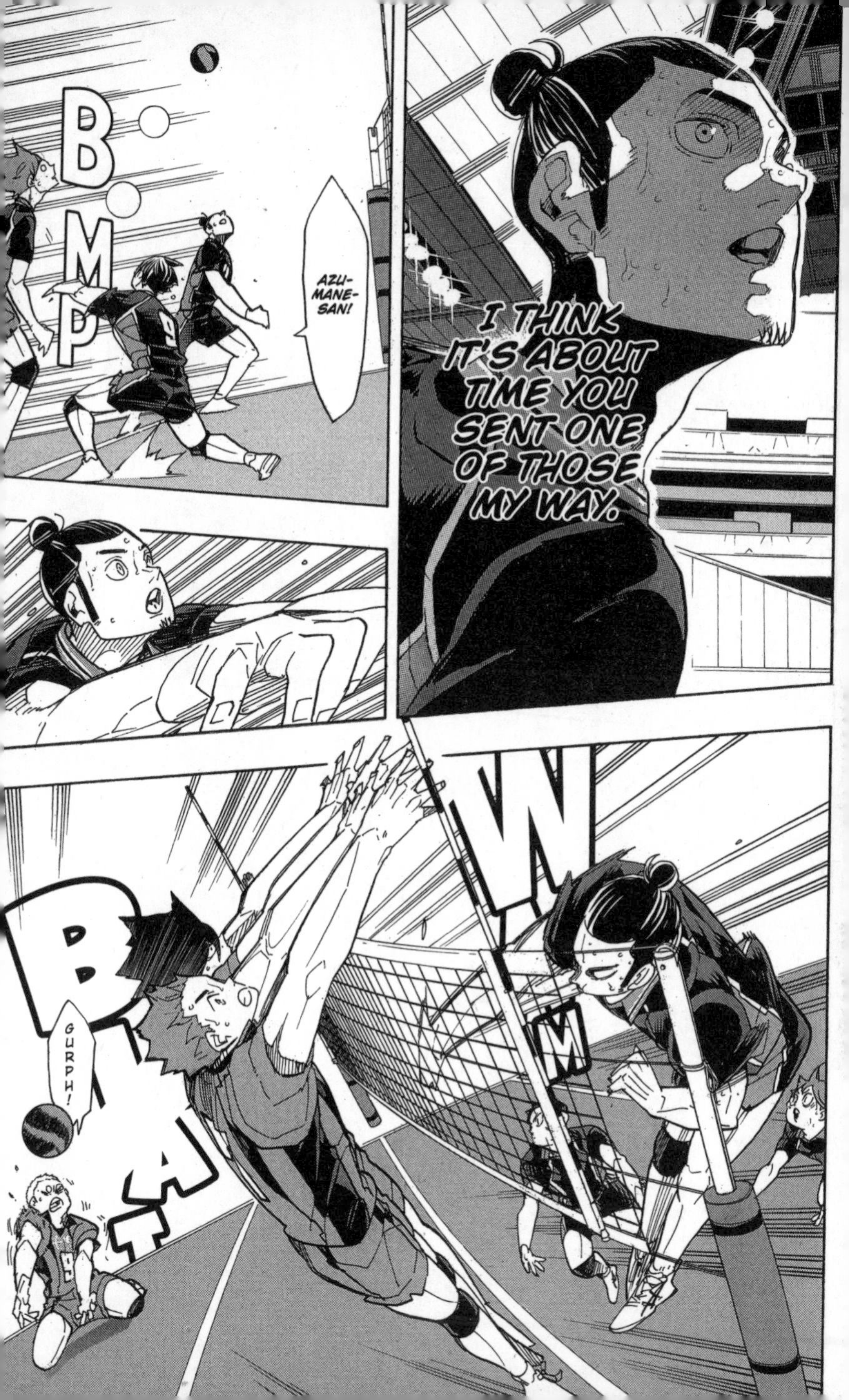
I THINK IT'S ABOUT TIME YOU SENT ONE OF THOSE MY WAY.
BMP
AZUMANE-SAN!
GURPH!

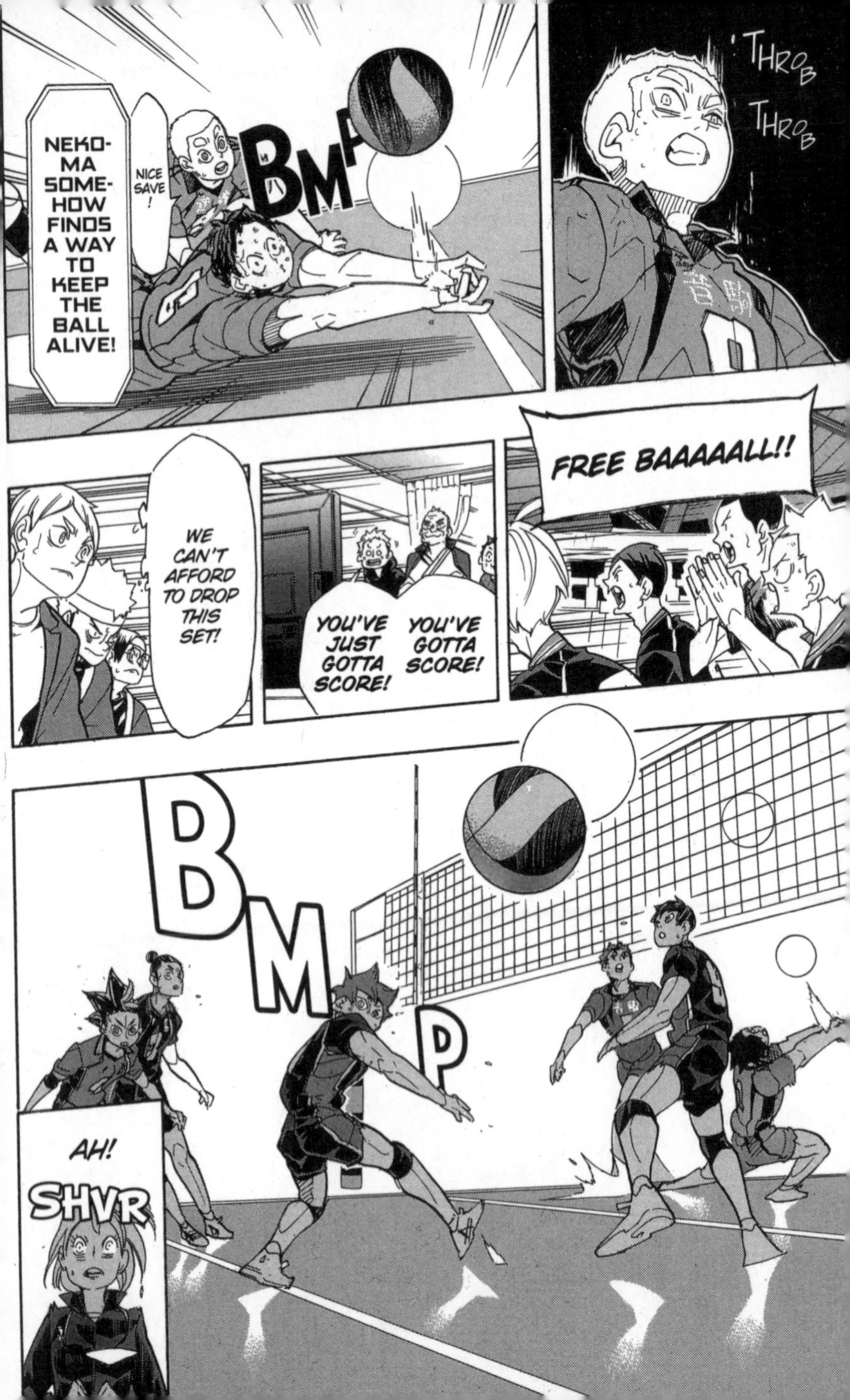
THROB
THROB
BMP
NICE SAVE!
NEKOMA SOMEHOW FINDS A WAY TO KEEP THE BALL ALIVE!
FREE BAAAAALL!!
YOU'VE GOTTA SCORE!
YOU'VE JUST GOTTA SCORE!
WE CAN'T AFFORD TO DROP THIS SET!
BMP
AH!
SHVR

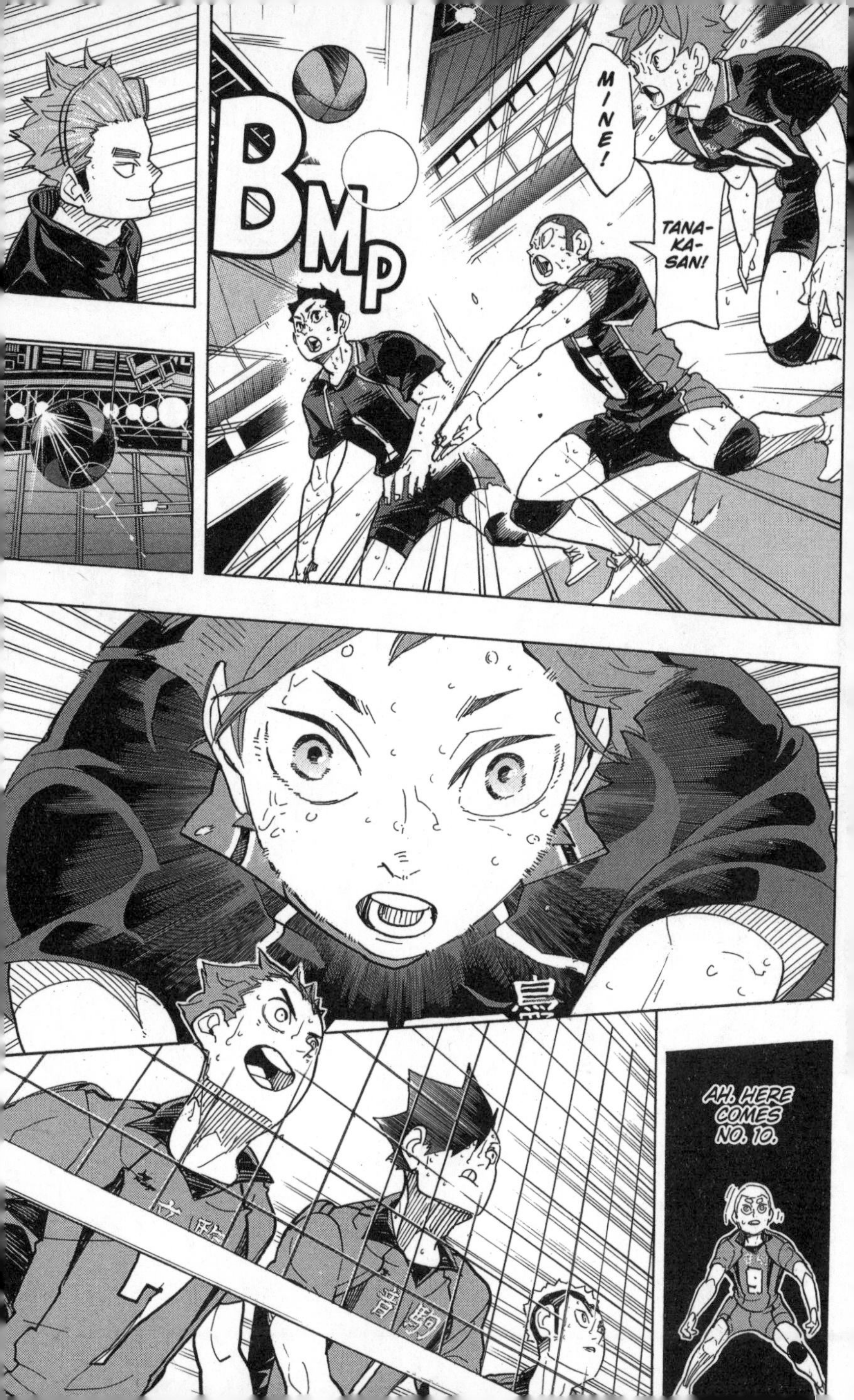
MINE!
TANAKA-SAN!
BMP
AH. HERE COMES NO. 10.

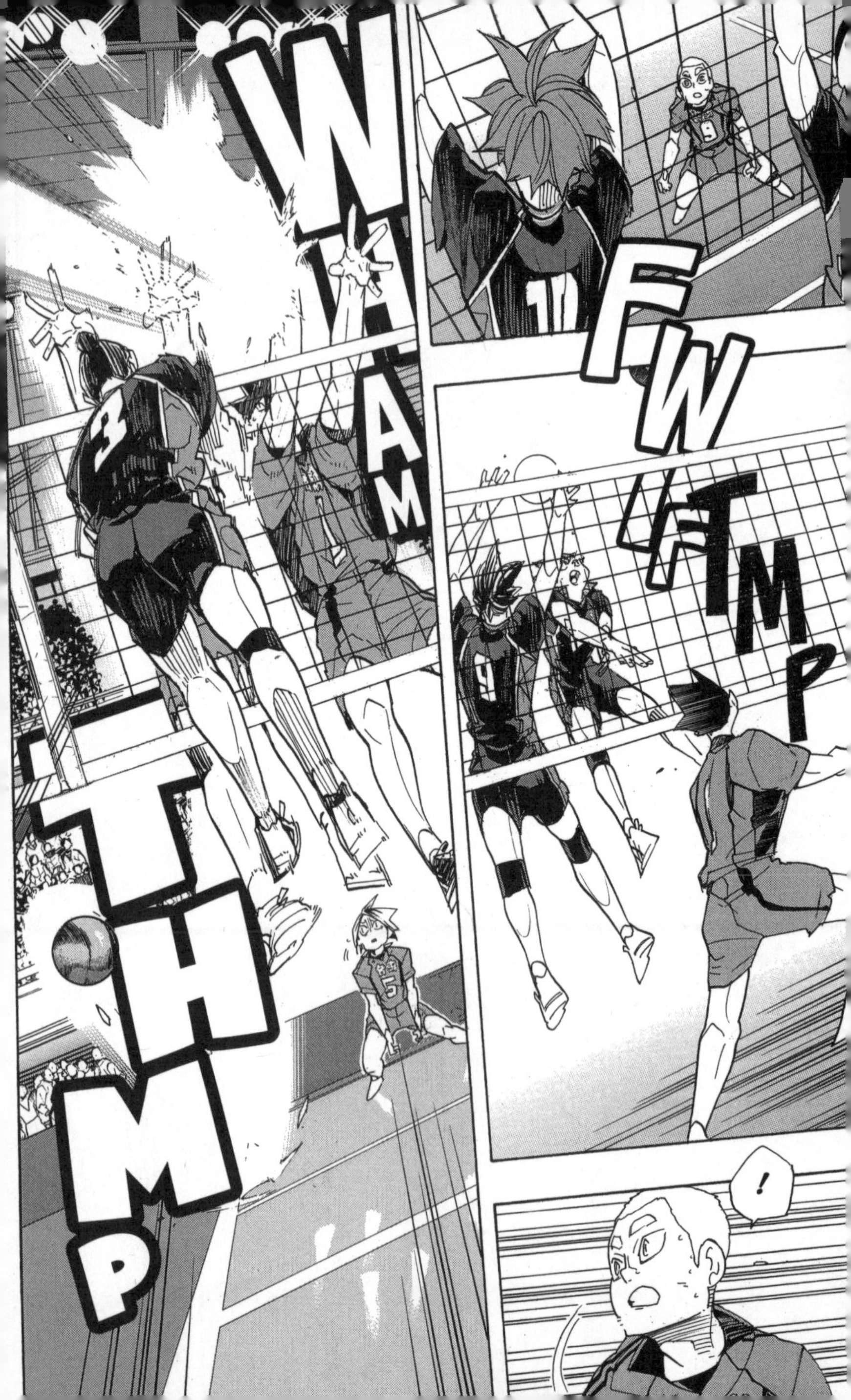
FWTMP
!
WHAM
THMP

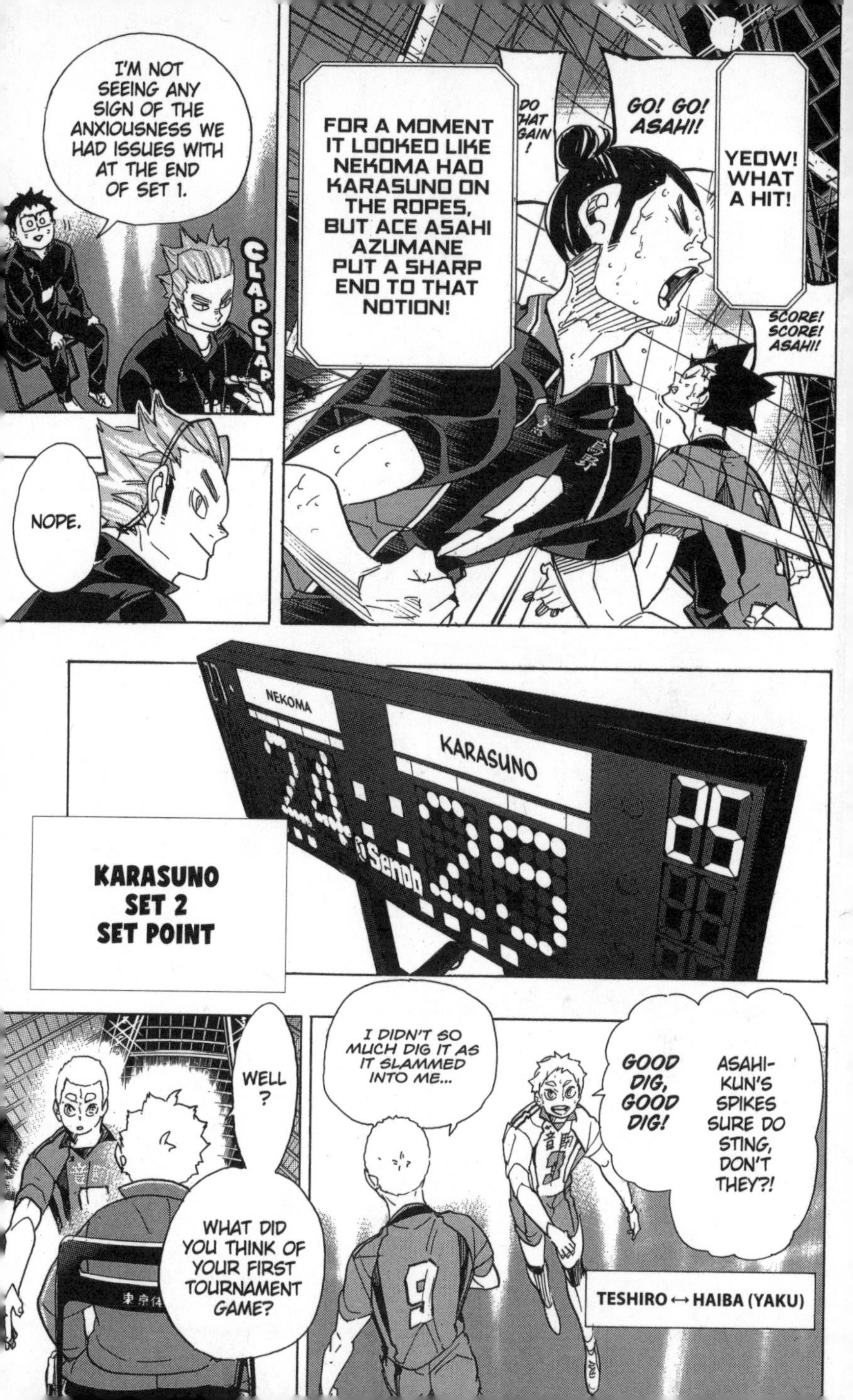
YEOW! WHAT A HIT!
GO! GO! ASAHI!
FOR A MOMENT IT LOOKED LIKE NEKOMA HAD KARASUNO ON THE ROPES, BUT ACE ASAHI AZUMANE PUT A SHARP END TO THAT NOTION!
SCORE! SCORE! ASAHI!
I'M NOT SEEING ANY SIGN OF THE ANXIOUSNESS WE HAD ISSUES WITH AT THE END OF SET 1.
CLAP CLAP
NOPE.
NEKOMA
KARASUNO
25
KARASUNO SET 2 SET POINT
GOOD DIG, GOOD DIG!
ASAHI-KUN'S SPIKES SURE DO STING, DON'T THEY?!
I DIDN'T SO MUCH DIG IT AS IT SLAMMED INTO ME...
TESHIRO ↔ HAIBA (YAKU)
WELL?
WHAT DID YOU THINK OF YOUR FIRST TOURNAMENT GAME?

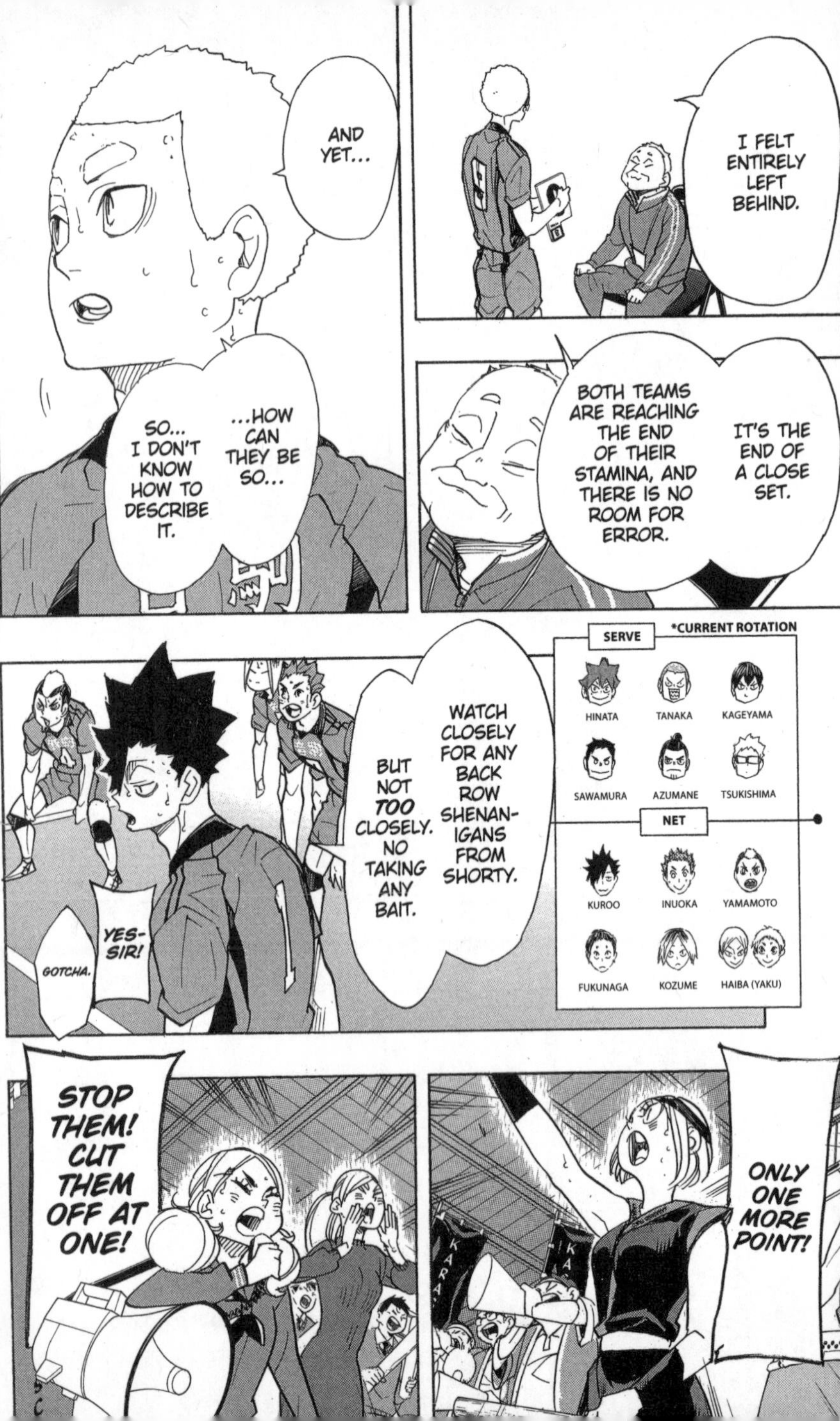
I FELT ENTIRELY LEFT BEHIND.
IT'S THE END OF A CLOSE SET.
BOTH TEAMS ARE REACHING THE END OF THEIR STAMINA, AND THERE IS NO ROOM FOR ERROR.
AND YET...
...HOW CAN THEY BE SO...
SO... I DON'T KNOW HOW TO DESCRIBE IT.
*CURRENT ROTATION
SERVE
HINATA
TANAKA
KAGEYAMA
SAWAMURA
AZUMANE
TSUKISHIMA
NET
KUROO
INUOKA
YAMAMOTO
FUKUNAGA
KOZUME
HAIBA (YAKU)
WATCH CLOSELY FOR ANY BACK ROW SHENANIGANS FROM SHORTY.
BUT NOT *TOO* CLOSELY. NO TAKING ANY BAIT.
YES-SIR!
GOTCHA.
ONLY ONE MORE POINT!
STOP THEM! CUT THEM OFF AT ONE!

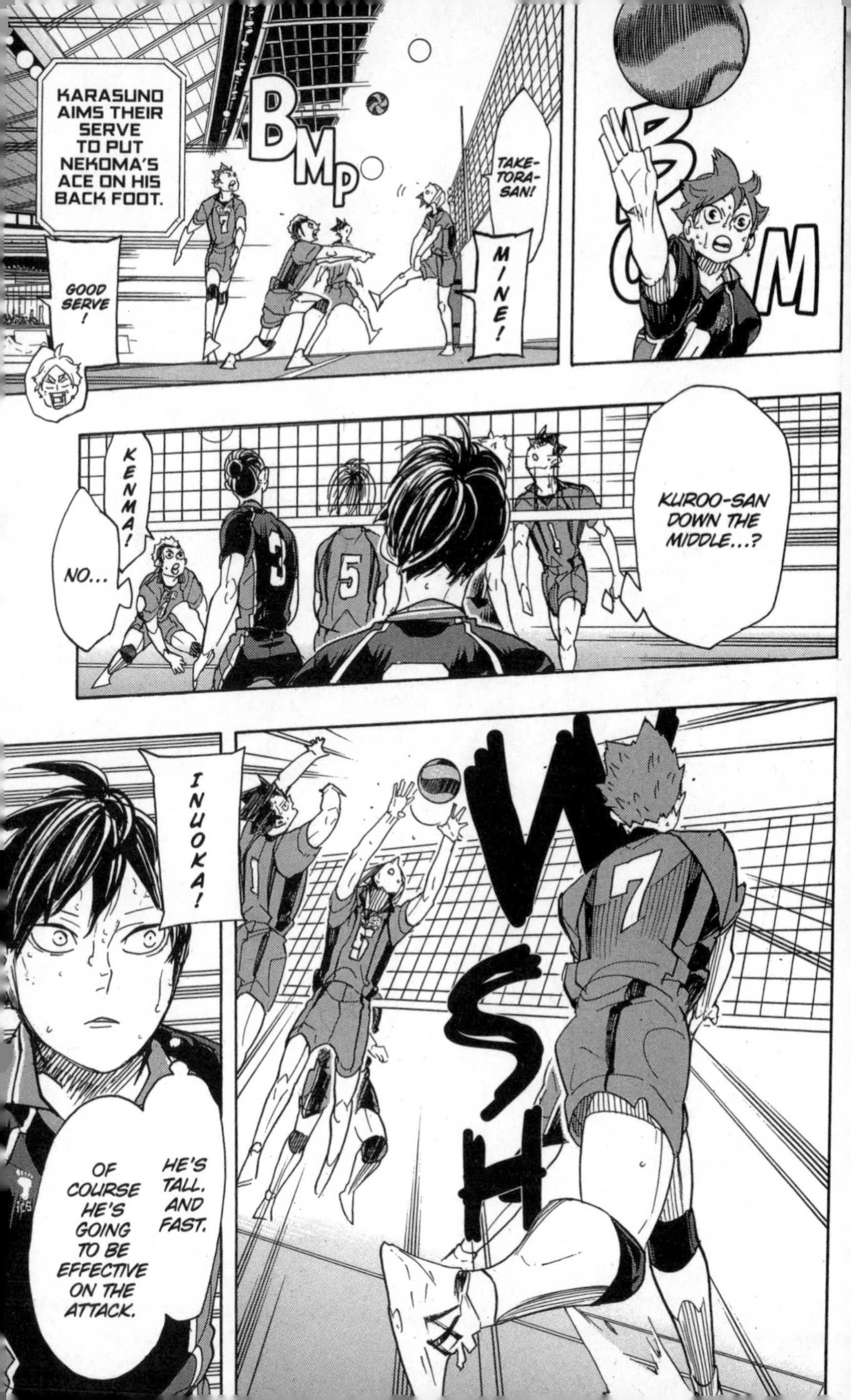
BOOM
TAKE-TORA-SAN!
MINE!
KARASUNO AIMS THEIR SERVE TO PUT NEKOMA'S ACE ON HIS BACK FOOT.
BMP
GOOD SERVE!
KUROO-SAN DOWN THE MIDDLE...?
KENMA!
NO...
WSH
INUOKA!
HE'S TALL. AND FAST.
OF COURSE HE'S GOING TO BE EFFECTIVE ON THE ATTACK.

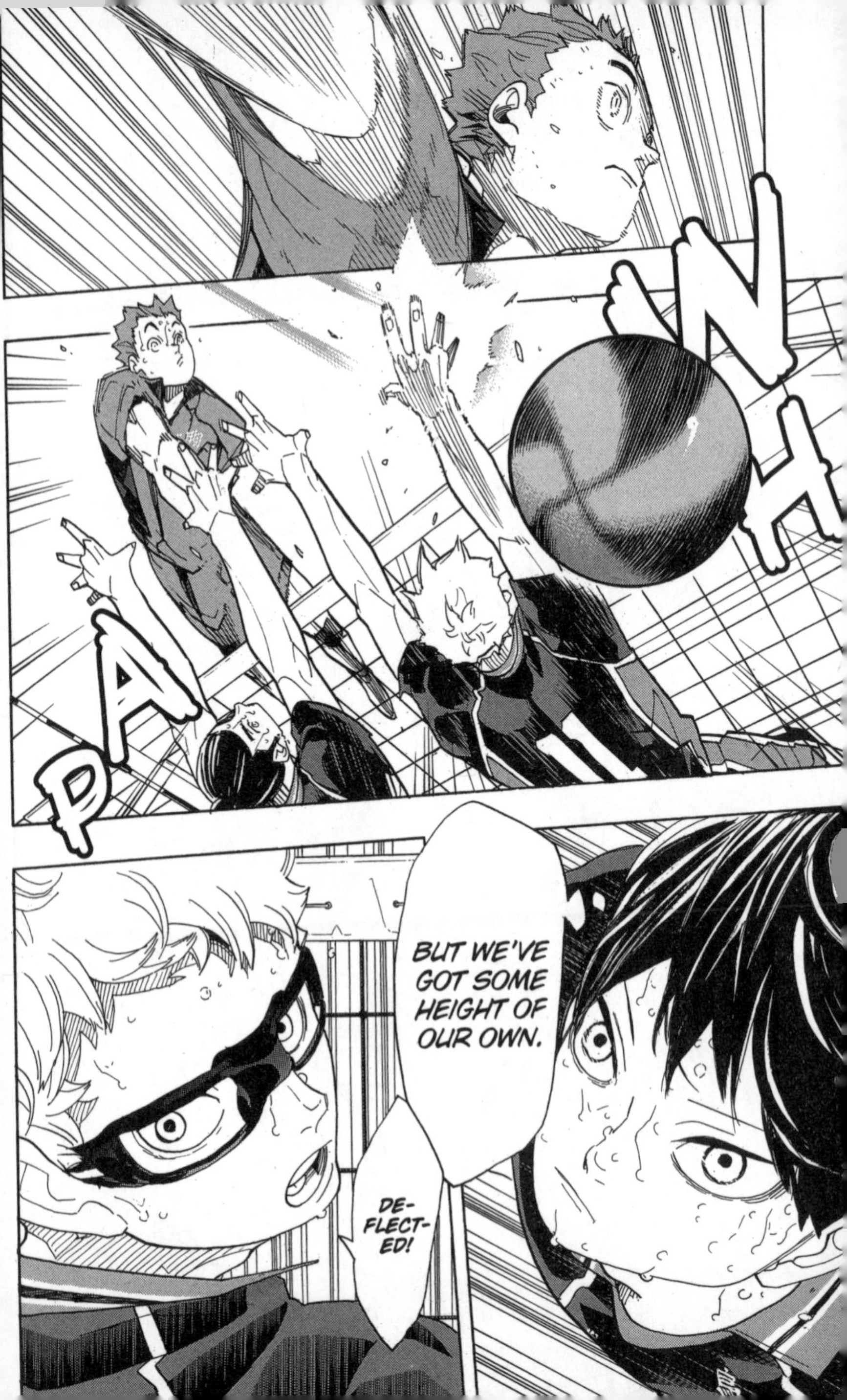
BUT WE'VE GOT SOME HEIGHT OF OUR OWN.
DE-FLECT-ED!

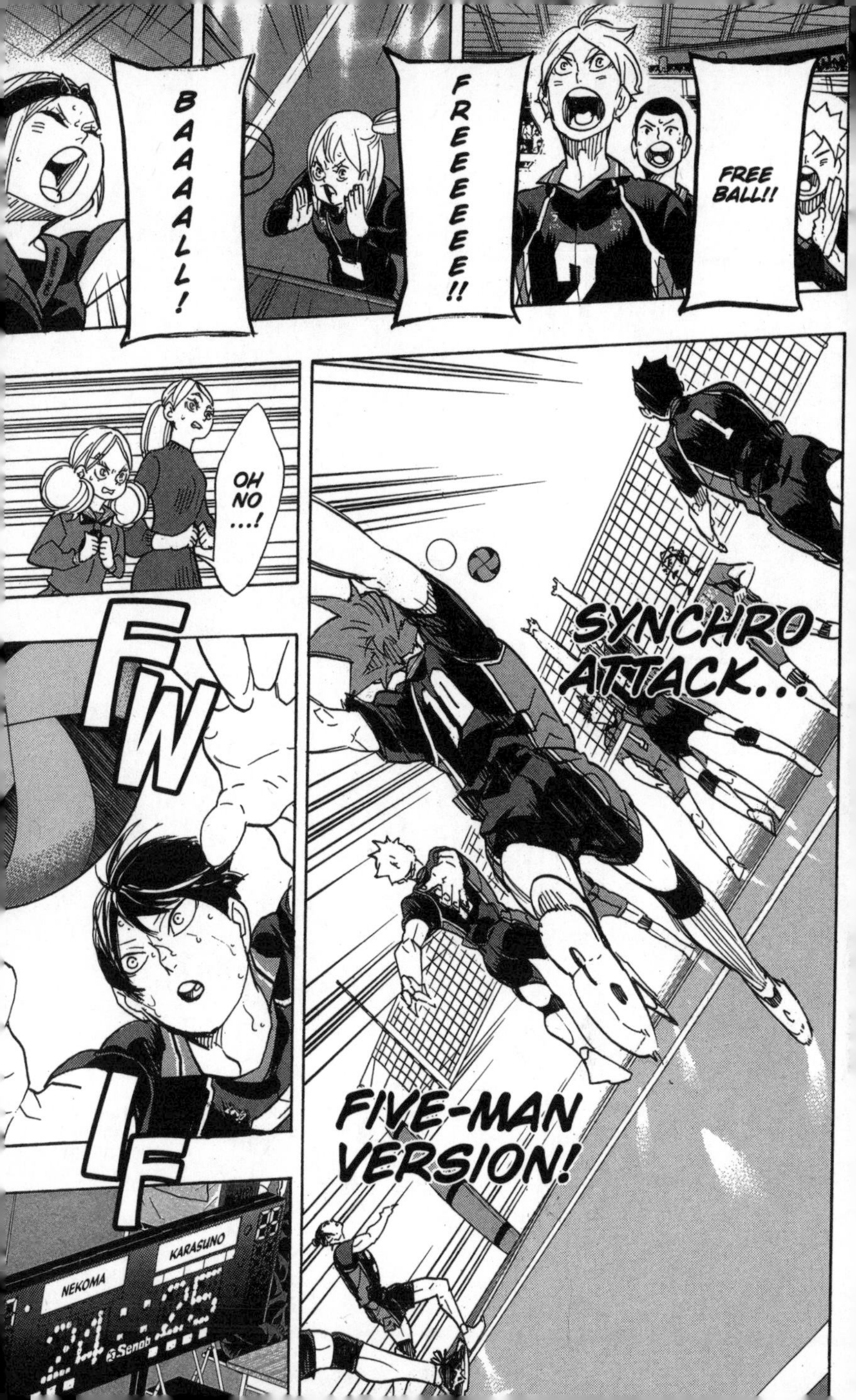
FREE BALL!!
FREEEEEEE!!
BAAAAALL!
SYNCHRO ATTACK...
FIVE-MAN VERSION!
OH NO ...!
FWIF
KARASUNO
NEKOMA
24
25

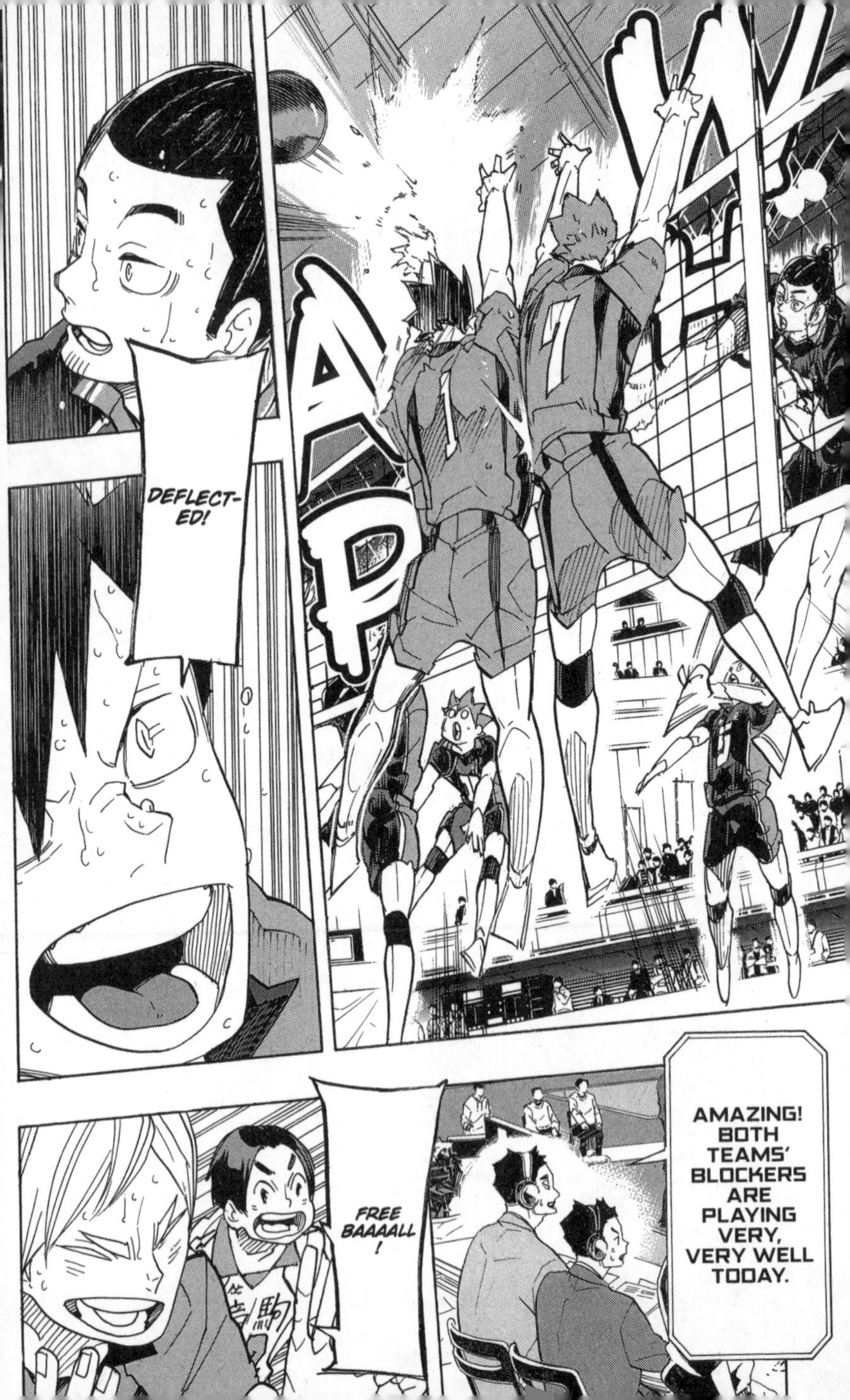
DEFLECT-ED!
AMAZING! BOTH TEAMS' BLOCKERS ARE PLAYING VERY, VERY WELL TODAY.
FREE BAAAALL!

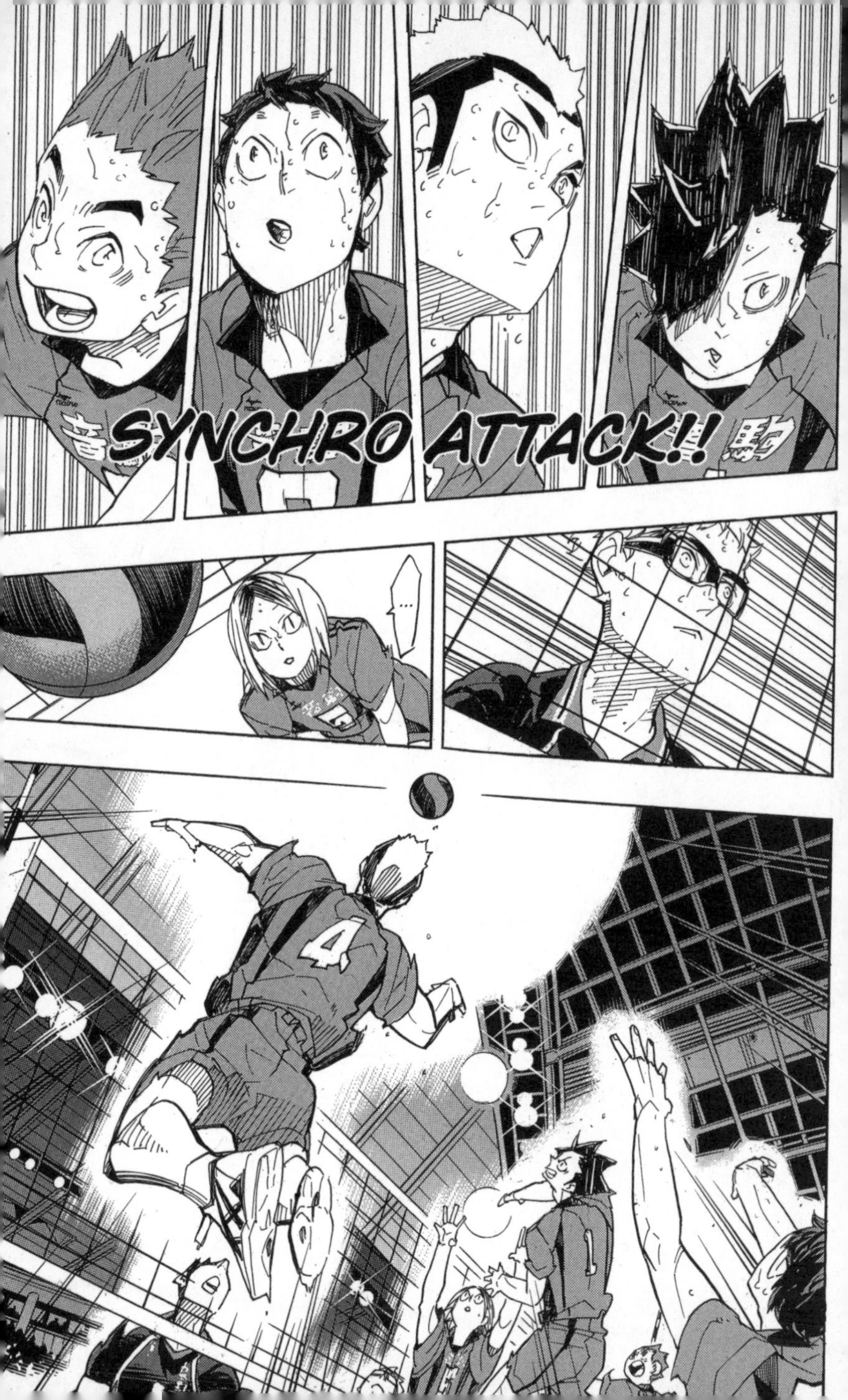
SYNCHRO ATTACK!!
...

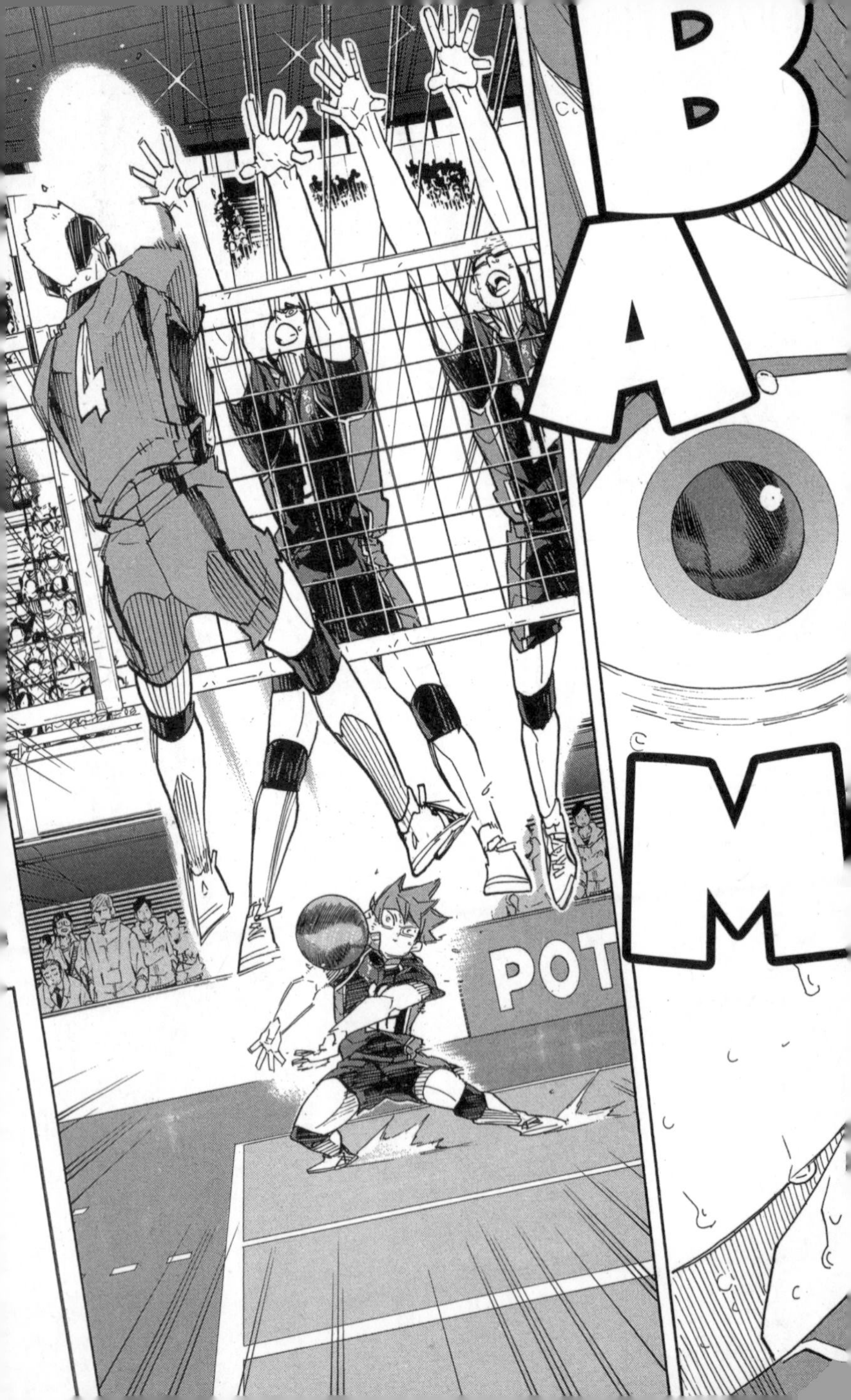
BAOM
POT

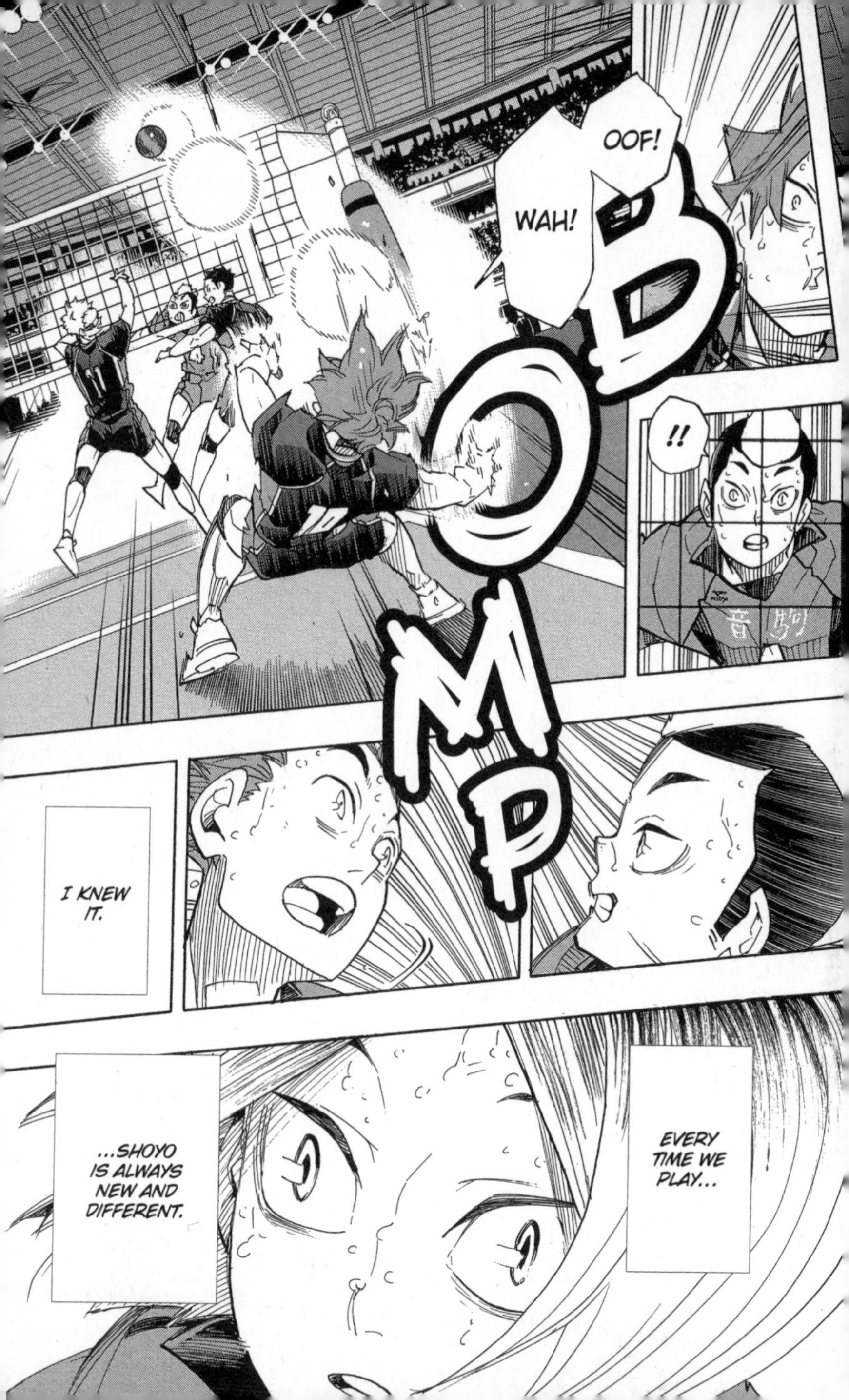
OOF!
WAH!
!!
BOOMP
I KNEW IT.
EVERY TIME WE PLAY...
...SHOYO IS ALWAYS NEW AND DIFFERENT.

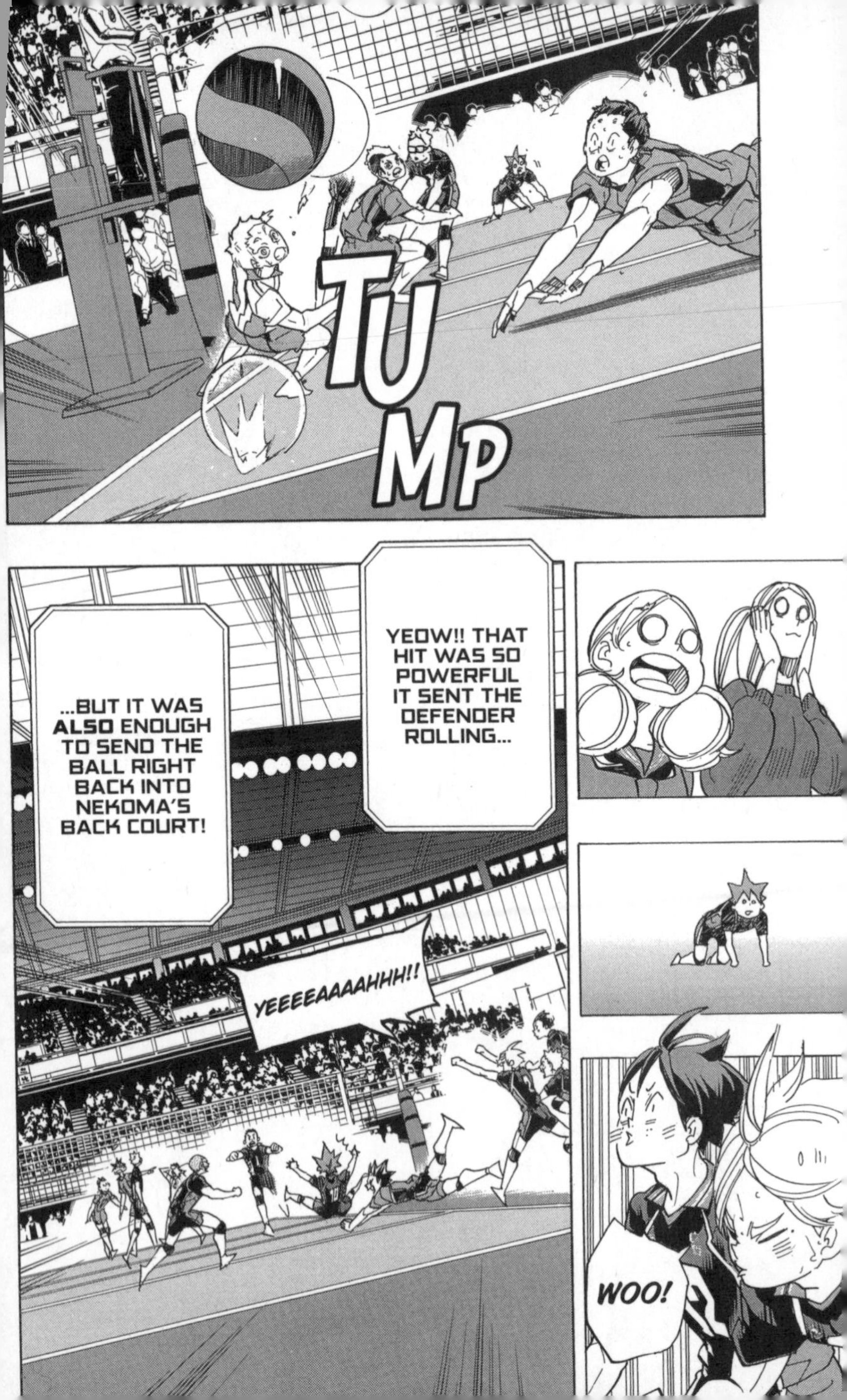
TUMP
WOO!
YEOW!! THAT HIT WAS SO POWERFUL IT SENT THE DEFENDER ROLLING...
...BUT IT WAS ALSO ENOUGH TO SEND THE BALL RIGHT BACK INTO NEKOMA'S BACK COURT!
YEEEEAAAAHHH!!

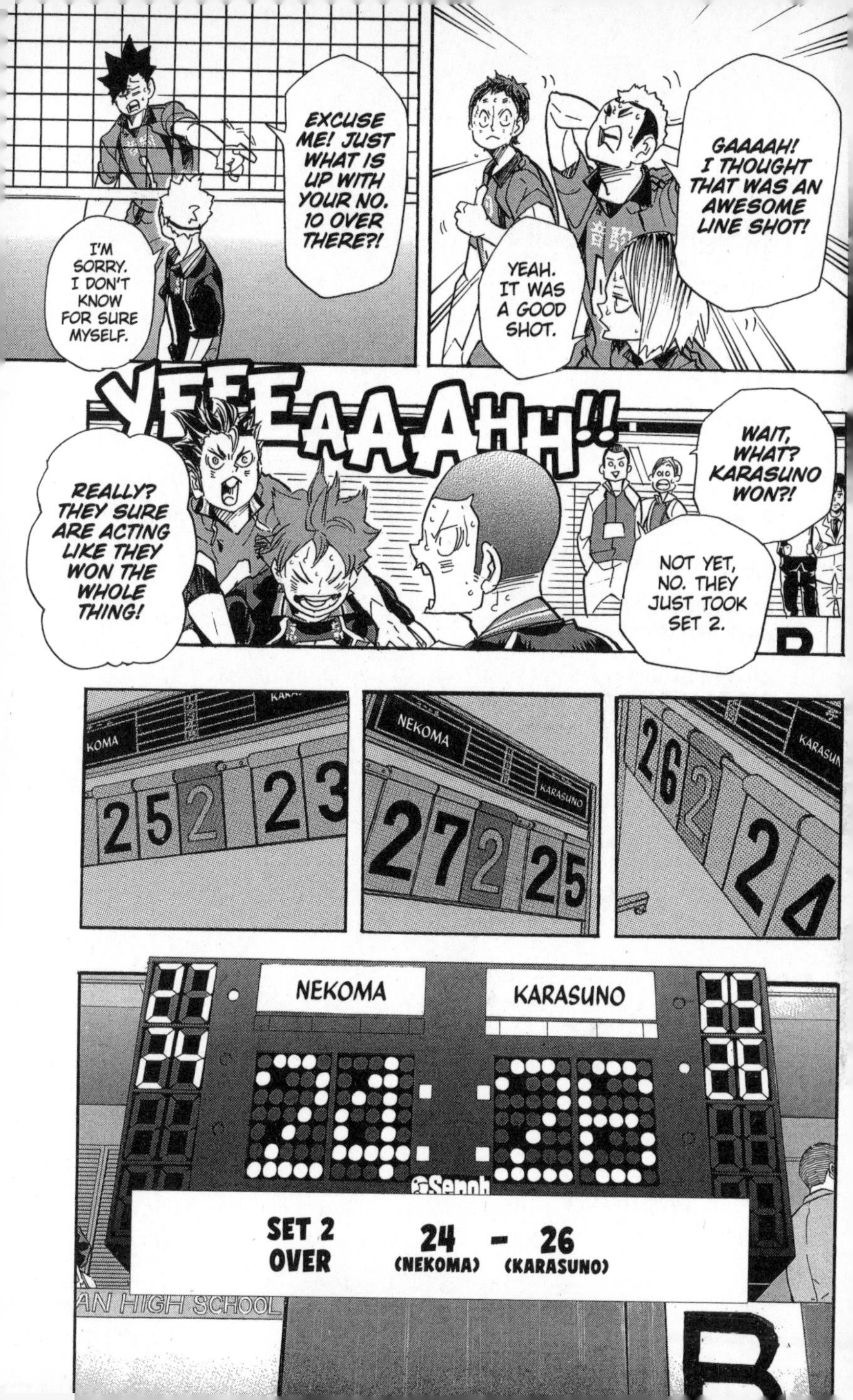
GAAAAH! I THOUGHT THAT WAS AN AWESOME LINE SHOT!
YEAH. IT WAS A GOOD SHOT.
EXCUSE ME! JUST WHAT IS UP WITH YOUR NO. 10 OVER THERE?!
I'M SORRY. I DON'T KNOW FOR SURE MYSELF.
YEEEAAAAHH!!
WAIT, WHAT? KARASUNO WON?!
NOT YET, NO. THEY JUST TOOK SET 2.
REALLY? THEY SURE ARE ACTING LIKE THEY WON THE WHOLE THING!
KARASUNO
26 2 24
NEKOMA
KARASUNO
27 2 25
KOMA
25 2 23
NEKOMA
KARASUNO
SET 2 OVER
24 - 26
(NEKOMA) (KARASUNO)
AN HIGH SCHOOL

TAMAHIKO TESHIRO

NEKOMA HIGH SCHOOL
CLASS 1-6

POSITION:
SETTER

HEIGHT: 5'8"

WEIGHT: 131 LBS.
(AS OF JANUARY, 1ST YEAR OF HIGH SCHOOL)

BIRTHDAY: JANUARY 14

FAVORITE FOOD:
SALT-GRILLED COD

CURRENT WORRY:
PEOPLE ASK HIM OUT OF THE BLUE, "WHY ARE YOU MAD?"

ABILITY PARAMETERS
(5-POINT SCALE)

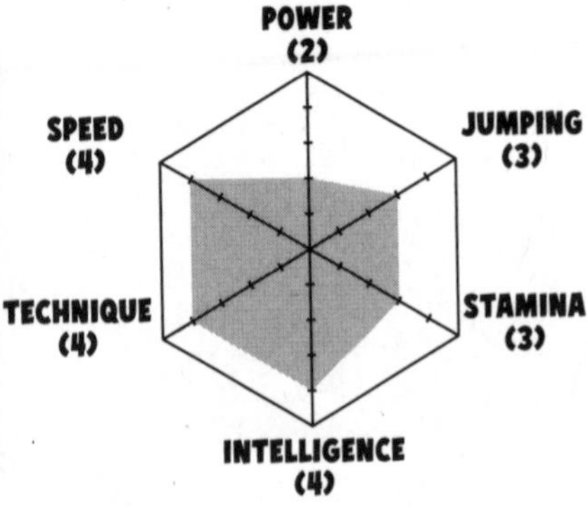
POWER (2)
JUMPING (3)
STAMINA (3)
INTELLIGENCE (4)
TECHNIQUE (4)
SPEED (4)

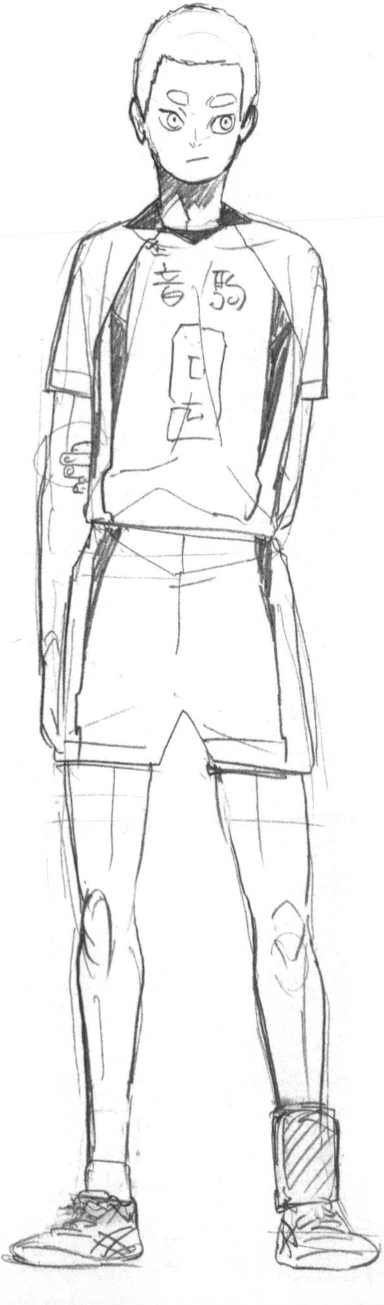

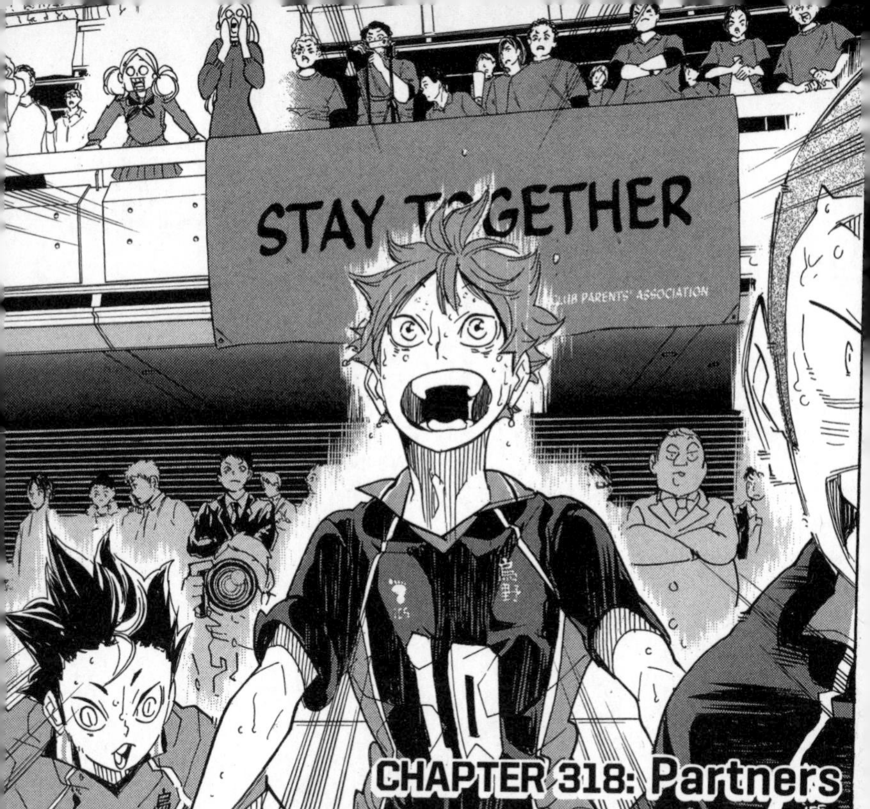
STAY T GETHER
CLUB PARENTS' ASSOCIATION
CHAPTER 318: Partners

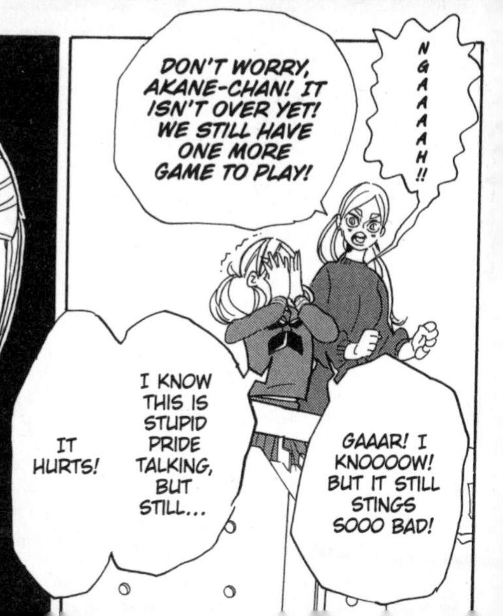
DON'T WORRY, AKANE-CHAN! IT ISN'T OVER YET! WE STILL HAVE ONE MORE GAME TO PLAY!
NGAAAAAH!!
GAAAR! I KNOOOOW! BUT IT STILL STINGS SOOO BAD!
I KNOW THIS IS STUPID PRIDE TALKING, BUT STILL...
IT HURTS!

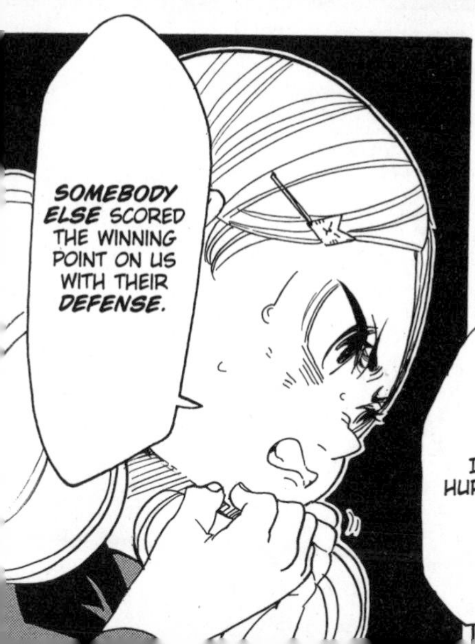
SOMEBODY ELSE SCORED THE WINNING POINT ON US WITH THEIR DEFENSE.

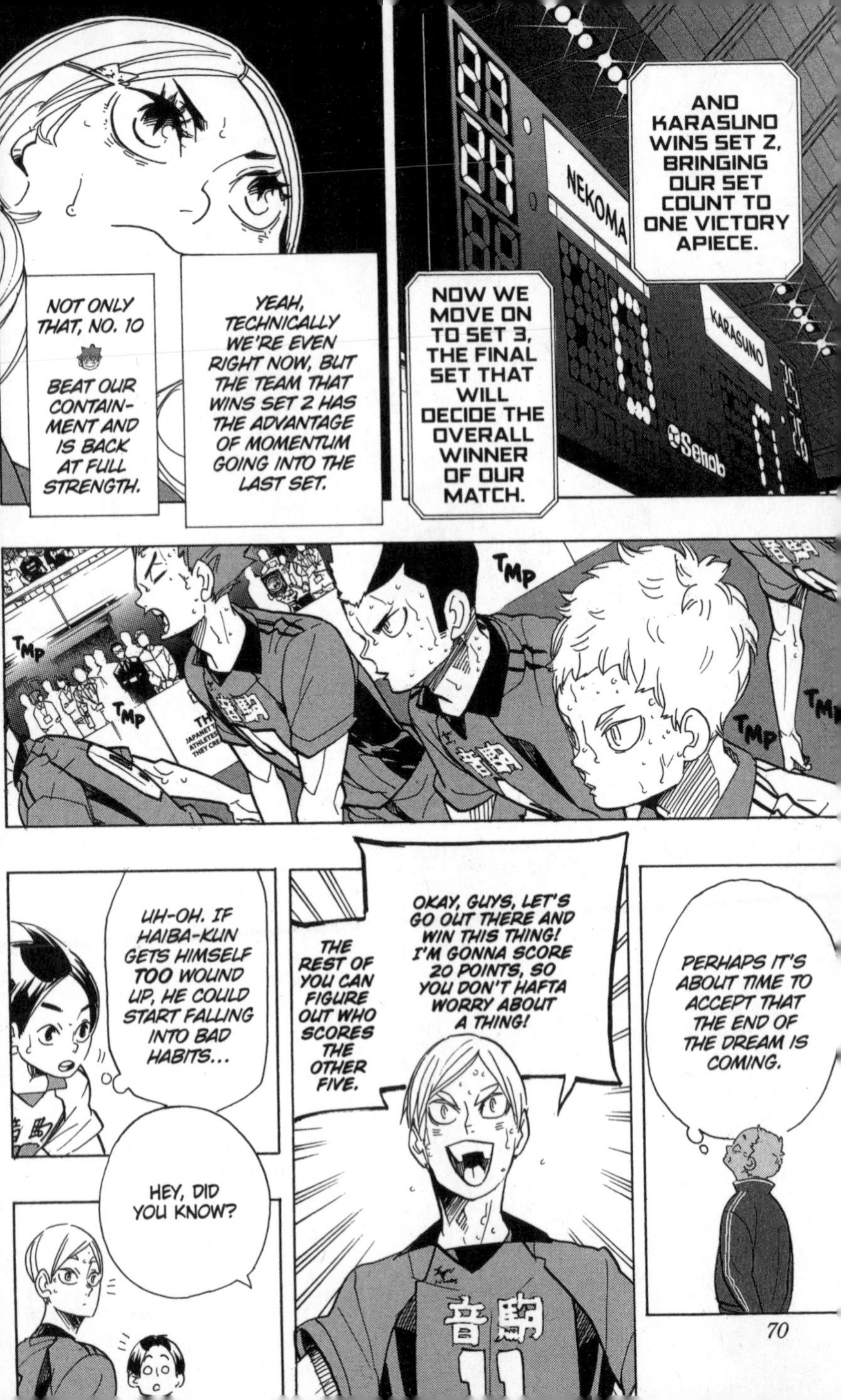
NEKOMA
KARASUNO
AND KARASUNO WINS SET 2, BRINGING OUR SET COUNT TO ONE VICTORY APIECE.
NOW WE MOVE ON TO SET 3, THE FINAL SET THAT WILL DECIDE THE OVERALL WINNER OF OUR MATCH.
YEAH, TECHNICALLY WE'RE EVEN RIGHT NOW, BUT THE TEAM THAT WINS SET 2 HAS THE ADVANTAGE OF MOMENTUM GOING INTO THE LAST SET.
NOT ONLY THAT, NO. 10
BEAT OUR CONTAINMENT AND IS BACK AT FULL STRENGTH.
TMP
TMP
TMP
TMP
TMP
PERHAPS IT'S ABOUT TIME TO ACCEPT THAT THE END OF THE DREAM IS COMING.
OKAY, GUYS, LET'S GO OUT THERE AND WIN THIS THING! I'M GONNA SCORE 20 POINTS, SO YOU DON'T HAFTA WORRY ABOUT A THING!
THE REST OF YOU CAN FIGURE OUT WHO SCORES THE OTHER FIVE.
UH-OH. IF HAIBA-KUN GETS HIMSELF TOO WOUND UP, HE COULD START FALLING INTO BAD HABITS...
HEY, DID YOU KNOW?

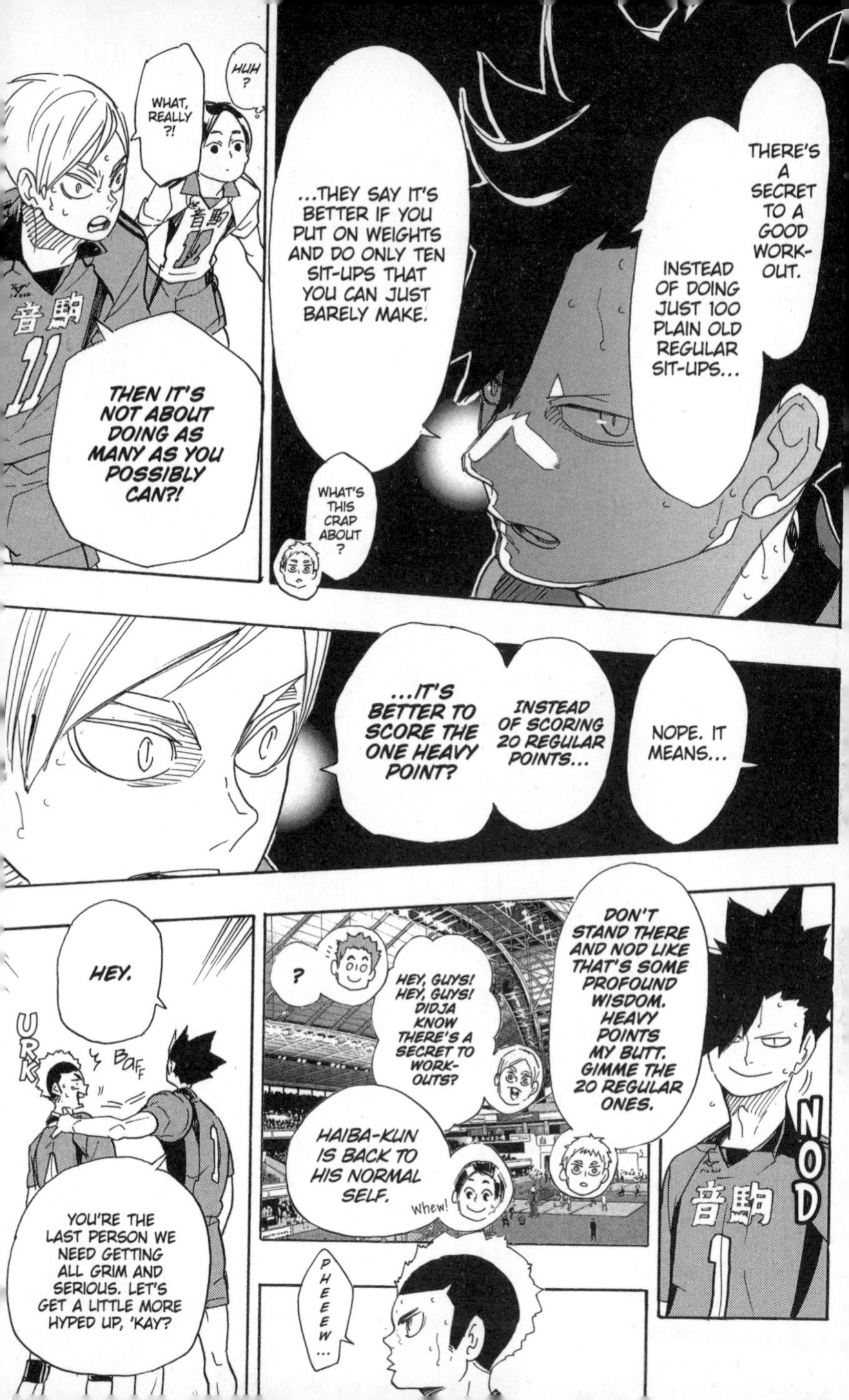
THERE'S A SECRET TO A GOOD WORKOUT.
INSTEAD OF DOING JUST 100 PLAIN OLD REGULAR SIT-UPS...
...THEY SAY IT'S BETTER IF YOU PUT ON WEIGHTS AND DO ONLY TEN SIT-UPS THAT YOU CAN JUST BARELY MAKE.
WHAT'S THIS CRAP ABOUT?
HUH?
WHAT, REALLY?!
THEN IT'S NOT ABOUT DOING AS MANY AS YOU POSSIBLY CAN?!
NOPE. IT MEANS...
INSTEAD OF SCORING 20 REGULAR POINTS...
...IT'S BETTER TO SCORE THE ONE HEAVY POINT?
DON'T STAND THERE AND NOD LIKE THAT'S SOME PROFOUND WISDOM. HEAVY POINTS MY BUTT. GIMME THE 20 REGULAR ONES.
NOD
?
HEY, GUYS! HEY, GUYS! DIDJA KNOW THERE'S A SECRET TO WORKOUTS?
HAIBA-KUN IS BACK TO HIS NORMAL SELF.
Whew!
PHEEEEW...
HEY.
URK
BAFF
YOU'RE THE LAST PERSON WE NEED GETTING ALL GRIM AND SERIOUS. LET'S GET A LITTLE MORE HYPED UP, 'KAY?

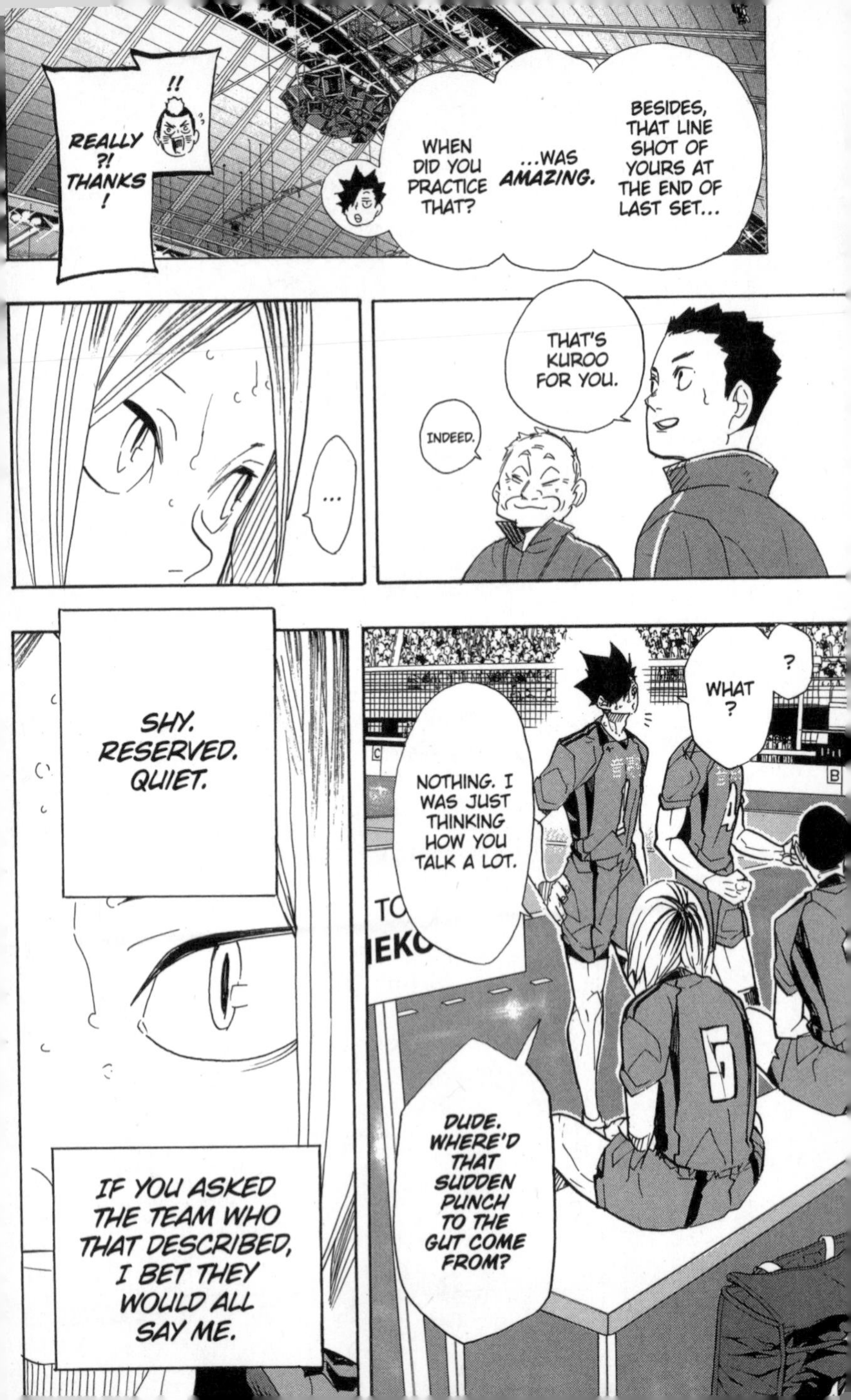
BESIDES, THAT LINE SHOT OF YOURS AT THE END OF LAST SET...
...WAS AMAZING.
WHEN DID YOU PRACTICE THAT?
!!
REALLY?! THANKS!
THAT'S KUROO FOR YOU.
INDEED.
...
WHAT? ?
NOTHING. I WAS JUST THINKING HOW YOU TALK A LOT.
DUDE. WHERE'D THAT SUDDEN PUNCH TO THE GUT COME FROM?
SHY. RESERVED. QUIET.
IF YOU ASKED THE TEAM WHO THAT DESCRIBED, I BET THEY WOULD ALL SAY ME.

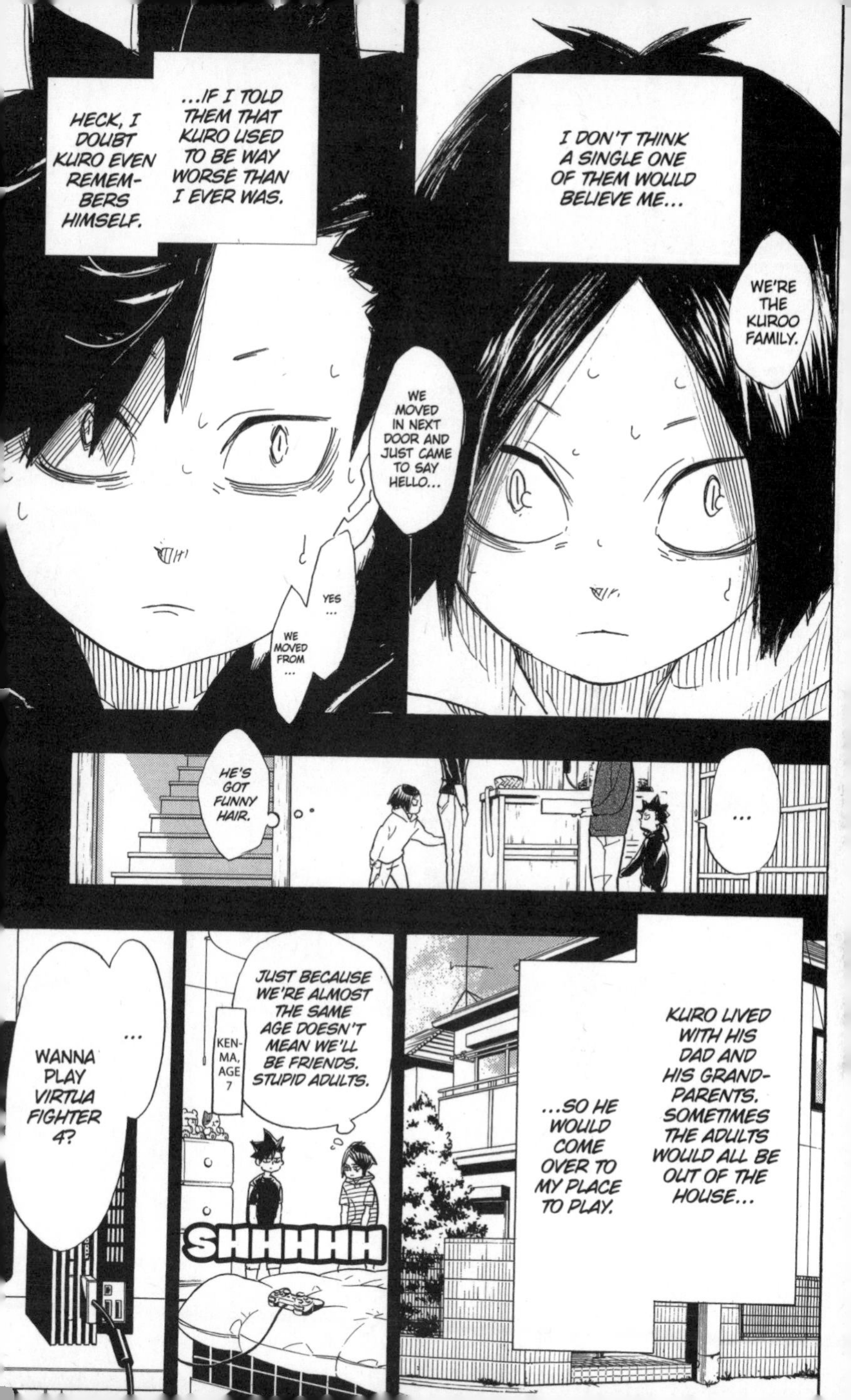

I DON'T THINK A SINGLE ONE OF THEM WOULD BELIEVE ME...
WE'RE THE KUROO FAMILY.
WE MOVED IN NEXT DOOR AND JUST CAME TO SAY HELLO...
...IF I TOLD THEM THAT KURO USED TO BE WAY WORSE THAN I EVER WAS.
HECK, I DOUBT KURO EVEN REMEMBERS HIMSELF.
YES ...
WE MOVED FROM ...
...
HE'S GOT FUNNY HAIR.
KURO LIVED WITH HIS DAD AND HIS GRANDPARENTS. SOMETIMES THE ADULTS WOULD ALL BE OUT OF THE HOUSE...
...SO HE WOULD COME OVER TO MY PLACE TO PLAY.
JUST BECAUSE WE'RE ALMOST THE SAME AGE DOESN'T MEAN WE'LL BE FRIENDS. STUPID ADULTS.
KENMA, AGE 7
SHHHHHH
...
WANNA PLAY VIRTUA FIGHTER 4?

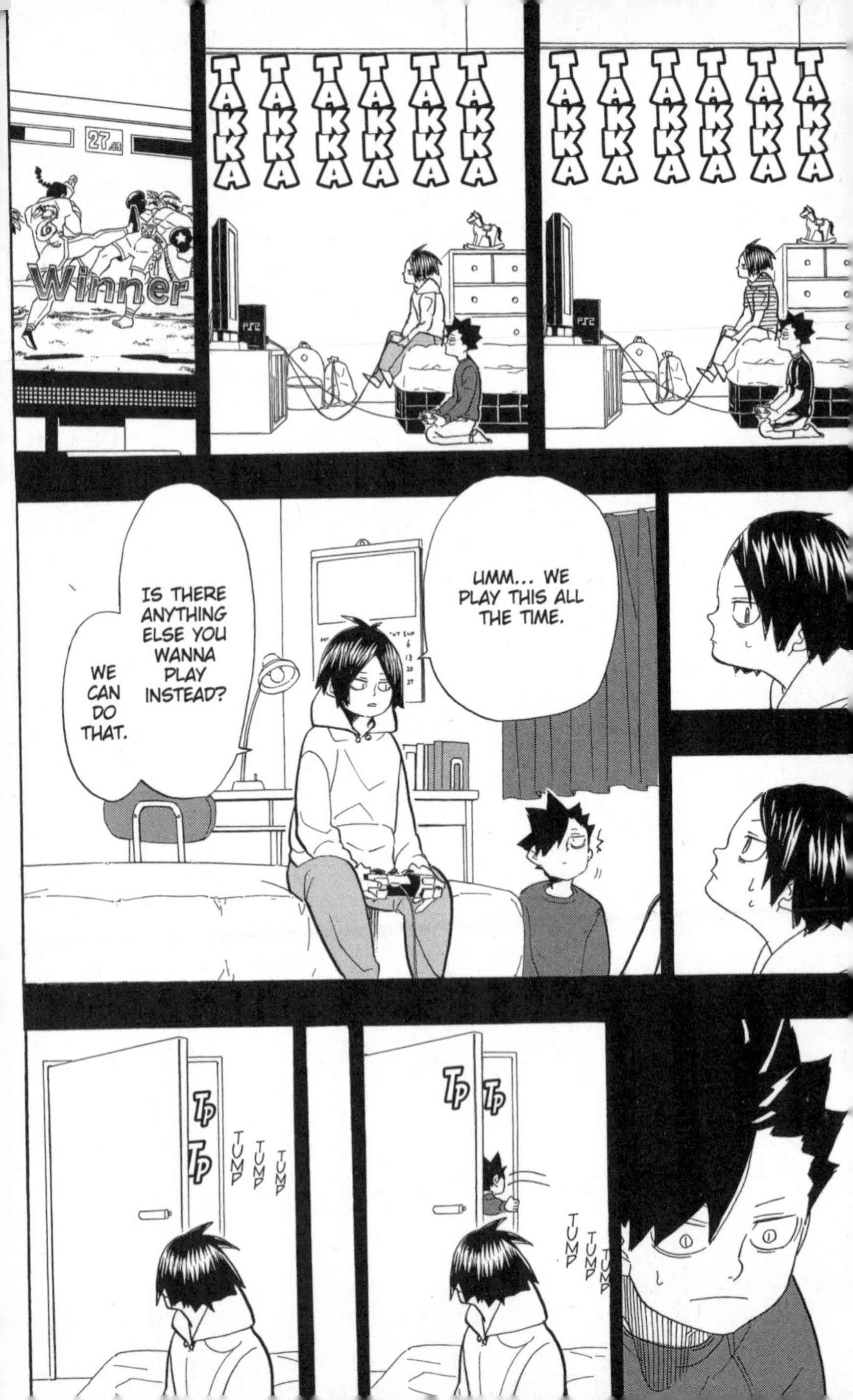
TAKKA TAKKA TAKKA TAKKA TAKKA TAKKA
TAKKA TAKKA TAKKA TAKKA TAKKA TAKKA
Winner
UMM... WE PLAY THIS ALL THE TIME.
IS THERE ANYTHING ELSE YOU WANNA PLAY INSTEAD?
WE CAN DO THAT.
Tp Tp
TUMP TUMP TUMP
Tp Tp
TUMP TUMP TUMP

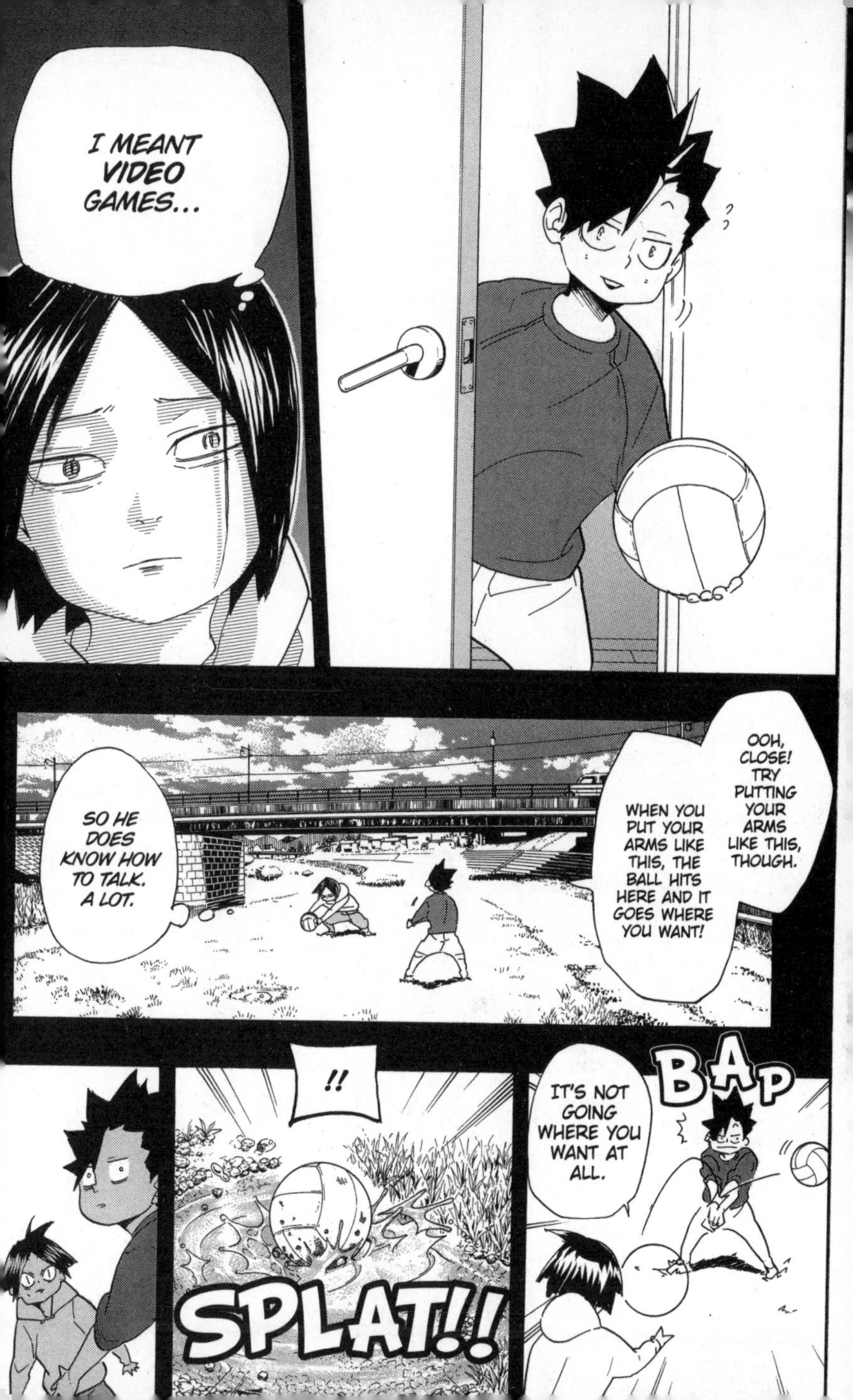
I MEANT VIDEO GAMES...
OOH, CLOSE! TRY PUTTING YOUR ARMS LIKE THIS, THOUGH.
WHEN YOU PUT YOUR ARMS LIKE THIS, THE BALL HITS HERE AND IT GOES WHERE YOU WANT!
SO HE DOES KNOW HOW TO TALK. A LOT.
BAP
IT'S NOT GOING WHERE YOU WANT AT ALL.
!!
SPLAT!!

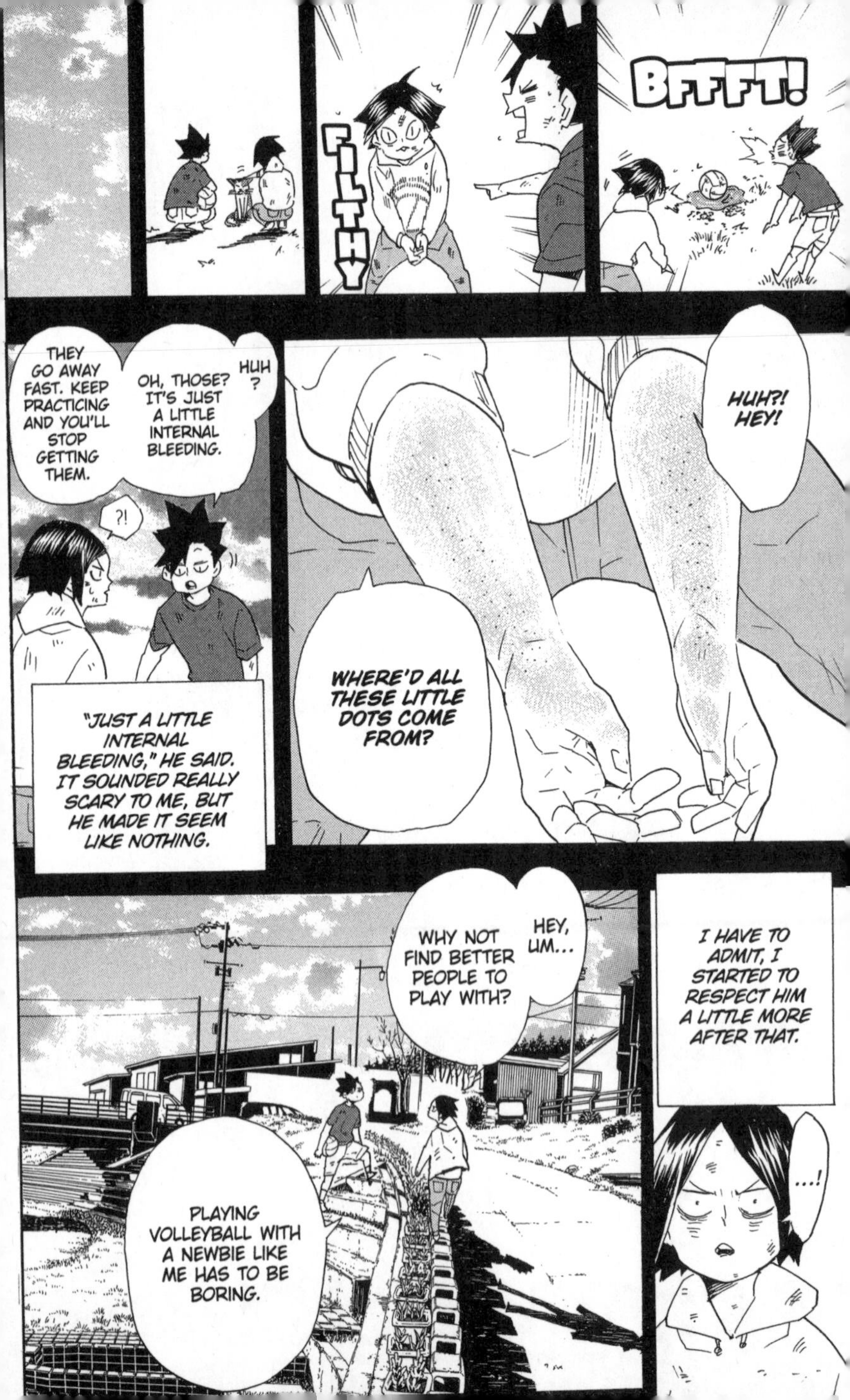
BFFFT!
FILTHY
HUH?! HEY!
WHERE'D ALL THESE LITTLE DOTS COME FROM?
HUH ?
OH, THOSE? IT'S JUST A LITTLE INTERNAL BLEEDING.
THEY GO AWAY FAST. KEEP PRACTICING AND YOU'LL STOP GETTING THEM.
?!
"JUST A LITTLE INTERNAL BLEEDING," HE SAID. IT SOUNDED REALLY SCARY TO ME, BUT HE MADE IT SEEM LIKE NOTHING.
I HAVE TO ADMIT, I STARTED TO RESPECT HIM A LITTLE MORE AFTER THAT.
...!
HEY, UM...
WHY NOT FIND BETTER PEOPLE TO PLAY WITH?
PLAYING VOLLEYBALL WITH A NEWBIE LIKE ME HAS TO BE BORING.

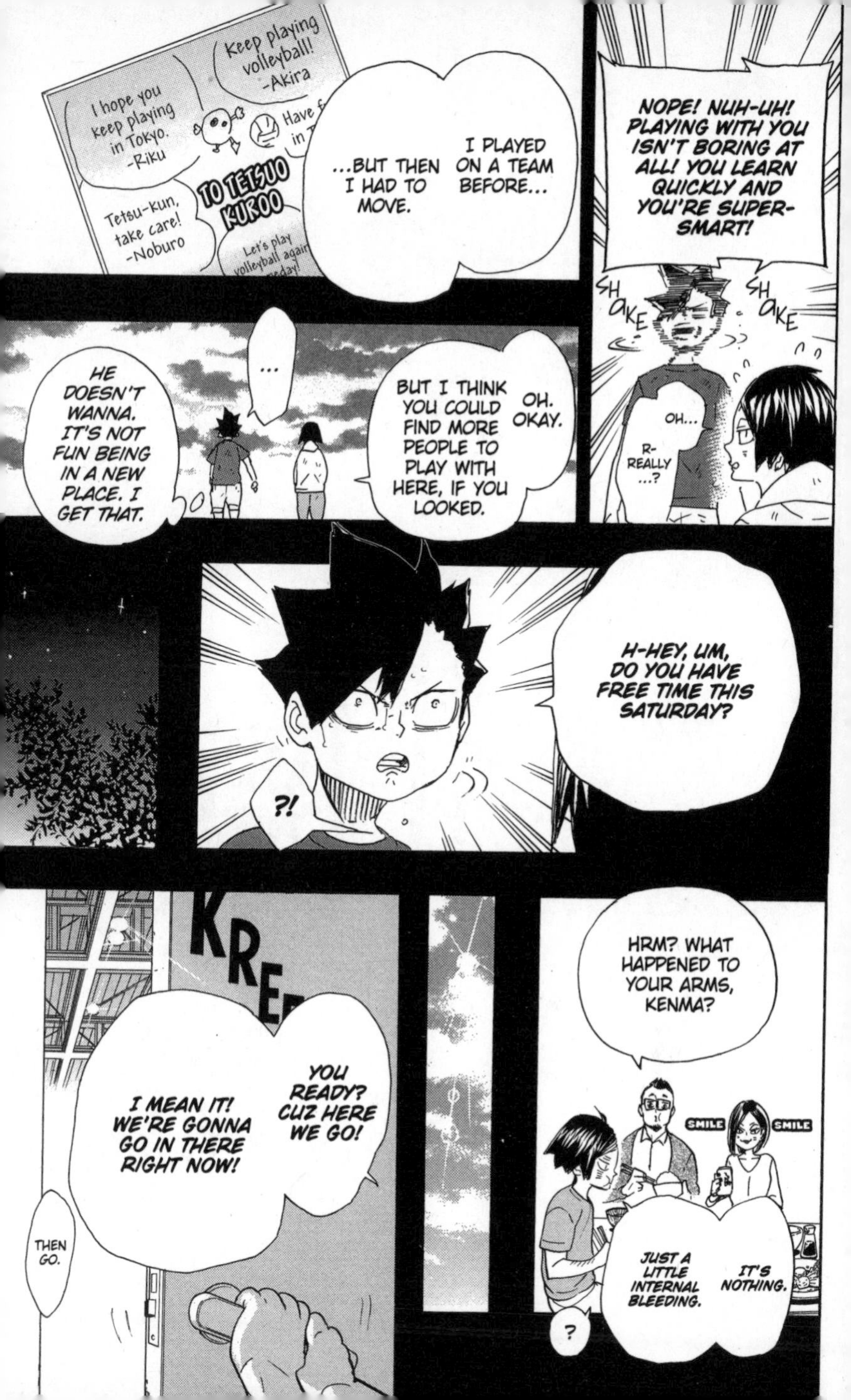

NOPE! NUH-UH! PLAYING WITH YOU ISN'T BORING AT ALL! YOU LEARN QUICKLY AND YOU'RE SUPER-SMART!
SHAKE
SHAKE
OH...
R-REALLY...?
Keep playing volleyball! -Akira
I hope you keep playing in Tokyo. -Riku
TO TETSUO KUROO
Tetsu-kun, take care! -Noburo
I PLAYED ON A TEAM BEFORE...
...BUT THEN I HAD TO MOVE.
OH. OKAY.
BUT I THINK YOU COULD FIND MORE PEOPLE TO PLAY WITH HERE, IF YOU LOOKED.
...
HE DOESN'T WANNA. IT'S NOT FUN BEING IN A NEW PLACE. I GET THAT.
H-HEY, UM, DO YOU HAVE FREE TIME THIS SATURDAY?
?!
HRM? WHAT HAPPENED TO YOUR ARMS, KENMA?
SMILE
SMILE
IT'S NOTHING.
JUST A LITTLE INTERNAL BLEEDING.
?
KRE
YOU READY? CUZ HERE WE GO!
I MEAN IT! WE'RE GONNA GO IN THERE RIGHT NOW!
THEN GO.

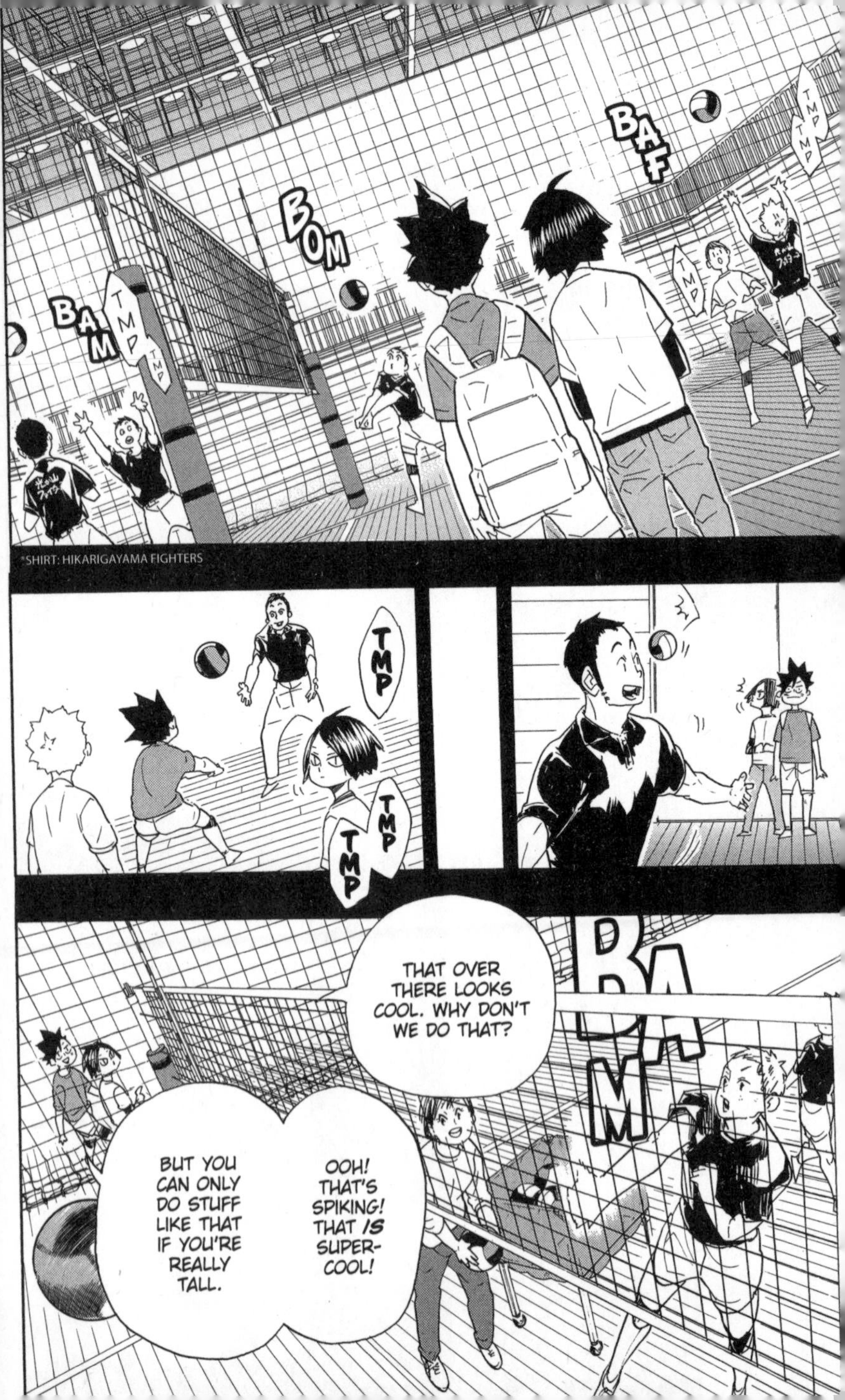
TMP TMP TMP
BAF
TMP
BOM
BAM
TMP
TMP
TMP TMP
TMP TMP
BAM
THAT OVER THERE LOOKS COOL. WHY DON'T WE DO THAT?
OOH! THAT'S SPIKING! THAT IS SUPER-COOL!
BUT YOU CAN ONLY DO STUFF LIKE THAT IF YOU'RE REALLY TALL.
*SHIRT: HIKARIGAYAMA FIGHTERS

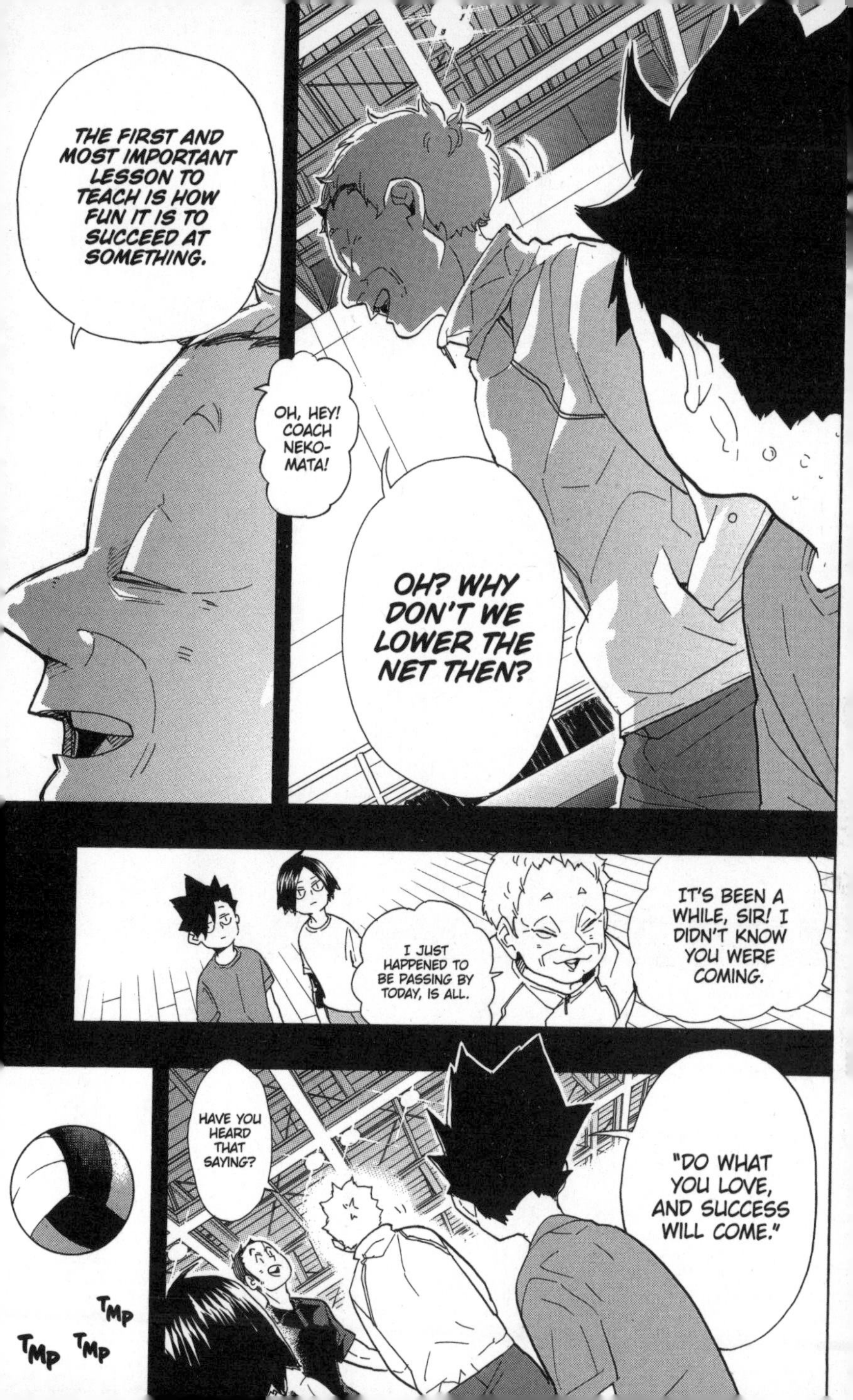
OH? WHY DON'T WE LOWER THE NET THEN?
OH, HEY! COACH NEKO-MATA!
THE FIRST AND MOST IMPORTANT LESSON TO TEACH IS HOW FUN IT IS TO SUCCEED AT SOMETHING.
IT'S BEEN A WHILE, SIR! I DIDN'T KNOW YOU WERE COMING.
I JUST HAPPENED TO BE PASSING BY TODAY, IS ALL.
"DO WHAT YOU LOVE, AND SUCCESS WILL COME."
HAVE YOU HEARD THAT SAYING?
TMP
TMP
TMP

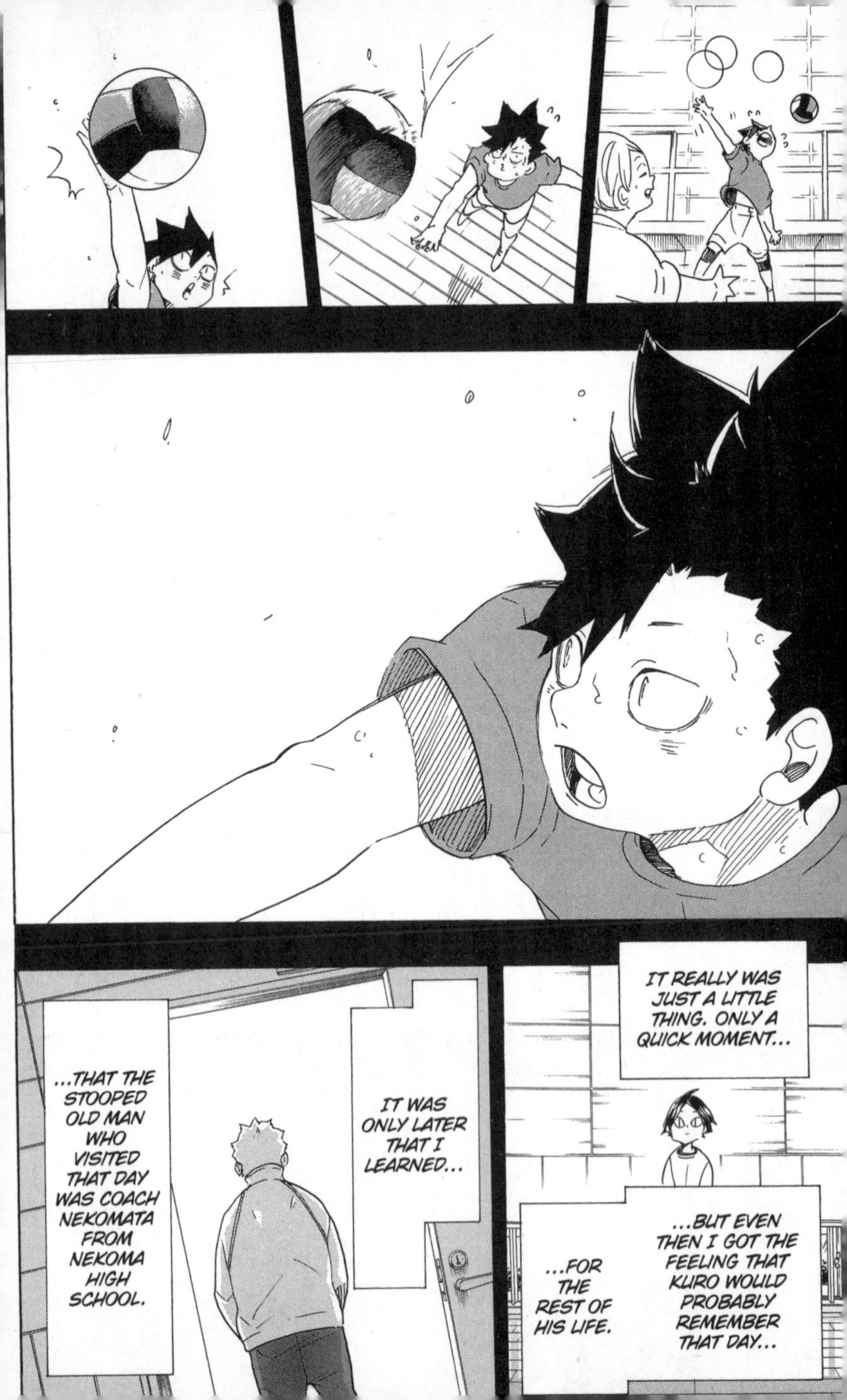
IT REALLY WAS JUST A LITTLE THING. ONLY A QUICK MOMENT...
...BUT EVEN THEN I GOT THE FEELING THAT KURO WOULD PROBABLY REMEMBER THAT DAY...
...FOR THE REST OF HIS LIFE.
IT WAS ONLY LATER THAT I LEARNED...
...THAT THE STOOPED OLD MAN WHO VISITED THAT DAY WAS COACH NEKOMATA FROM NEKOMA HIGH SCHOOL.

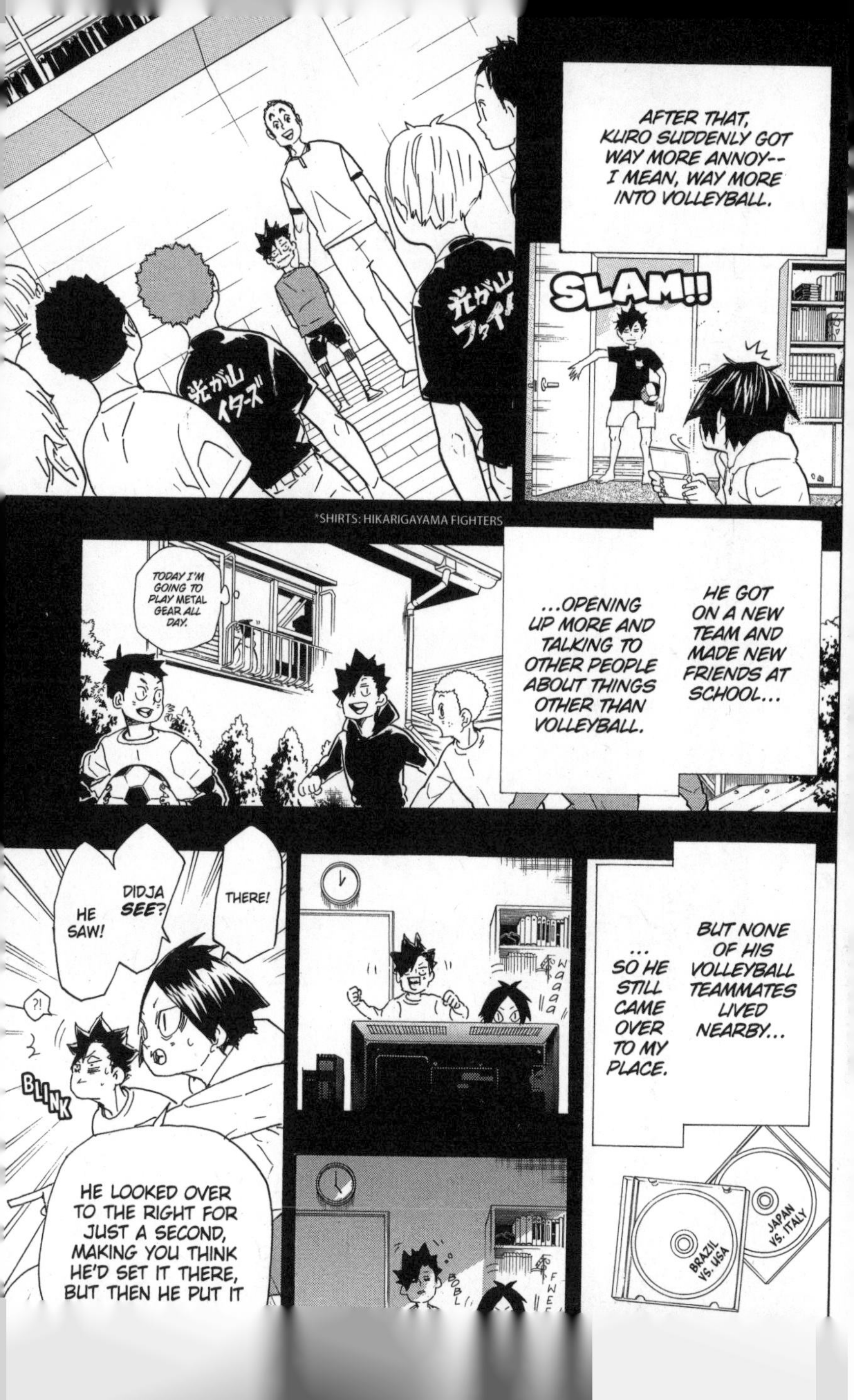
AFTER THAT, KURO SUDDENLY GOT WAY MORE ANNOY-- I MEAN, WAY MORE INTO VOLLEYBALL.
SLAM!!
HE GOT ON A NEW TEAM AND MADE NEW FRIENDS AT SCHOOL...
...OPENING UP MORE AND TALKING TO OTHER PEOPLE ABOUT THINGS OTHER THAN VOLLEYBALL.
TODAY I'M GOING TO PLAY METAL GEAR ALL DAY.
BUT NONE OF HIS VOLLEYBALL TEAMMATES LIVED NEARBY...
...SO HE STILL CAME OVER TO MY PLACE.
JAPAN VS. ITALY
BRAZIL VS. USA
Waaaaa
THERE!
DIDJA SEE?
HE SAW!
?!
BLINK
HE LOOKED OVER TO THE RIGHT FOR JUST A SECOND, MAKING YOU THINK HE'D SET IT THERE, BUT THEN HE PUT IT

*SHIRTS: HIKARIGAYAMA FIGHTERS

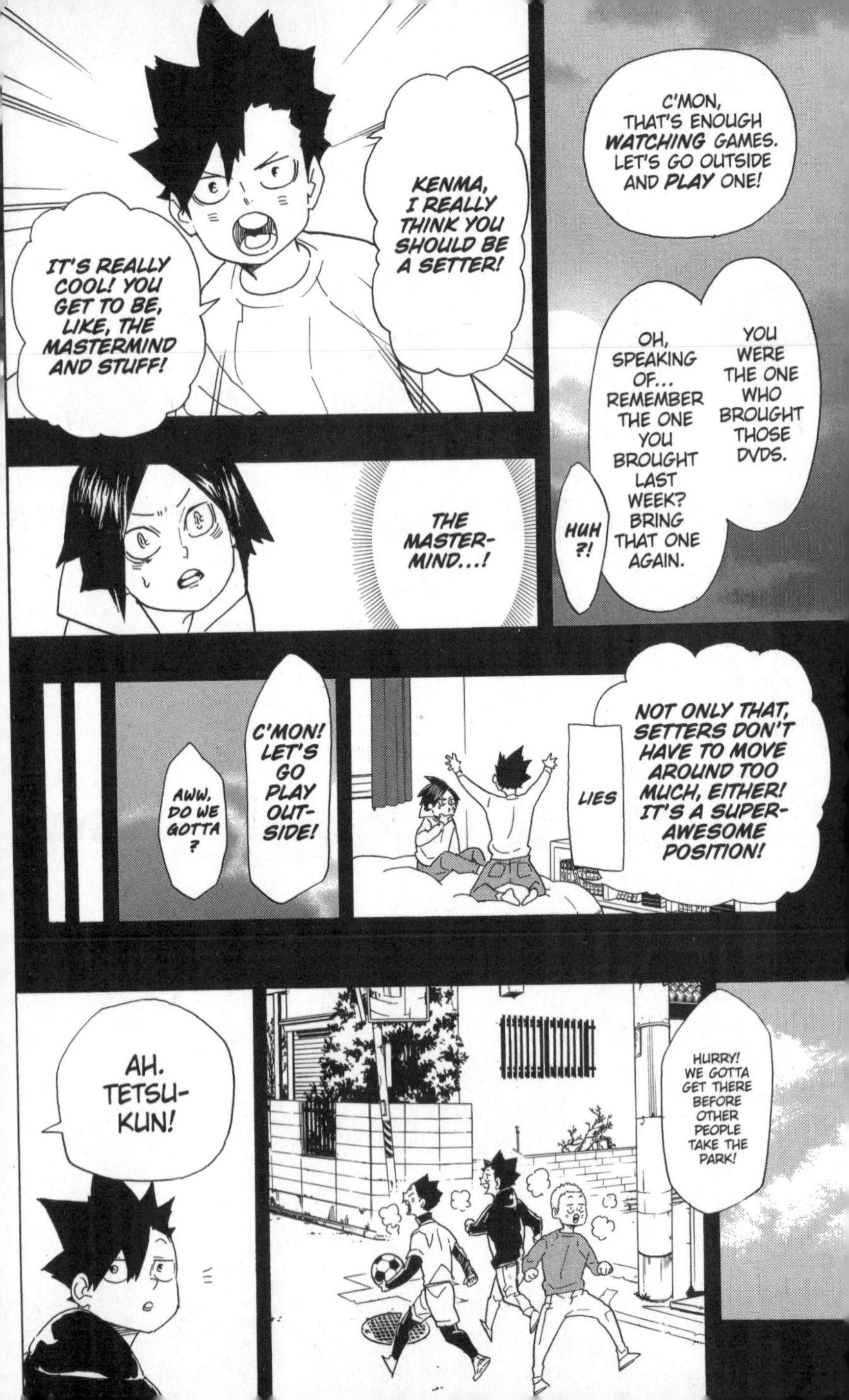
C'MON, THAT'S ENOUGH WATCHING GAMES. LET'S GO OUTSIDE AND PLAY ONE!
YOU WERE THE ONE WHO BROUGHT THOSE DVDS.
OH, SPEAKING OF... REMEMBER THE ONE YOU BROUGHT LAST WEEK? BRING THAT ONE AGAIN.
HUH?!
KENMA, I REALLY THINK YOU SHOULD BE A SETTER!
IT'S REALLY COOL! YOU GET TO BE, LIKE, THE MASTERMIND AND STUFF!
THE MASTER-MIND...!
NOT ONLY THAT, SETTERS DON'T HAVE TO MOVE AROUND TOO MUCH, EITHER! IT'S A SUPER-AWESOME POSITION!
LIES
C'MON! LET'S GO PLAY OUT-SIDE!
AWW, DO WE GOTTA?
HURRY! WE GOTTA GET THERE BEFORE OTHER PEOPLE TAKE THE PARK!
AH. TETSU-KUN!

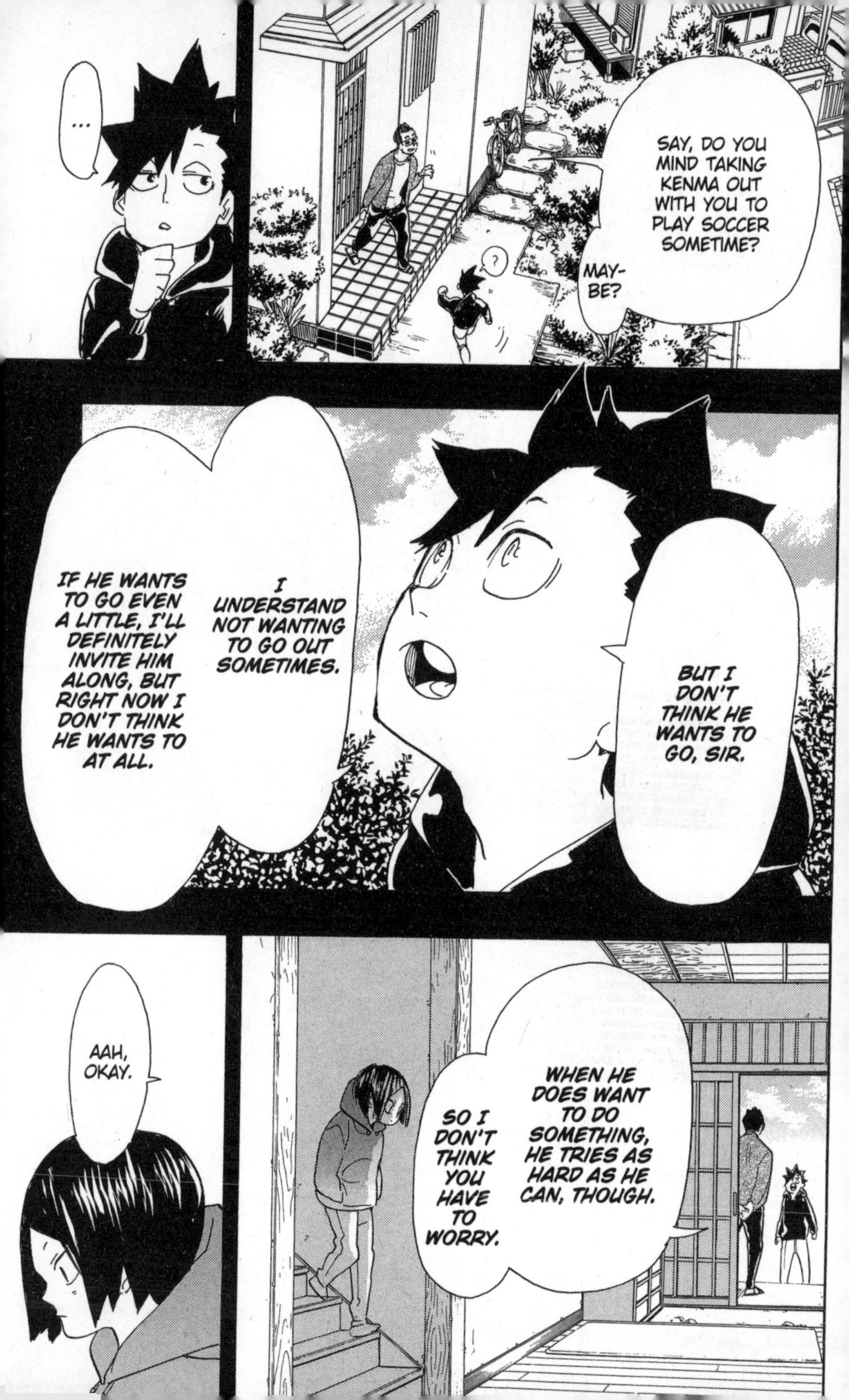
SAY, DO YOU MIND TAKING KENMA OUT WITH YOU TO PLAY SOCCER SOMETIME?
?
MAY-BE?
...
BUT I DON'T THINK HE WANTS TO GO, SIR.
I UNDERSTAND NOT WANTING TO GO OUT SOMETIMES.
IF HE WANTS TO GO EVEN A LITTLE, I'LL DEFINITELY INVITE HIM ALONG, BUT RIGHT NOW I DON'T THINK HE WANTS TO AT ALL.
WHEN HE DOES WANT TO DO SOMETHING, HE TRIES AS HARD AS HE CAN, THOUGH.
SO I DON'T THINK YOU HAVE TO WORRY.
AAH, OKAY.

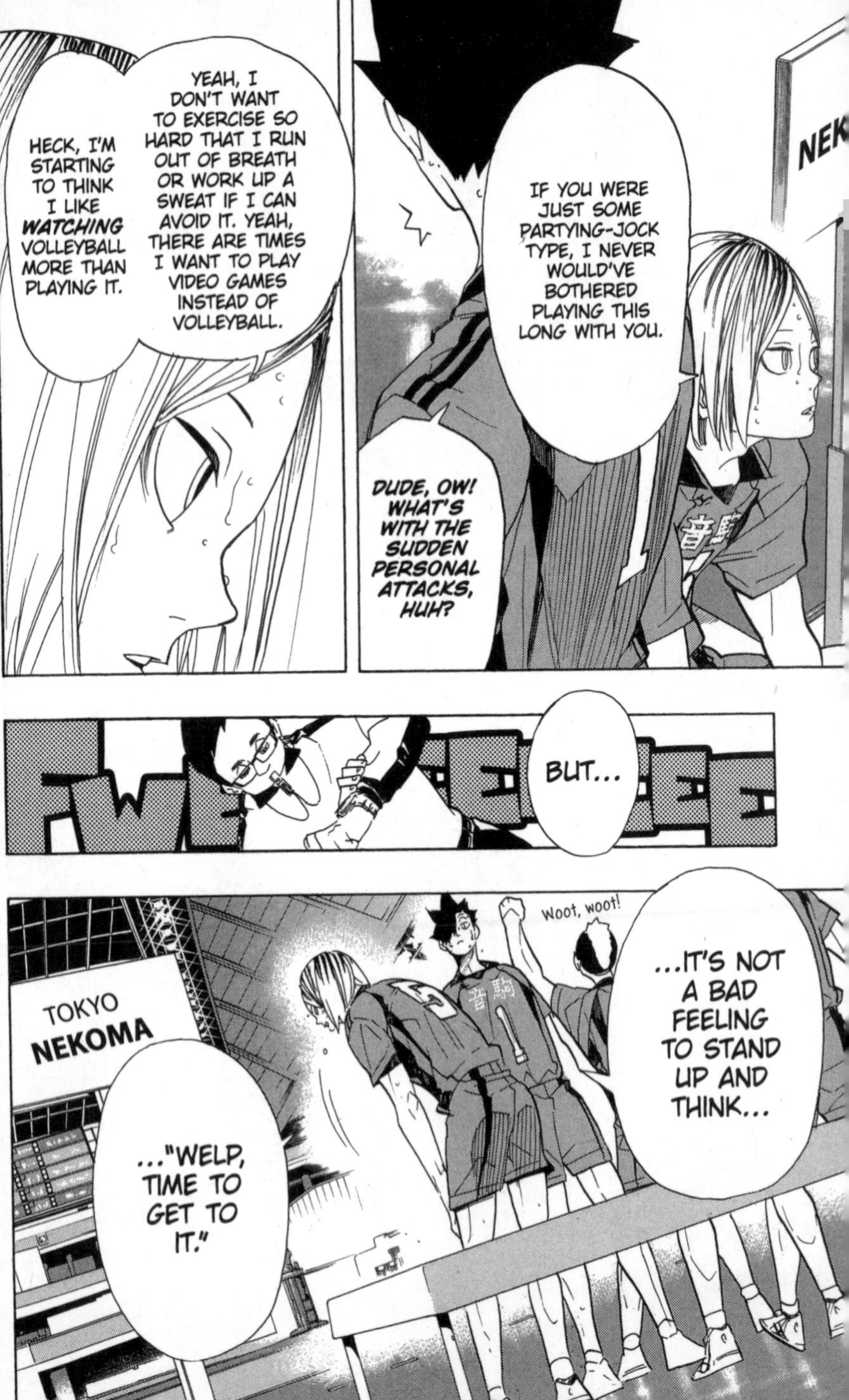
NEK
IF YOU WERE JUST SOME PARTYING-JOCK TYPE, I NEVER WOULD'VE BOTHERED PLAYING THIS LONG WITH YOU.
DUDE, OW! WHAT'S WITH THE SUDDEN PERSONAL ATTACKS, HUH?
YEAH, I DON'T WANT TO EXERCISE SO HARD THAT I RUN OUT OF BREATH OR WORK UP A SWEAT IF I CAN AVOID IT. YEAH, THERE ARE TIMES I WANT TO PLAY VIDEO GAMES INSTEAD OF VOLLEYBALL.
HECK, I'M STARTING TO THINK I LIKE *WATCHING* VOLLEYBALL MORE THAN PLAYING IT.
BUT...
FWEEEEH
Woot, woot!
...IT'S NOT A BAD FEELING TO STAND UP AND THINK...
TOKYO NEKOMA
..."WELP, TIME TO GET TO IT."

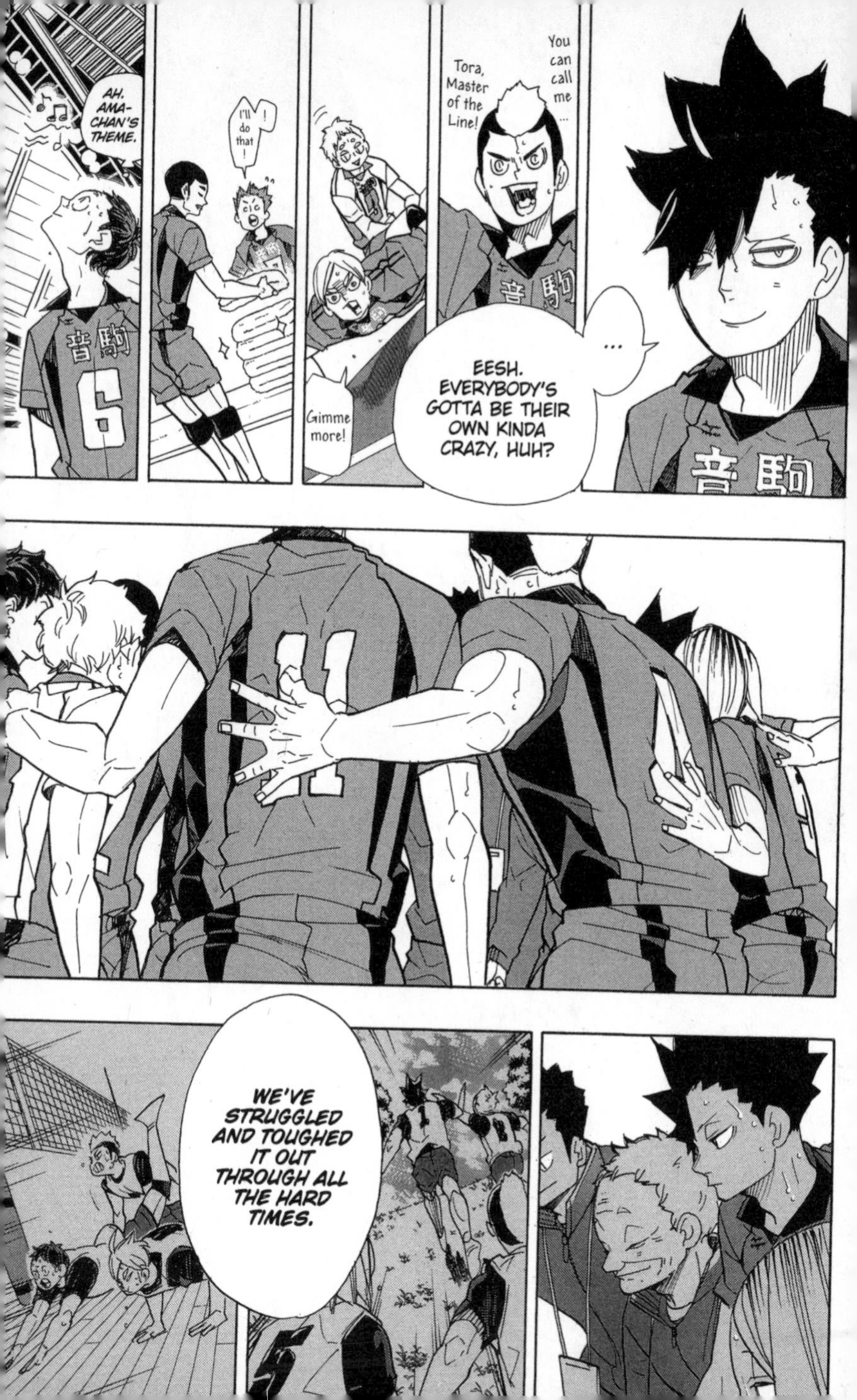
...
EESH. EVERYBODY'S GOTTA BE THEIR OWN KINDA CRAZY, HUH?
You can call me ...
Tora, Master of the Line!
Gimme more!
I'll do that!
AH. AMA-CHAN'S THEME.
WE'VE STRUGGLED AND TOUGHED IT OUT THROUGH ALL THE HARD TIMES.

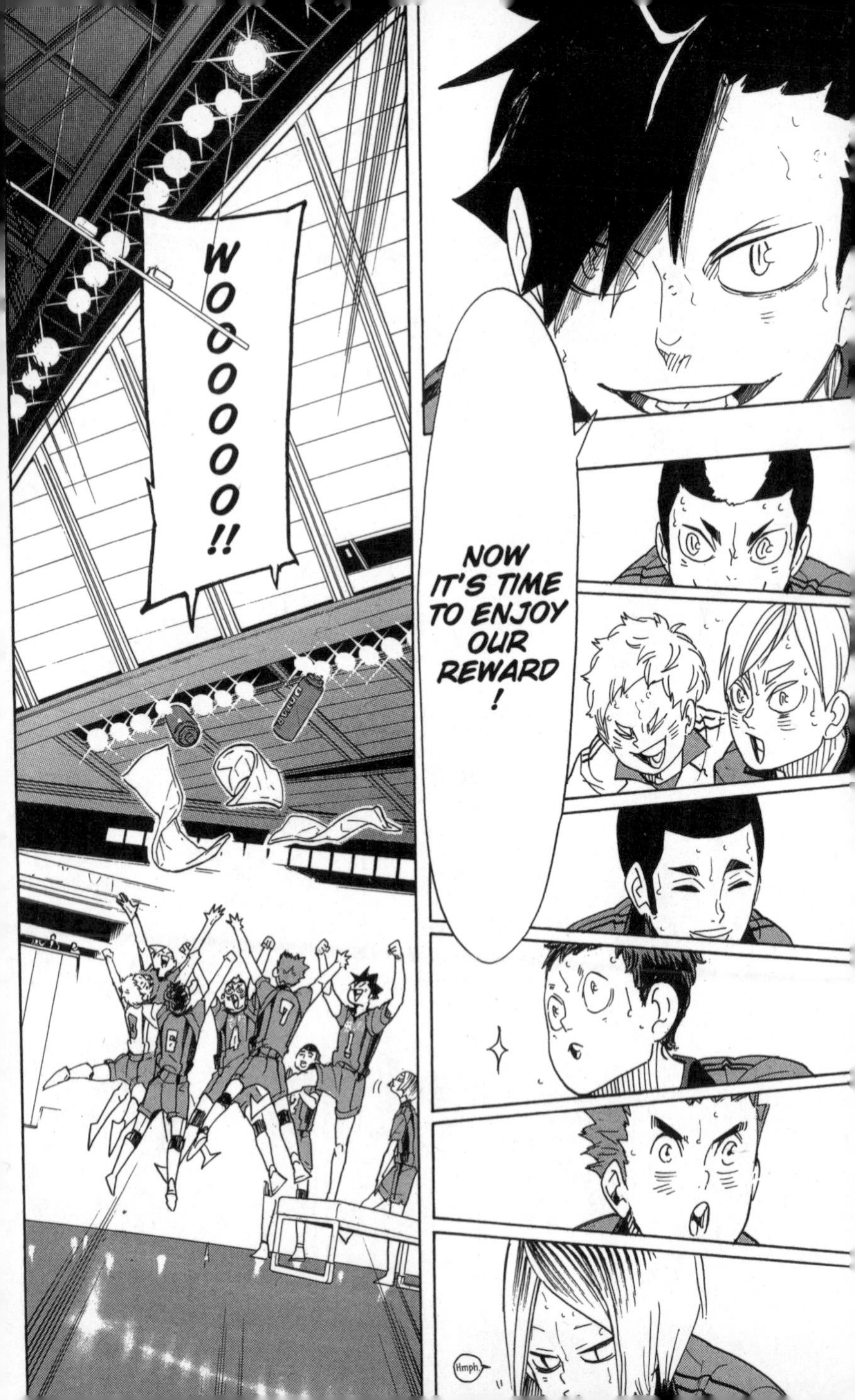
NOW IT'S TIME TO ENJOY OUR REWARD!
Hmph
WOOOOOO!!

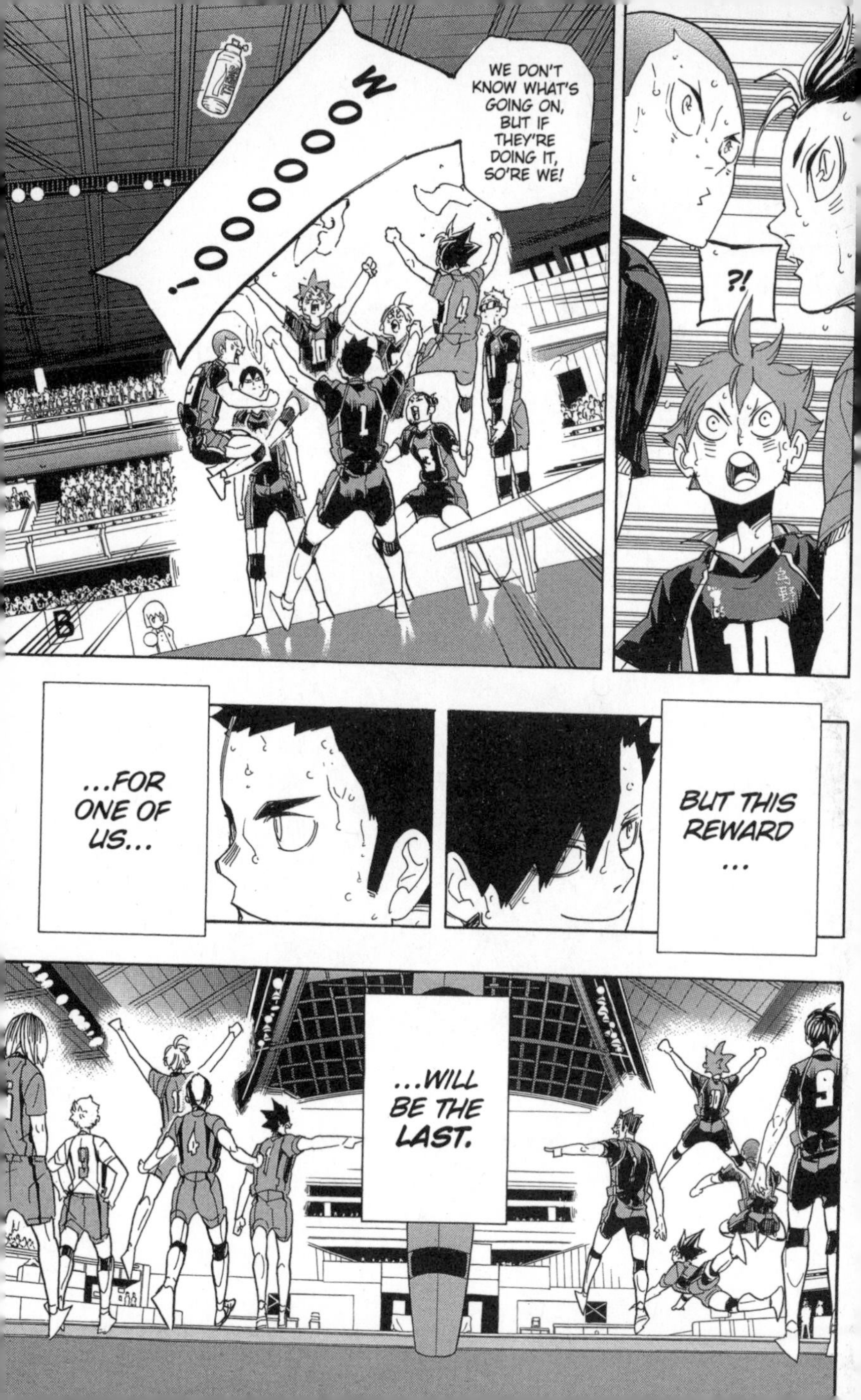
?!
WE DON'T KNOW WHAT'S GOING ON, BUT IF THEY'RE DOING IT, SO'RE WE!
WOOOOOO!
BUT THIS REWARD ...
...FOR ONE OF US...
...WILL BE THE LAST.

HELLO FROM BEYOND THE (PAGE) EDGE!! GUESS WHICH PANEL THIS IS!!

FROM CHAPTER 318

I...THINK THAT'S FUKUNAGA'S HAND?

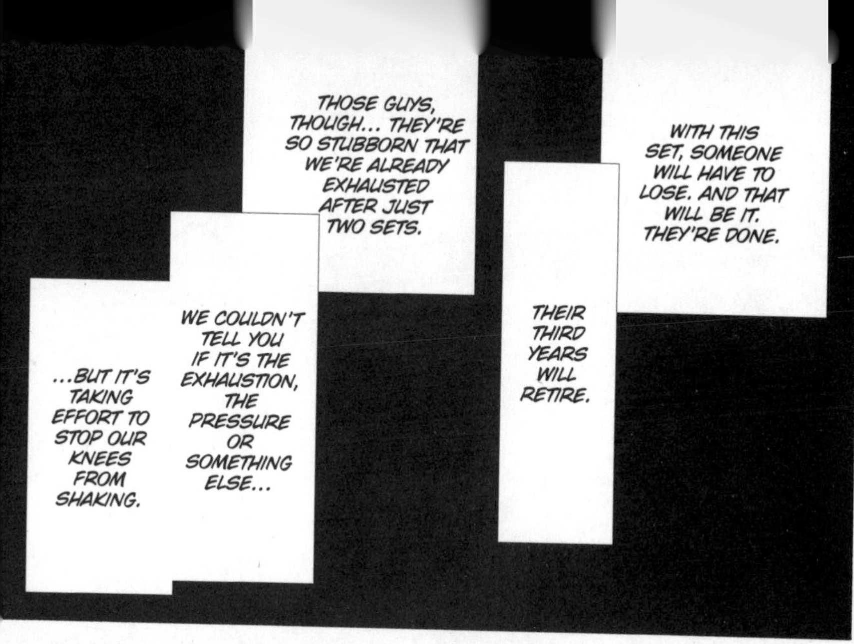
WITH THIS SET, SOMEONE WILL HAVE TO LOSE. AND THAT WILL BE IT. THEY'RE DONE.
THEIR THIRD YEARS WILL RETIRE.
THOSE GUYS, THOUGH... THEY'RE SO STUBBORN THAT WE'RE ALREADY EXHAUSTED AFTER JUST TWO SETS.
WE COULDN'T TELL YOU IF IT'S THE EXHAUSTION, THE PRESSURE OR SOMETHING ELSE...
...BUT IT'S TAKING EFFORT TO STOP OUR KNEES FROM SHAKING.

CHAPTER 319

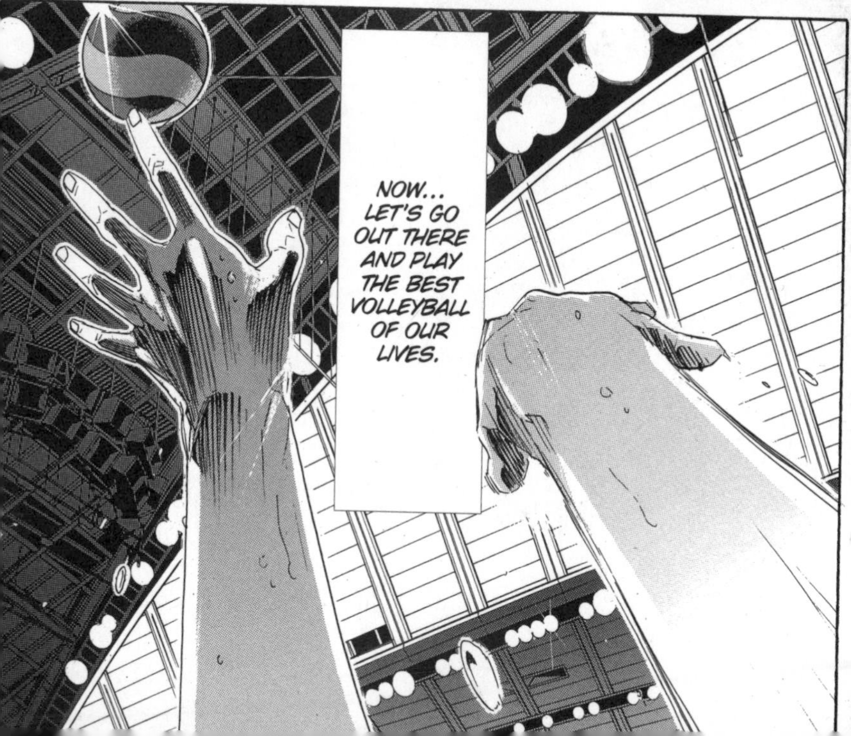
NOW... LET'S GO OUT THERE AND PLAY THE BEST VOLLEYBALL OF OUR LIVES.

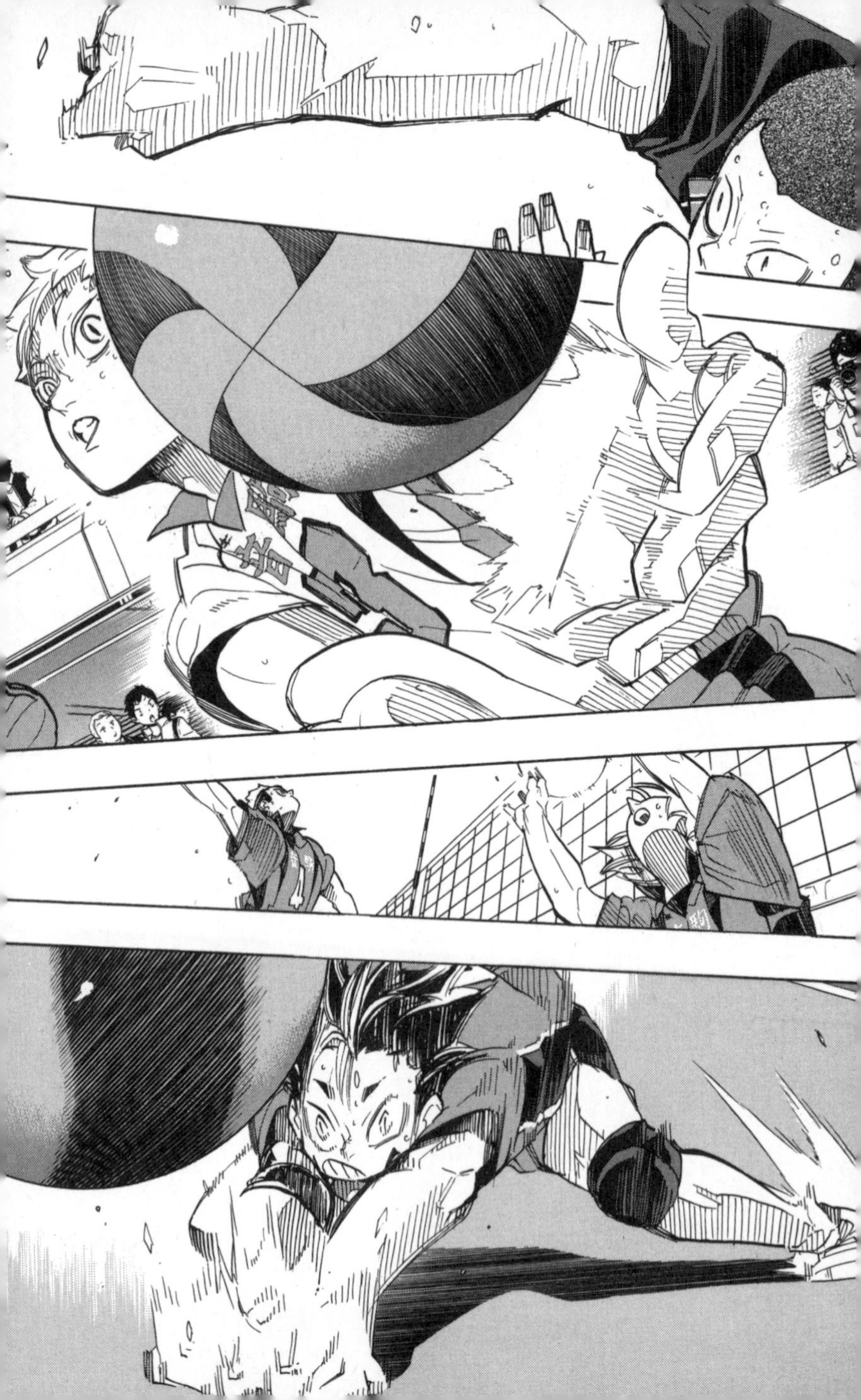

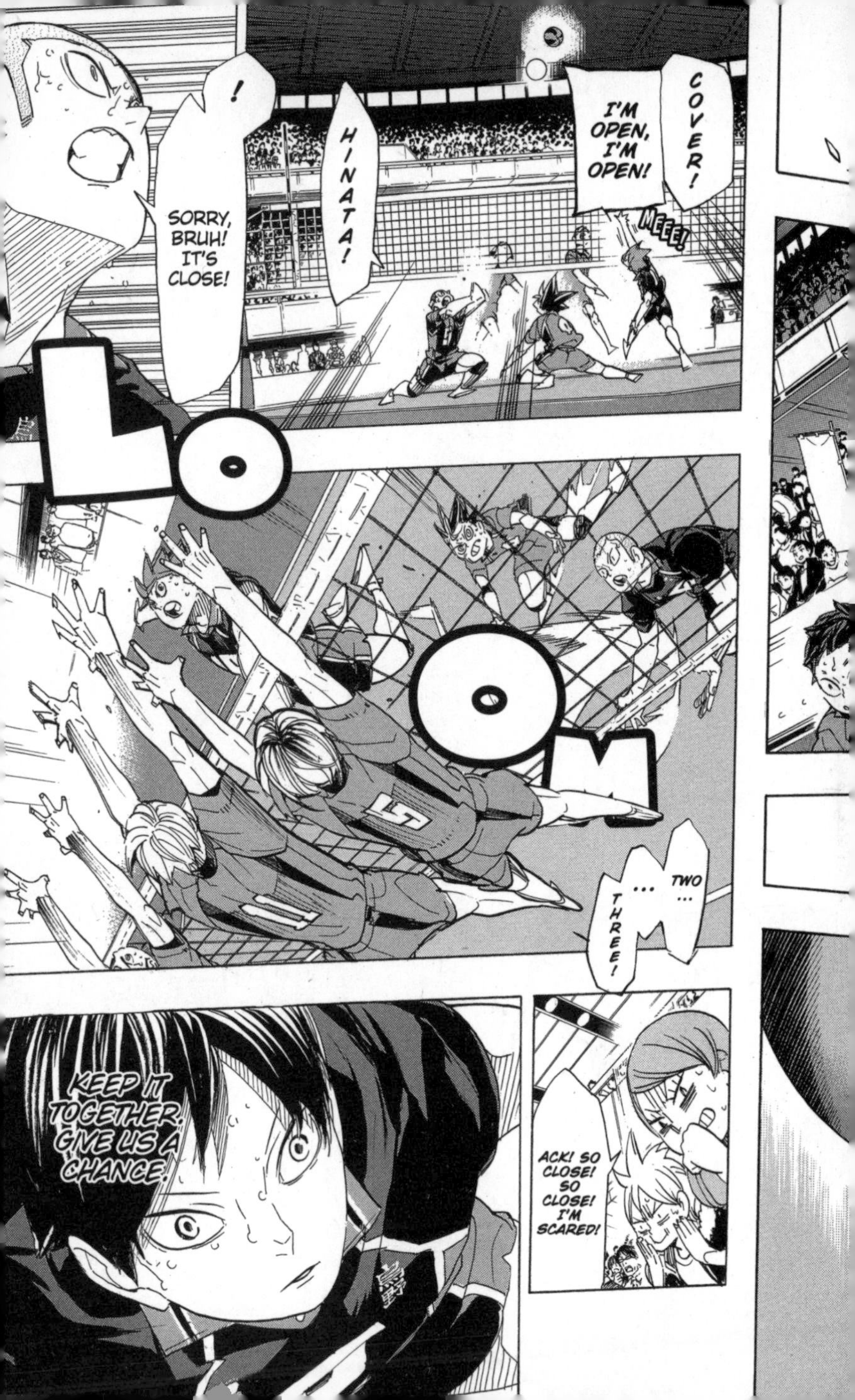

COVER!
I'M OPEN, I'M OPEN!
MEEEE!
HINATA!
!
SORRY, BRUH! IT'S CLOSE!
LOOM
TWO...
...THREE!
ACK! SO CLOSE! SO CLOSE! I'M SCARED!
KEEP IT TOGETHER. GIVE US A CHANCE.

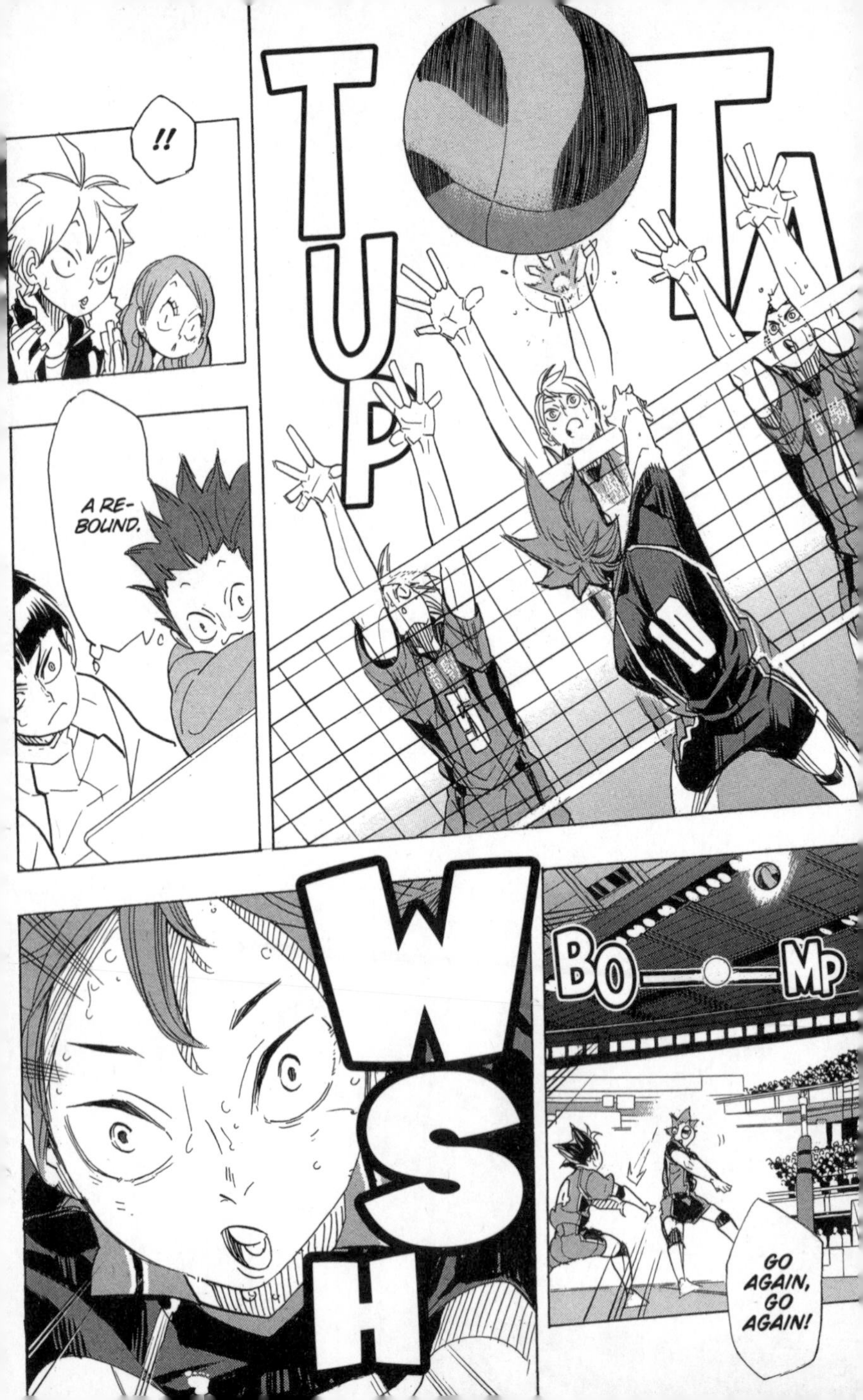
TUP
!!
A RE-BOUND.
BOMP
GO AGAIN, GO AGAIN!
WSH

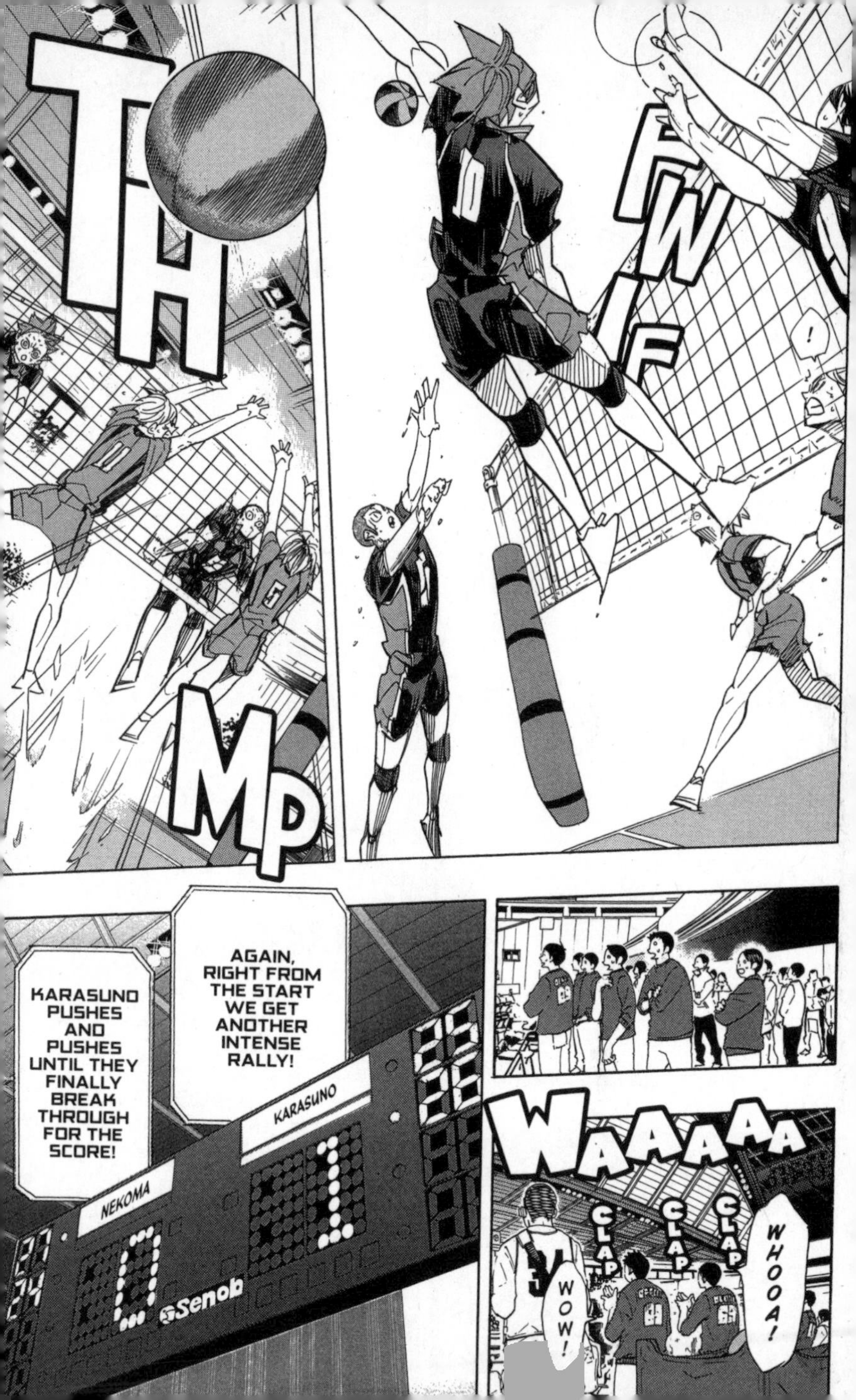
FWIF
!
THUMP
WAAAAA
WHOOA!
CLAP CLAP CLAP
WOW!
AGAIN, RIGHT FROM THE START WE GET ANOTHER INTENSE RALLY!
KARASUNO PUSHES AND PUSHES UNTIL THEY FINALLY BREAK THROUGH FOR THE SCORE!
KARASUNO
NEKOMA
1
0
Senob

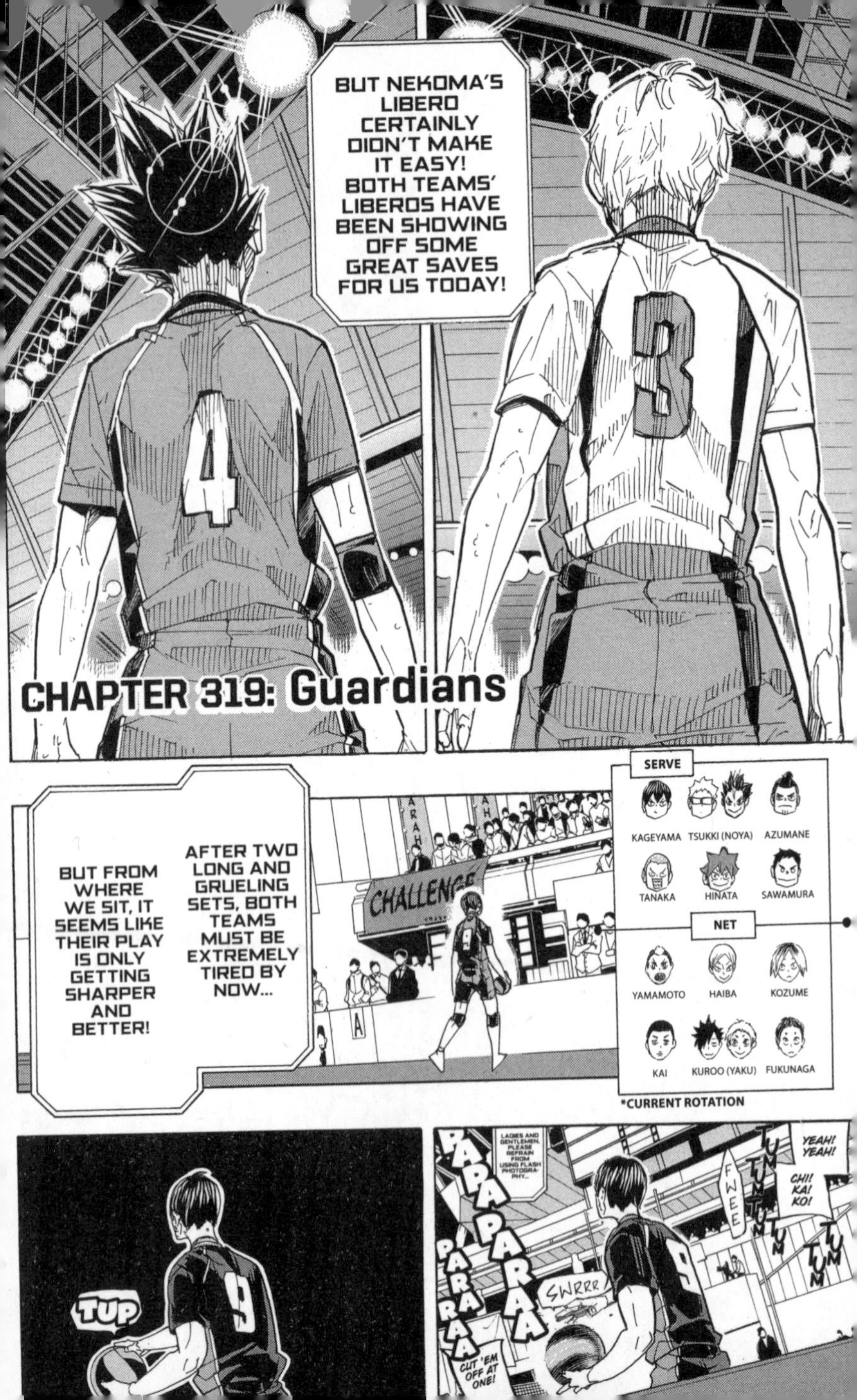
BUT NEKOMA'S LIBERO CERTAINLY DIDN'T MAKE IT EASY! BOTH TEAMS' LIBEROS HAVE BEEN SHOWING OFF SOME GREAT SAVES FOR US TODAY!
CHAPTER 319: Guardians
SERVE
KAGEYAMA
TSUKKI (NOYA)
AZUMANE
TANAKA
HINATA
SAWAMURA
NET
YAMAMOTO
HAIBA
KOZUME
KAI
KUROO (YAKU)
FUKUNAGA
*CURRENT ROTATION
AFTER TWO LONG AND GRUELING SETS, BOTH TEAMS MUST BE EXTREMELY TIRED BY NOW...
BUT FROM WHERE WE SIT, IT SEEMS LIKE THEIR PLAY IS ONLY GETTING SHARPER AND BETTER!
CHALLENGE
LADIES AND GENTLEMEN, PLEASE REFRAIN FROM USING FLASH PHOTOGRAPHY.
YEAH! YEAH!
CHI! KAI! KO!
TUM TUM TUM TUM
TUM TUM TUM
FWEE
PAPAPAPARAA
PAPARARAA
SWRRR
CUT 'EM OFF AT ONE!
TUP

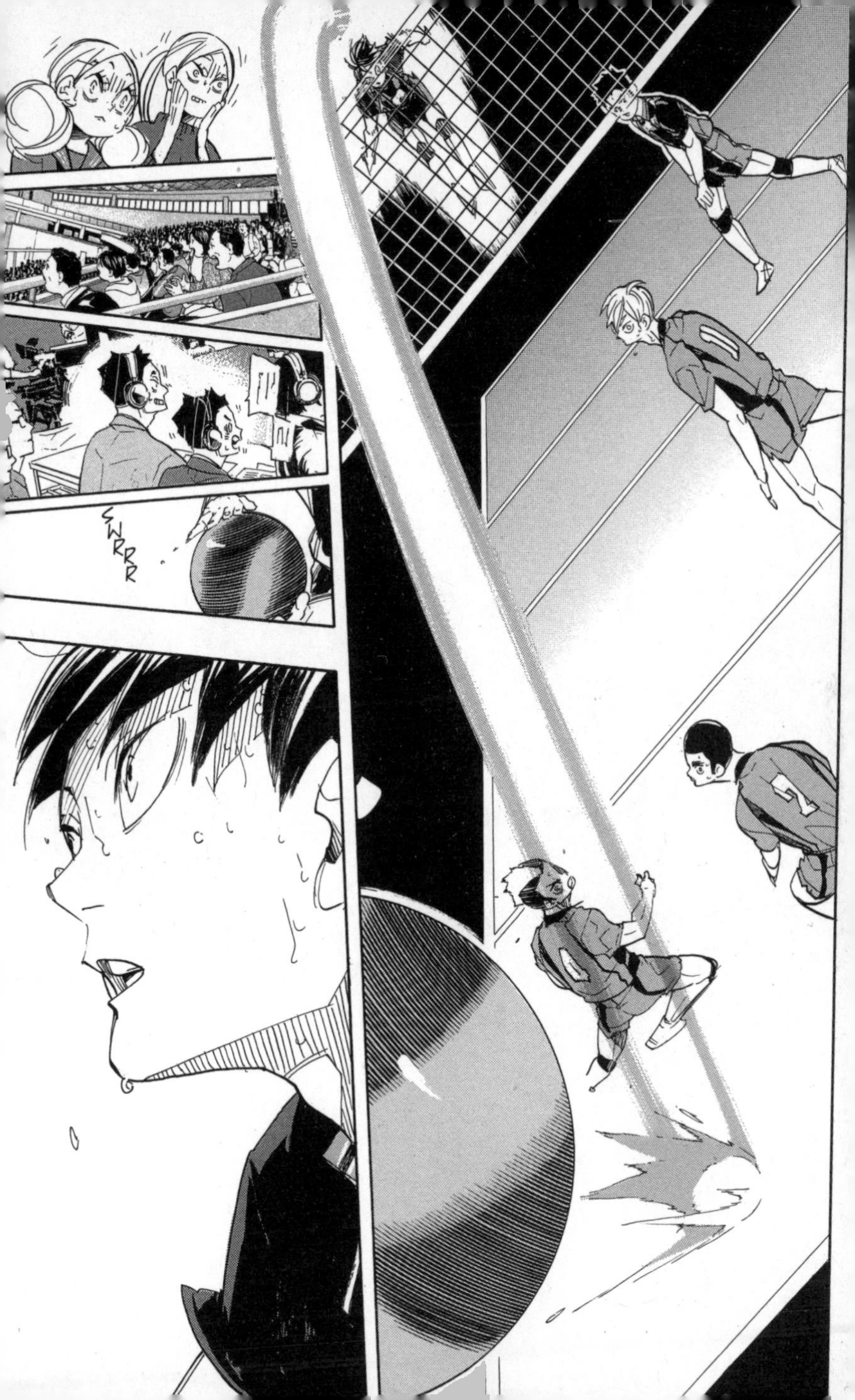
SWRRR

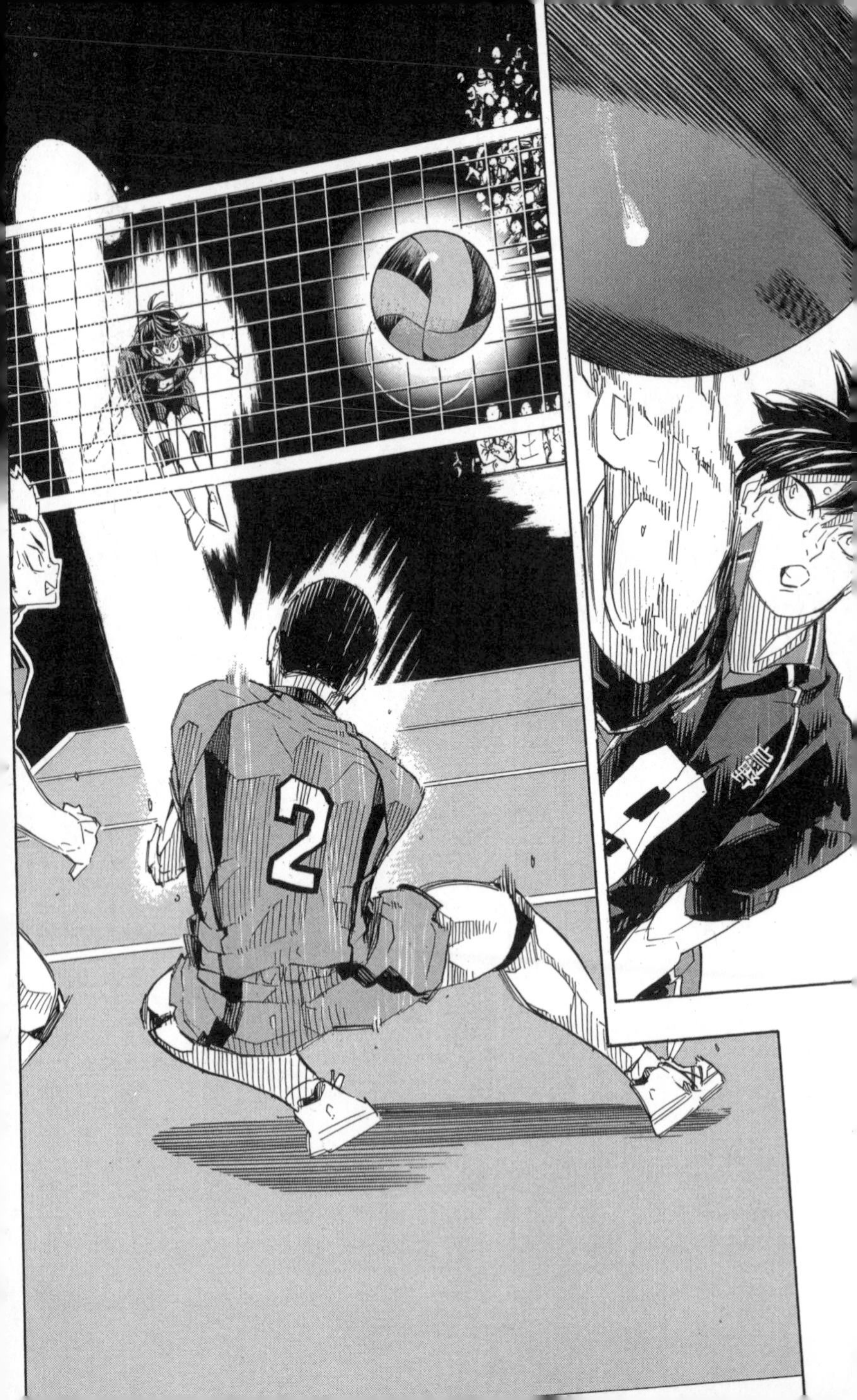

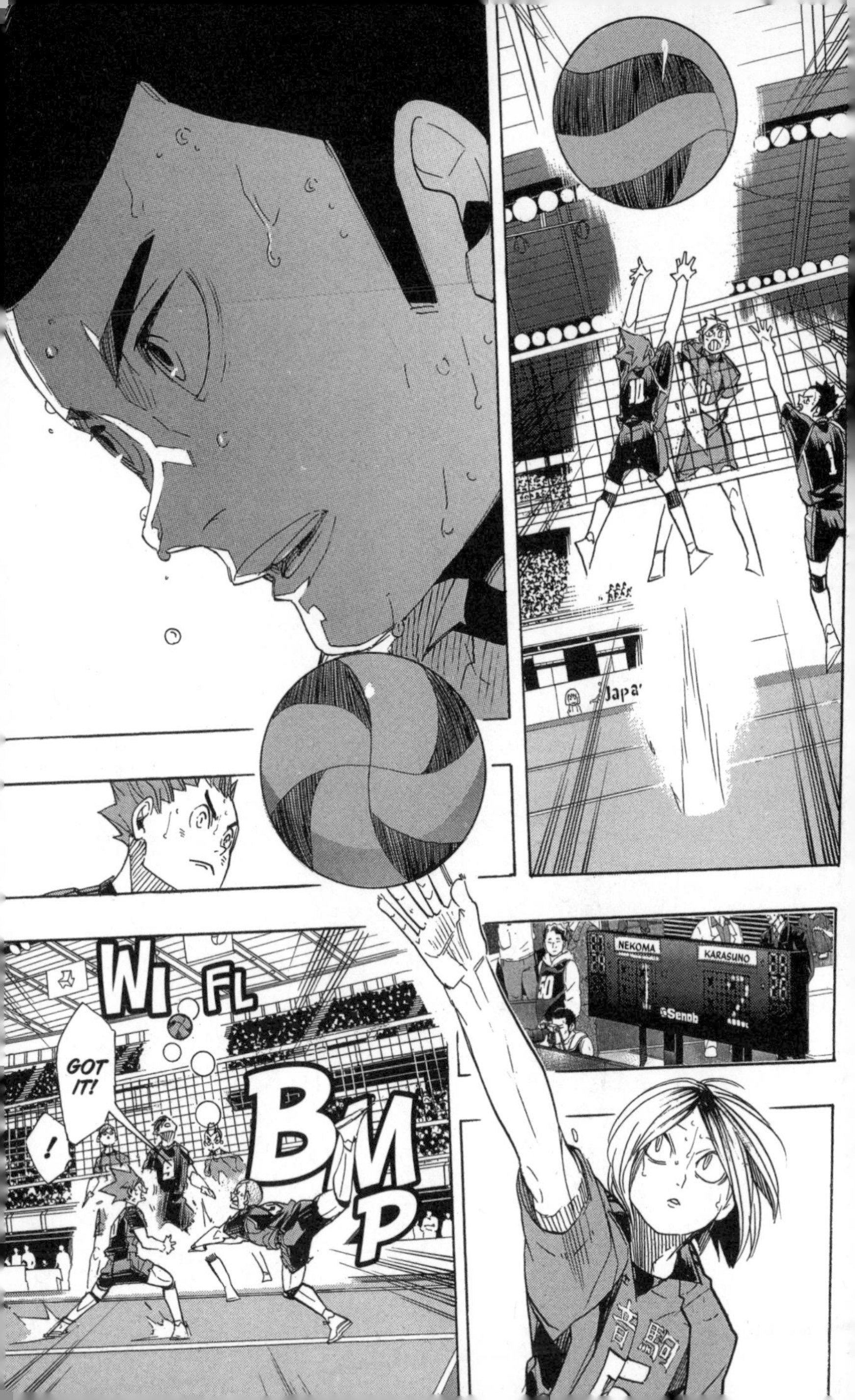

Japa
NEKOMA
KARASUNO
Senob
WI
FL
GOT IT!
!
BMP

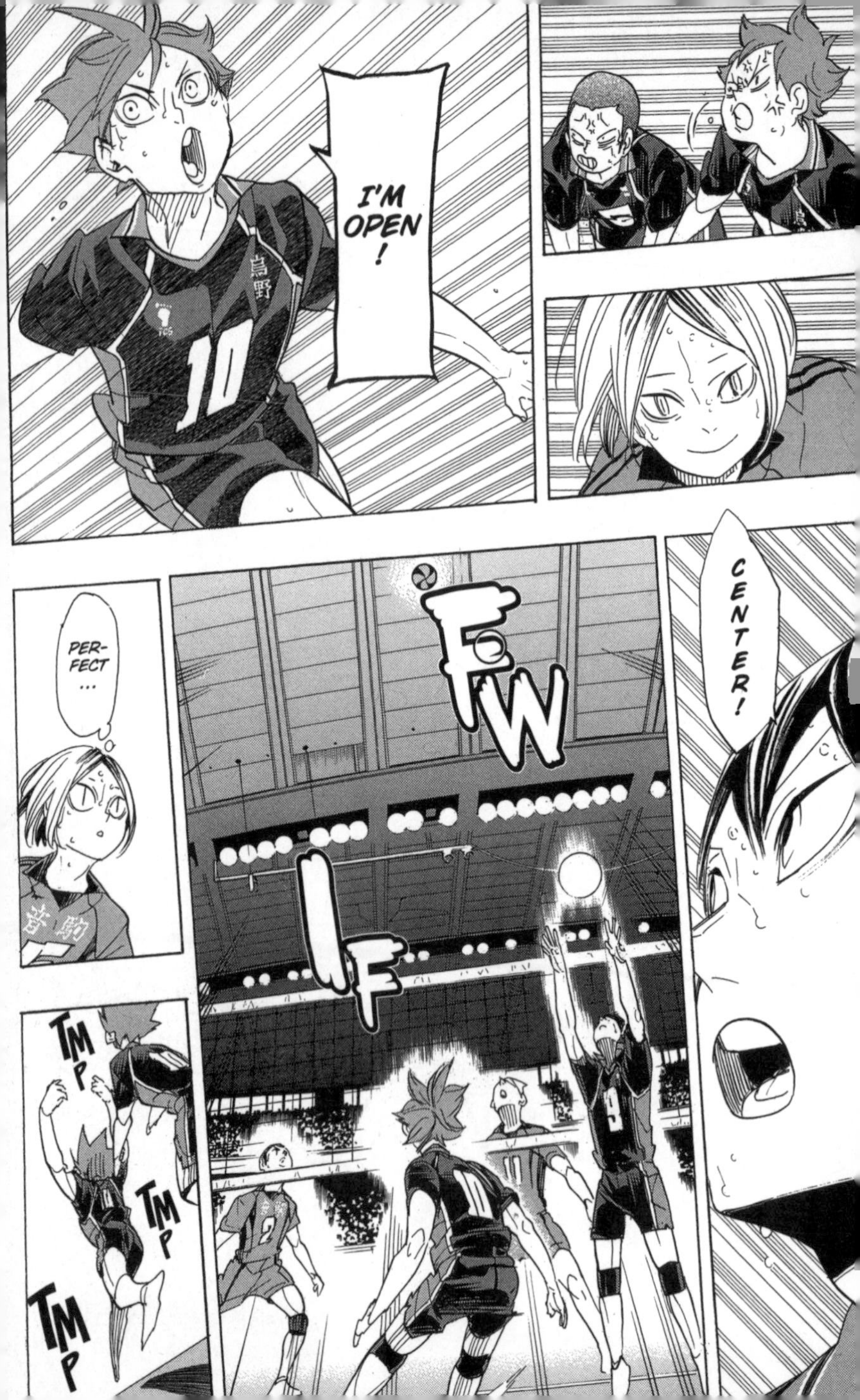

I'M OPEN!
CENTER!
FW
F
PER-FECT...
TMP
TMP
TMP

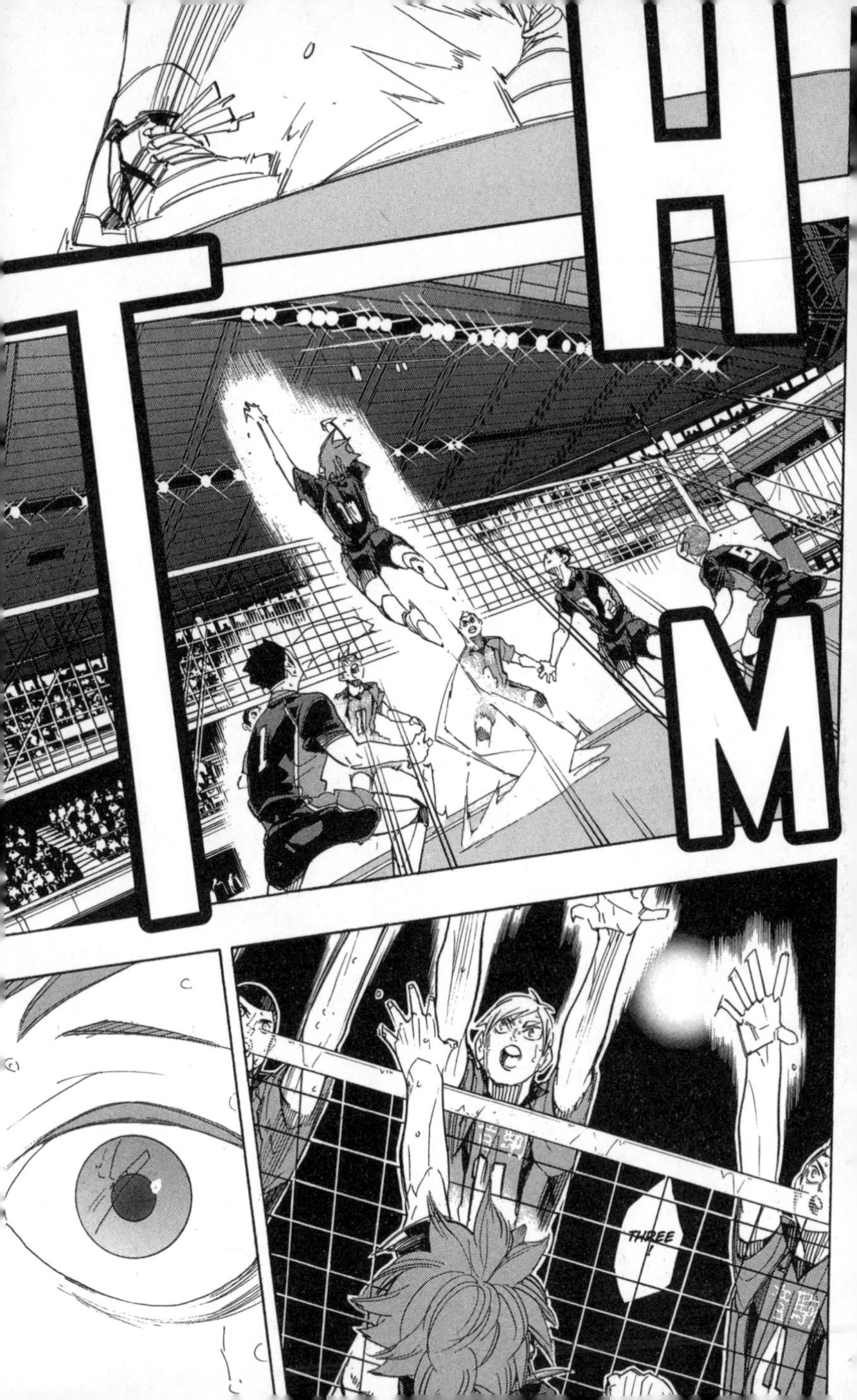
THREE

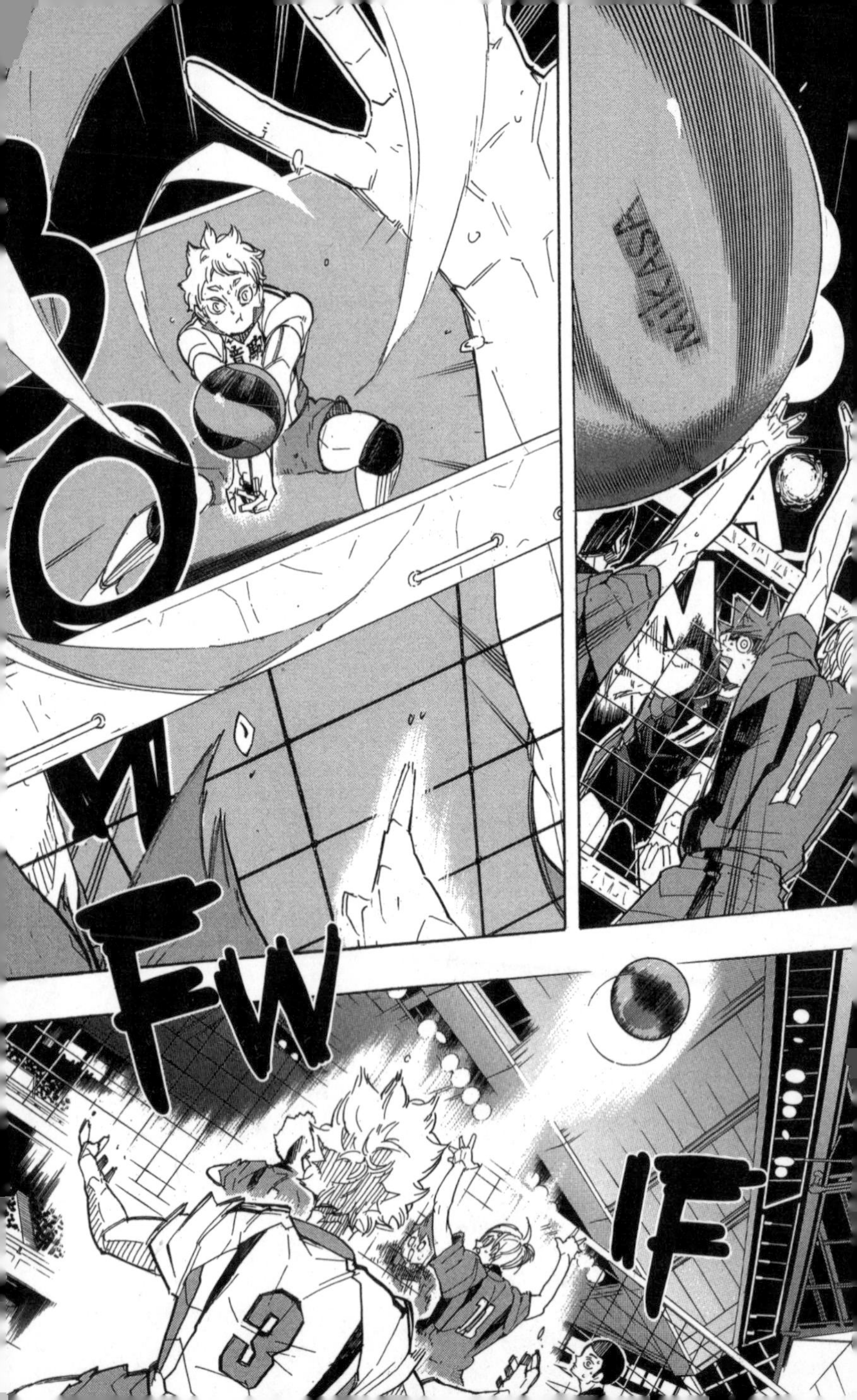
MIKASA
FWIF

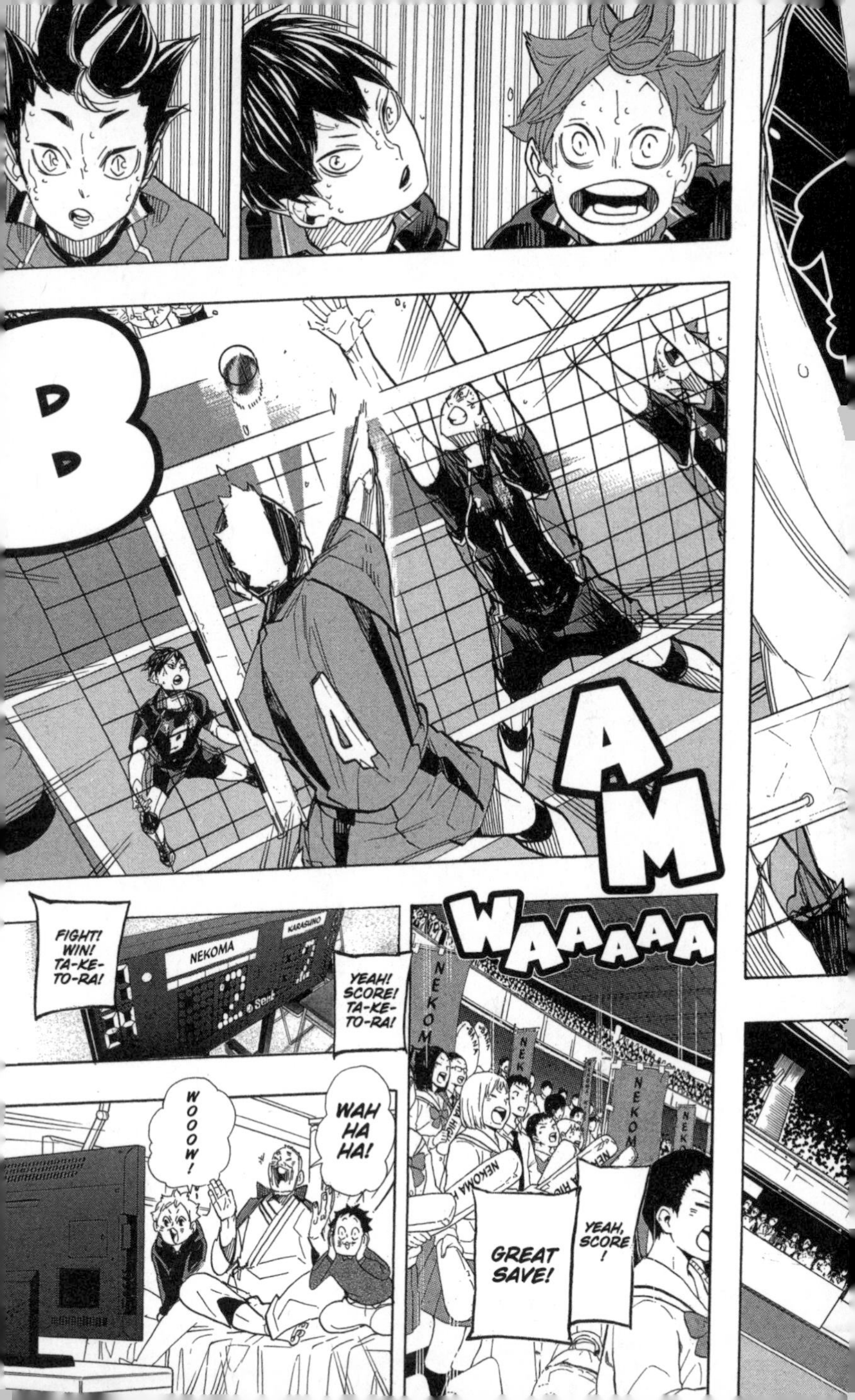

B
A
M
WAAAAAA
YEAH! SCORE! TA-KE-TO-RA!
YEAH, SCORE!
GREAT SAVE!
KARASUNO
NEKOMA
FIGHT! WIN! TA-KE-TO-RA!
WAH HA HA!
WOOOOW!

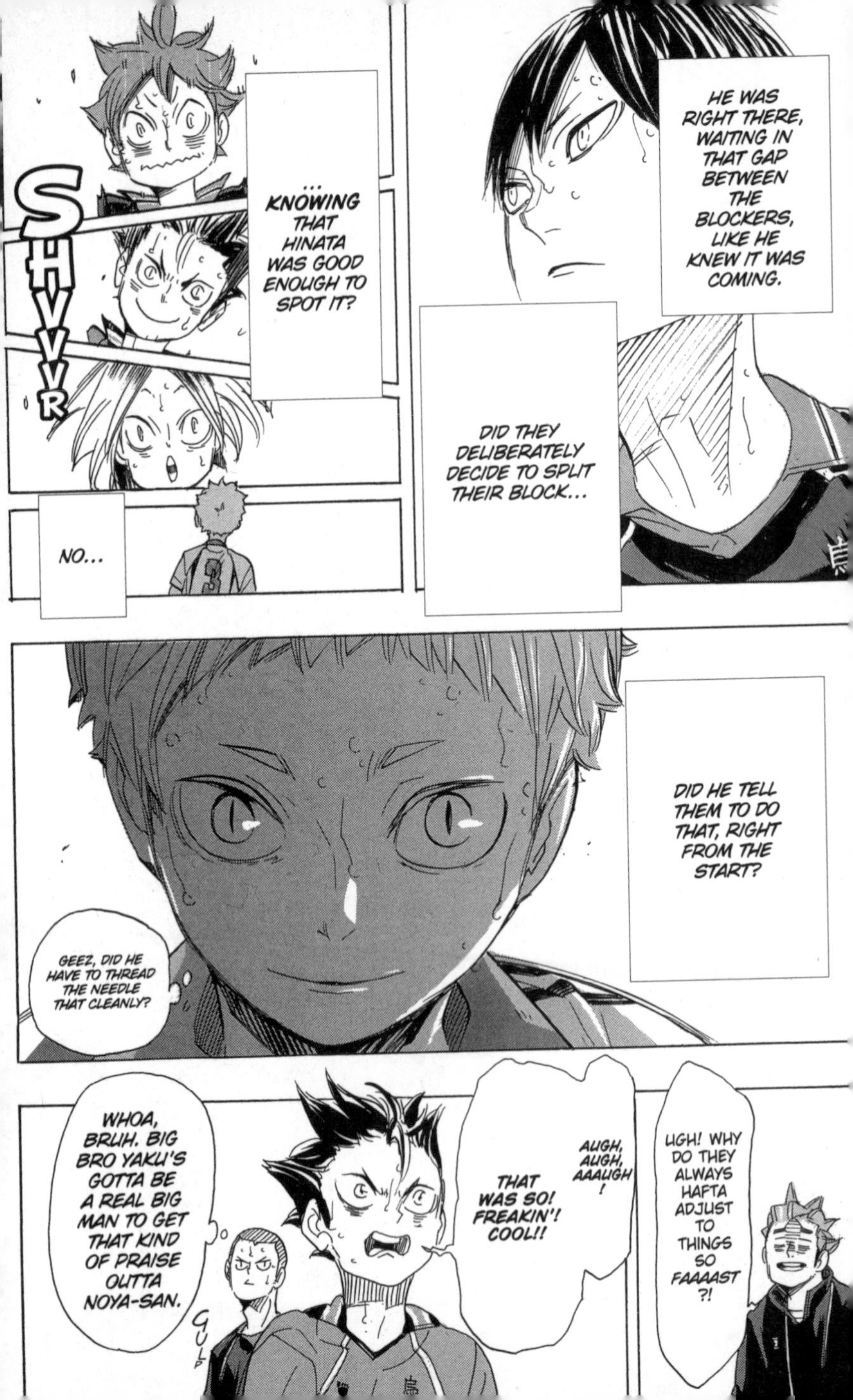
HE WAS RIGHT THERE, WAITING IN THAT GAP BETWEEN THE BLOCKERS, LIKE HE KNEW IT WAS COMING.
DID THEY DELIBERATELY DECIDE TO SPLIT THEIR BLOCK...
... KNOWING THAT HINATA WAS GOOD ENOUGH TO SPOT IT?
SHVVVR
NO...
DID HE TELL THEM TO DO THAT, RIGHT FROM THE START?
GEEZ, DID HE HAVE TO THREAD THE NEEDLE THAT CLEANLY?
UGH! WHY DO THEY ALWAYS HAFTA ADJUST TO THINGS SO FAAAAST?!
AUGH, AUGH, AAAUGH!
THAT WAS SO! FREAKIN'! COOL!!
WHOA, BRUH. BIG BRO YAKU'S GOTTA BE A REAL BIG MAN TO GET THAT KIND OF PRAISE OUTTA NOYA-SAN.
GULP

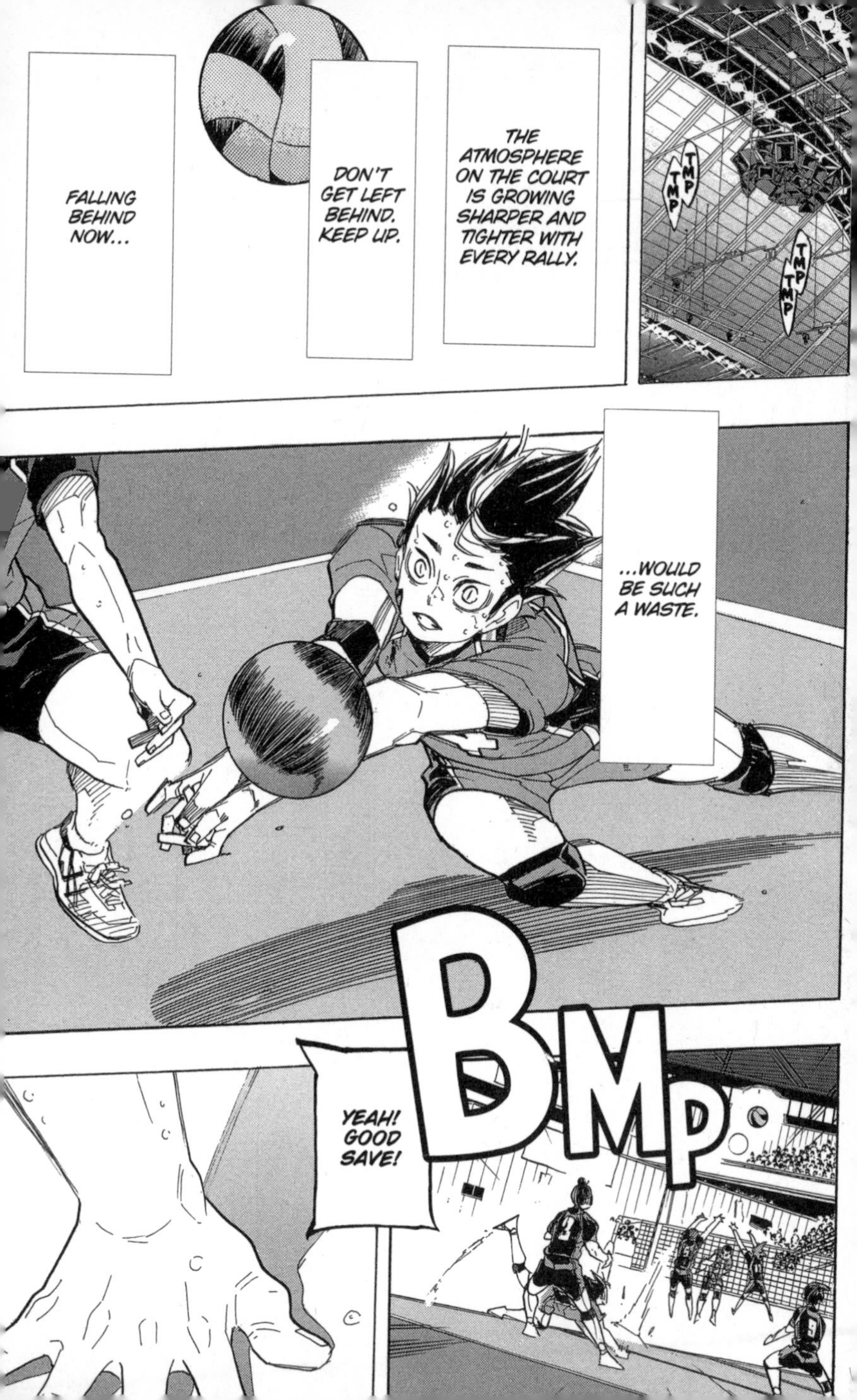
TMP TMP TMP
TMP TMP TMP
THE ATMOSPHERE ON THE COURT IS GROWING SHARPER AND TIGHTER WITH EVERY RALLY.
DON'T GET LEFT BEHIND. KEEP UP.
FALLING BEHIND NOW...
...WOULD BE SUCH A WASTE.
BMP
YEAH! GOOD SAVE!

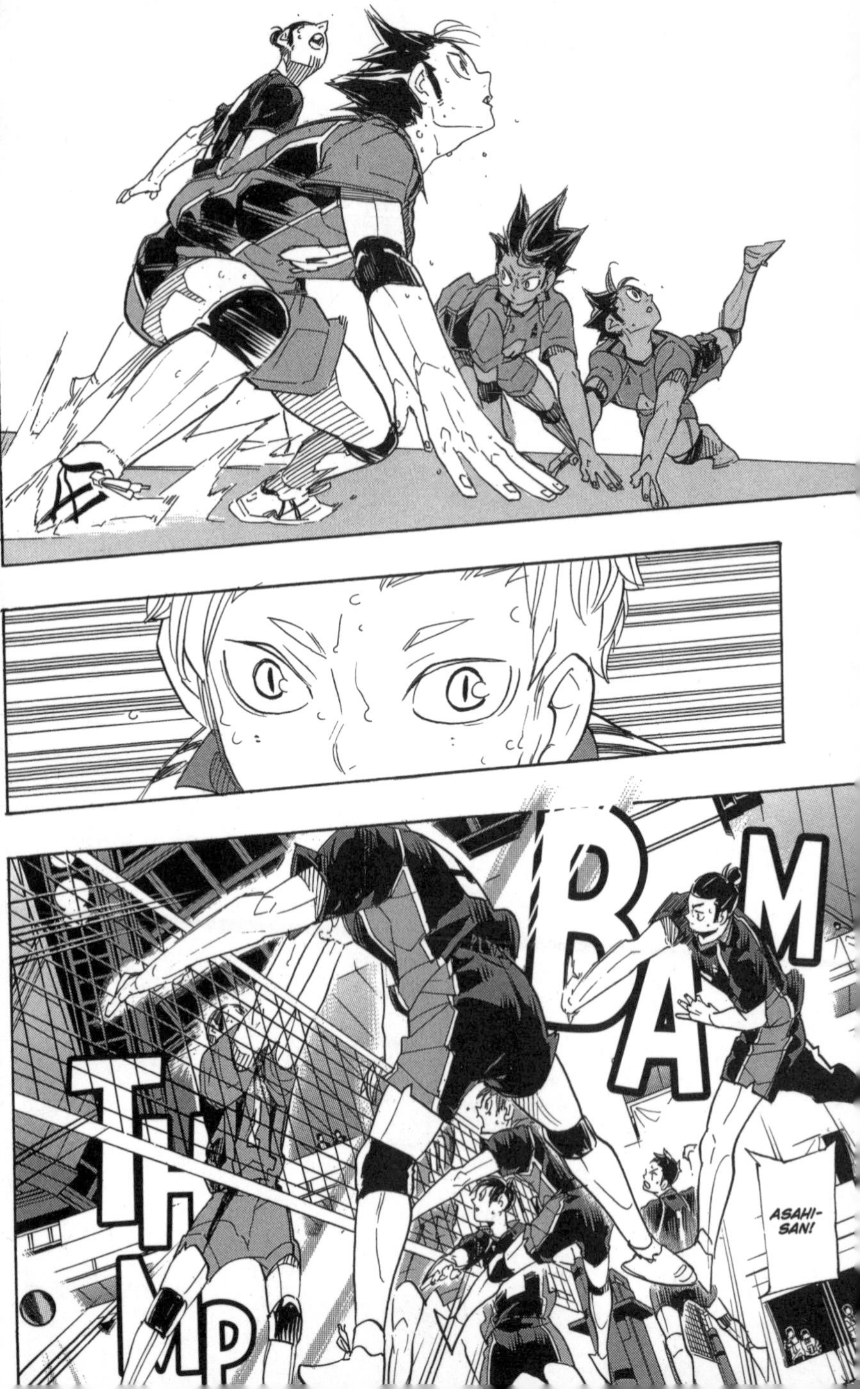
BAM
ASAHI-SAN!
THUMP

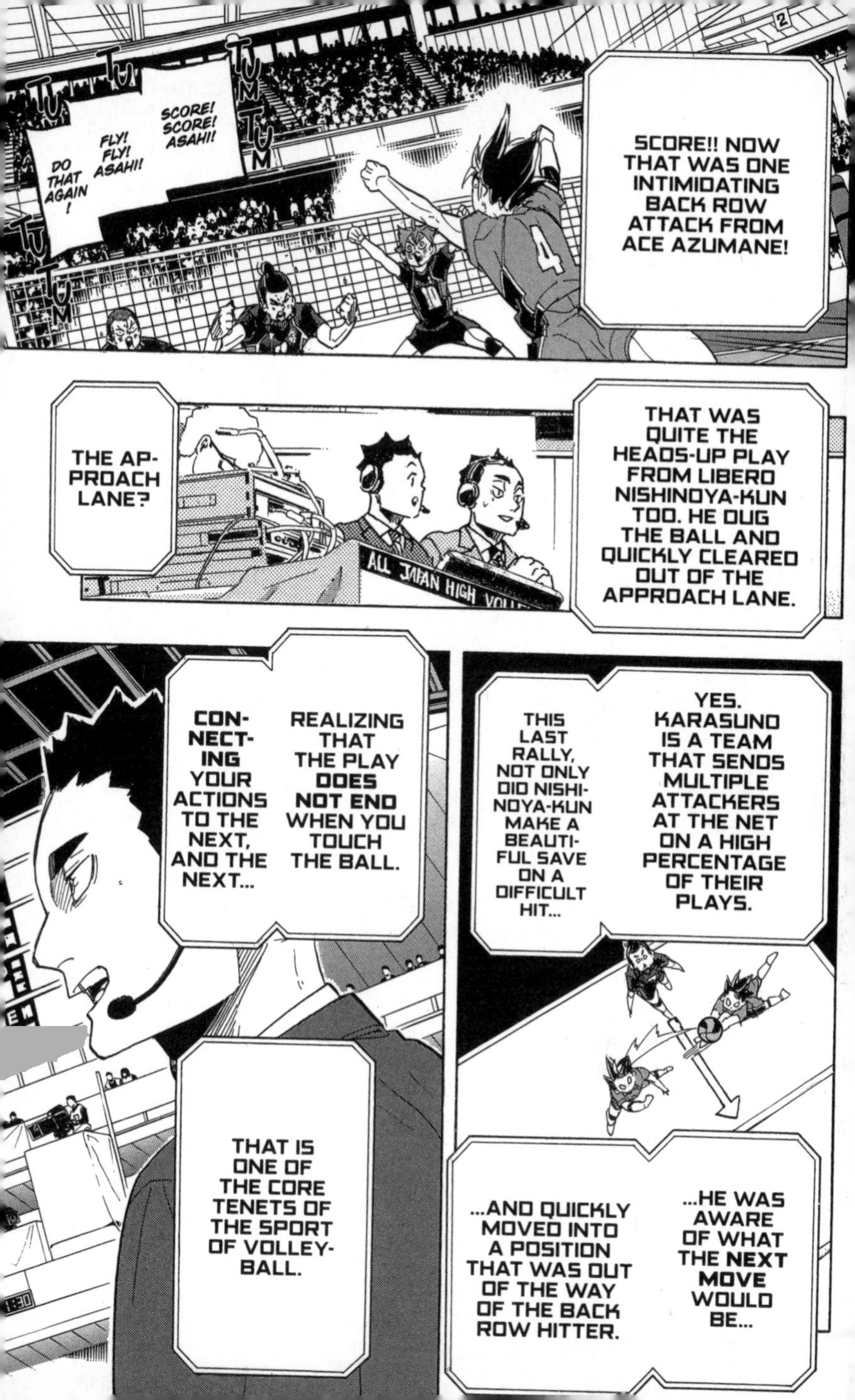
SCORE!! NOW THAT WAS ONE INTIMIDATING BACK ROW ATTACK FROM ACE AZUMANE!
TUMTUM
SCORE! SCORE! ASAHI!!
TU TU
FLY! FLY! ASAHI!
DO THAT AGAIN!
TUTUM
THAT WAS QUITE THE HEADS-UP PLAY FROM LIBERO NISHINOYA-KUN TOO. HE DUG THE BALL AND QUICKLY CLEARED OUT OF THE APPROACH LANE.
THE AP-PROACH LANE?
YES. KARASUNO IS A TEAM THAT SENDS MULTIPLE ATTACKERS AT THE NET ON A HIGH PERCENTAGE OF THEIR PLAYS.
THIS LAST RALLY, NOT ONLY DID NISHI-NOYA-KUN MAKE A BEAUTI-FUL SAVE ON A DIFFICULT HIT...
...HE WAS AWARE OF WHAT THE NEXT MOVE WOULD BE...
...AND QUICKLY MOVED INTO A POSITION THAT WAS OUT OF THE WAY OF THE BACK ROW HITTER.
REALIZING THAT THE PLAY DOES NOT END WHEN YOU TOUCH THE BALL.
CON-NECT-ING YOUR ACTIONS TO THE NEXT, AND THE NEXT...
THAT IS ONE OF THE CORE TENETS OF THE SPORT OF VOLLEY-BALL.

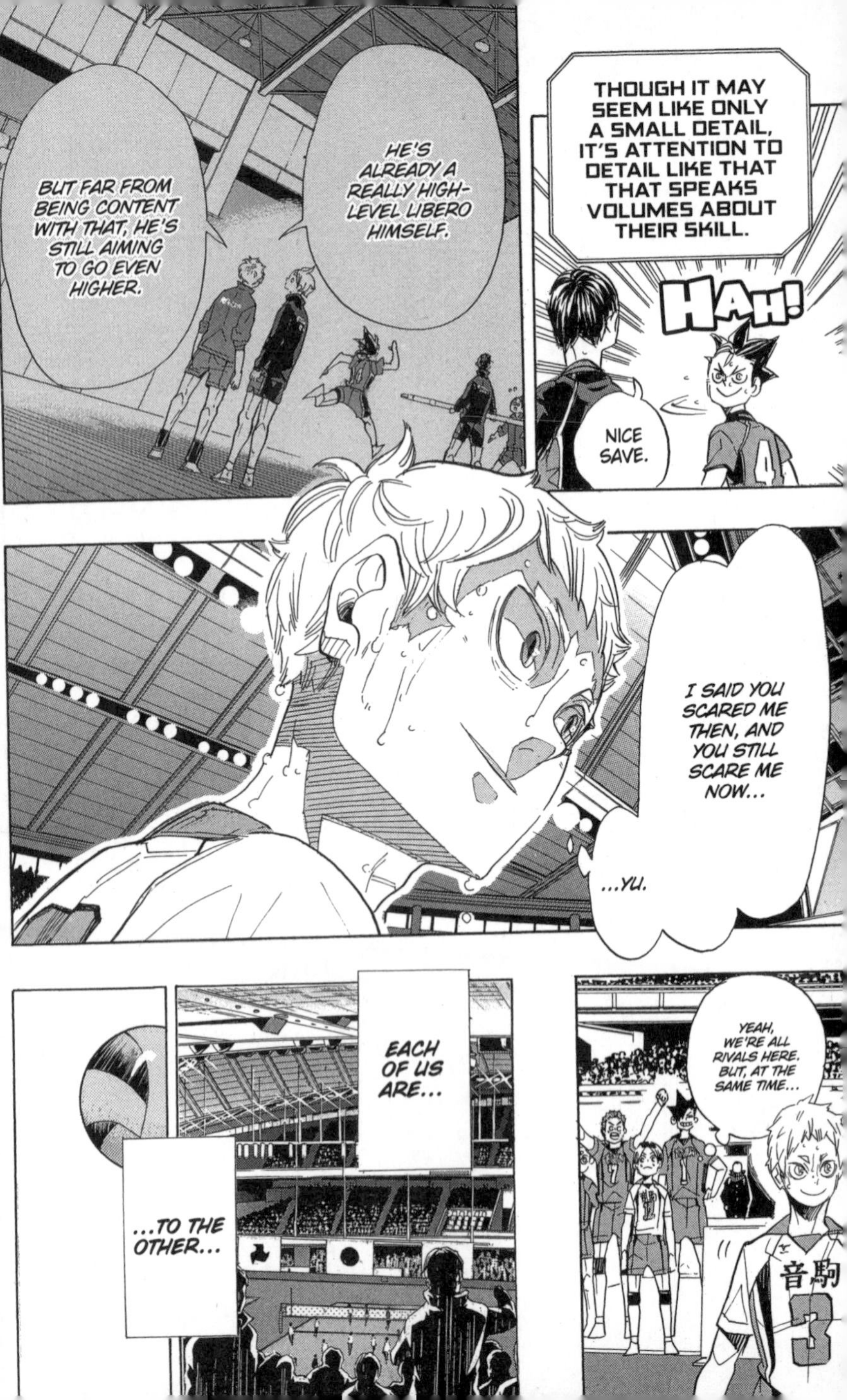
THOUGH IT MAY SEEM LIKE ONLY A SMALL DETAIL, IT'S ATTENTION TO DETAIL LIKE THAT THAT SPEAKS VOLUMES ABOUT THEIR SKILL.
HAH!
NICE SAVE.
HE'S ALREADY A REALLY HIGH-LEVEL LIBERO HIMSELF.
BUT FAR FROM BEING CONTENT WITH THAT, HE'S STILL AIMING TO GO EVEN HIGHER.
I SAID YOU SCARED ME THEN, AND YOU STILL SCARE ME NOW...
...YU.
YEAH, WE'RE ALL RIVALS HERE. BUT, AT THE SAME TIME...
音駒
3
EACH OF US ARE...
...TO THE OTHER...

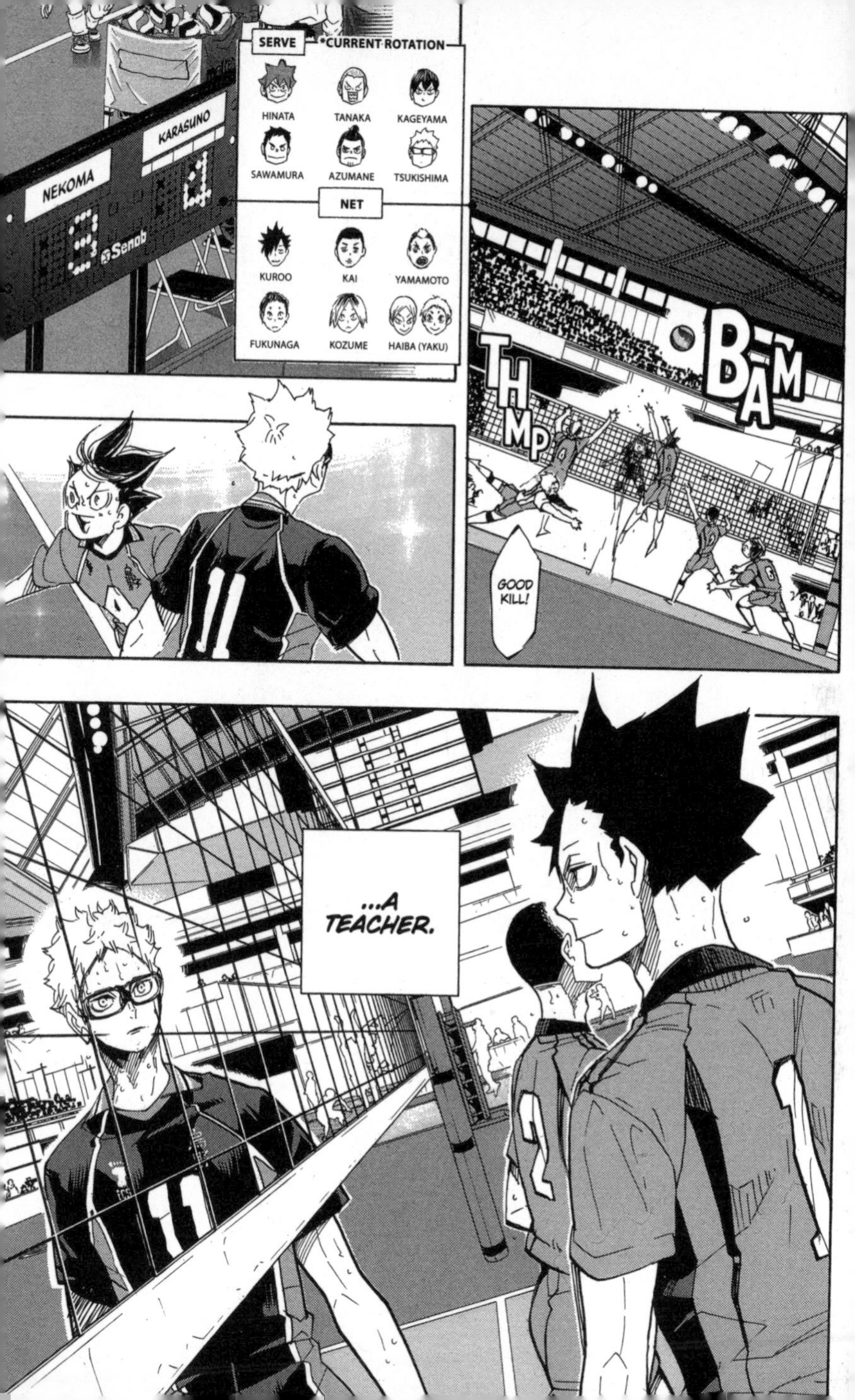

THMP
BAM
GOOD KILL!
NEKOMA
KARASUNO
Senob
SERVE
*CURRENT ROTATION
HINATA
TANAKA
KAGEYAMA
SAWAMURA
AZUMANE
TSUKISHIMA
NET
KUROO
KAI
YAMAMOTO
FUKUNAGA
KOZUME
HAIBA (YAKU)
...A TEACHER.

HELLO FROM BEYOND THE (PAGE) EDGE!!
GUESS WHICH PANEL THIS IS!!

少年ジャンプ原稿
319

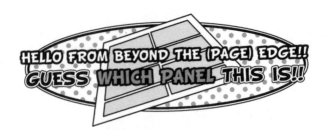

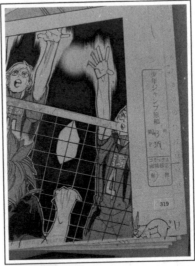

FROM CHAPTER 319

I THINK THAT'S...YAKUL? I SEEM TO REMEMBER THAT, THE WEEK I WAS WORKING ON THIS CHAPTER, THEY WERE SHOWING *PRINCESS MONONOKE* ON TV.

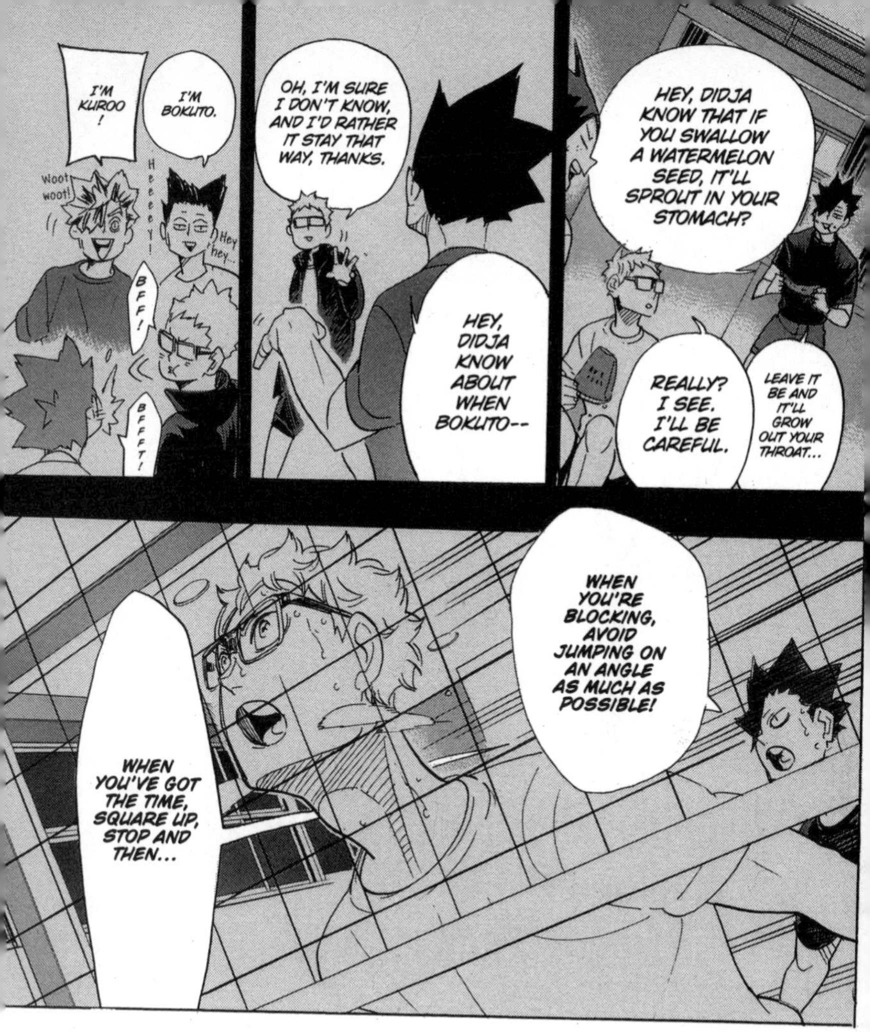
HEY, DIDJA KNOW THAT IF YOU SWALLOW A WATERMELON SEED, IT'LL SPROUT IN YOUR STOMACH?
LEAVE IT BE AND IT'LL GROW OUT YOUR THROAT...
REALLY? I SEE. I'LL BE CAREFUL.
HEY, DIDJA KNOW ABOUT WHEN BOKUTO--
OH, I'M SURE I DON'T KNOW, AND I'D RATHER IT STAY THAT WAY, THANKS.
I'M BOKUTO.
Hey hey...
Heeeey!
I'M KUROO!
Woot woot!
BFF!
BFFFT!
WHEN YOU'RE BLOCKING, AVOID JUMPING ON AN ANGLE AS MUCH AS POSSIBLE!
WHEN YOU'VE GOT THE TIME, SQUARE UP, STOP AND THEN...

CHAPTER 320

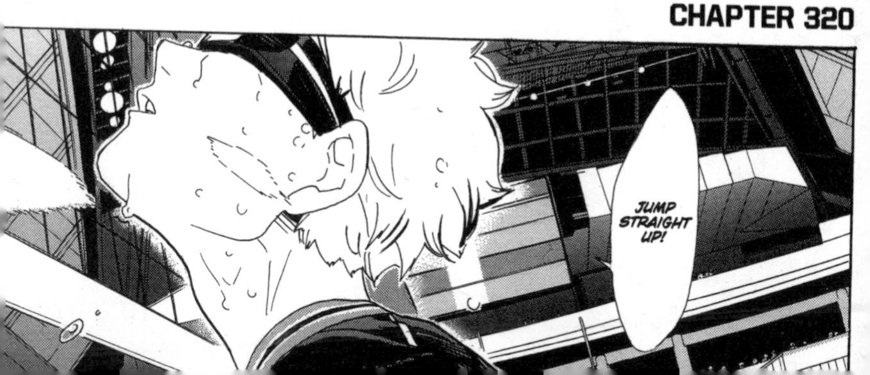
JUMP STRAIGHT UP!

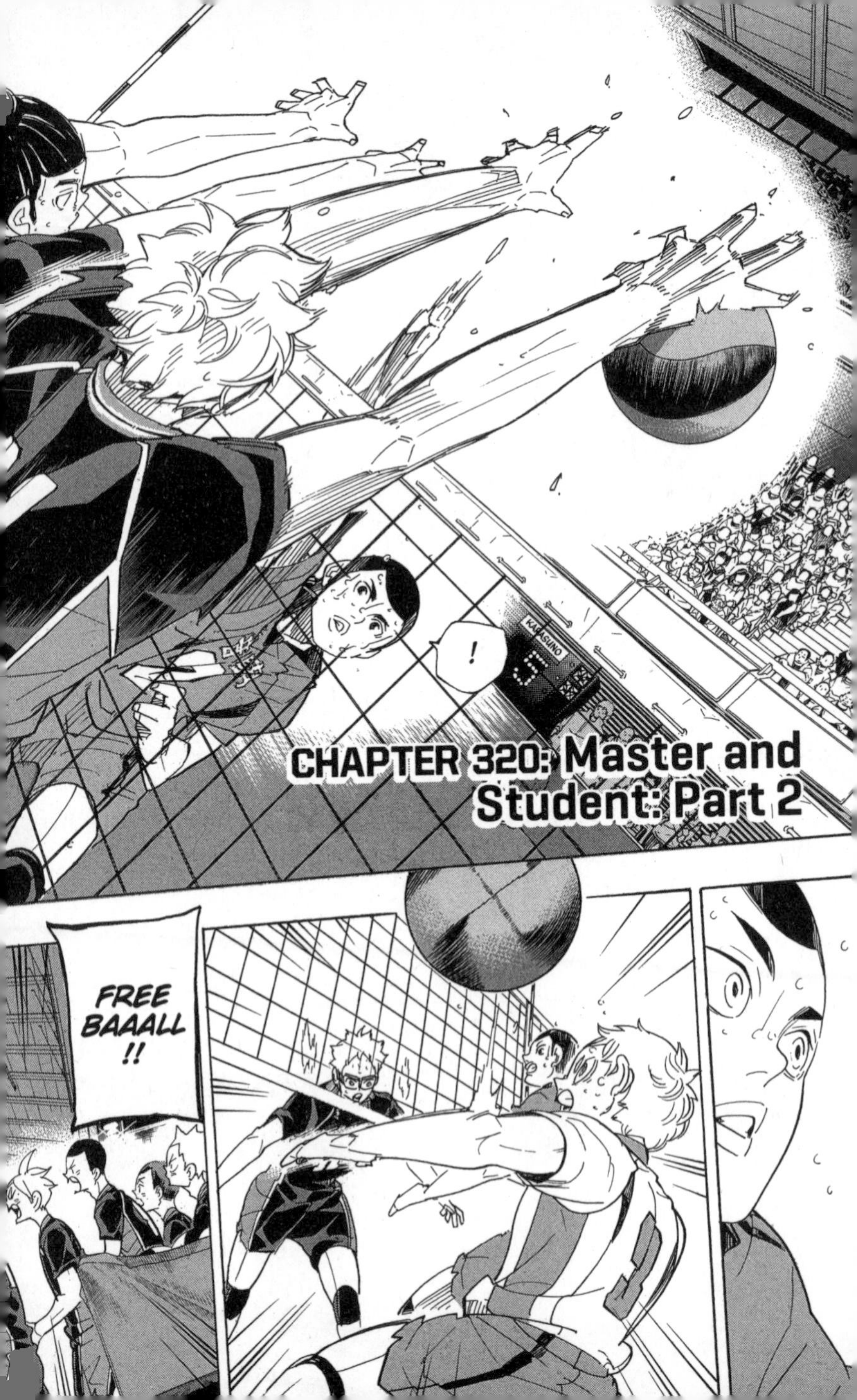
!
CHAPTER 320: Master and Student: Part 2
FREE BAAALL !!

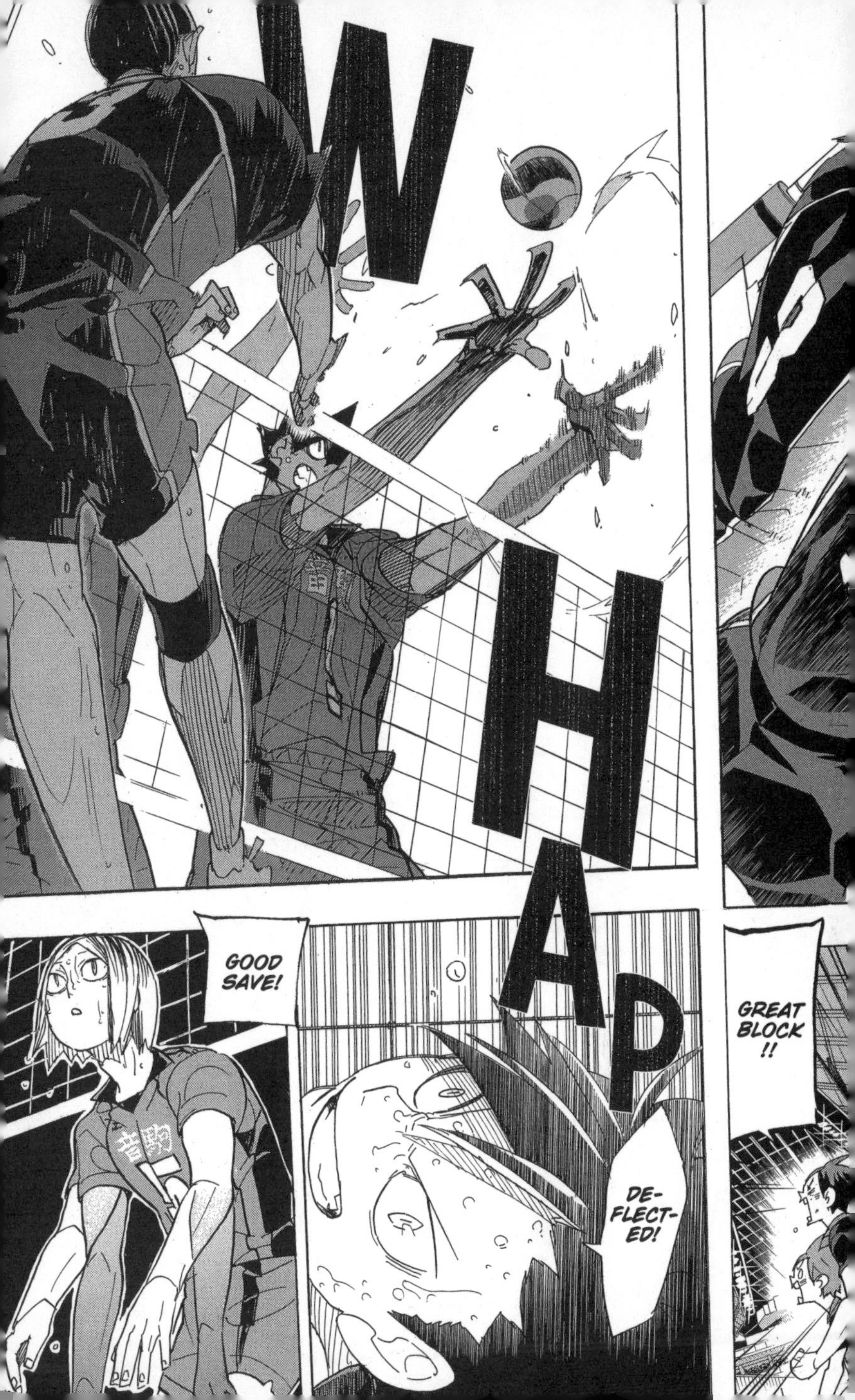
WHHAP
GREAT BLOCK !!
DE-FLECT-ED!
GOOD SAVE!

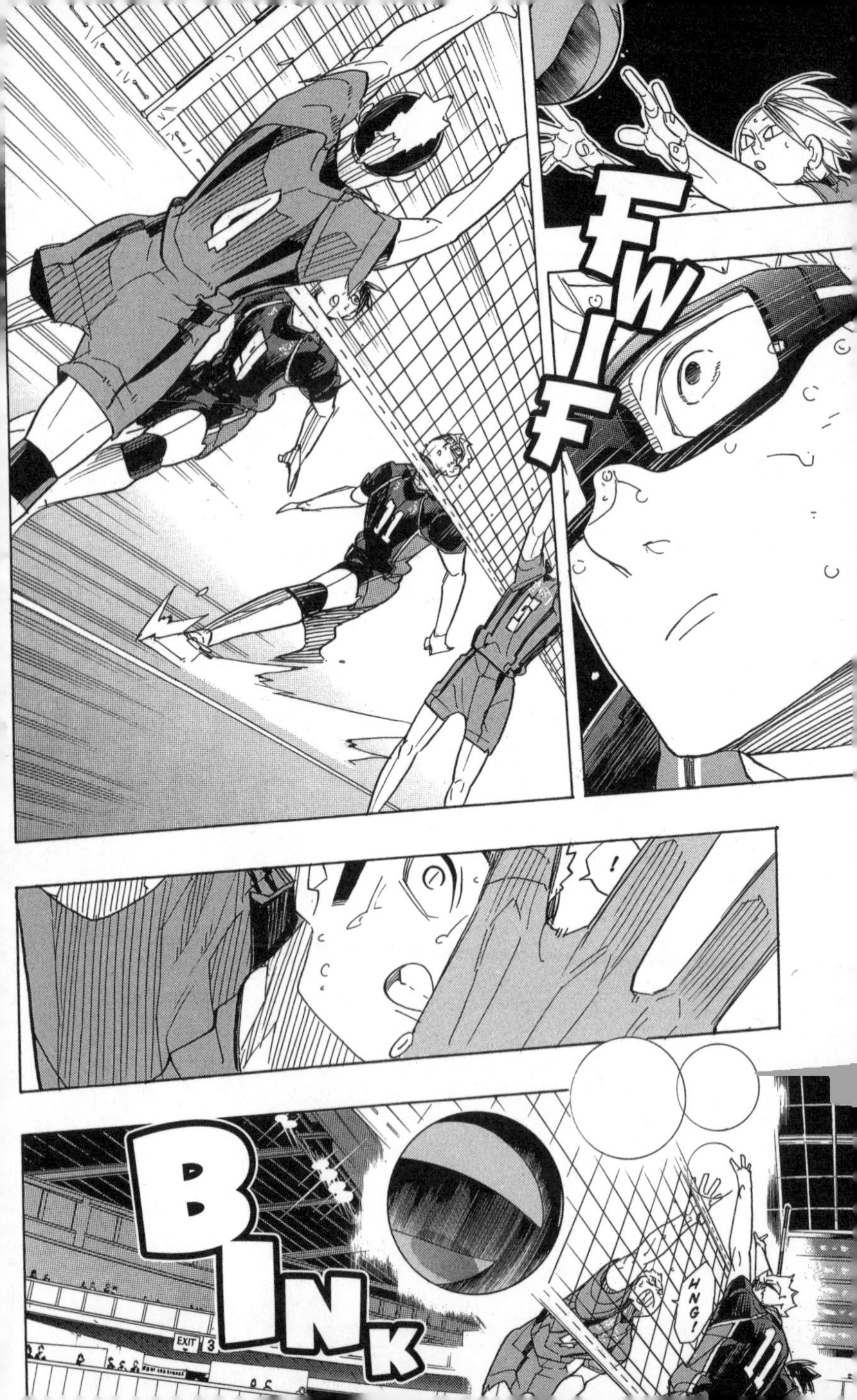
FWIFF
!
BINK
HNG!

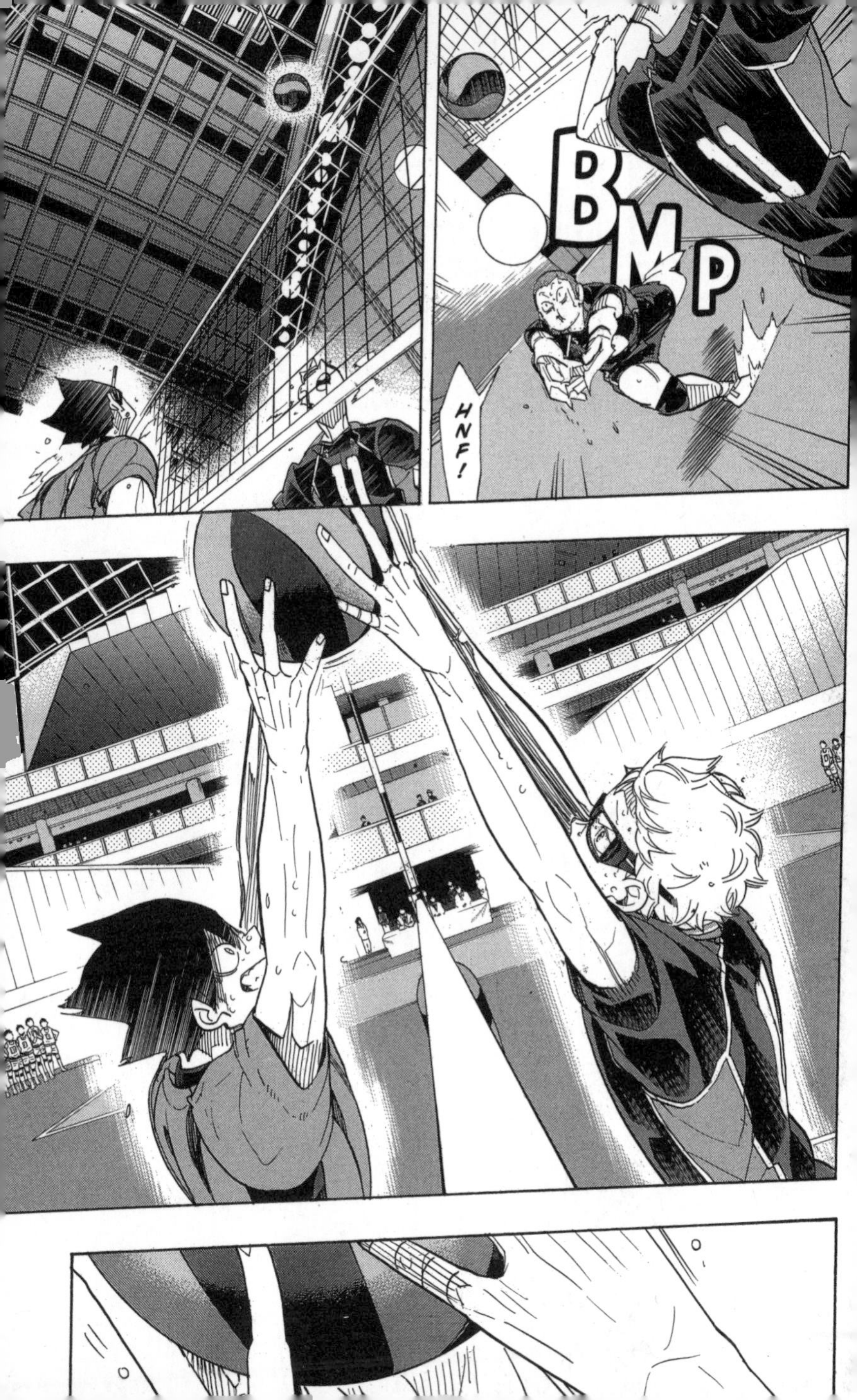
BMP
HNF!

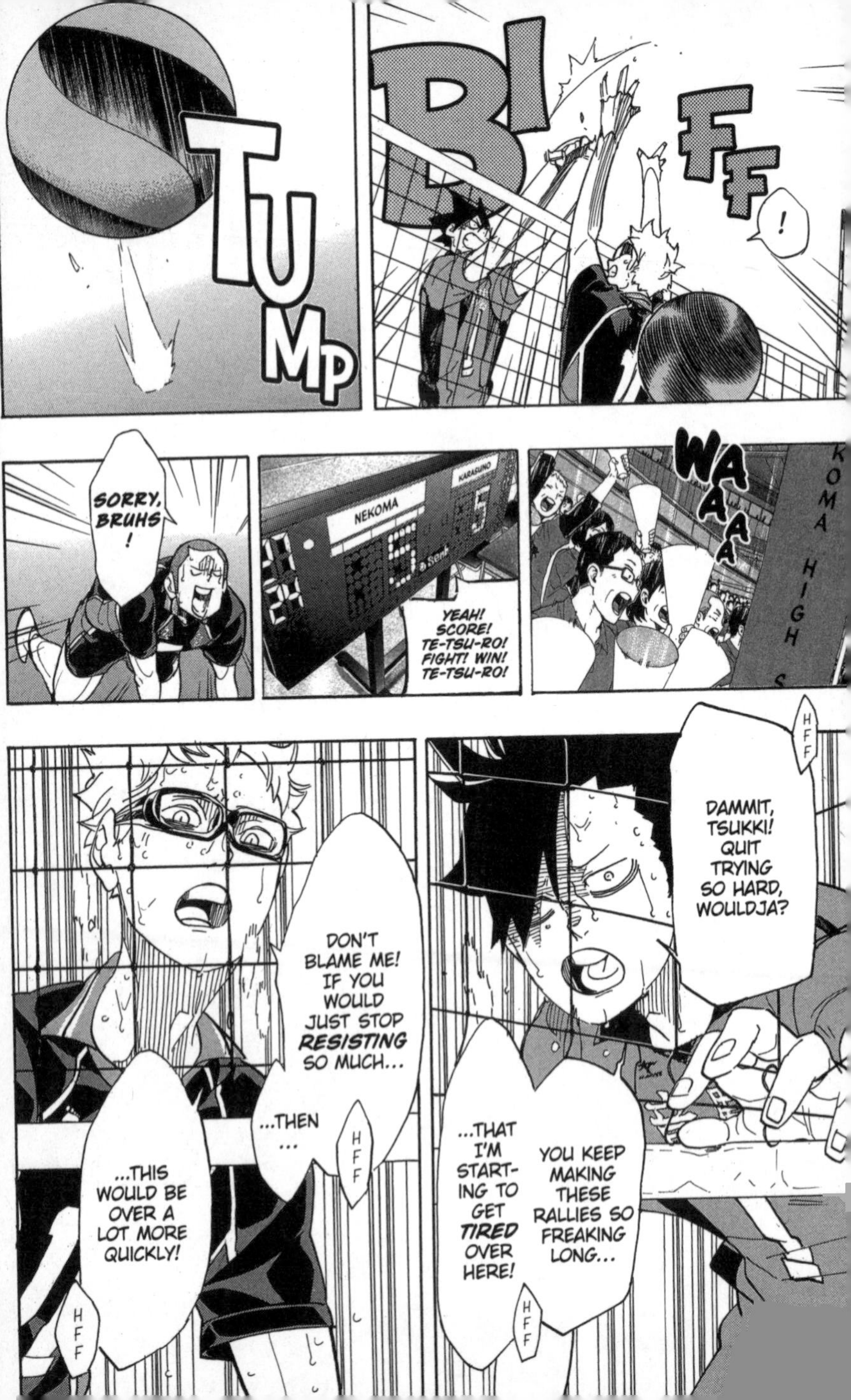
BLIFFF
!
TUMP
WAAAAA
KOMA HIGH S
NEKOMA
KARASUNO
YEAH! SCORE! TE-TSU-RO! FIGHT! WIN! TE-TSU-RO!
SORRY, BRUHS!
HFF
DAMMIT, TSUKKI! QUIT TRYING SO HARD, WOULDJA?
YOU KEEP MAKING THESE RALLIES SO FREAKING LONG...
...THAT I'M STARTING TO GET ***TIRED*** OVER HERE!
HFF
DON'T BLAME ME! IF YOU WOULD JUST STOP ***RESISTING*** SO MUCH...
...THEN...
HFF
...THIS WOULD BE OVER A LOT MORE QUICKLY!
HFF

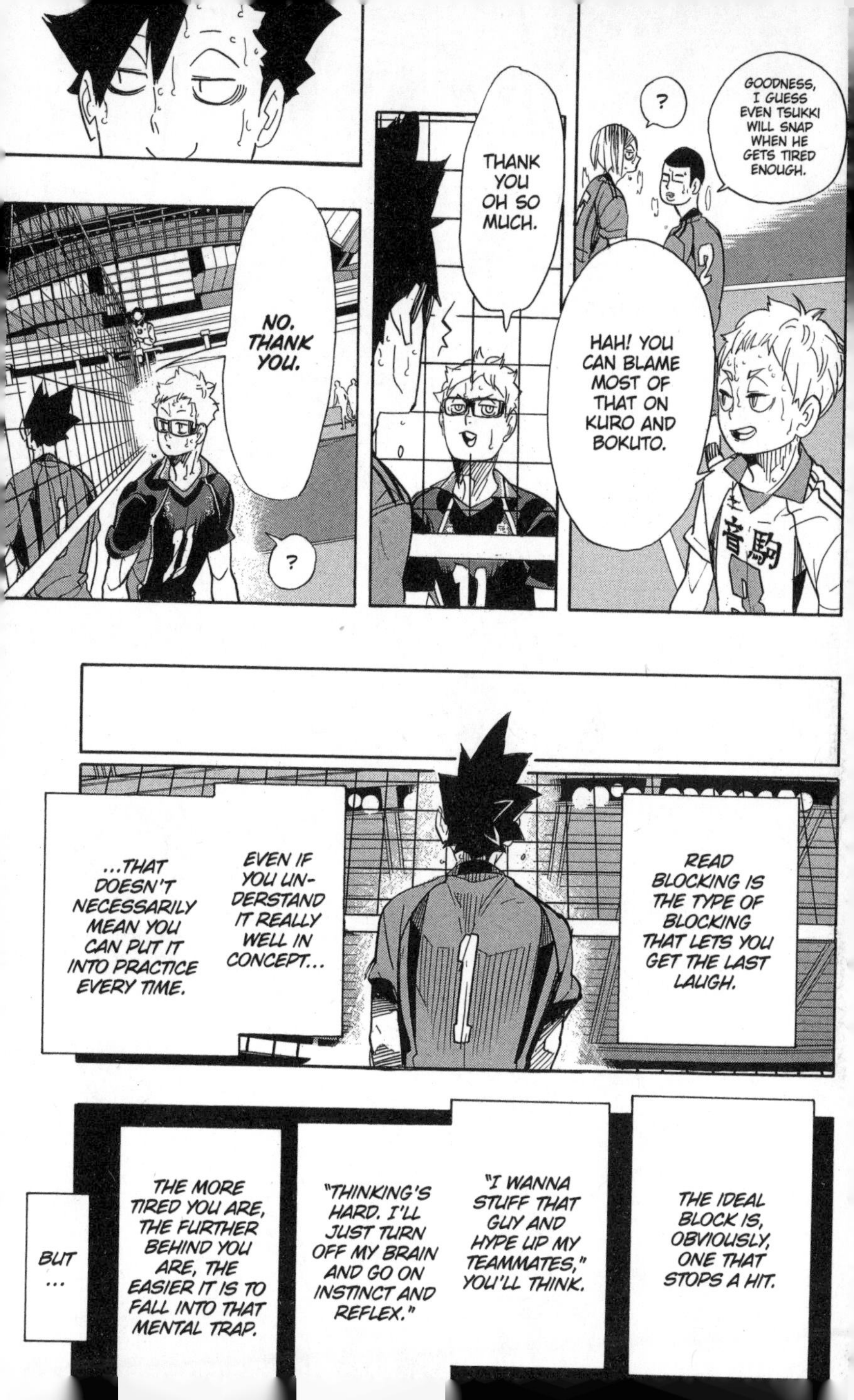
GOODNESS, I GUESS EVEN TSUKKI WILL SNAP WHEN HE GETS TIRED ENOUGH.
?
HAH! YOU CAN BLAME MOST OF THAT ON KURO AND BOKUTO.
THANK YOU OH SO MUCH.
NO. THANK YOU.
?
READ BLOCKING IS THE TYPE OF BLOCKING THAT LETS YOU GET THE LAST LAUGH.
EVEN IF YOU UNDERSTAND IT REALLY WELL IN CONCEPT...
...THAT DOESN'T NECESSARILY MEAN YOU CAN PUT IT INTO PRACTICE EVERY TIME.
THE IDEAL BLOCK IS, OBVIOUSLY, ONE THAT STOPS A HIT.
"I WANNA STUFF THAT GUY AND HYPE UP MY TEAMMATES," YOU'LL THINK.
"THINKING'S HARD. I'LL JUST TURN OFF MY BRAIN AND GO ON INSTINCT AND REFLEX."
THE MORE TIRED YOU ARE, THE FURTHER BEHIND YOU ARE, THE EASIER IT IS TO FALL INTO THAT MENTAL TRAP.
BUT ...

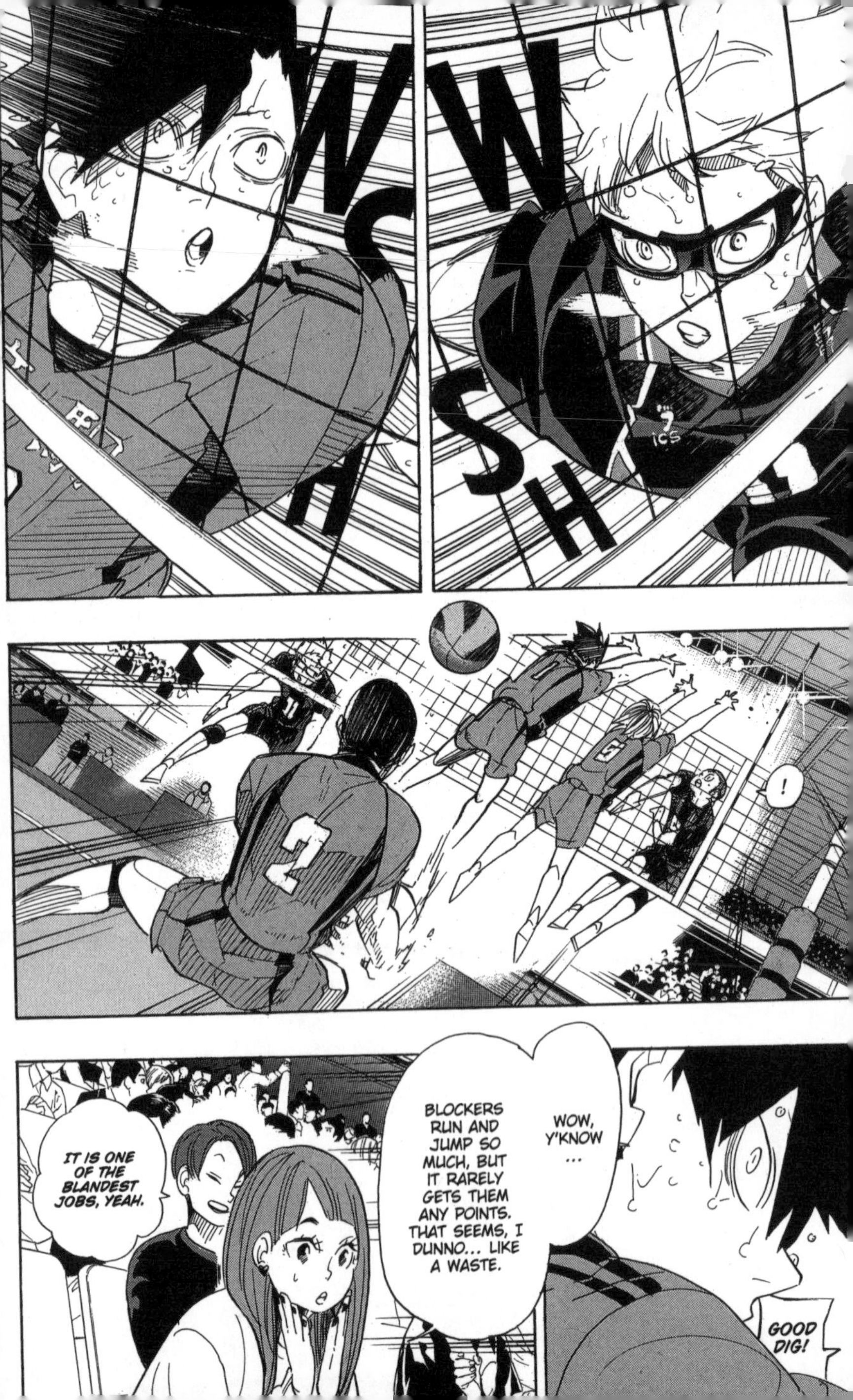
WSH
WSH
!
WOW, Y'KNOW ...
BLOCKERS RUN AND JUMP SO MUCH, BUT IT RARELY GETS THEM ANY POINTS. THAT SEEMS, I DUNNO... LIKE A WASTE.
IT IS ONE OF THE BLANDEST JOBS, YEAH.
GOOD DIG!

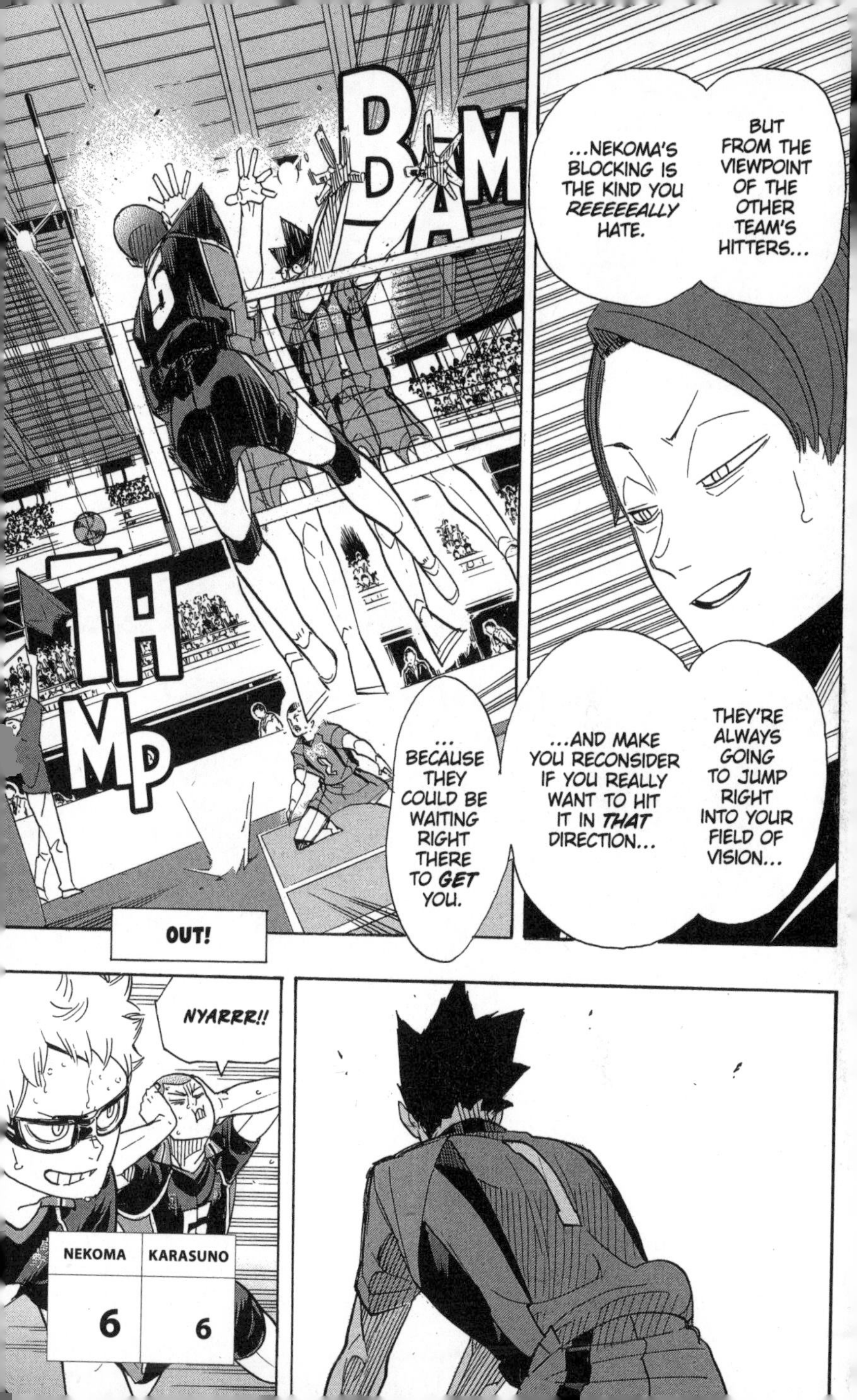
BUT FROM THE VIEWPOINT OF THE OTHER TEAM'S HITTERS...
...NEKOMA'S BLOCKING IS THE KIND YOU REEEEEALLY HATE.
THEY'RE ALWAYS GOING TO JUMP RIGHT INTO YOUR FIELD OF VISION...
...AND MAKE YOU RECONSIDER IF YOU REALLY WANT TO HIT IT IN THAT DIRECTION...
...BECAUSE THEY COULD BE WAITING RIGHT THERE TO GET YOU.
BAM
THMP
OUT!
NYARRR!!
NEKOMA 6
KARASUNO 6

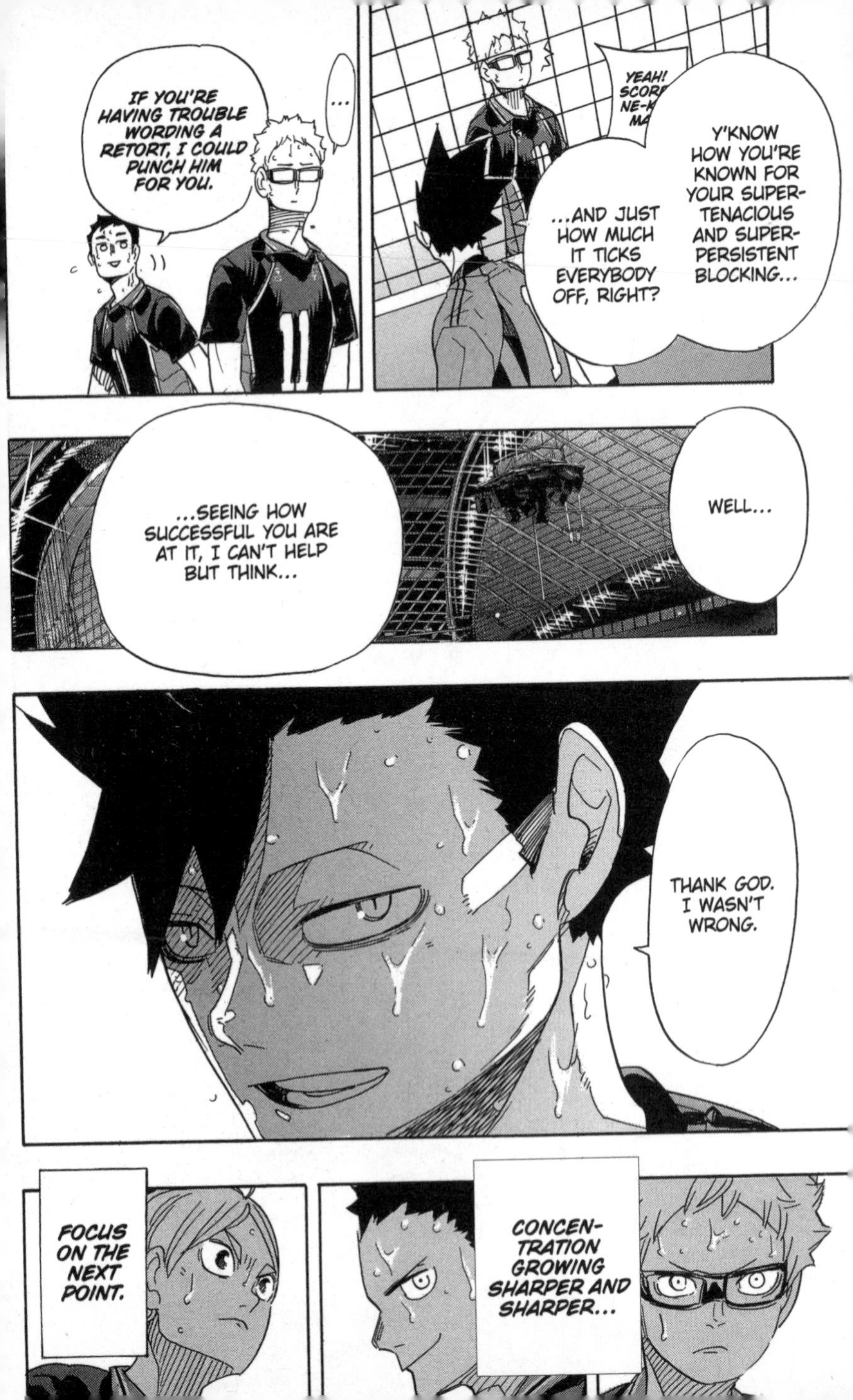
YEAH!
Y'KNOW HOW YOU'RE KNOWN FOR YOUR SUPER-TENACIOUS AND SUPER-PERSISTENT BLOCKING...
...AND JUST HOW MUCH IT TICKS EVERYBODY OFF, RIGHT?
...
IF YOU'RE HAVING TROUBLE WORDING A RETORT, I COULD PUNCH HIM FOR YOU.
WELL...
...SEEING HOW SUCCESSFUL YOU ARE AT IT, I CAN'T HELP BUT THINK...
THANK GOD. I WASN'T WRONG.
CONCEN-TRATION GROWING SHARPER AND SHARPER...
FOCUS ON THE NEXT POINT.

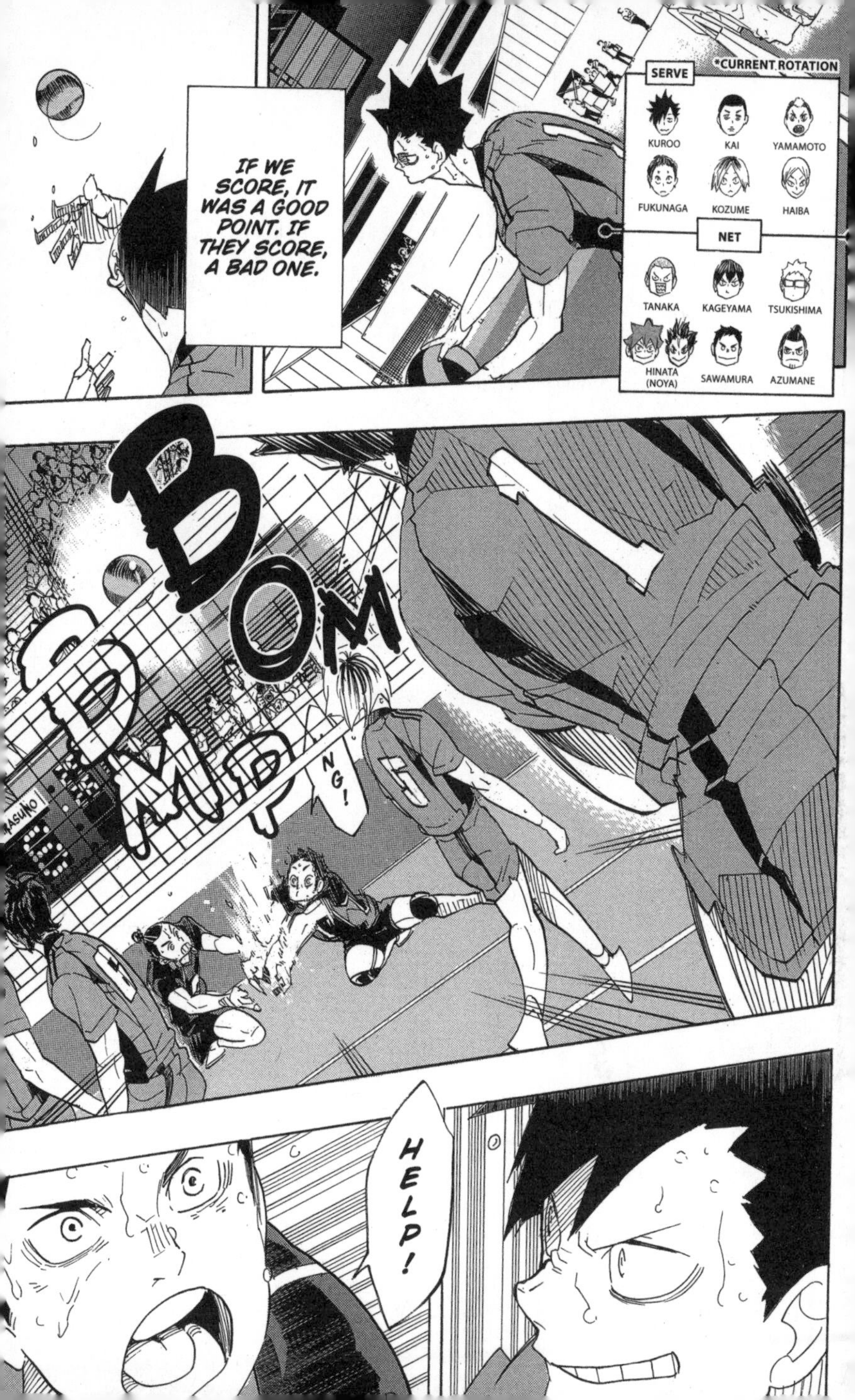
*CURRENT ROTATION
SERVE
KUROO
KAI
YAMAMOTO
FUKUNAGA
KOZUME
HAIBA
NET
TANAKA
KAGEYAMA
TSUKISHIMA
HINATA (NOYA)
SAWAMURA
AZUMANE
IF WE SCORE, IT WAS A GOOD POINT. IF THEY SCORE, A BAD ONE.
BOOM
NG!
HELP!

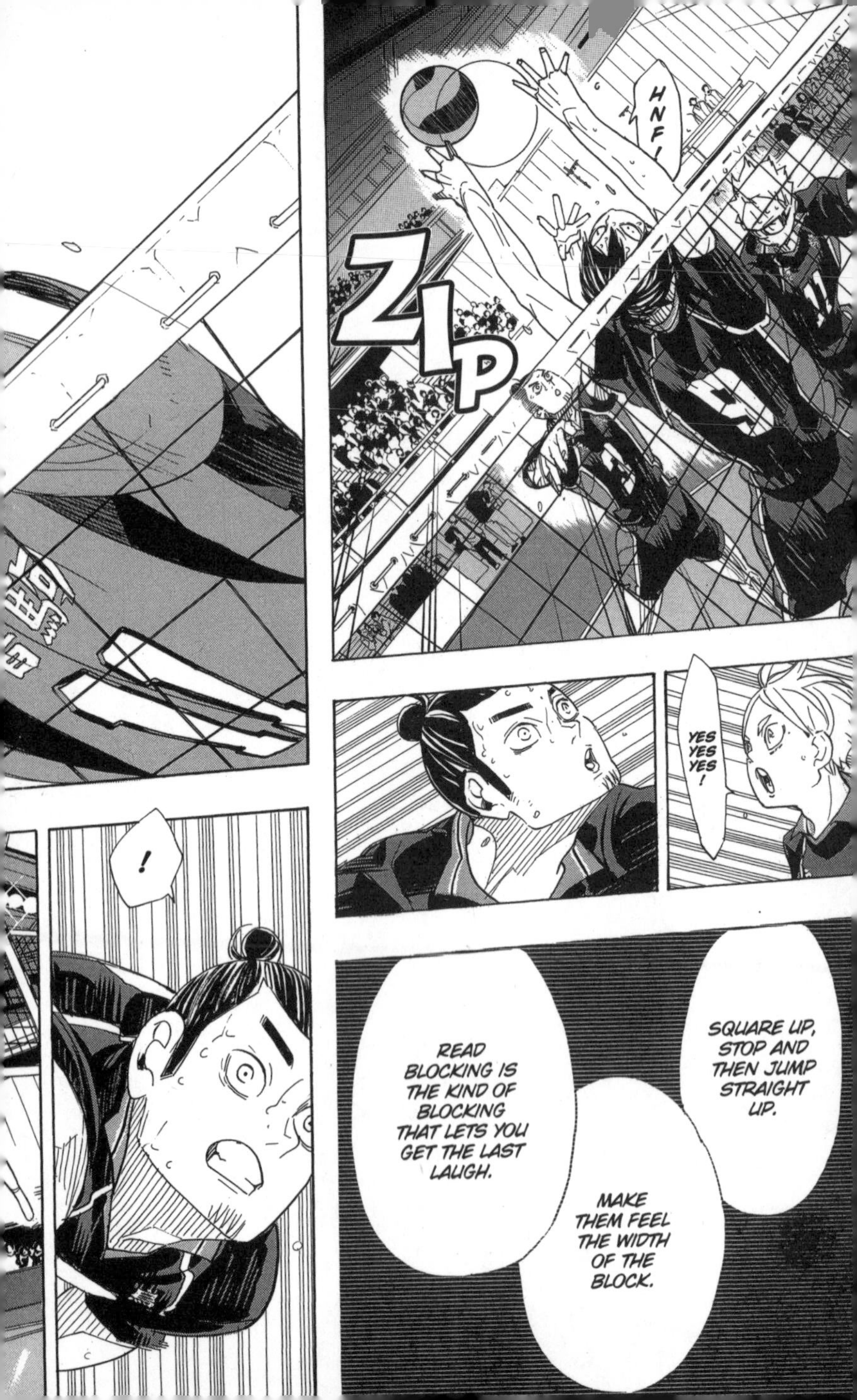
HNF!
ZIP
YES YES YES!
SQUARE UP, STOP AND THEN JUMP STRAIGHT UP.
READ BLOCKING IS THE KIND OF BLOCKING THAT LETS YOU GET THE LAST LAUGH.
MAKE THEM FEEL THE WIDTH OF THE BLOCK.
!

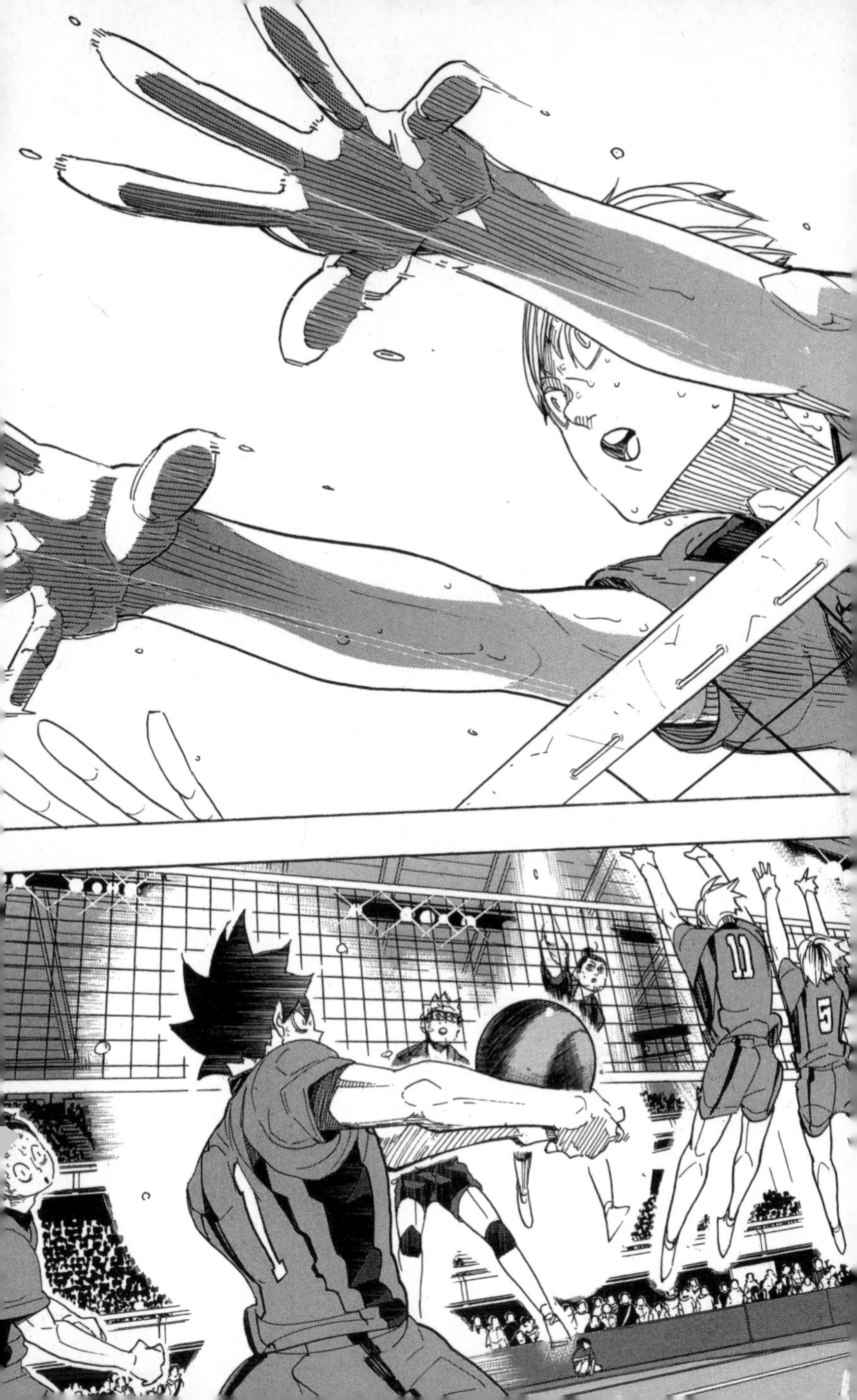

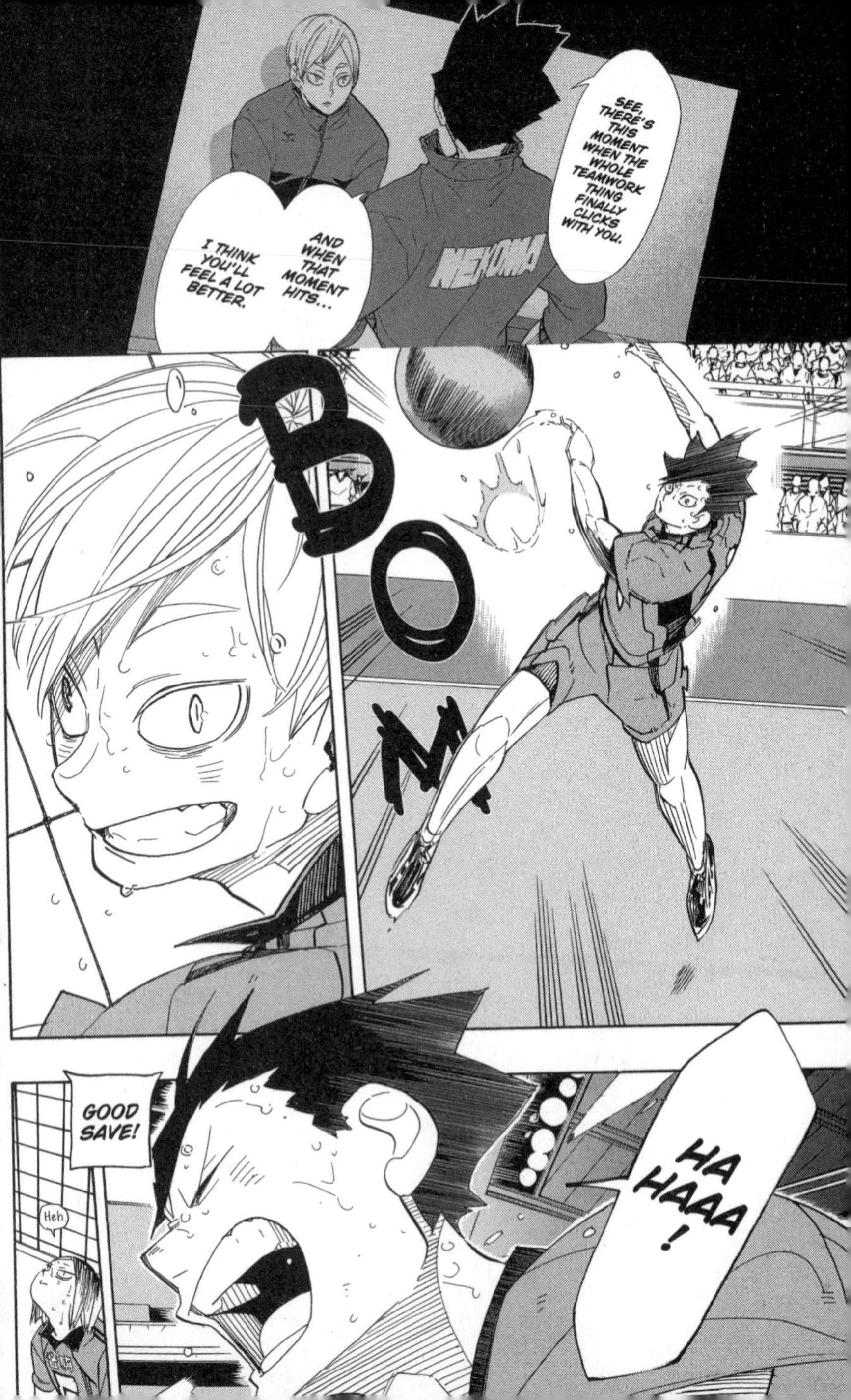
SEE, THERE'S THIS MOMENT WHEN THE WHOLE TEAMWORK THING FINALLY CLICKS WITH YOU.
AND WHEN THAT MOMENT HITS...
I THINK YOU'LL FEEL A LOT BETTER.
BOOM
HA HAAA!
GOOD SAVE!
Heh.

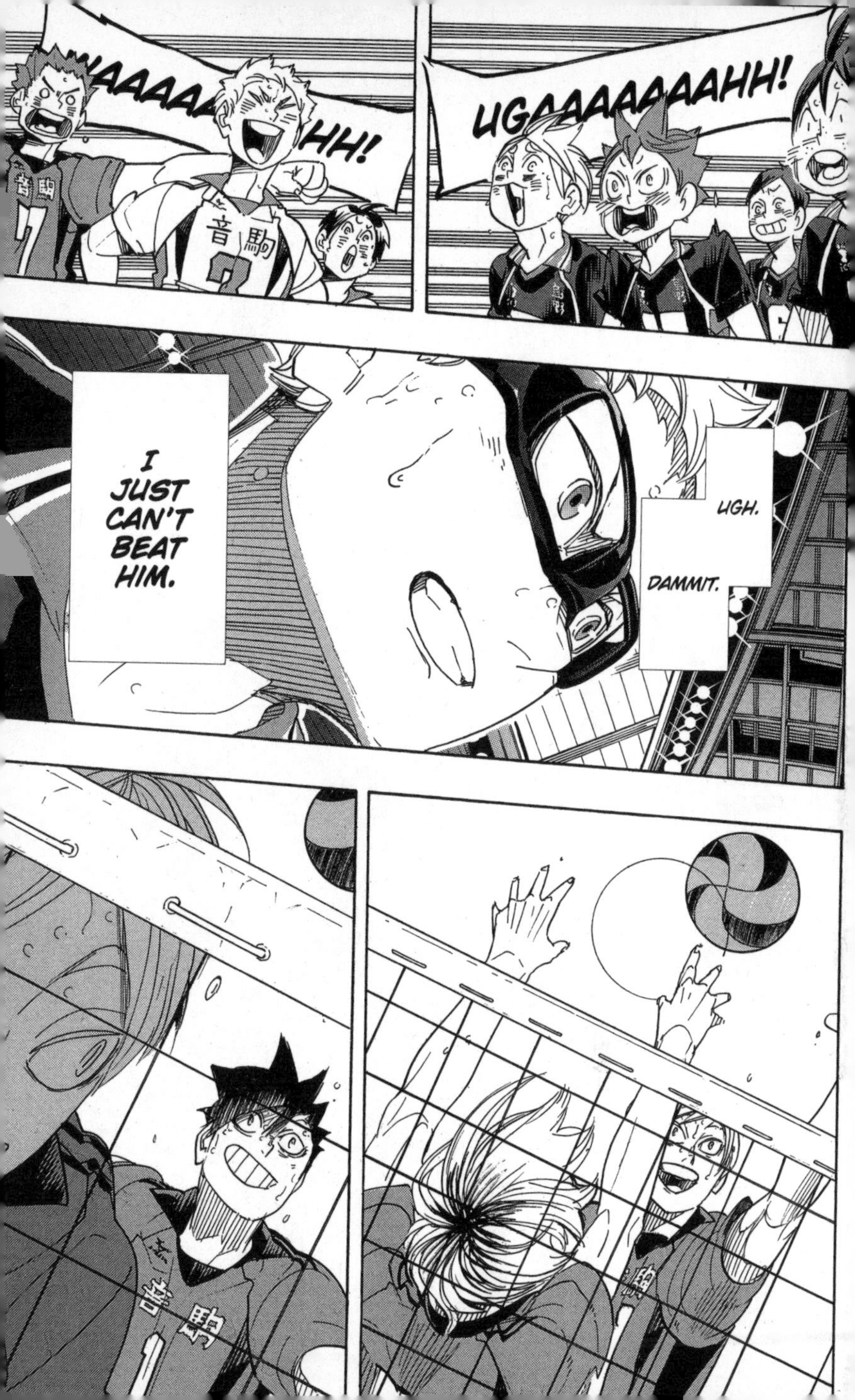
UGAAAAAAAAHH!
AAAAAA HH!
UGH.
DAMMIT.
I JUST CAN'T BEAT HIM.

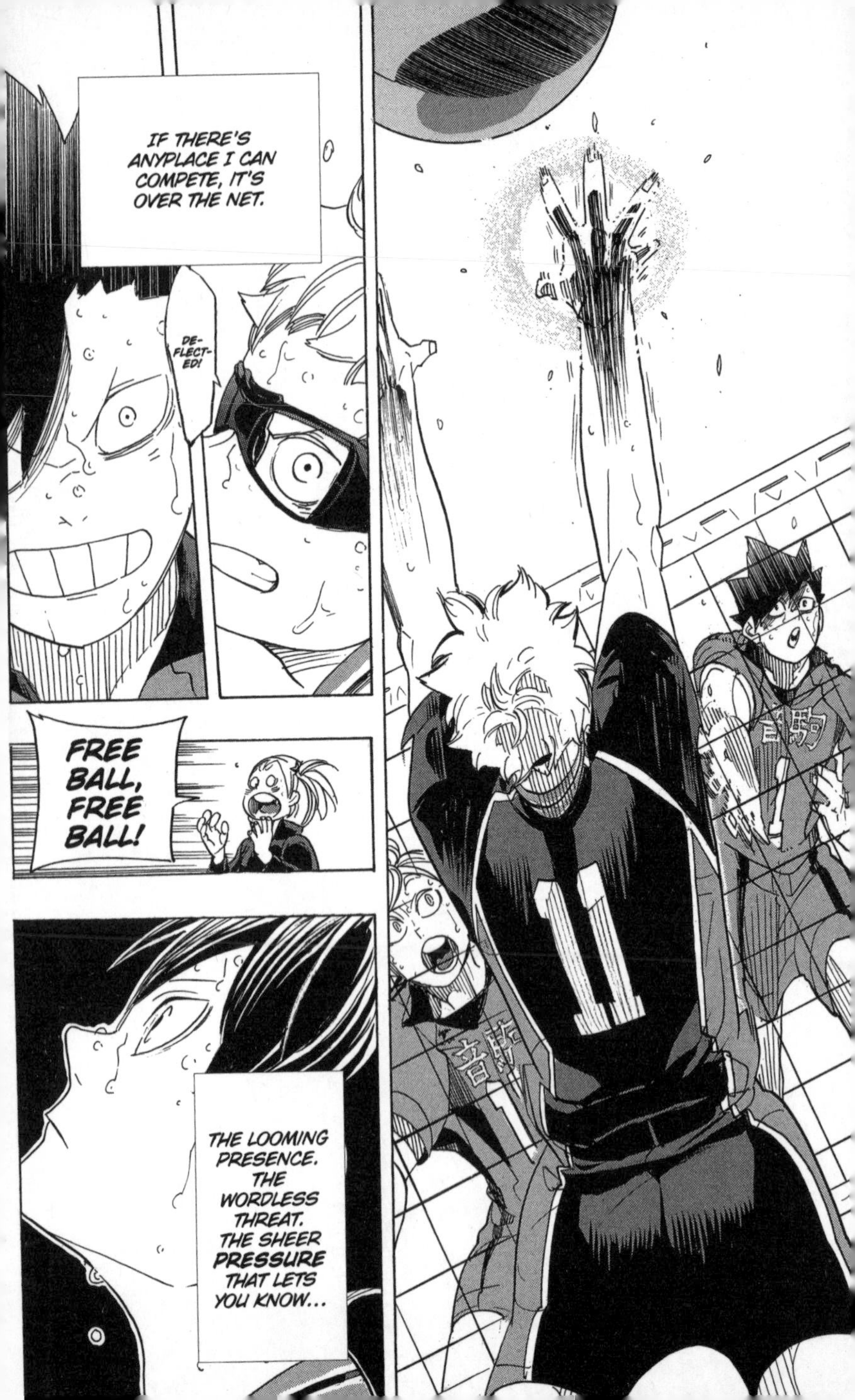
IF THERE'S ANYPLACE I CAN COMPETE, IT'S OVER THE NET.
DE-FLECT-ED!
FREE BALL, FREE BALL!
THE LOOMING PRESENCE. THE WORDLESS THREAT. THE SHEER PRESSURE THAT LETS YOU KNOW...

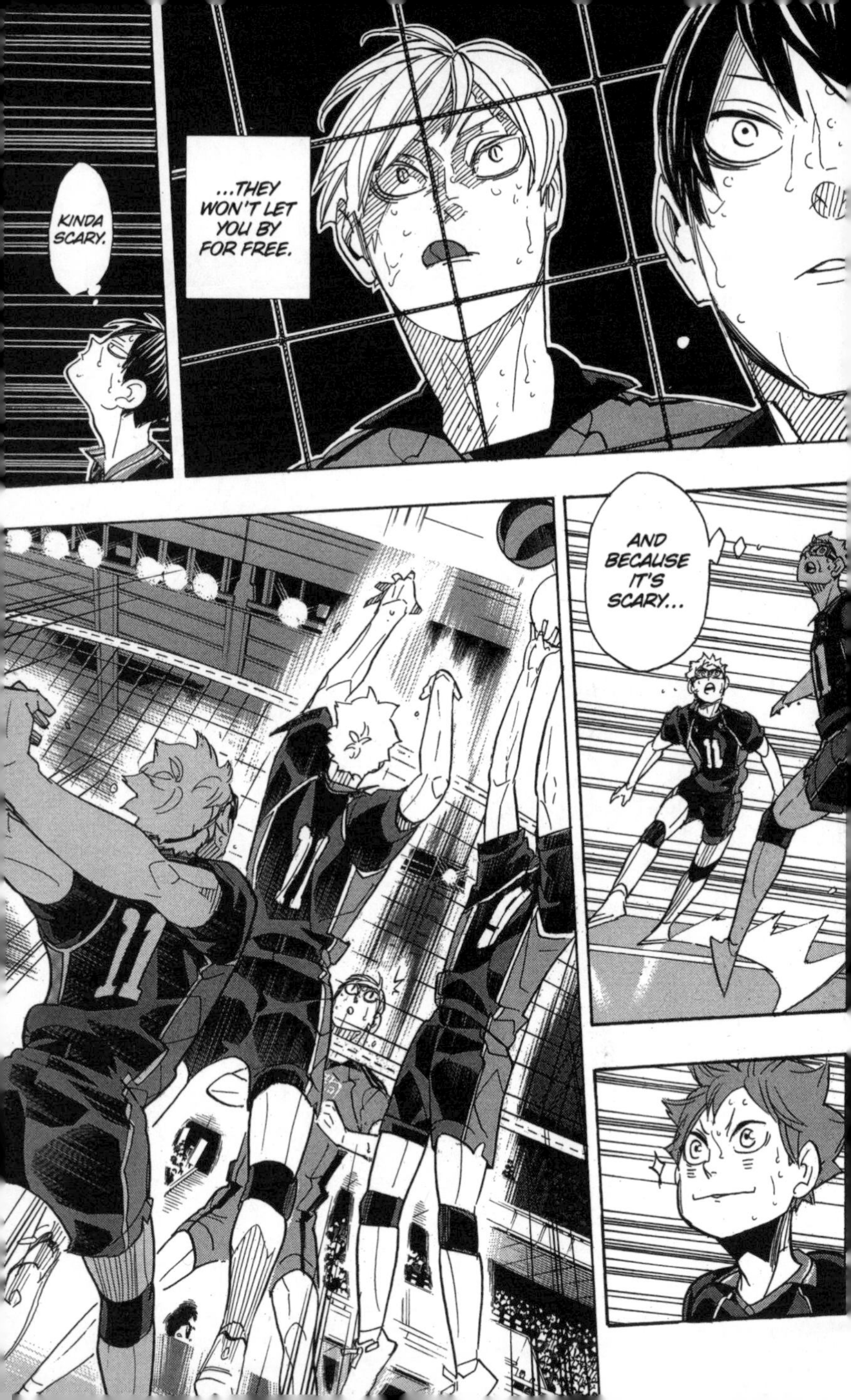
...THEY WON'T LET YOU BY FOR FREE.
KINDA SCARY.
AND BECAUSE IT'S SCARY...

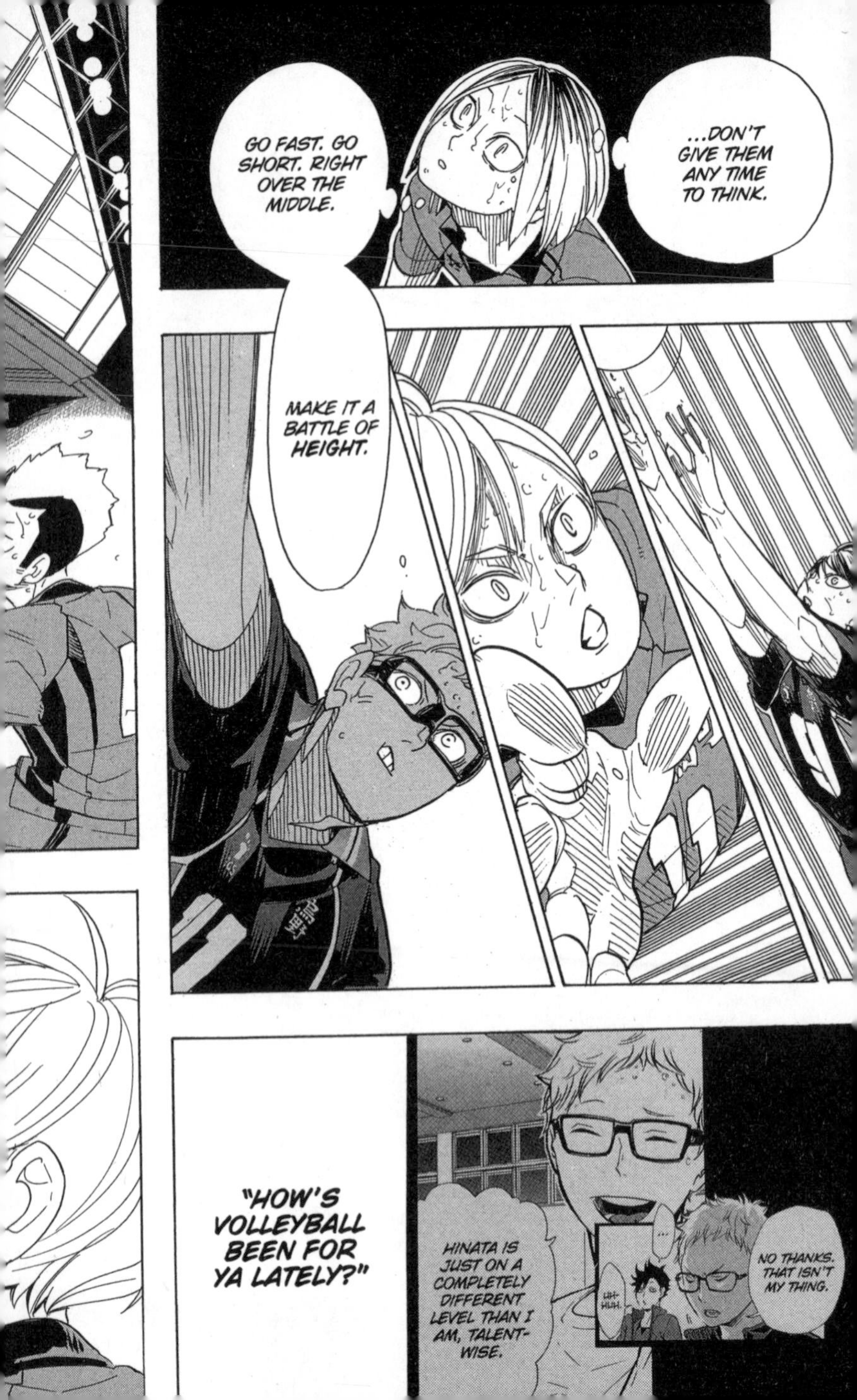

...DON'T GIVE THEM ANY TIME TO THINK.
GO FAST. GO SHORT. RIGHT OVER THE MIDDLE.
MAKE IT A BATTLE OF HEIGHT.
NO THANKS. THAT ISN'T MY THING.
...
UH-HUH.
HINATA IS JUST ON A COMPLETELY DIFFERENT LEVEL THAN I AM, TALENT-WISE.
"HOW'S VOLLEYBALL BEEN FOR YA LATELY?"

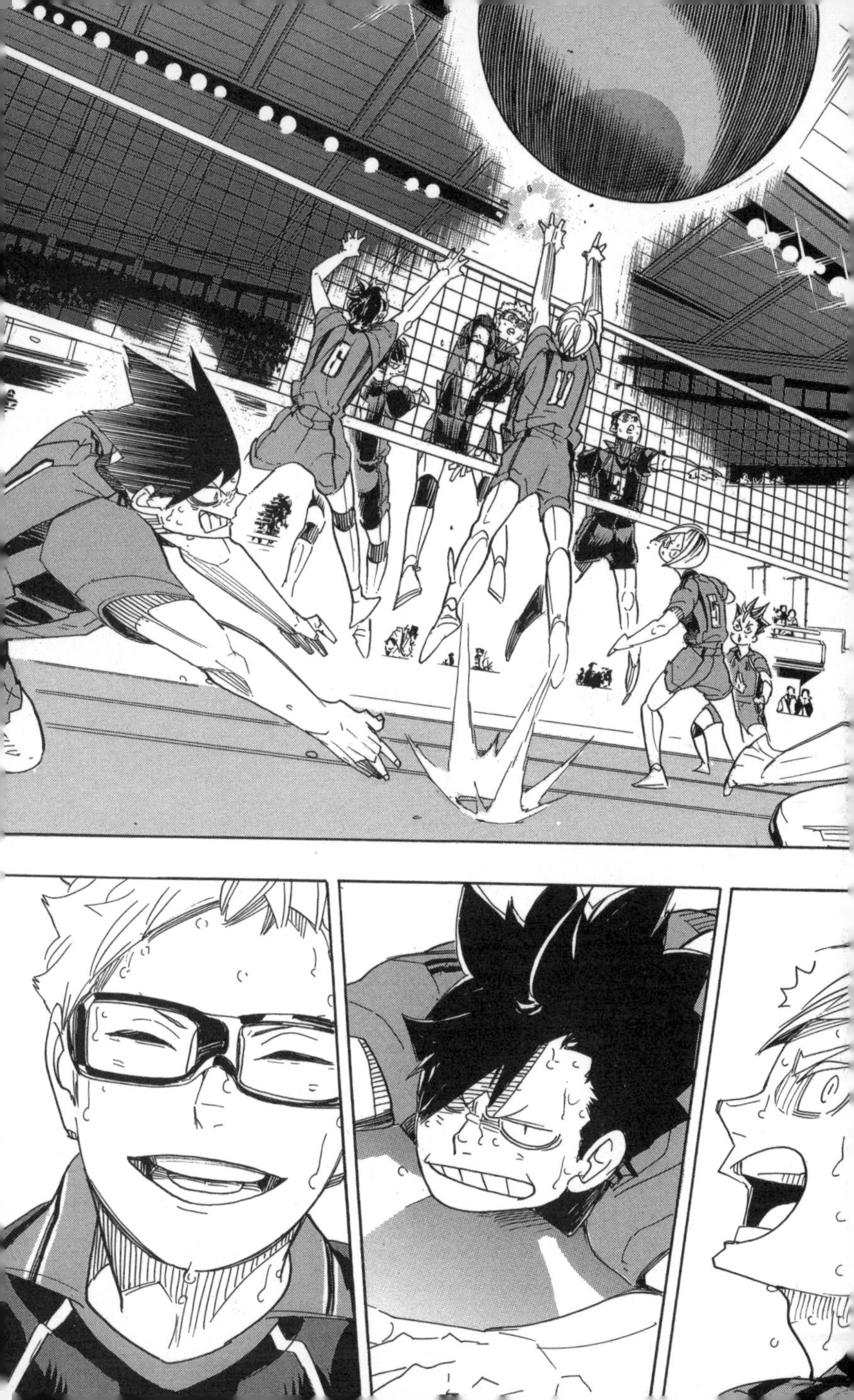

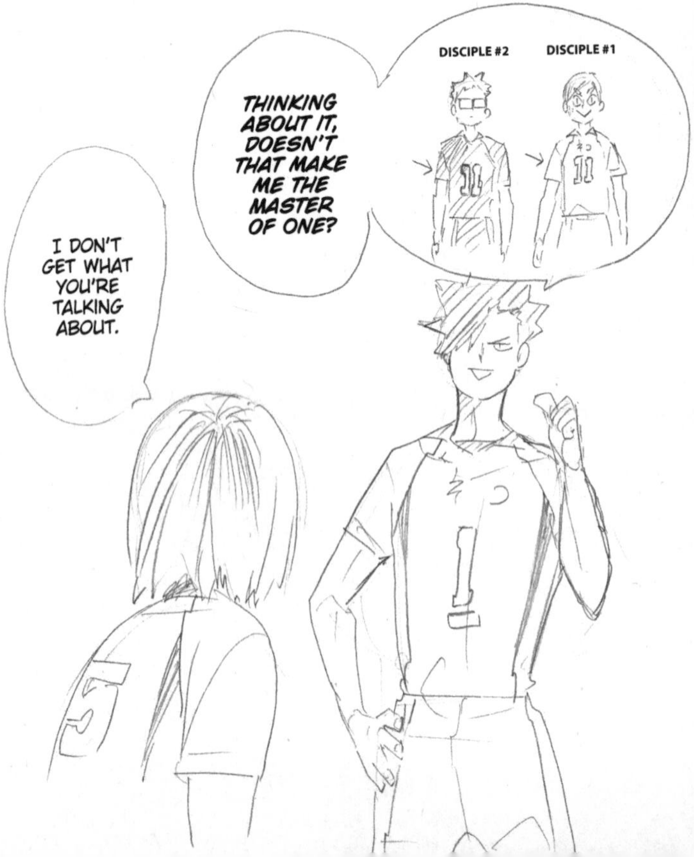
THINKING ABOUT IT, DOESN'T THAT MAKE ME THE MASTER OF ONE?
DISCIPLE #1
DISCIPLE #2
I DON'T GET WHAT YOU'RE TALKING ABOUT.

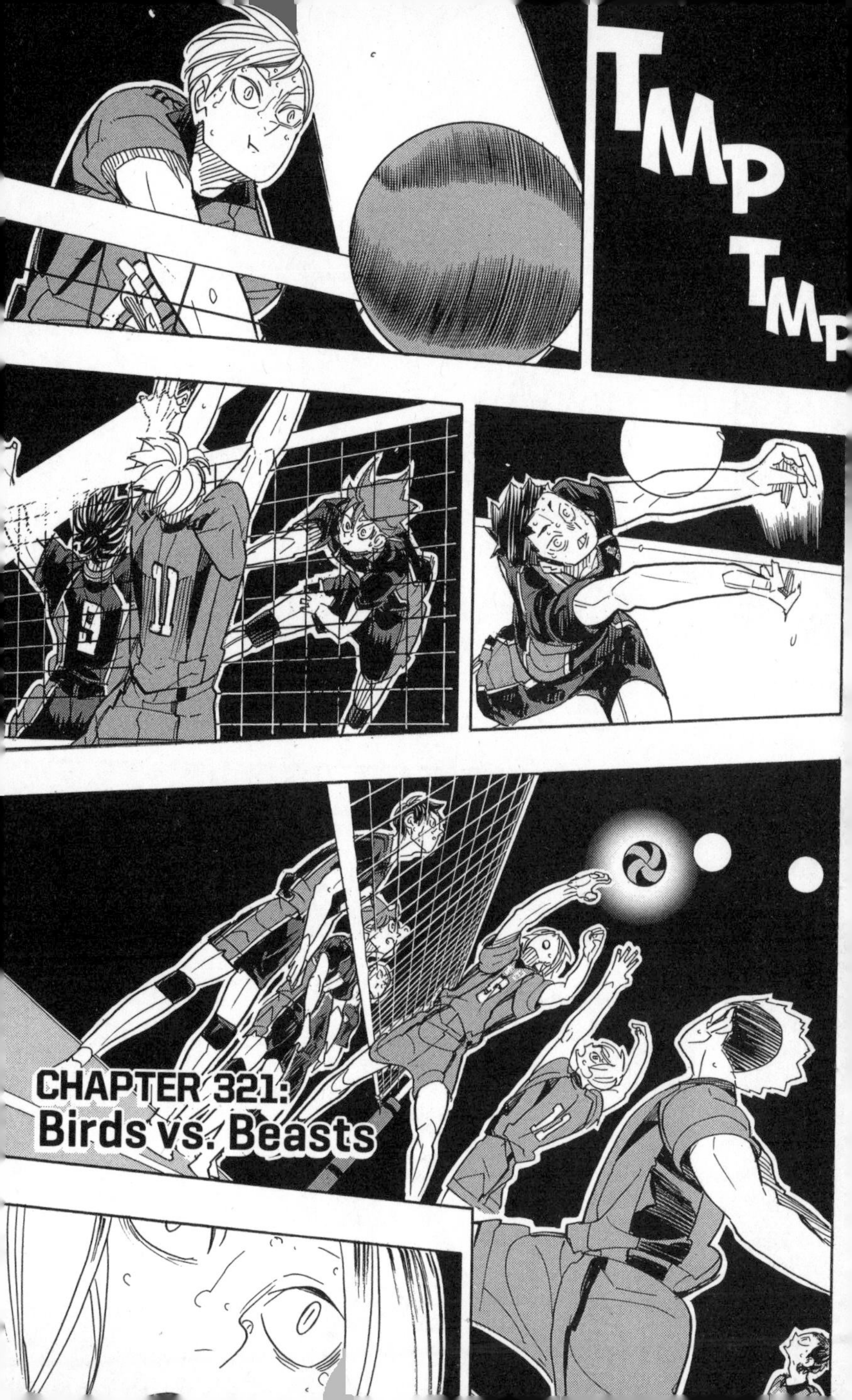
TMP TMP
CHAPTER 321:
Birds vs. Beasts

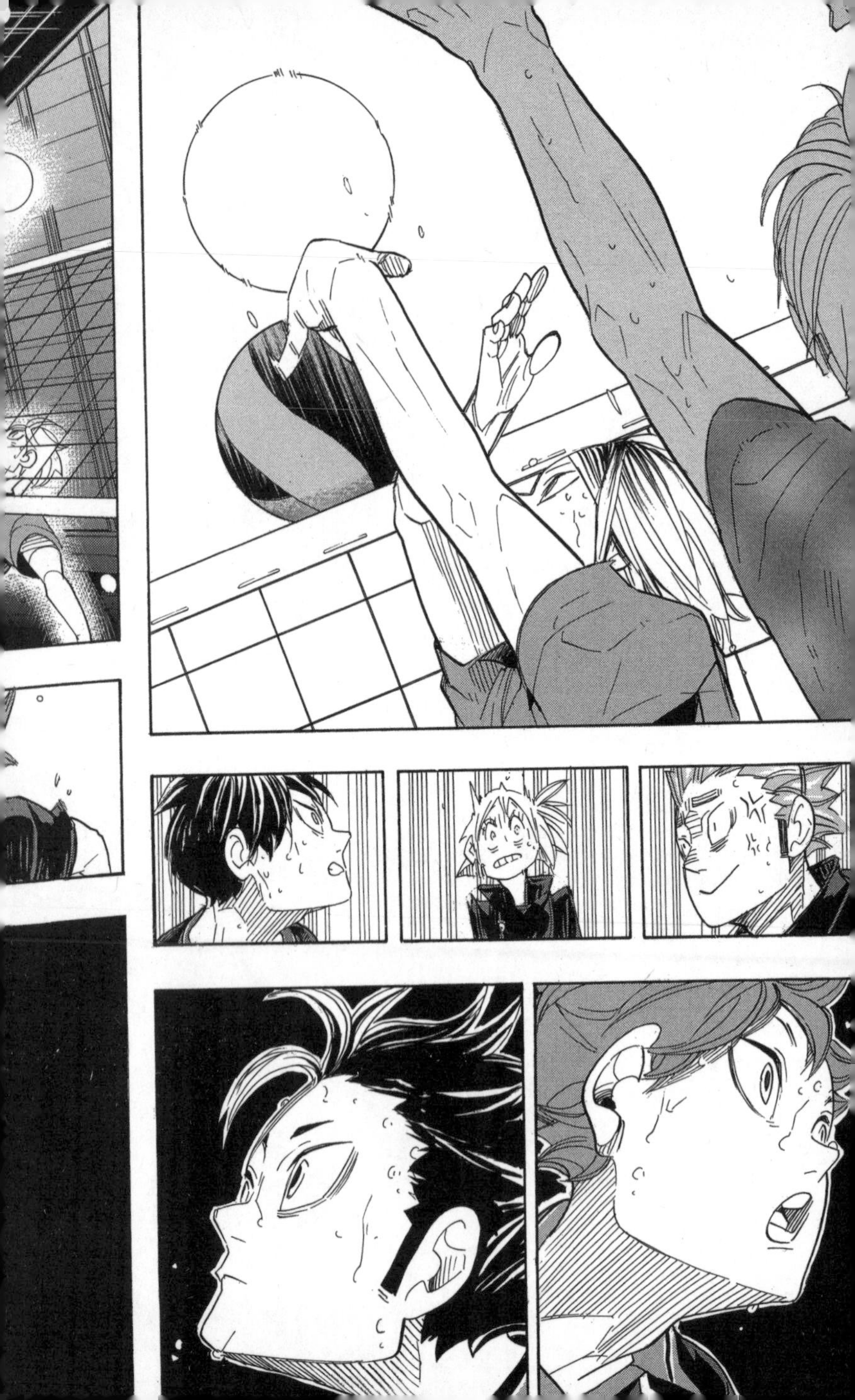

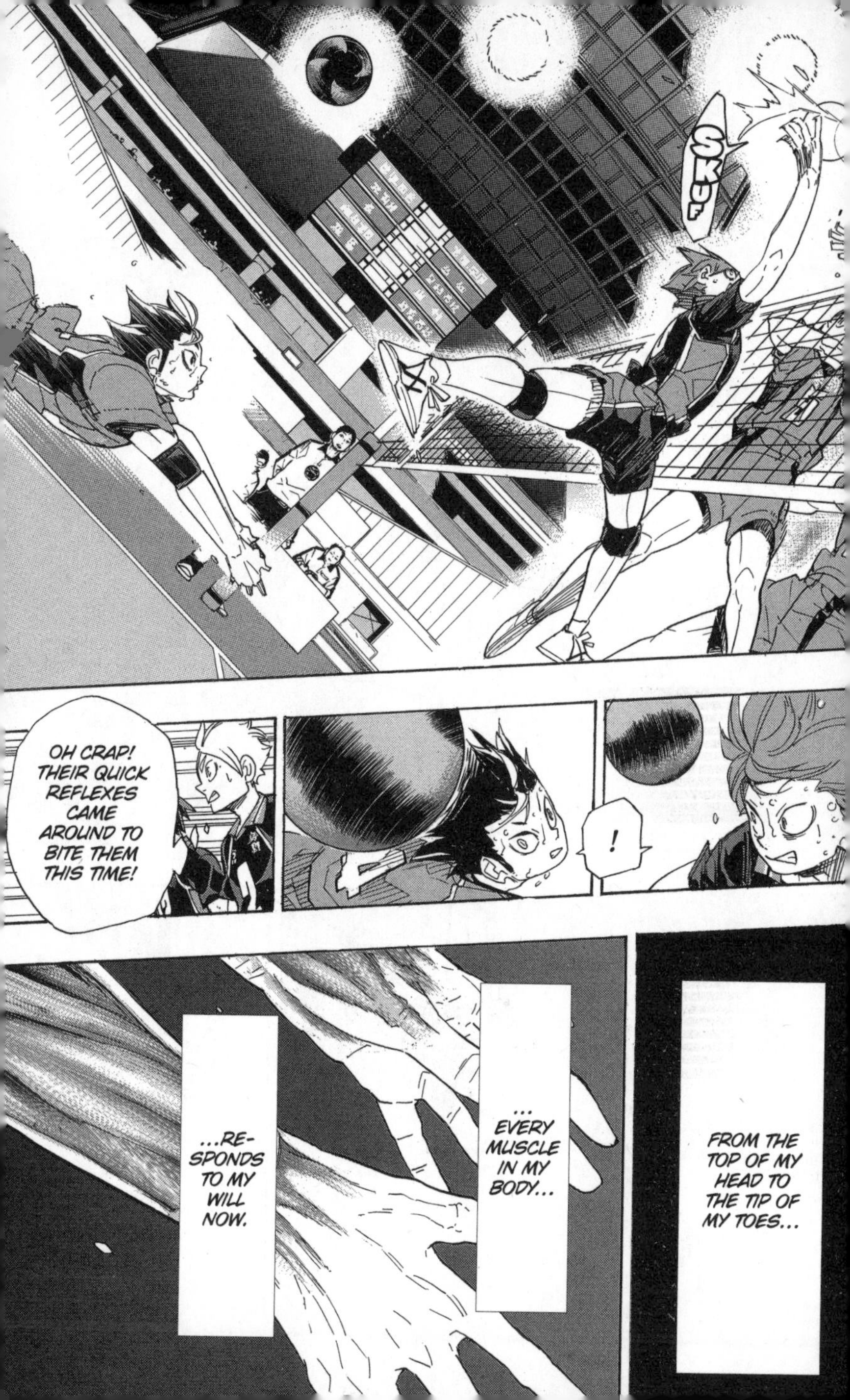
SKUF
!
OH CRAP! THEIR QUICK REFLEXES CAME AROUND TO BITE THEM THIS TIME!
FROM THE TOP OF MY HEAD TO THE TIP OF MY TOES...
...EVERY MUSCLE IN MY BODY...
...RE-SPONDS TO MY WILL NOW.

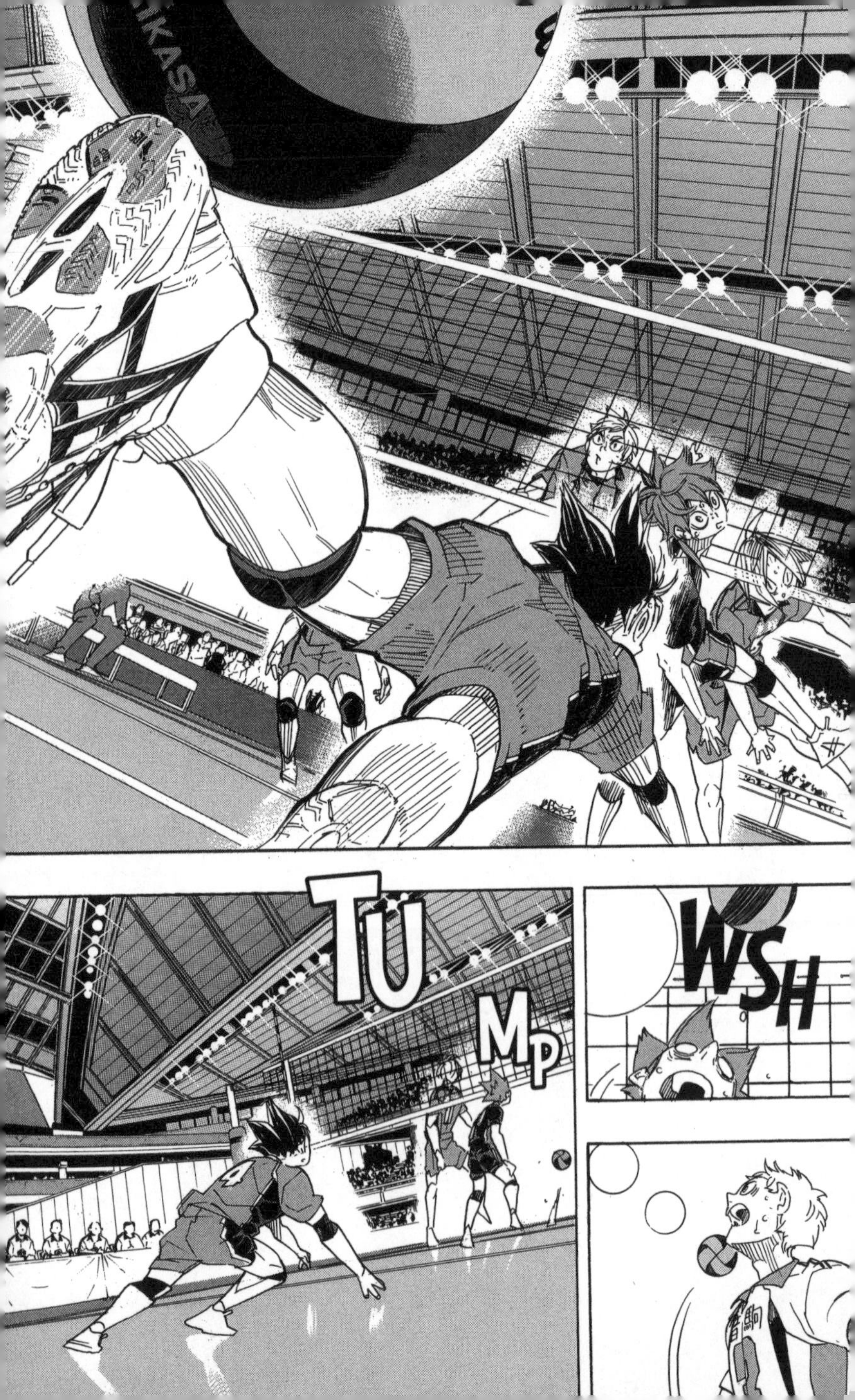
WSH
TUMP

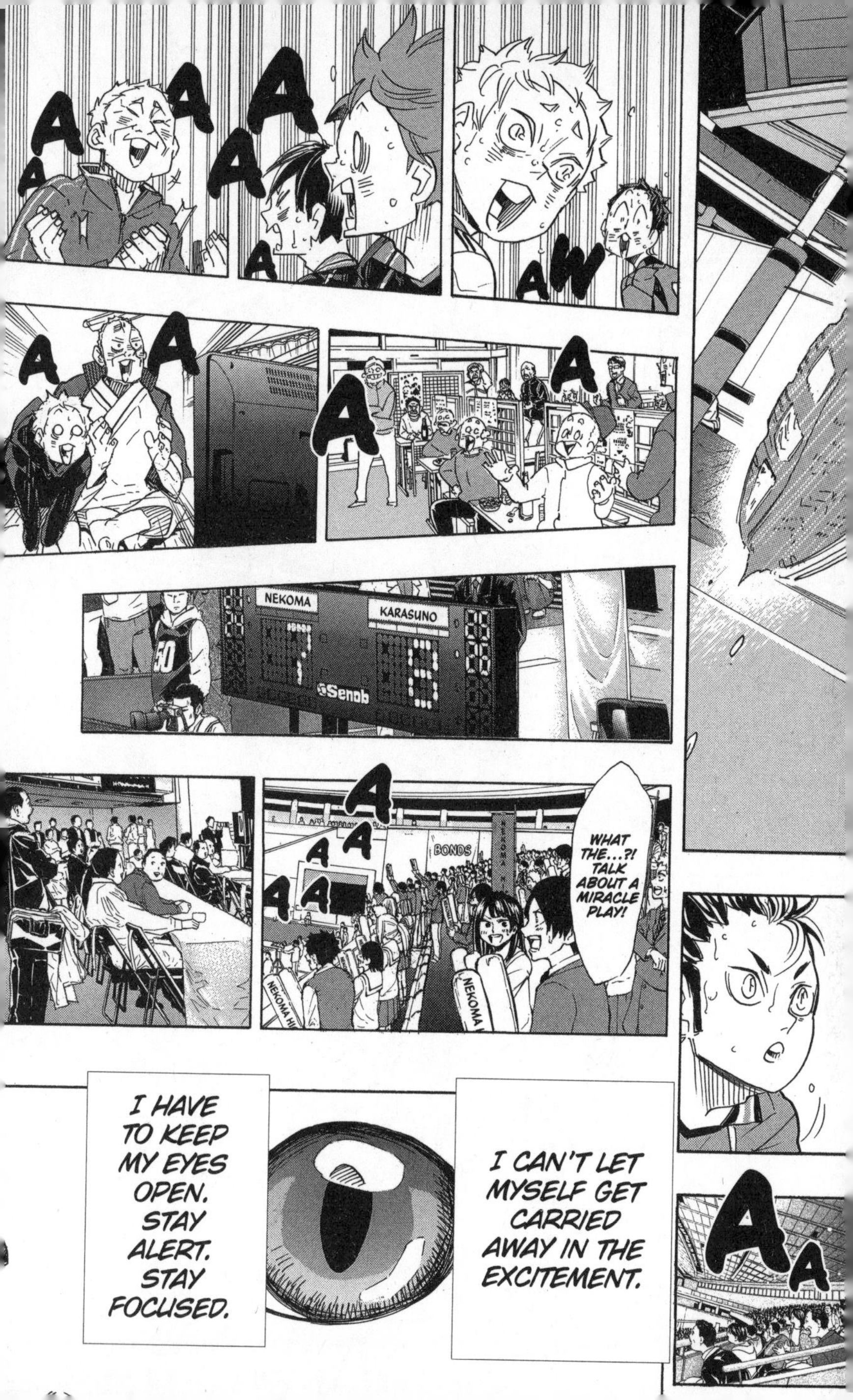

AW
AAAA
AAAA
AA
AA
NEKOMA
KARASUNO
AAAA
BONDS
WHAT THE...?! TALK ABOUT A MIRACLE PLAY!
AA
I CAN'T LET MYSELF GET CARRIED AWAY IN THE EXCITEMENT.
I HAVE TO KEEP MY EYES OPEN. STAY ALERT. STAY FOCUSED.

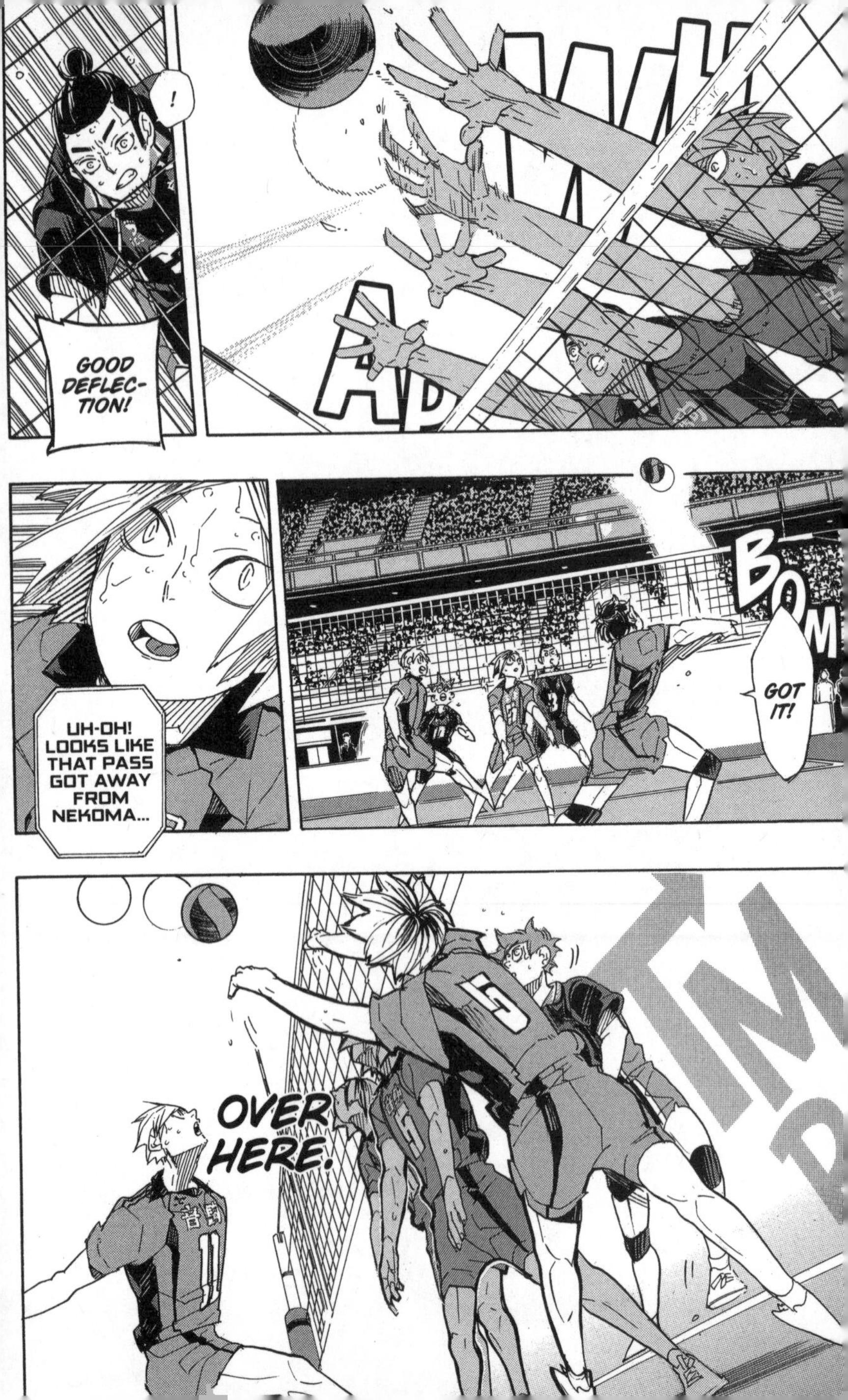
!
GOOD DEFLEC-TION!
GOT IT!
UH-OH! LOOKS LIKE THAT PASS GOT AWAY FROM NEKOMA...
OVER HERE.

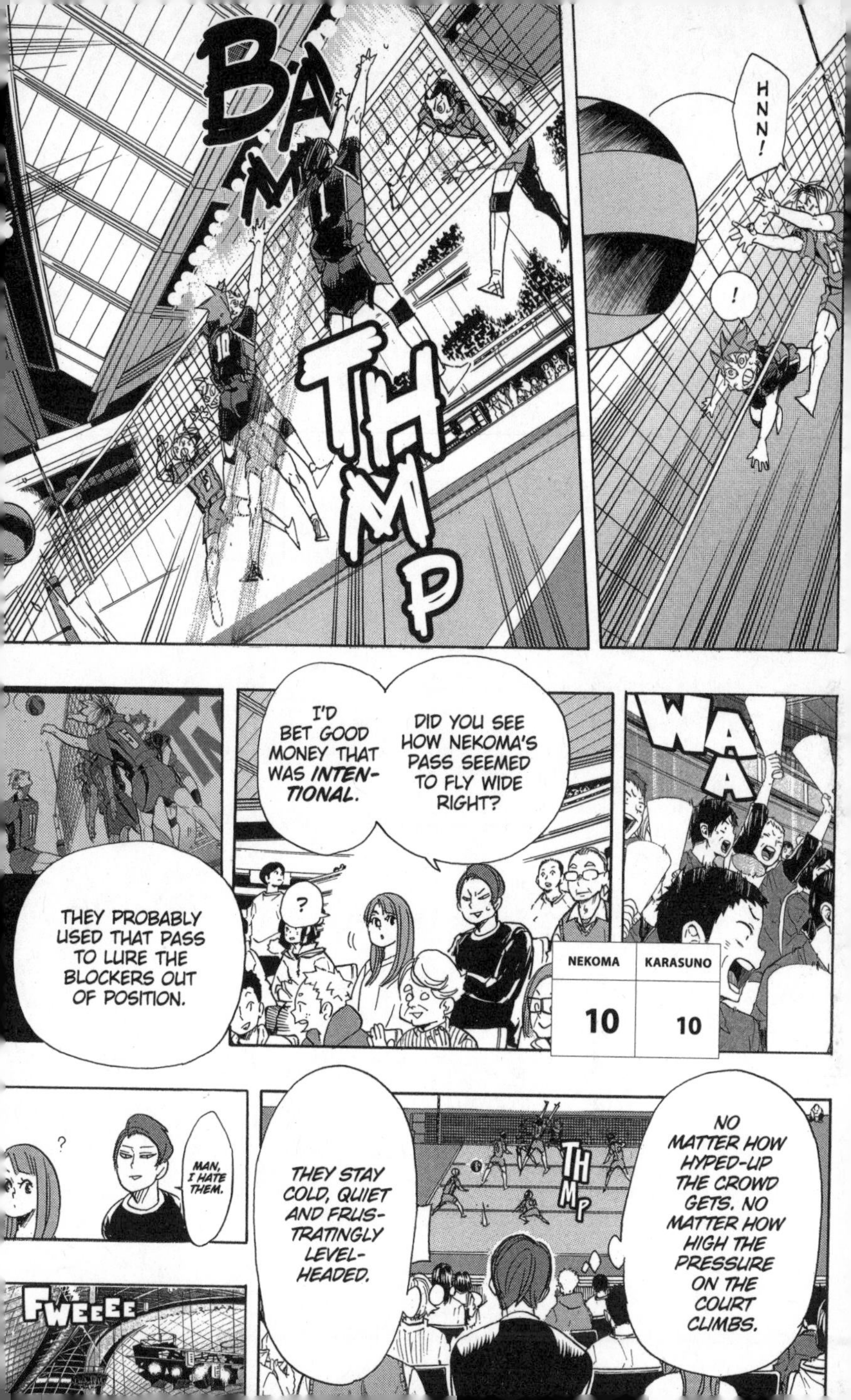
HNN!
!
BAM
THMP
WAA
DID YOU SEE HOW NEKOMA'S PASS SEEMED TO FLY WIDE RIGHT?
I'D BET GOOD MONEY THAT WAS *INTENTIONAL*.
?
THEY PROBABLY USED THAT PASS TO LURE THE BLOCKERS OUT OF POSITION.
NEKOMA 10
KARASUNO 10
NO MATTER HOW HYPED-UP THE CROWD GETS. NO MATTER HOW HIGH THE PRESSURE ON THE COURT CLIMBS.
THMP
THEY STAY COLD, QUIET AND FRUSTRATINGLY LEVEL-HEADED.
MAN, I HATE THEM.
?
FWEEEE

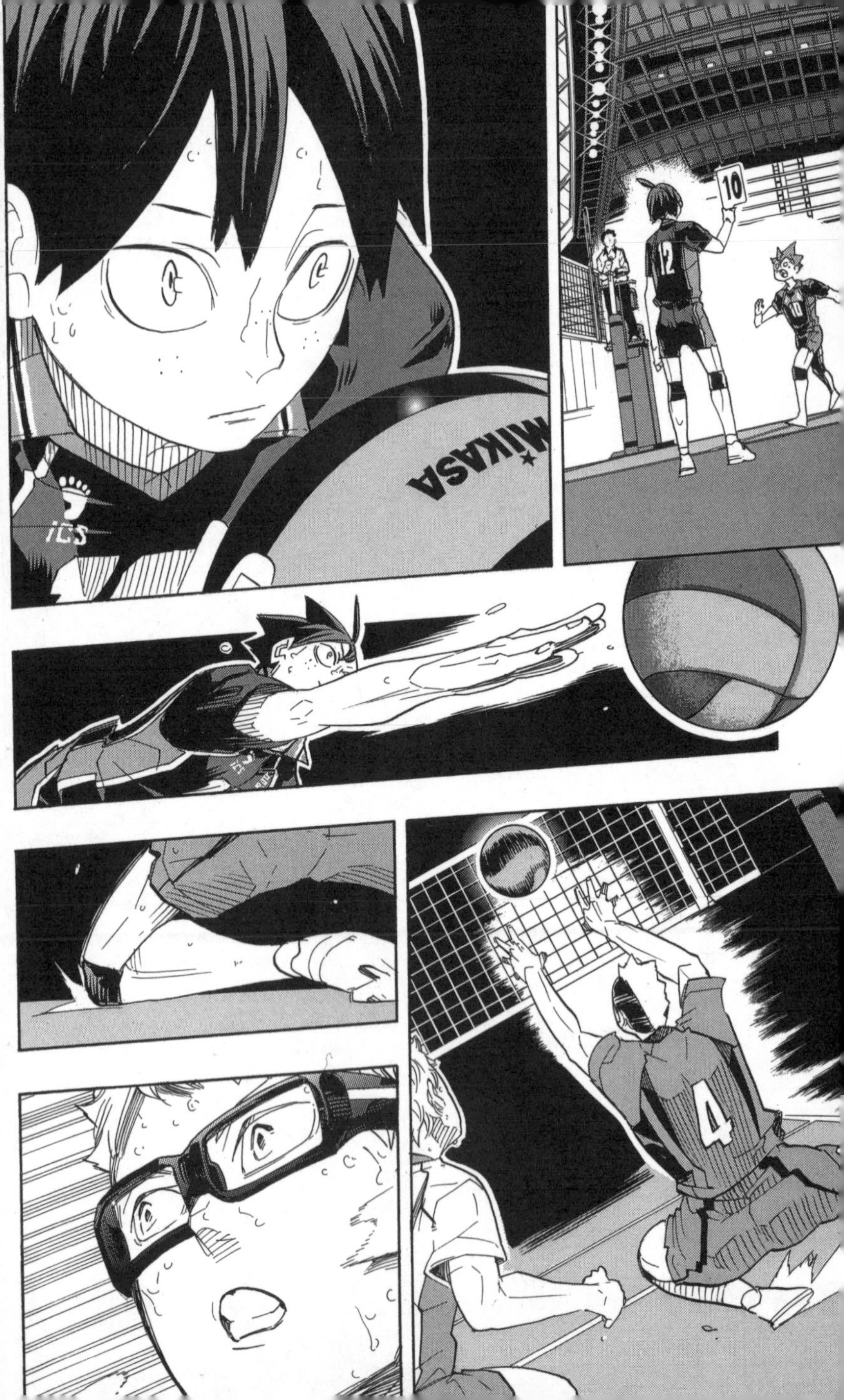
MIKASA

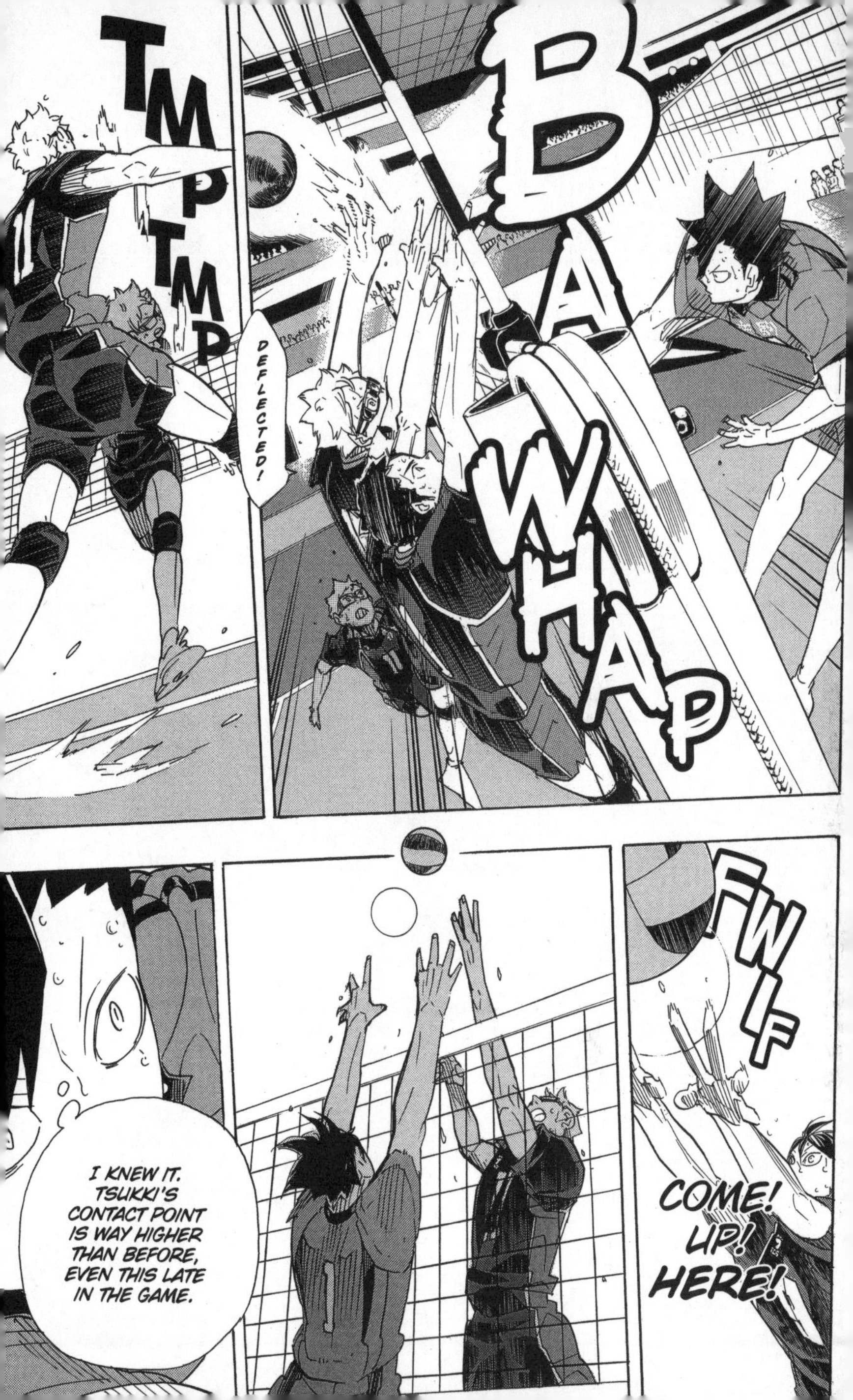
BAWHAP
DEFLECTED!
TMP TMP TMP
FWIF
COME! UP! HERE!
I KNEW IT. TSUKKI'S CONTACT POINT IS WAY HIGHER THAN BEFORE, EVEN THIS LATE IN THE GAME.

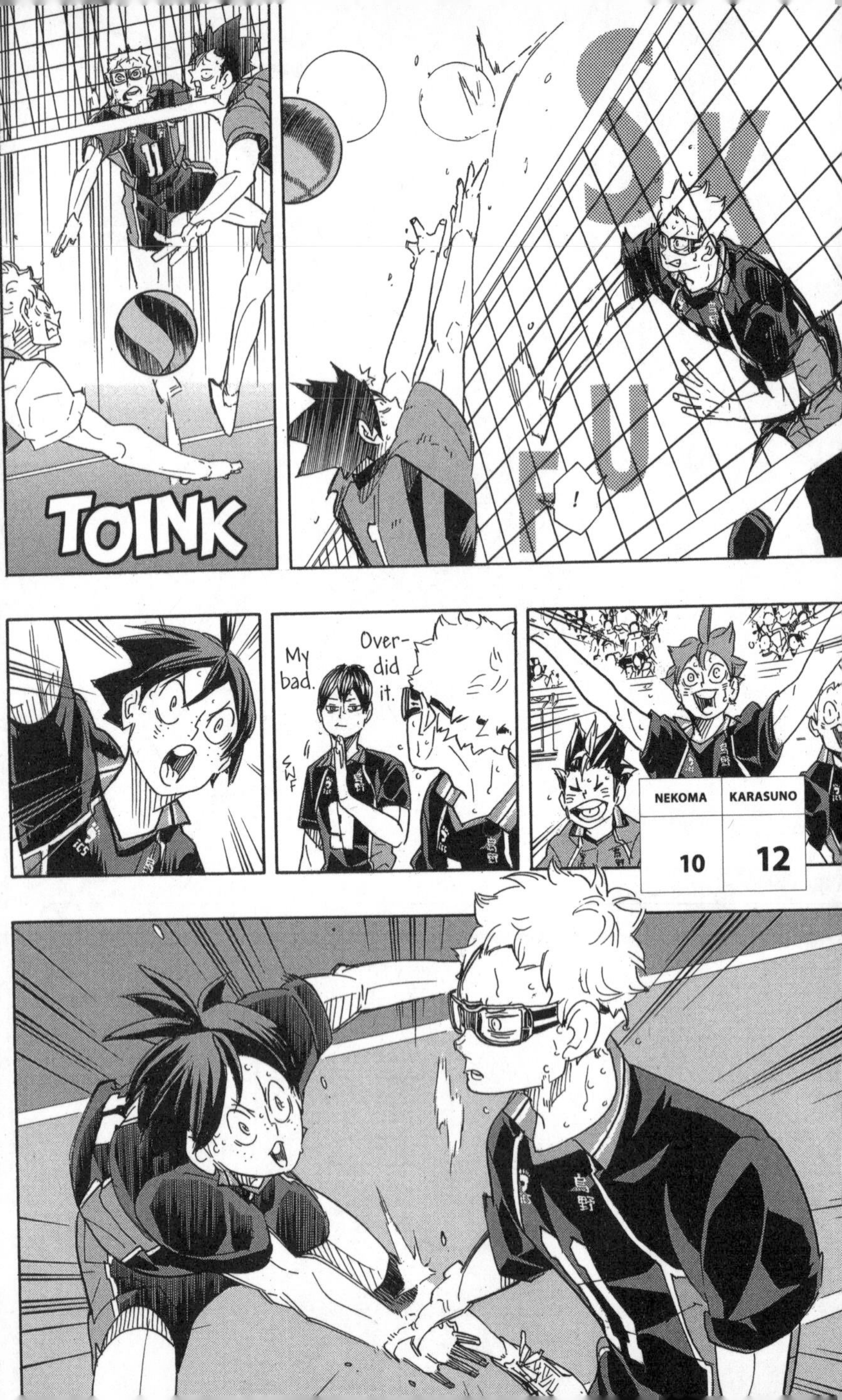
!
TOINK
NEKOMA 10
KARASUNO 12
Over-did it.
My bad.
SWF

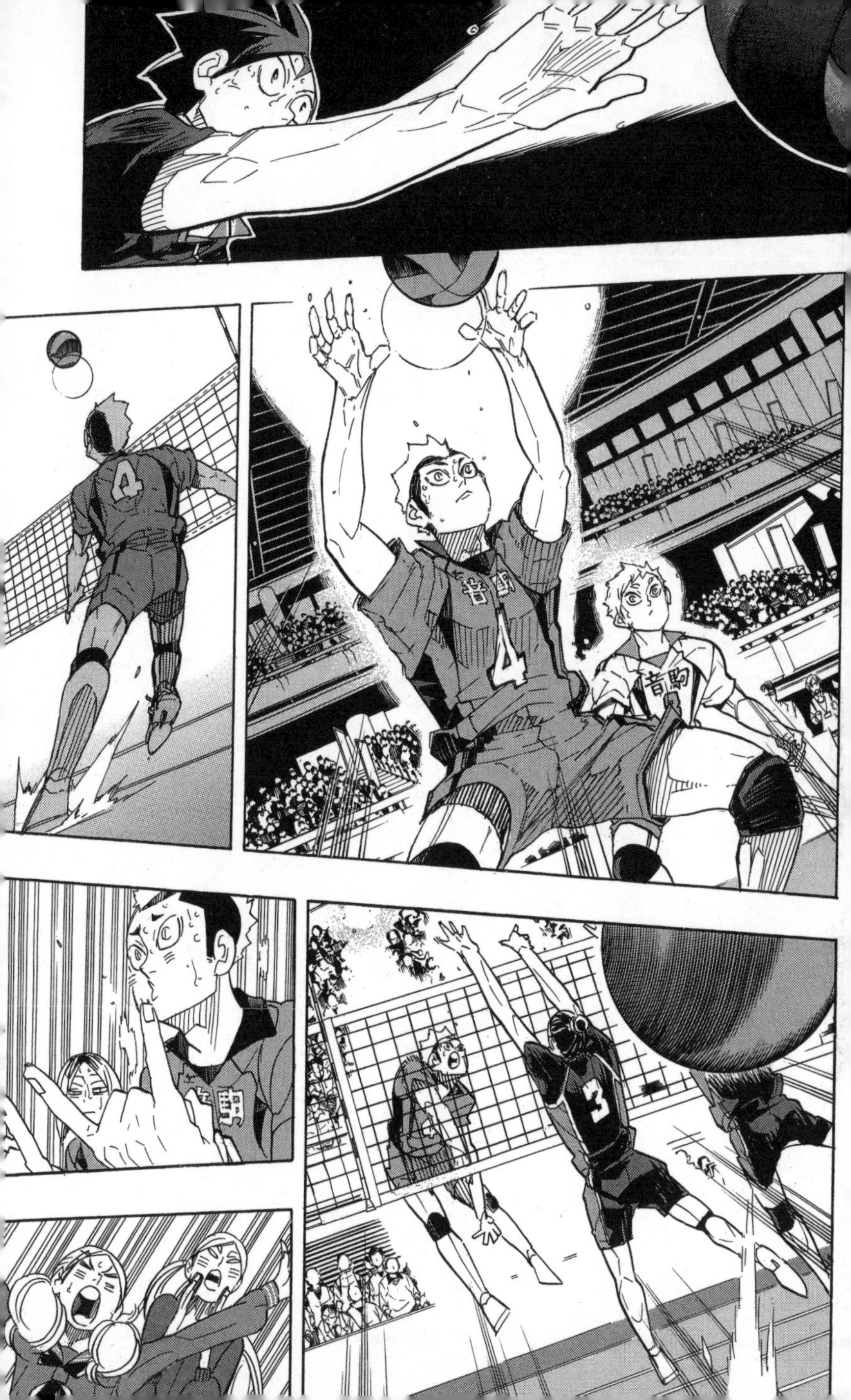
音駒
音駒

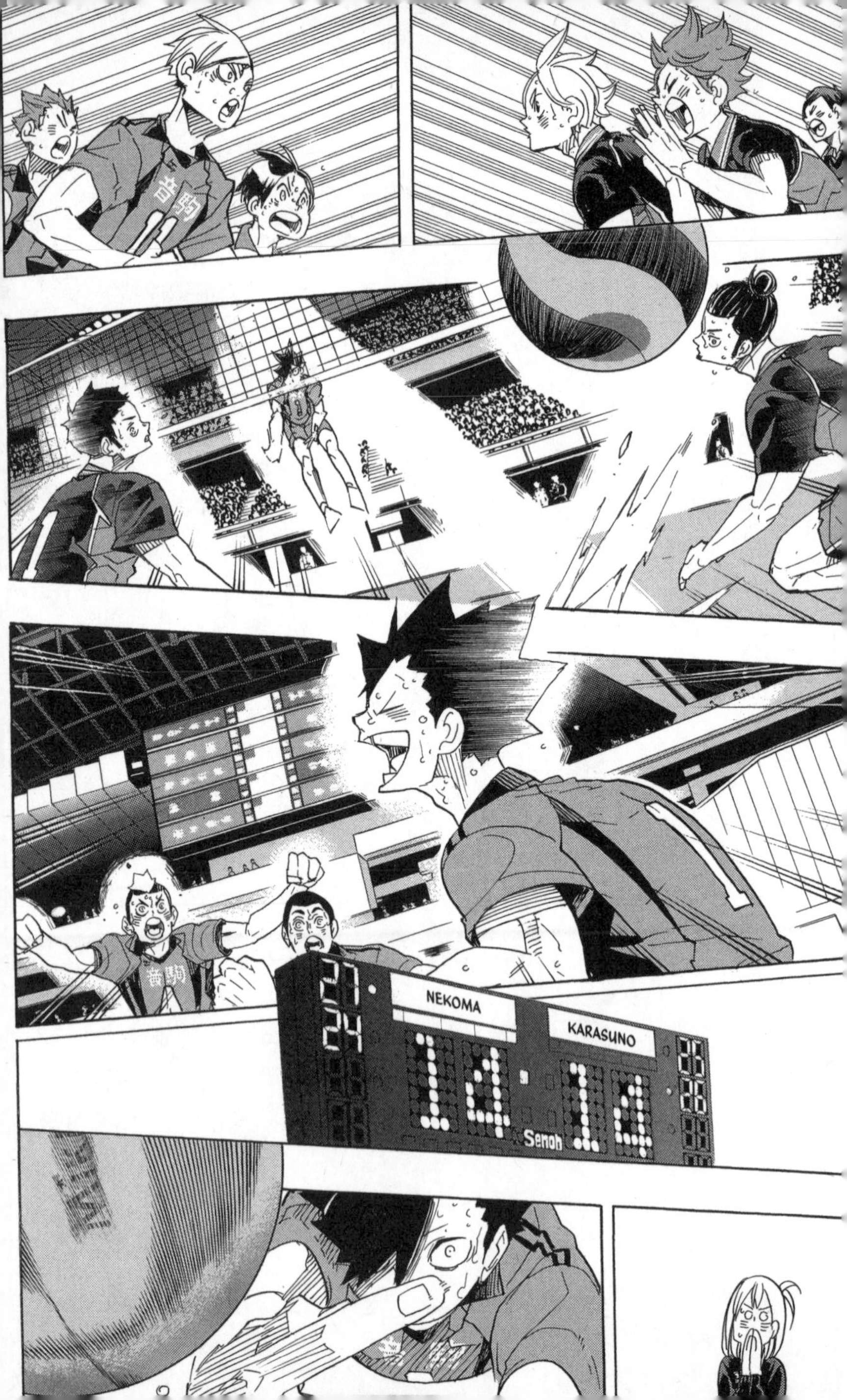
NEKOMA
KARASUNO
Senoh

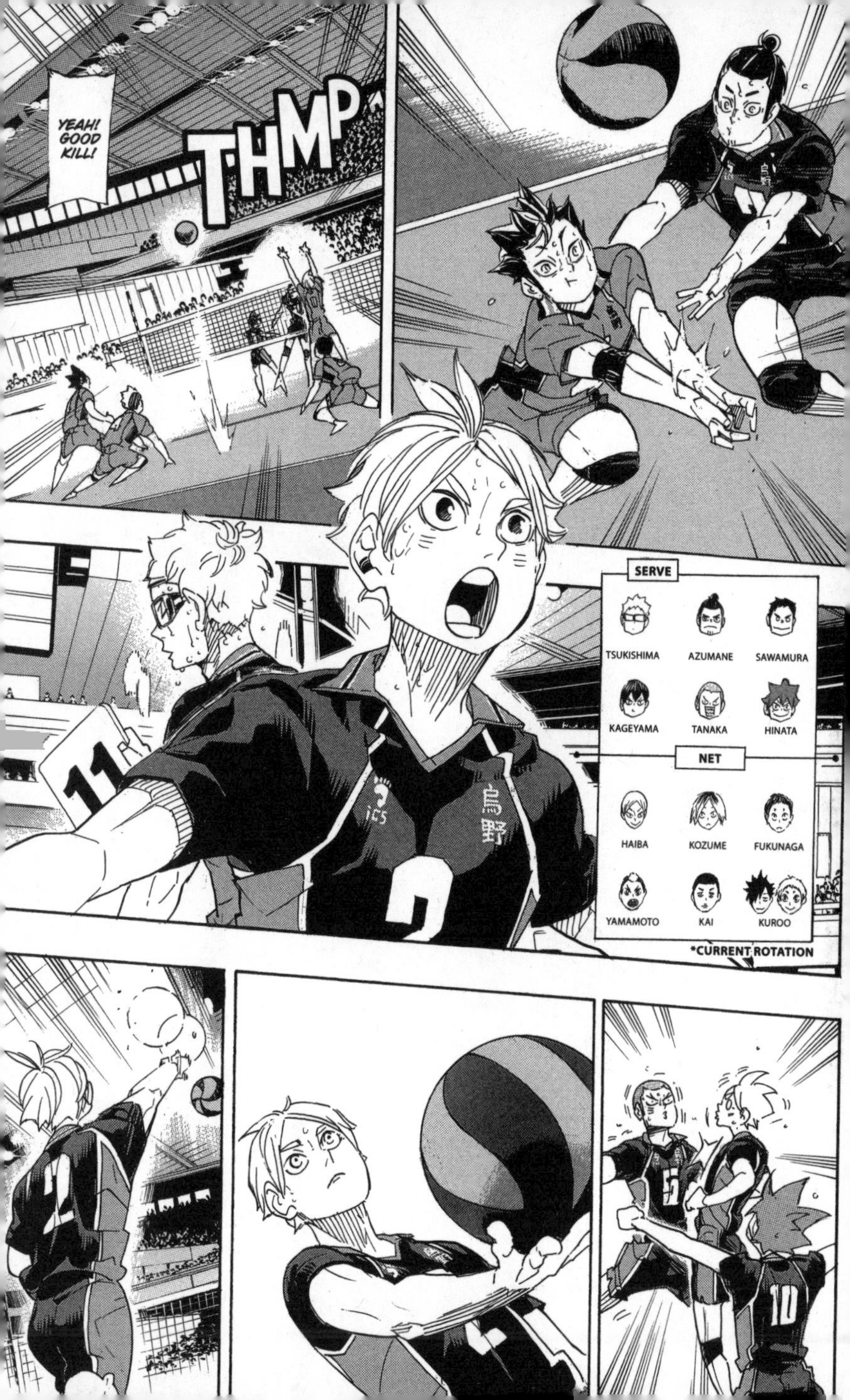
YEAH! GOOD KILL!
THMP
11
SERVE
TSUKISHIMA
AZUMANE
SAWAMURA
KAGEYAMA
TANAKA
HINATA
NET
HAIBA
KOZUME
FUKUNAGA
YAMAMOTO
KAI
KUROO
*CURRENT ROTATION

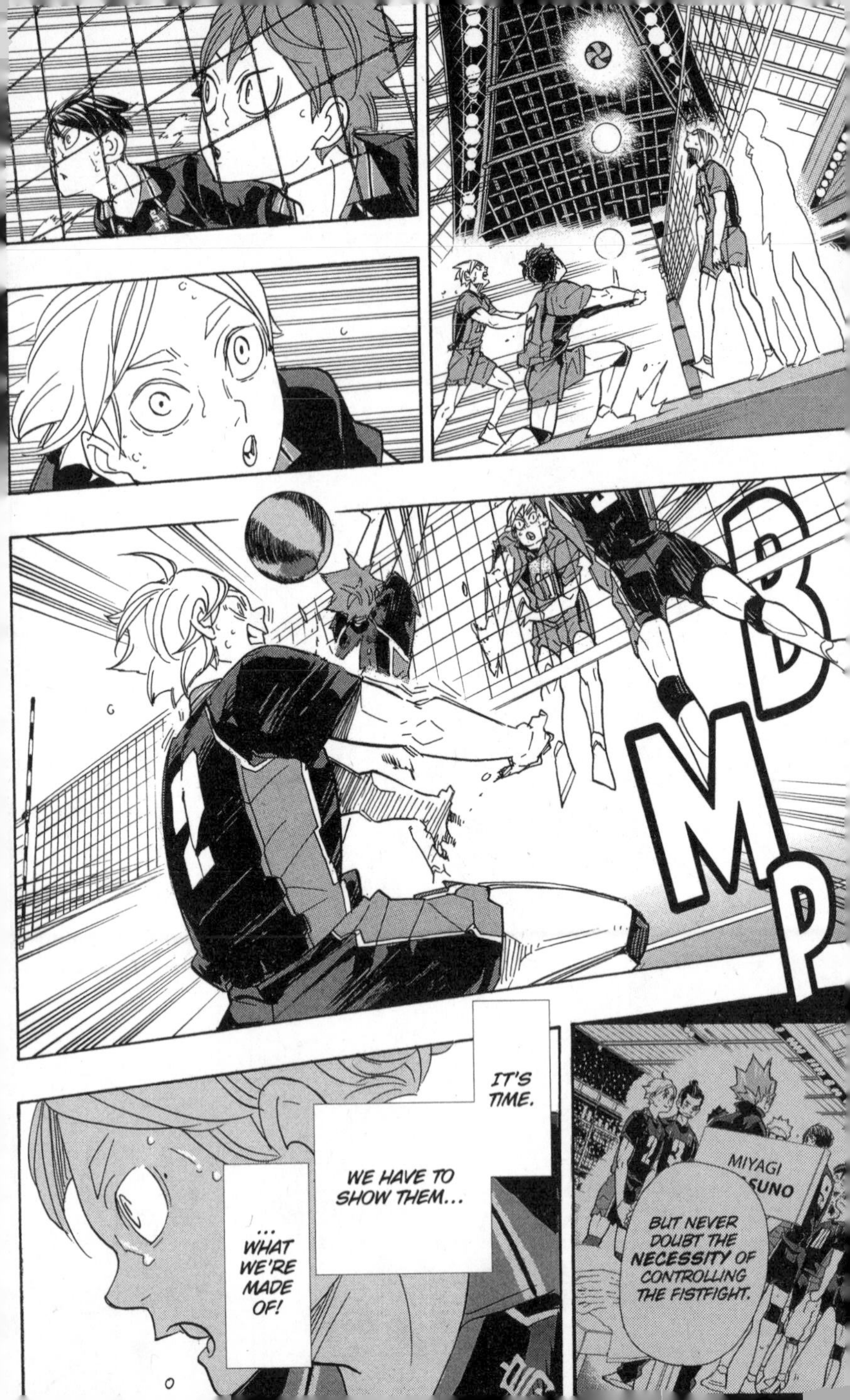
BMMP
MIYAGI
SUNO
BUT NEVER DOUBT THE NECESSITY OF CONTROLLING THE FISTFIGHT.
IT'S TIME.
WE HAVE TO SHOW THEM...
...WHAT WE'RE MADE OF!

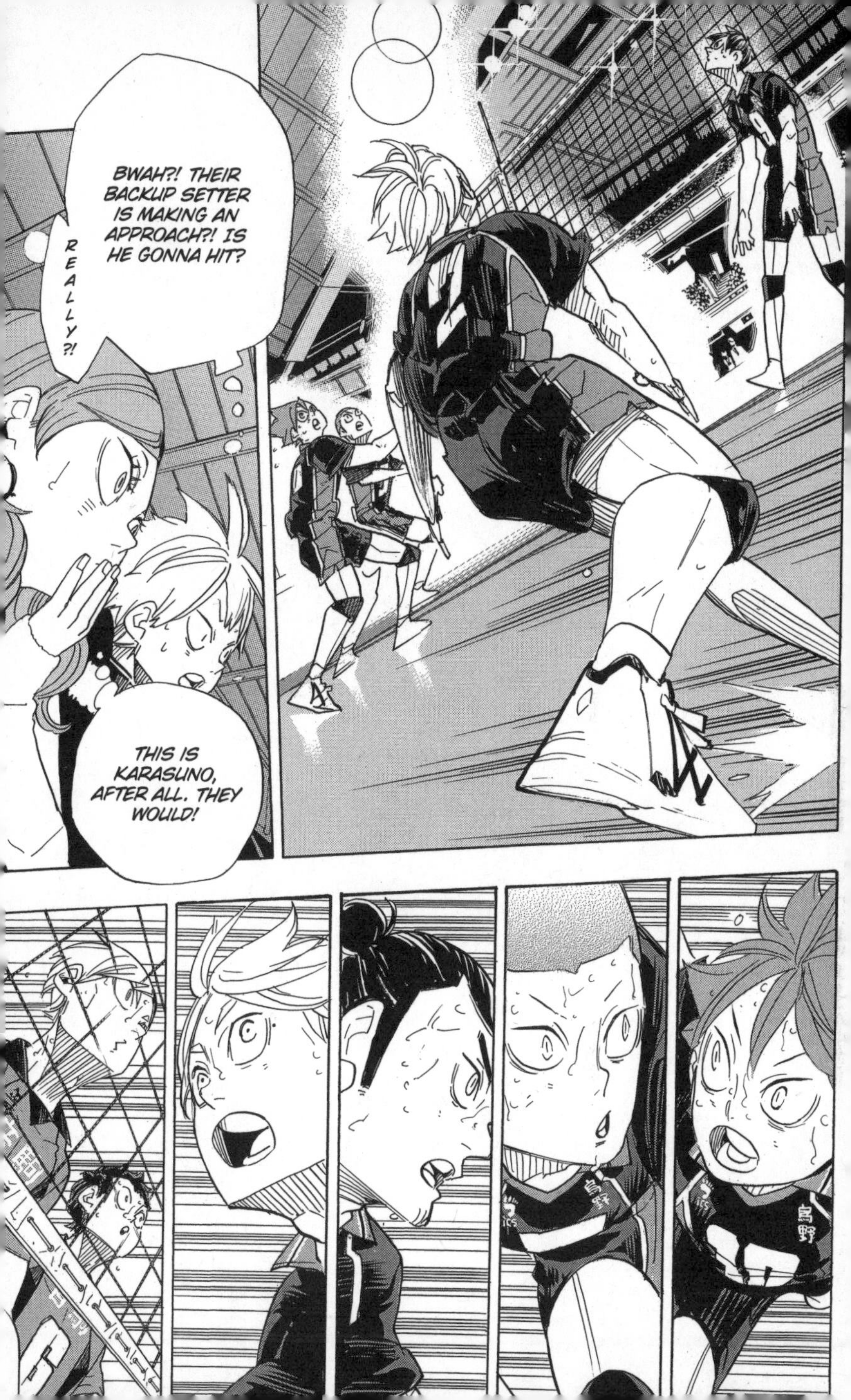
BWAH?! THEIR BACKUP SETTER IS MAKING AN APPROACH?! IS HE GONNA HIT?
REALLY?!
THIS IS KARASUNO, AFTER ALL. THEY WOULD!

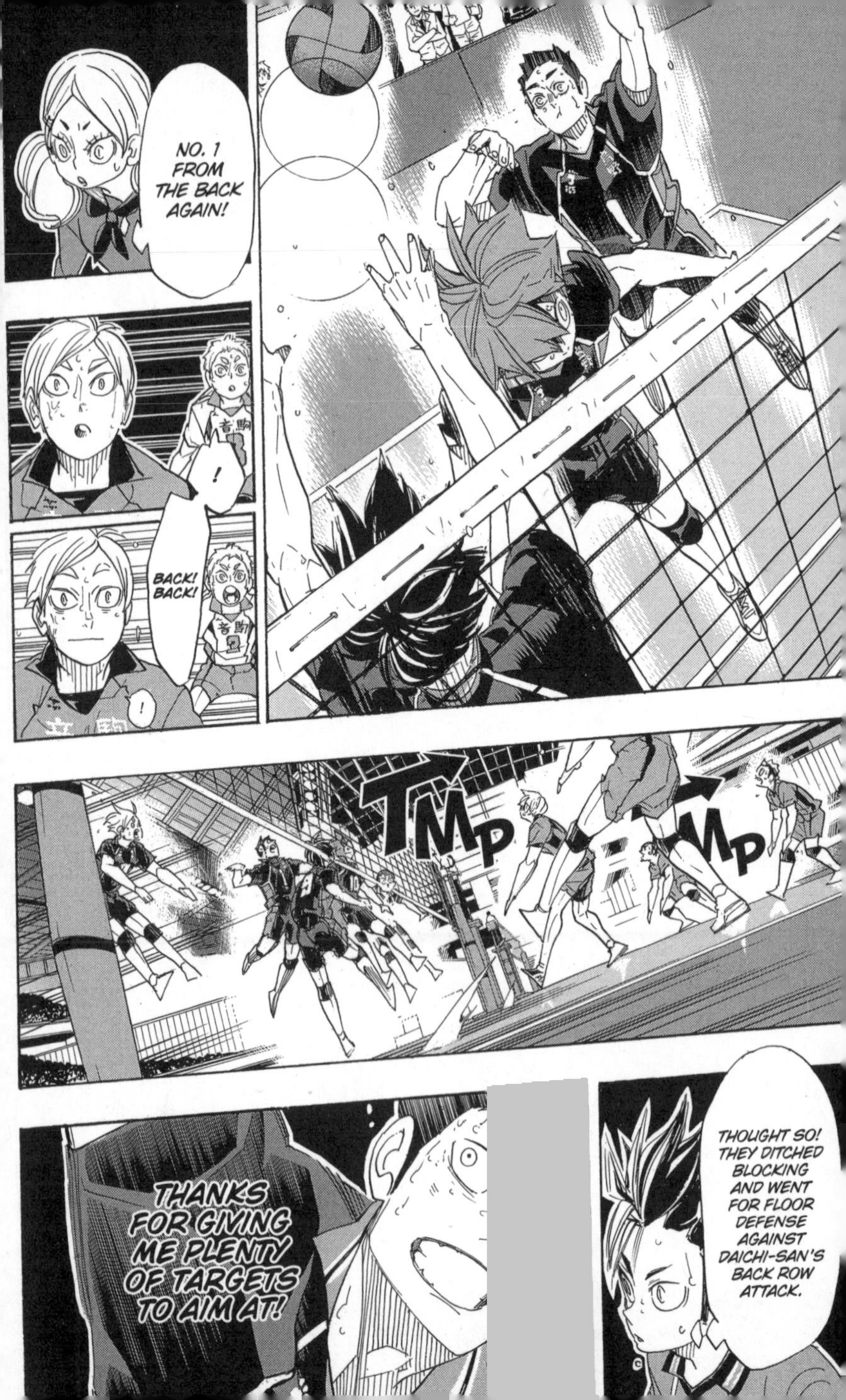
NO. 1 FROM THE BACK AGAIN!
!
BACK! BACK!
!
TMP
TMP
THOUGHT SO! THEY DITCHED BLOCKING AND WENT FOR FLOOR DEFENSE AGAINST DAICHI-SAN'S BACK ROW ATTACK.
THANKS FOR GIVING ME PLENTY OF TARGETS TO AIM AT!

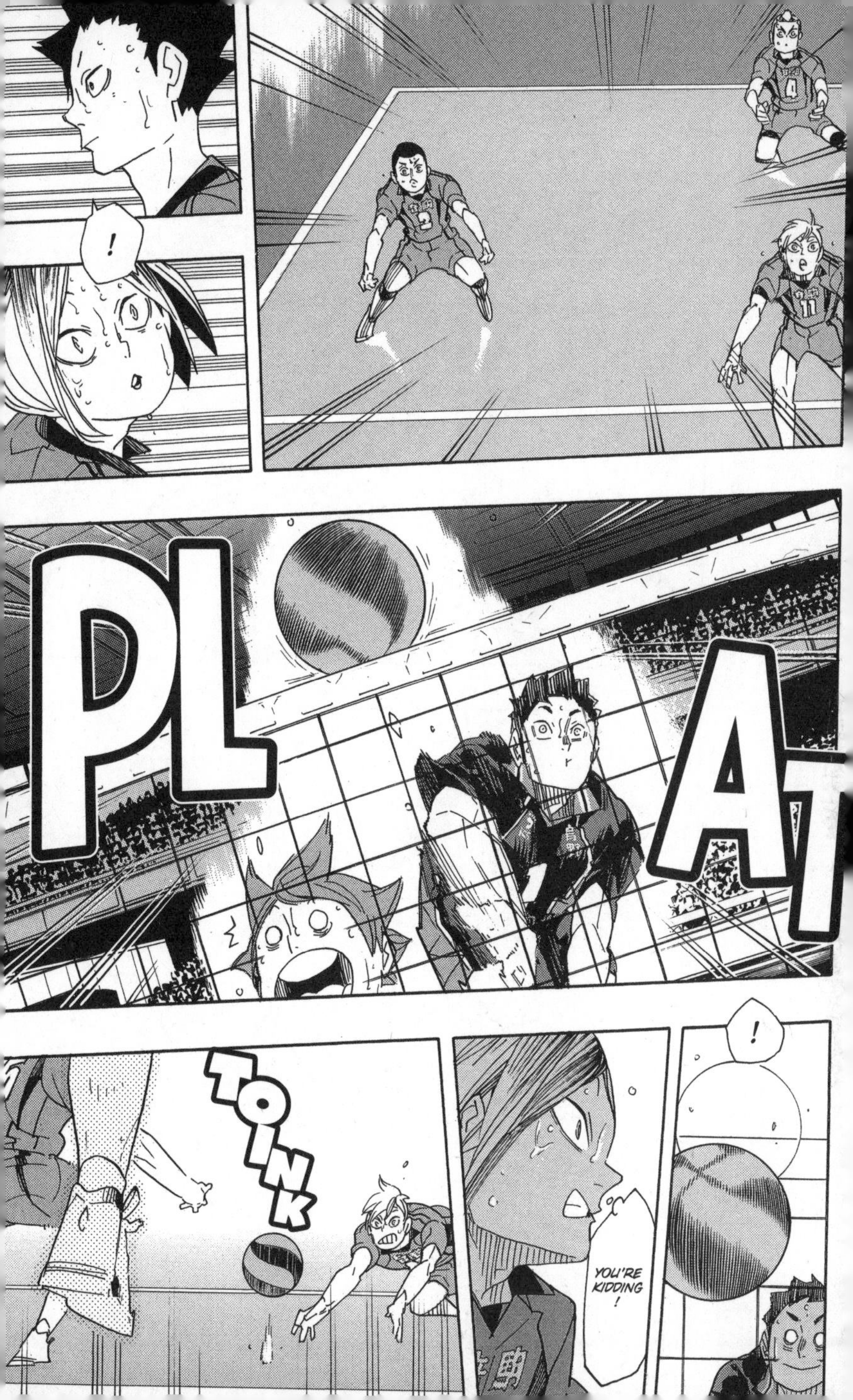
!
PLAT
!
YOU'RE KIDDING!
TOINK

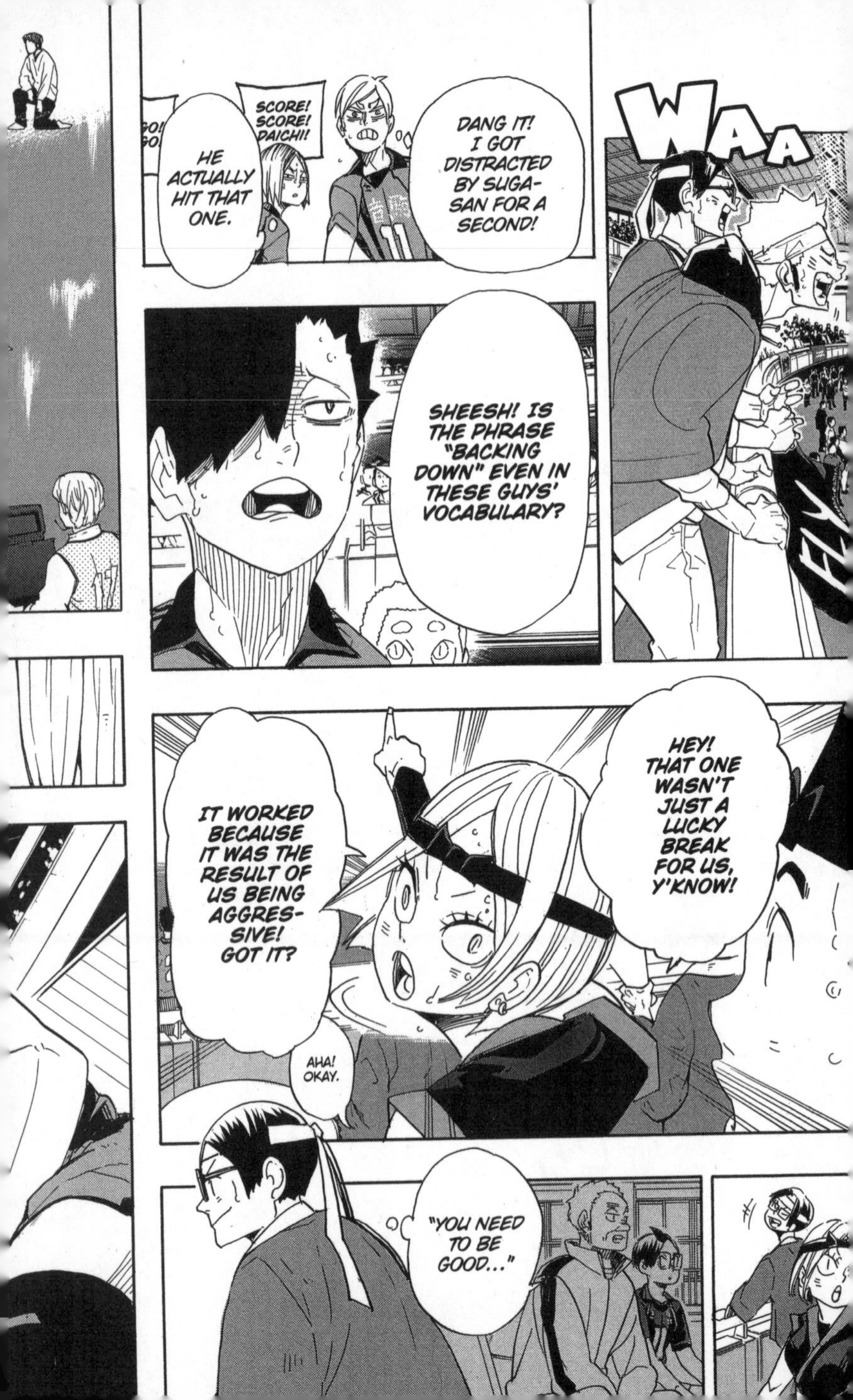
WAA
DANG IT! I GOT DISTRACTED BY SUGA-SAN FOR A SECOND!
SCORE! SCORE! DAICHI!
HE ACTUALLY HIT THAT ONE.
SHEESH! IS THE PHRASE "BACKING DOWN" EVEN IN THESE GUYS' VOCABULARY?
HEY! THAT ONE WASN'T JUST A LUCKY BREAK FOR US, Y'KNOW!
IT WORKED BECAUSE IT WAS THE RESULT OF US BEING AGGRES-SIVE! GOT IT?
AHA! OKAY.
"YOU NEED TO BE GOOD..."

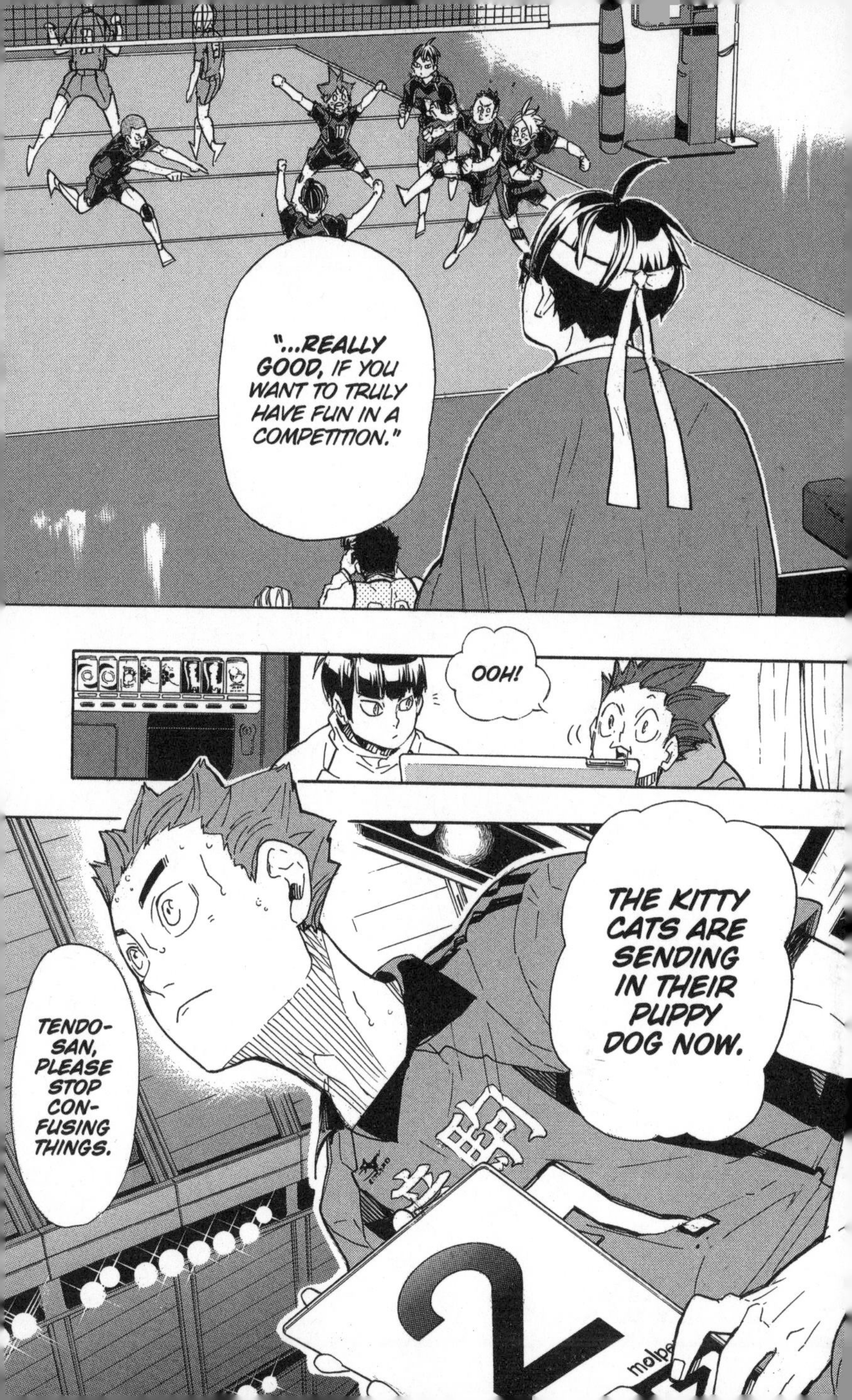
"...REALLY GOOD, IF YOU WANT TO TRULY HAVE FUN IN A COMPETITION."
OOH!
THE KITTY CATS ARE SENDING IN THEIR PUPPY DOG NOW.
TENDO-SAN, PLEASE STOP CON-FUSING THINGS.
2
molpe

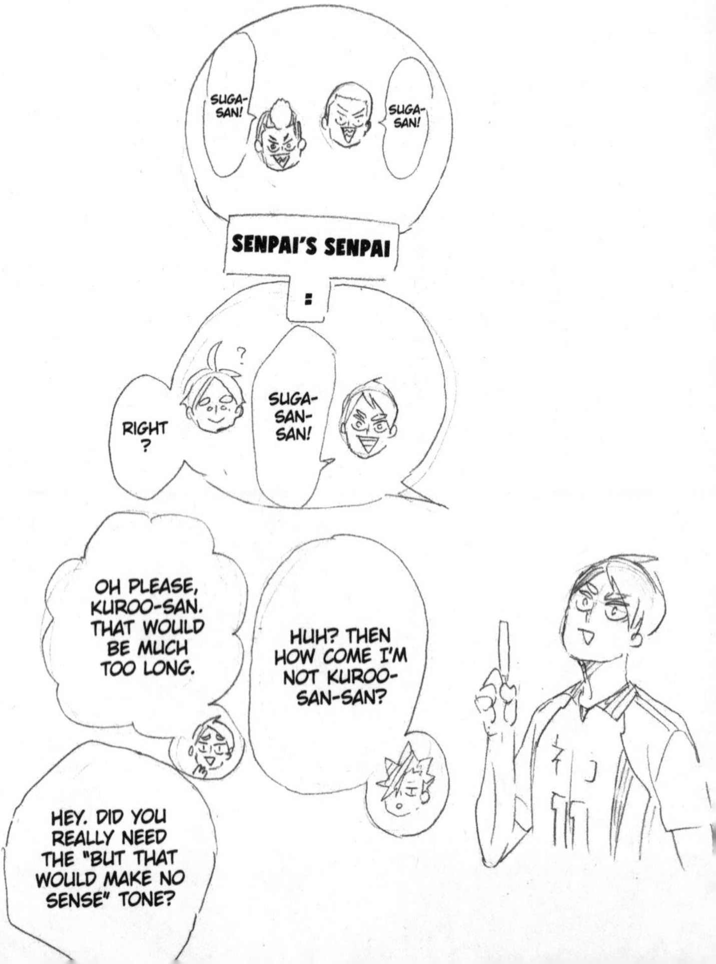
SUGA-SAN!
SUGA-SAN!
SENPAI'S SENPAI
:
SUGA-SAN-SAN!
?
RIGHT?
HUH? THEN HOW COME I'M NOT KUROO-SAN-SAN?
OH PLEASE, KUROO-SAN. THAT WOULD BE MUCH TOO LONG.
HEY. DID YOU REALLY NEED THE "BUT THAT WOULD MAKE NO SENSE" TONE?

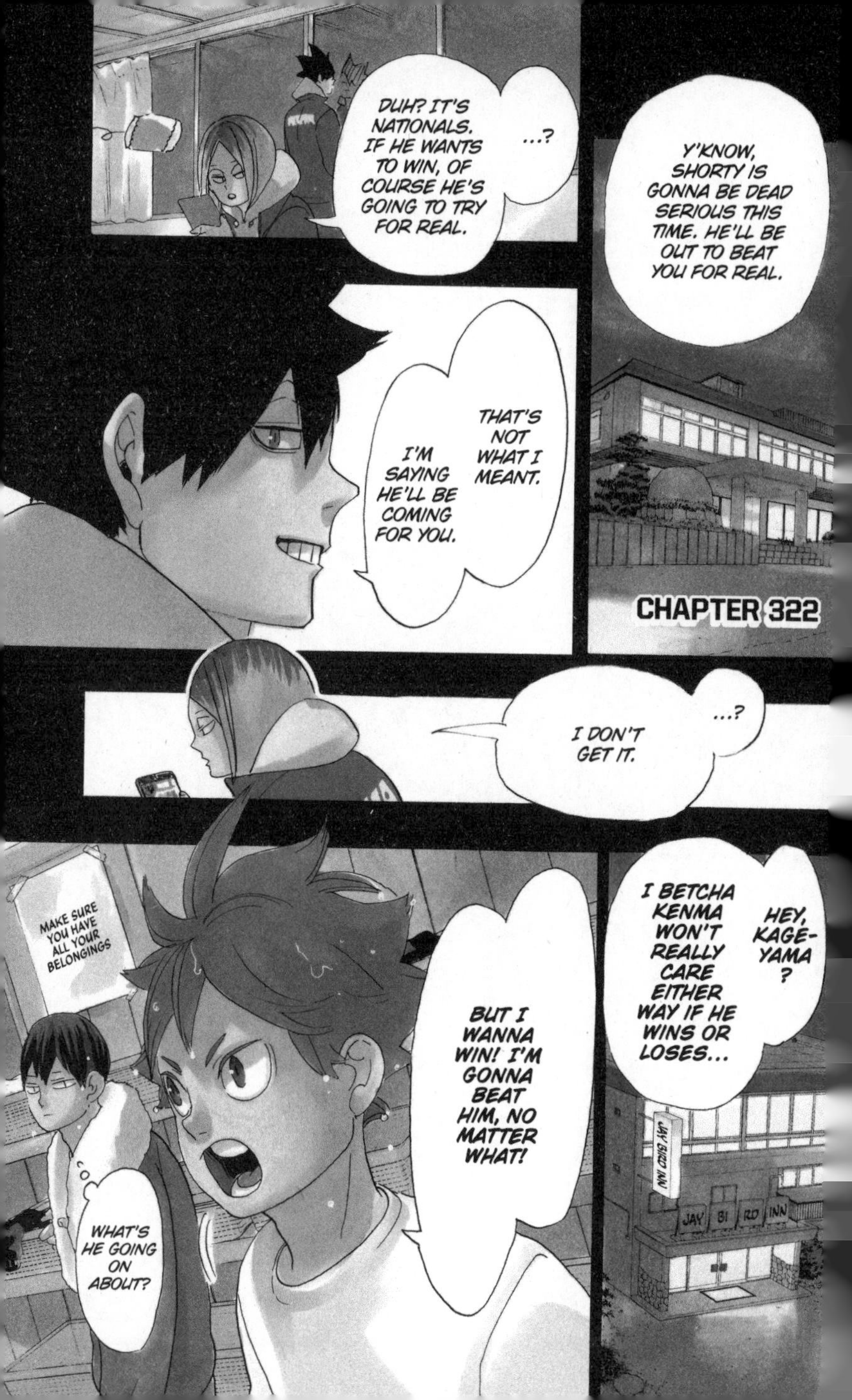
Y'KNOW, SHORTY IS GONNA BE DEAD SERIOUS THIS TIME. HE'LL BE OUT TO BEAT YOU FOR REAL.
CHAPTER 322
...?
DUH? IT'S NATIONALS. IF HE WANTS TO WIN, OF COURSE HE'S GOING TO TRY FOR REAL.
THAT'S NOT WHAT I MEANT.
I'M SAYING HE'LL BE COMING FOR YOU.
...?
I DON'T GET IT.
JAY BIRD INN
JAY BI RD INN
HEY, KAGE-YAMA?
I BETCHA KENMA WON'T REALLY CARE EITHER WAY IF HE WINS OR LOSES...
MAKE SURE YOU HAVE ALL YOUR BELONGINGS
BUT I WANNA WIN! I'M GONNA BEAT HIM, NO MATTER WHAT!
WHAT'S HE GOING ON ABOUT?

CHAPTER 322: I Win

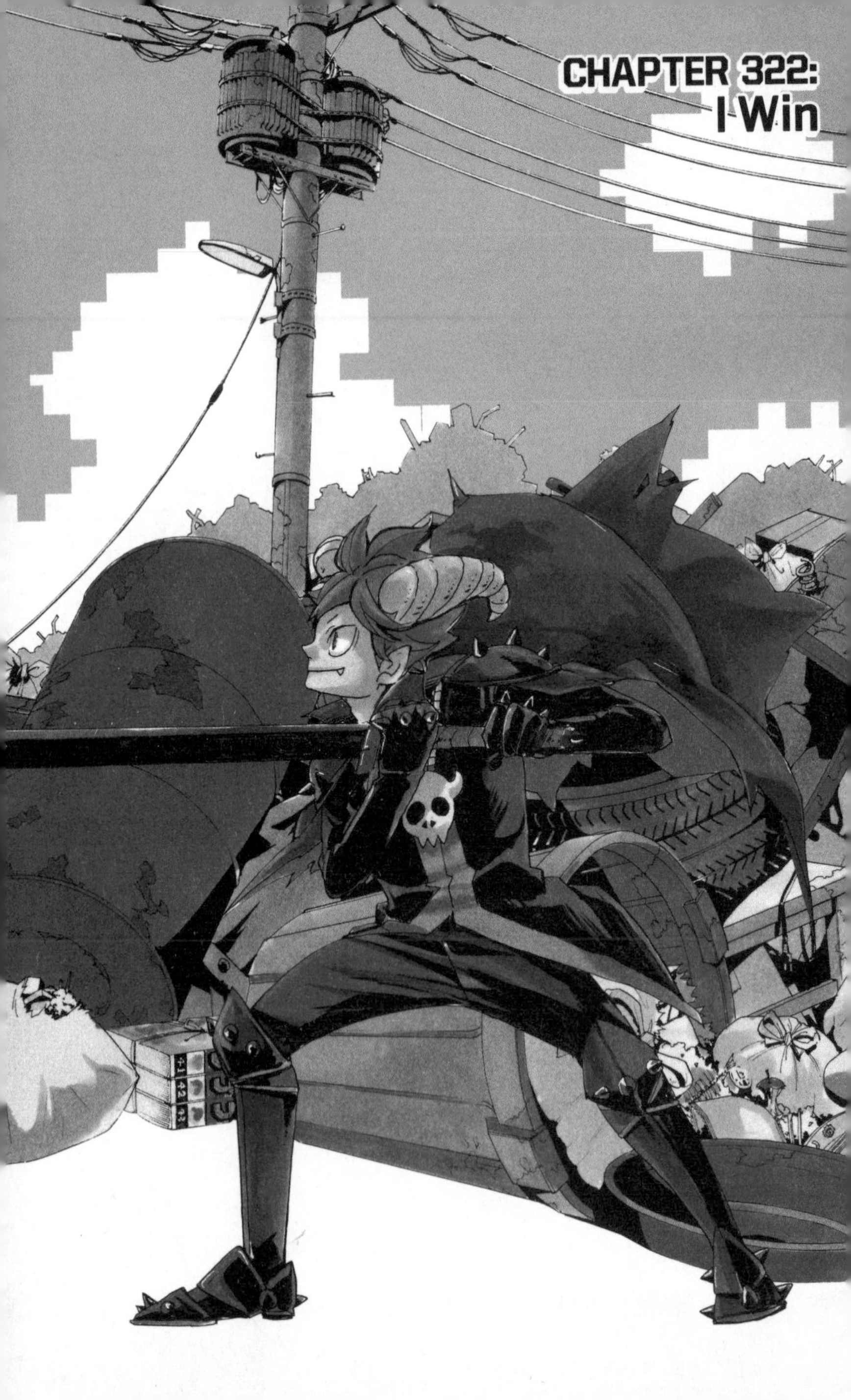

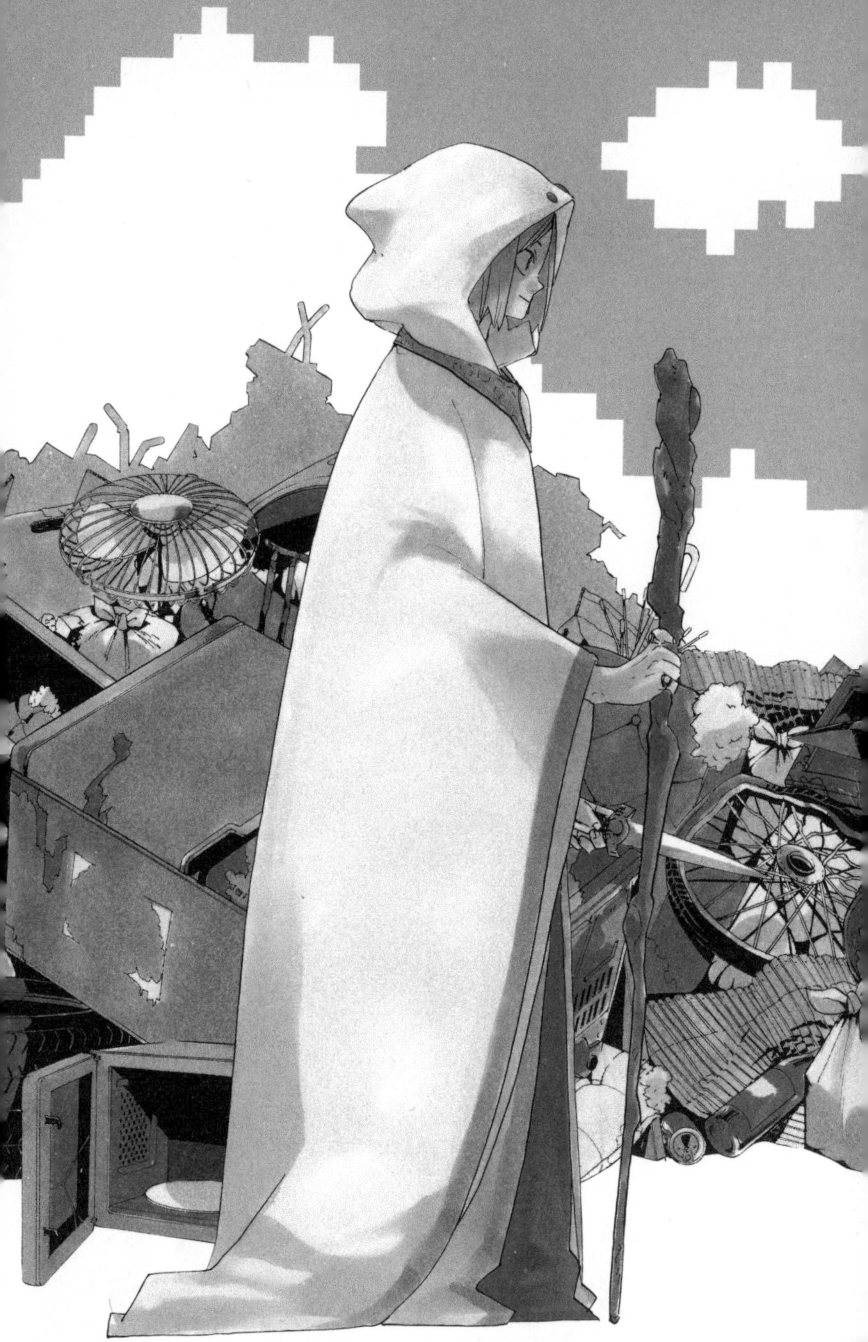

HAIKYU!!

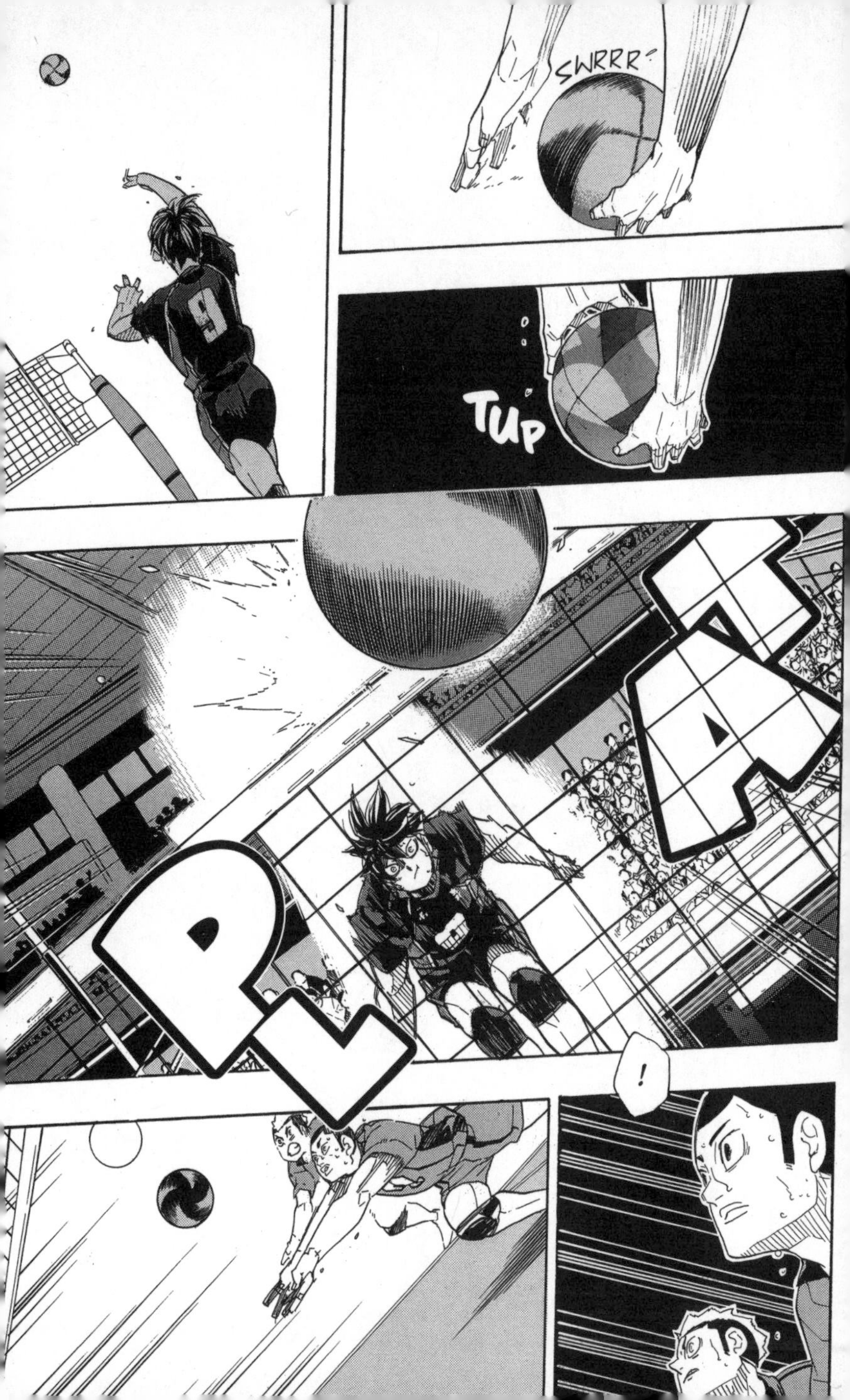
SWRRR
TUP
PLA
!

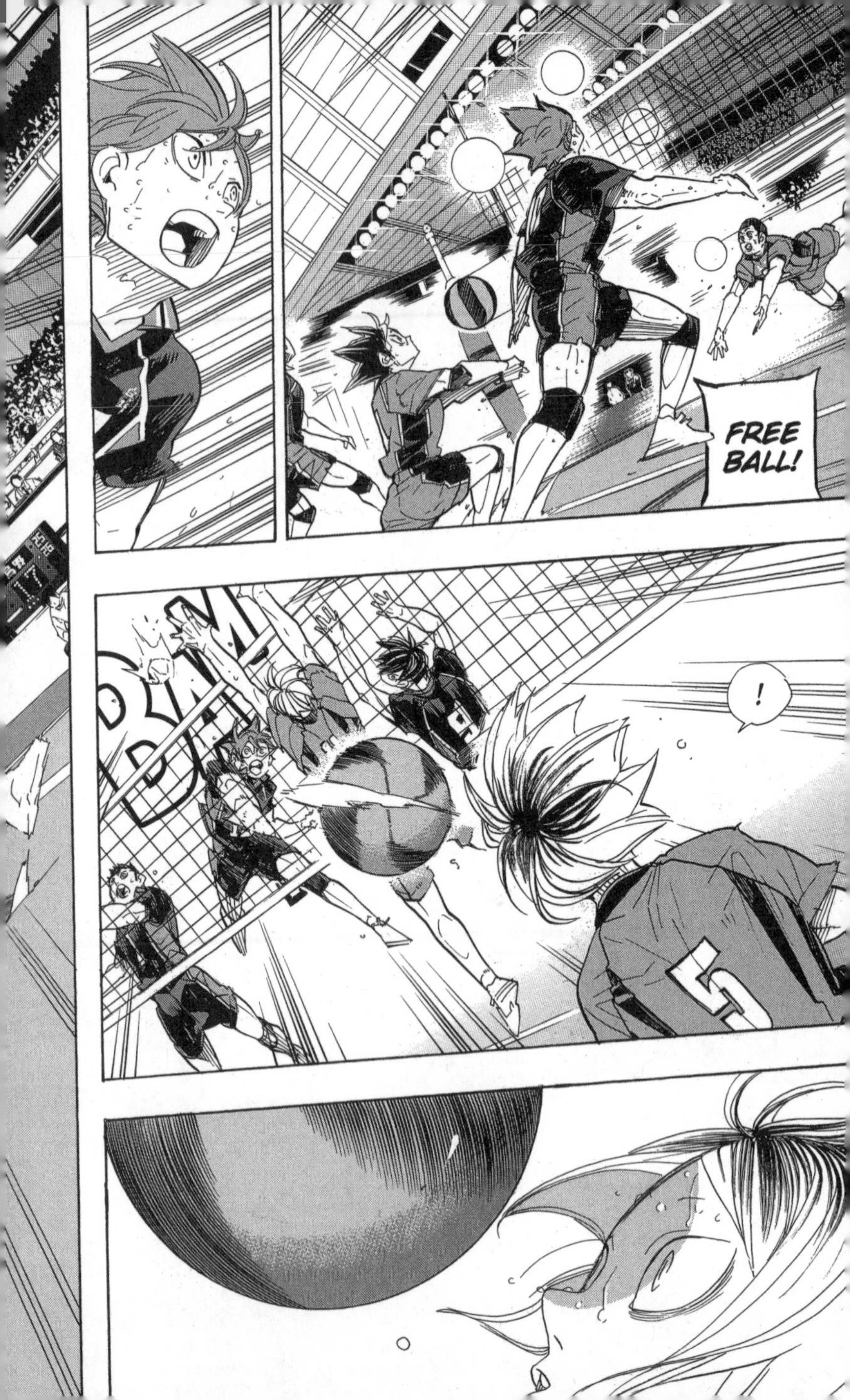
FREE BALL!
!
BAM

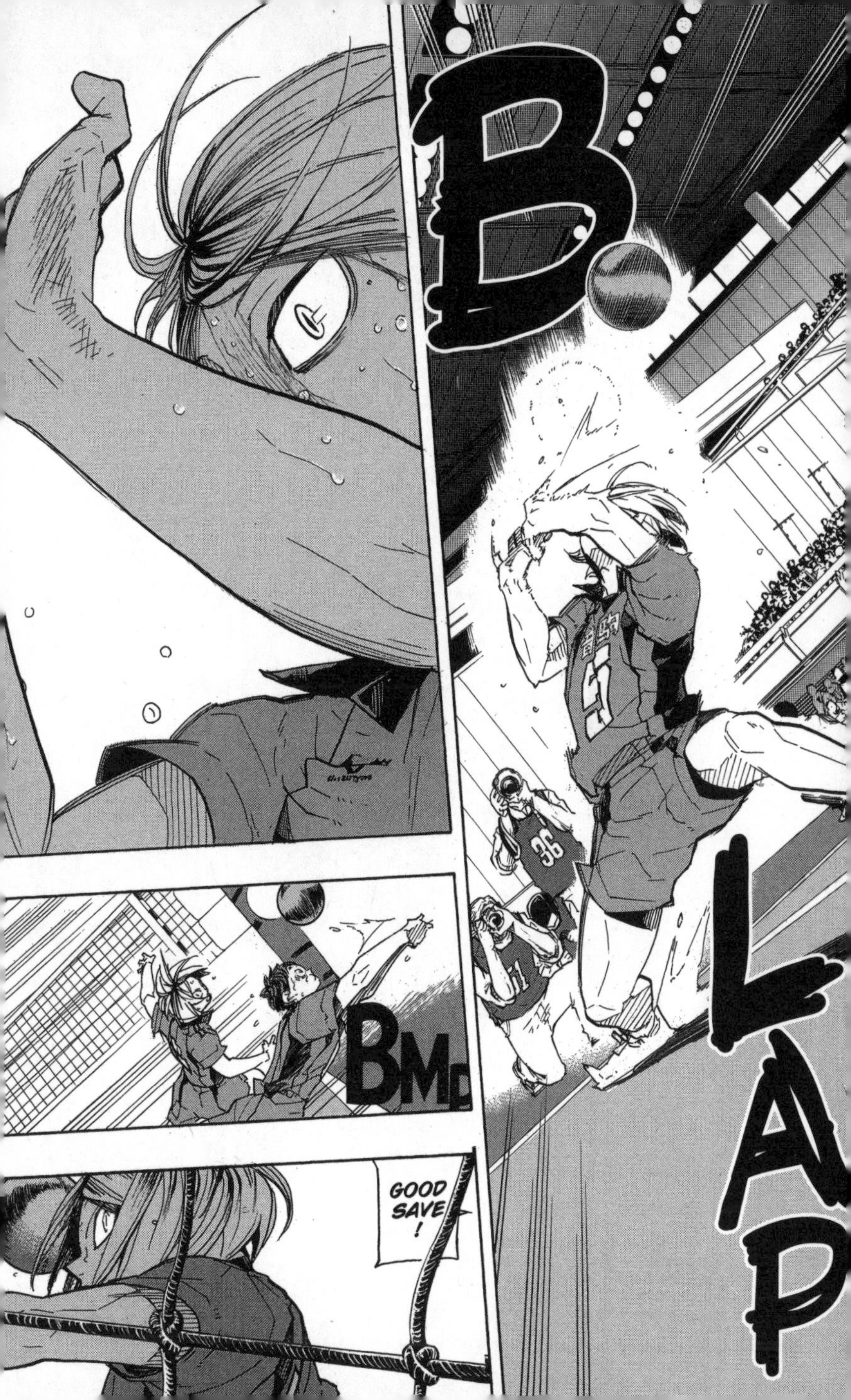
BLAP
BMP
GOOD SAVE!

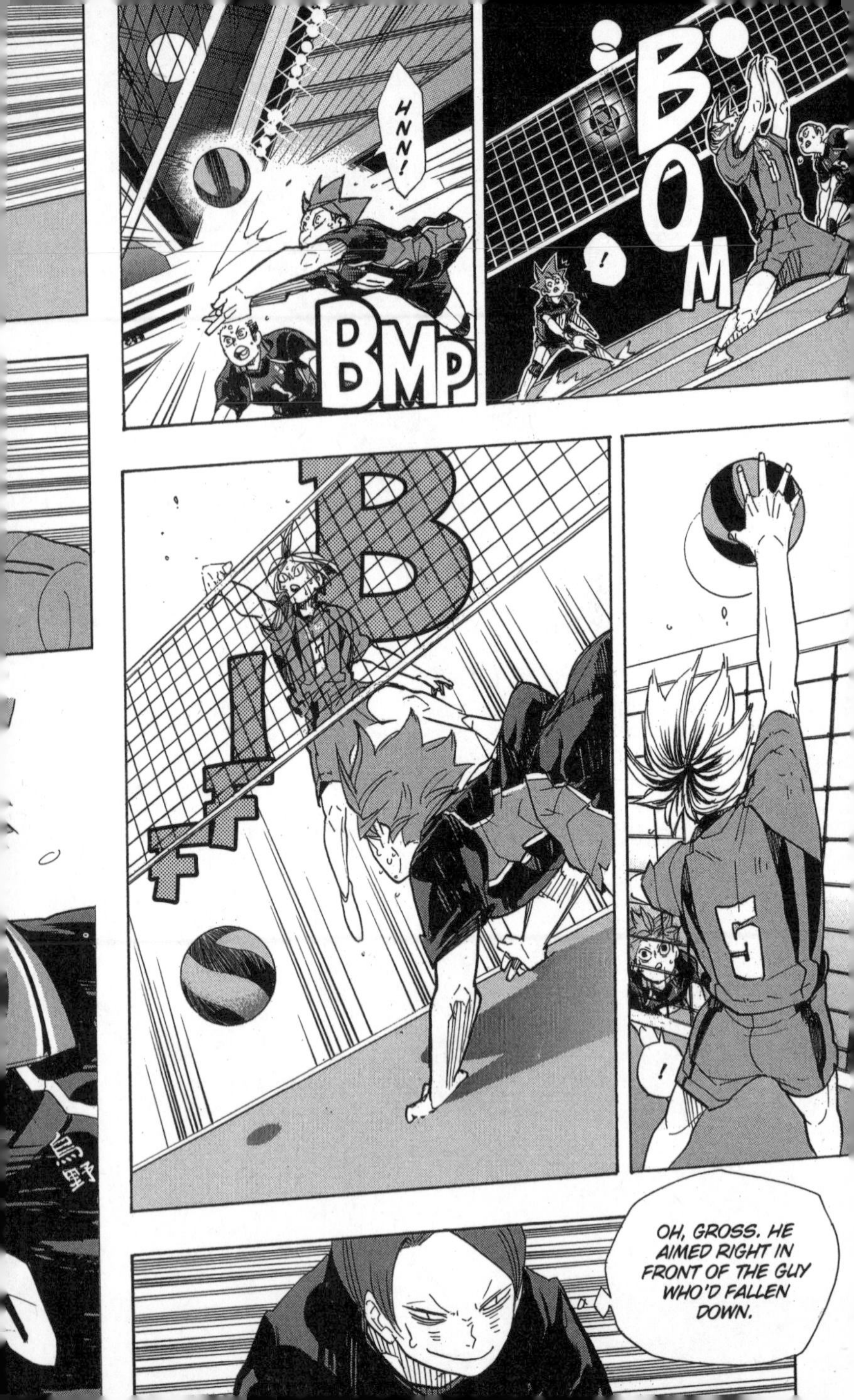
BOM
!
HNN!
BMP
!
B
OH, GROSS. HE AIMED RIGHT IN FRONT OF THE GUY WHO'D FALLEN DOWN.

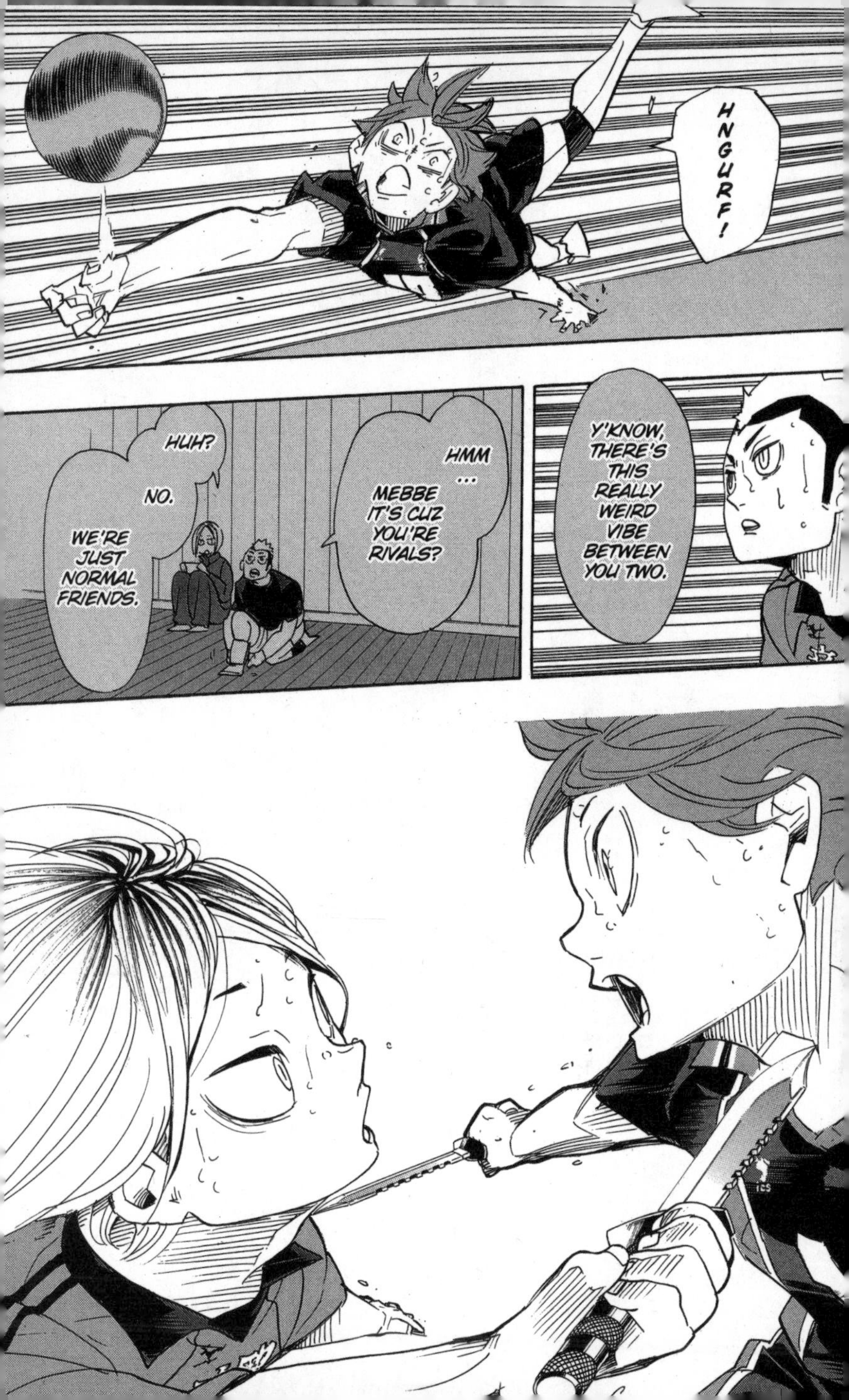
HNGURF!
Y'KNOW, THERE'S THIS REALLY WEIRD VIBE BETWEEN YOU TWO.
HMM ... MEBBE IT'S CUZ YOU'RE RIVALS?
HUH? NO. WE'RE JUST NORMAL FRIENDS.

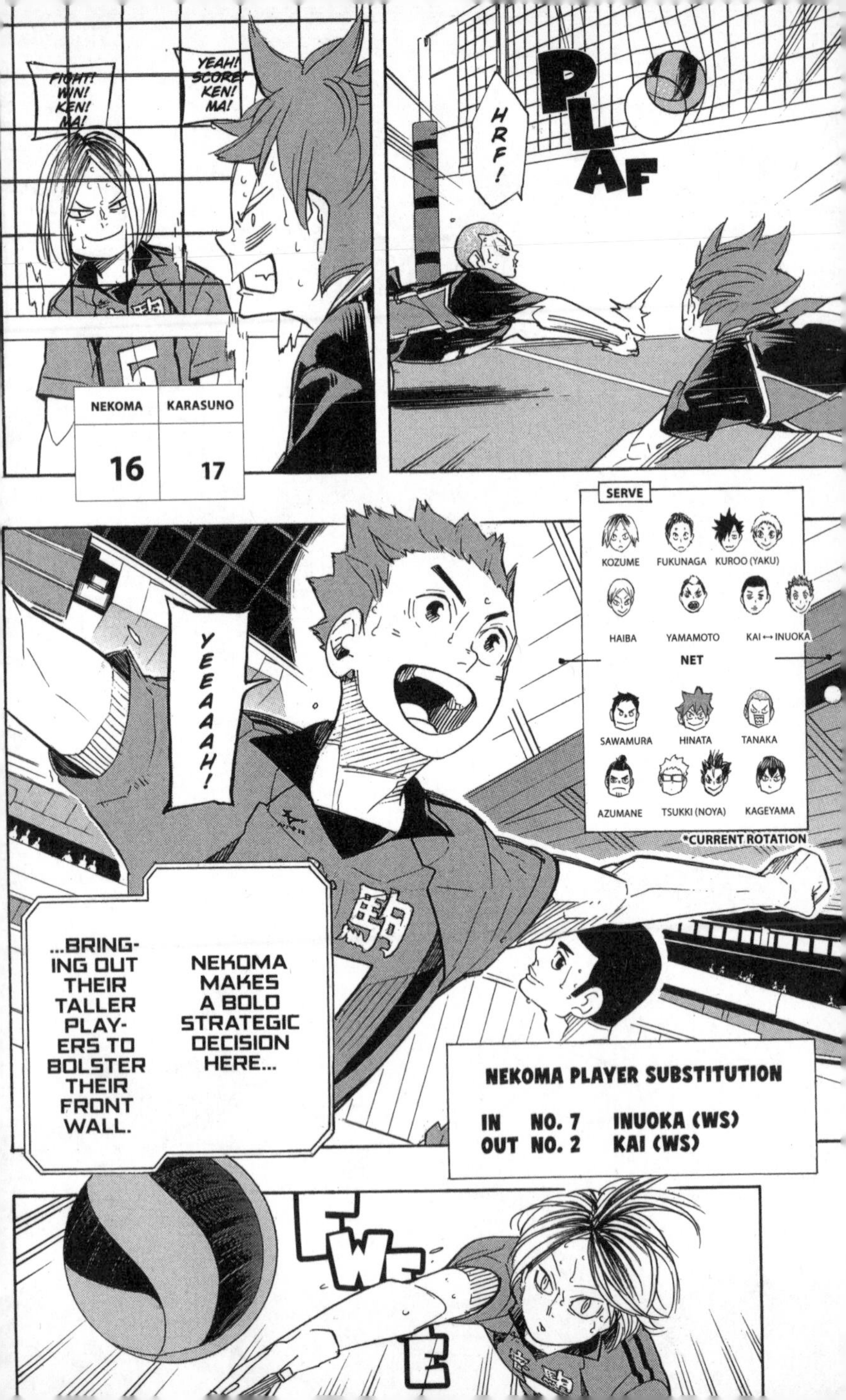
HRF!
PLAF
YEAH! SCORE! KEN! MA!
FIGHT! WIN! KEN! MA!
NEKOMA 16
KARASUNO 17
SERVE
KOZUME
FUKUNAGA
KUROO (YAKU)
HAIBA
YAMAMOTO
KAI ↔ INUOKA
NET
SAWAMURA
HINATA
TANAKA
AZUMANE
TSUKKI (NOYA)
KAGEYAMA
*CURRENT ROTATION
YEEAAAAH!
NEKOMA MAKES A BOLD STRATEGIC DECISION HERE...
...BRINGING OUT THEIR TALLER PLAYERS TO BOLSTER THEIR FRONT WALL.
NEKOMA PLAYER SUBSTITUTION
IN NO. 7 INUOKA (WS)
OUT NO. 2 KAI (WS)

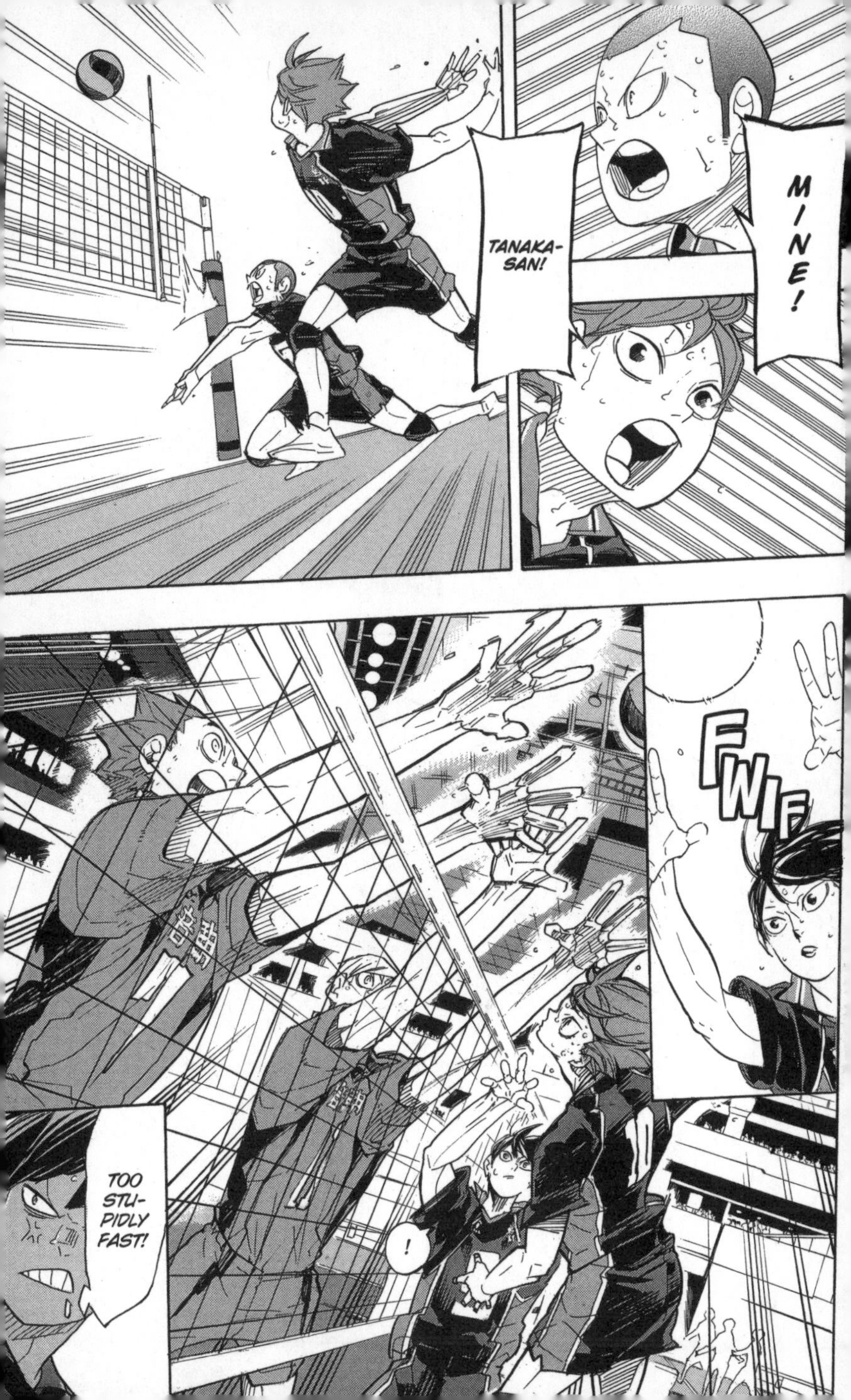
MINE!
TANAKA-SAN!
FWIF
!
TOO STU-PIDLY FAST!

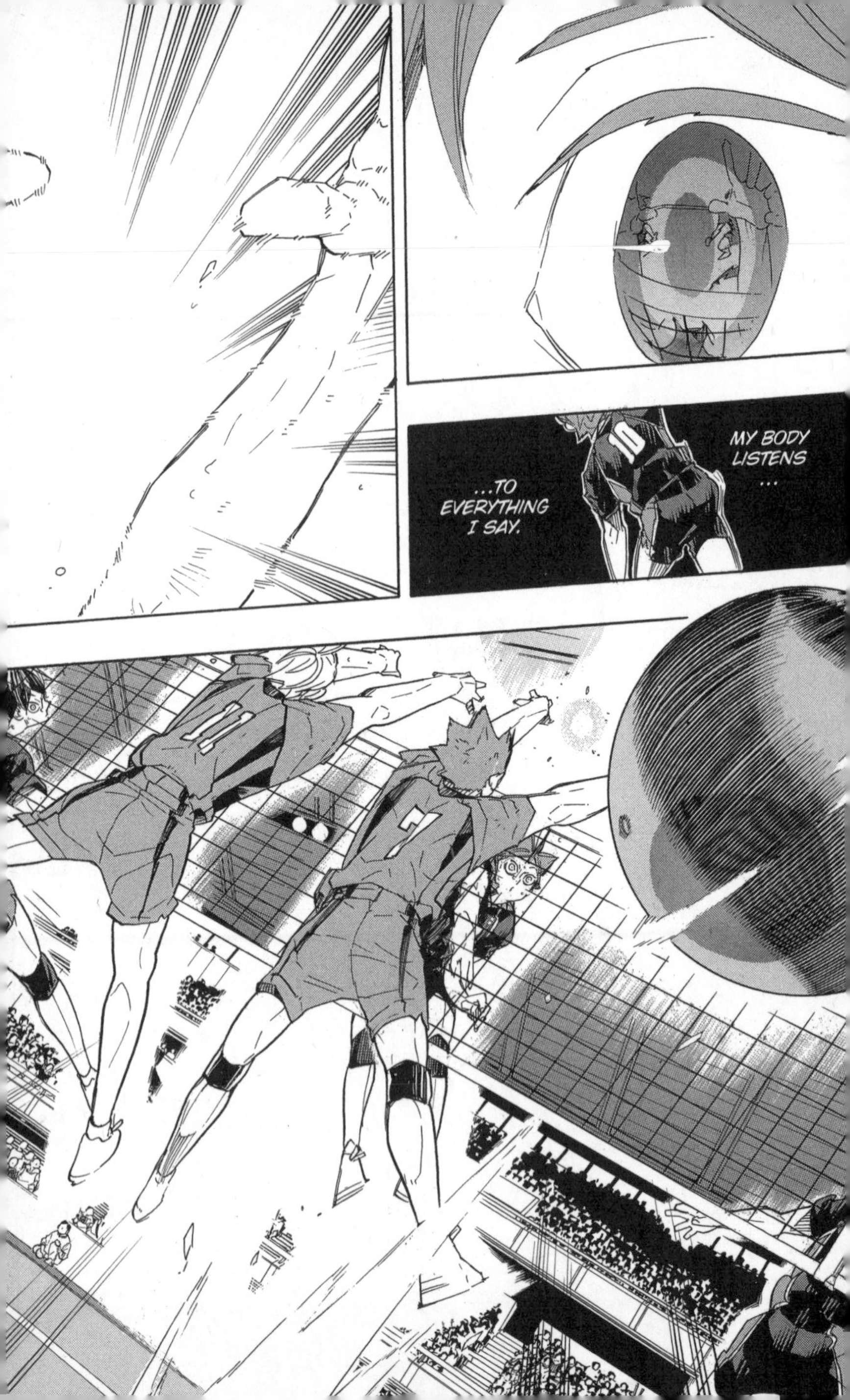
MY BODY LISTENS ...
...TO EVERYTHING I SAY.

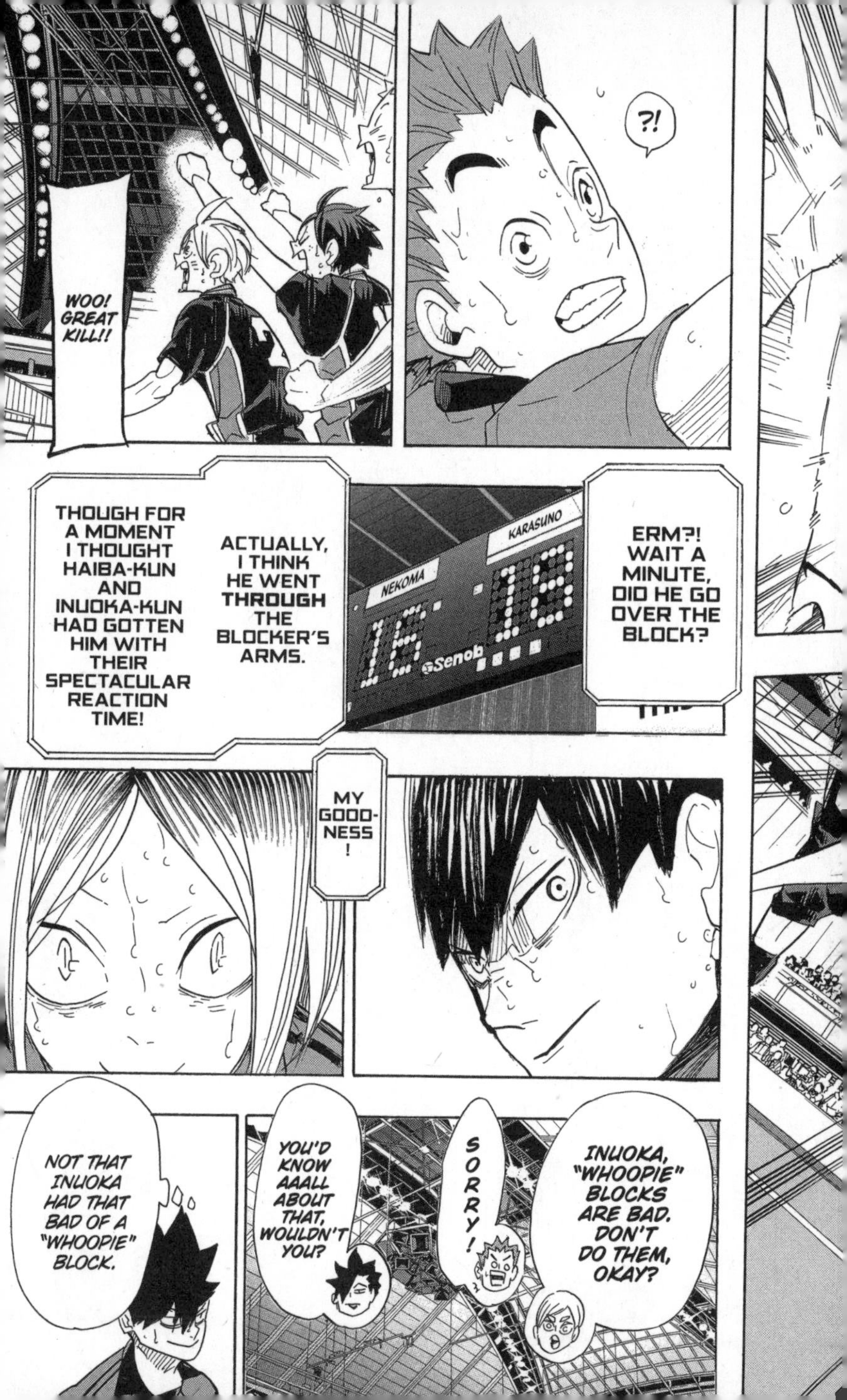

?!
WOO! GREAT KILL!!
ERM?! WAIT A MINUTE, DID HE GO OVER THE BLOCK?
KARASUNO
NEKOMA
Senob
ACTUALLY, I THINK HE WENT THROUGH THE BLOCKER'S ARMS.
THOUGH FOR A MOMENT I THOUGHT HAIBA-KUN AND INUOKA-KUN HAD GOTTEN HIM WITH THEIR SPECTACULAR REACTION TIME!
MY GOODNESS!
INUOKA, "WHOOPIE" BLOCKS ARE BAD. DON'T DO THEM, OKAY?
SORRY!
YOU'D KNOW AAALL ABOUT THAT, WOULDN'T YOU?
NOT THAT INUOKA HAD THAT BAD OF A "WHOOPIE" BLOCK.

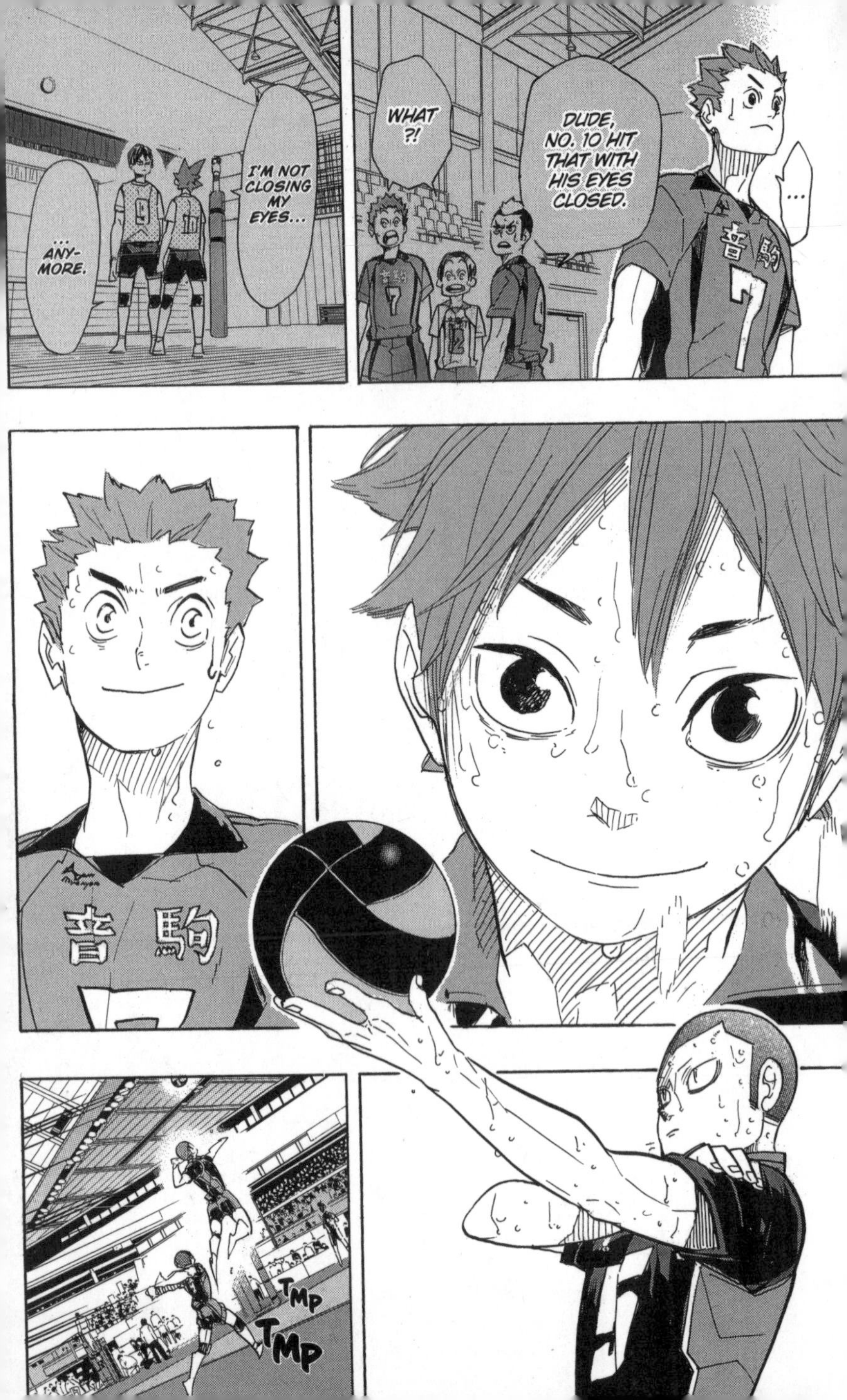
DUDE, NO. 10 HIT THAT WITH HIS EYES CLOSED.
...
WHAT ?!
I'M NOT CLOSING MY EYES...
...ANYMORE.
TMP
TMP

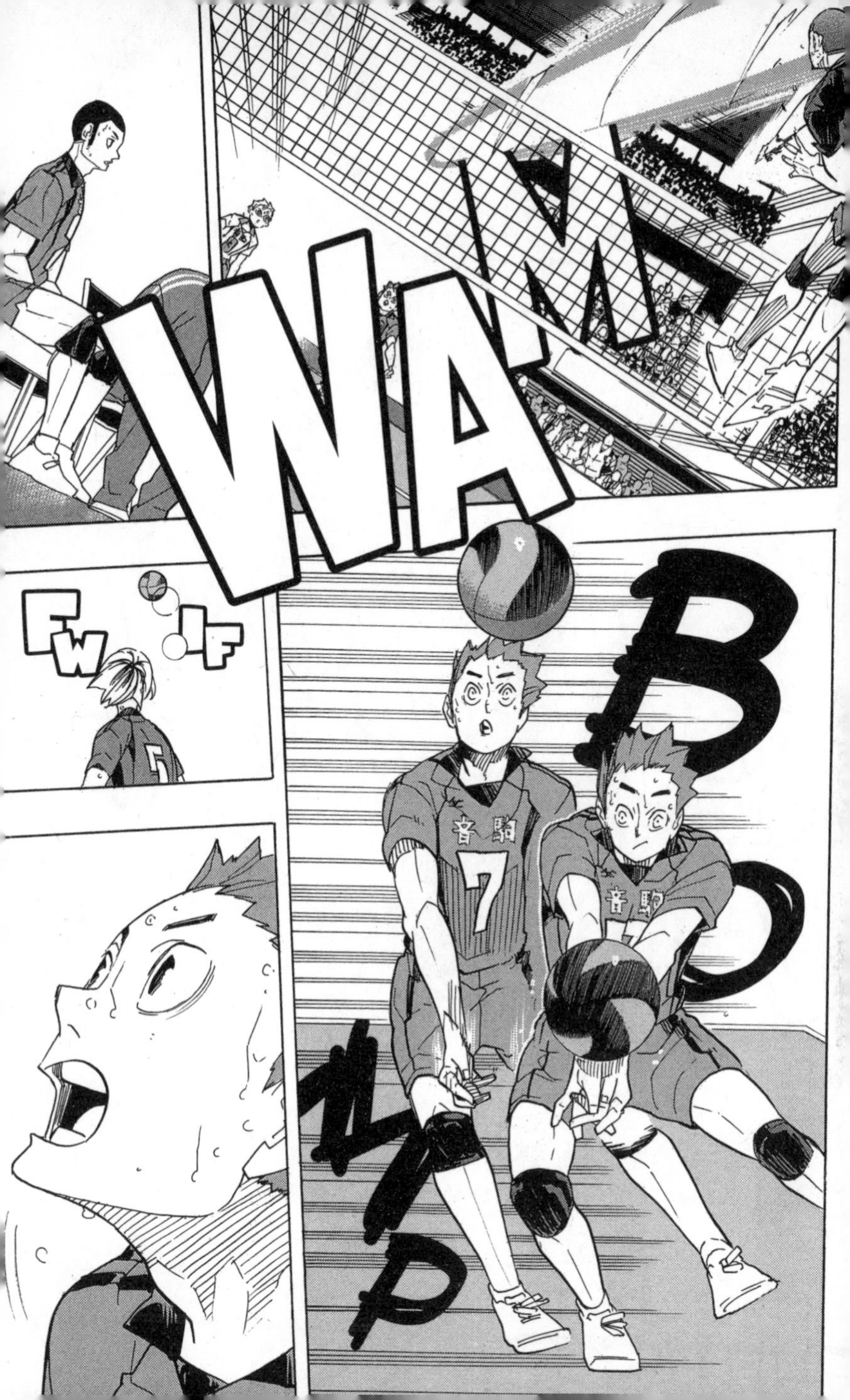
WAAAA
FWIF
音駒
7

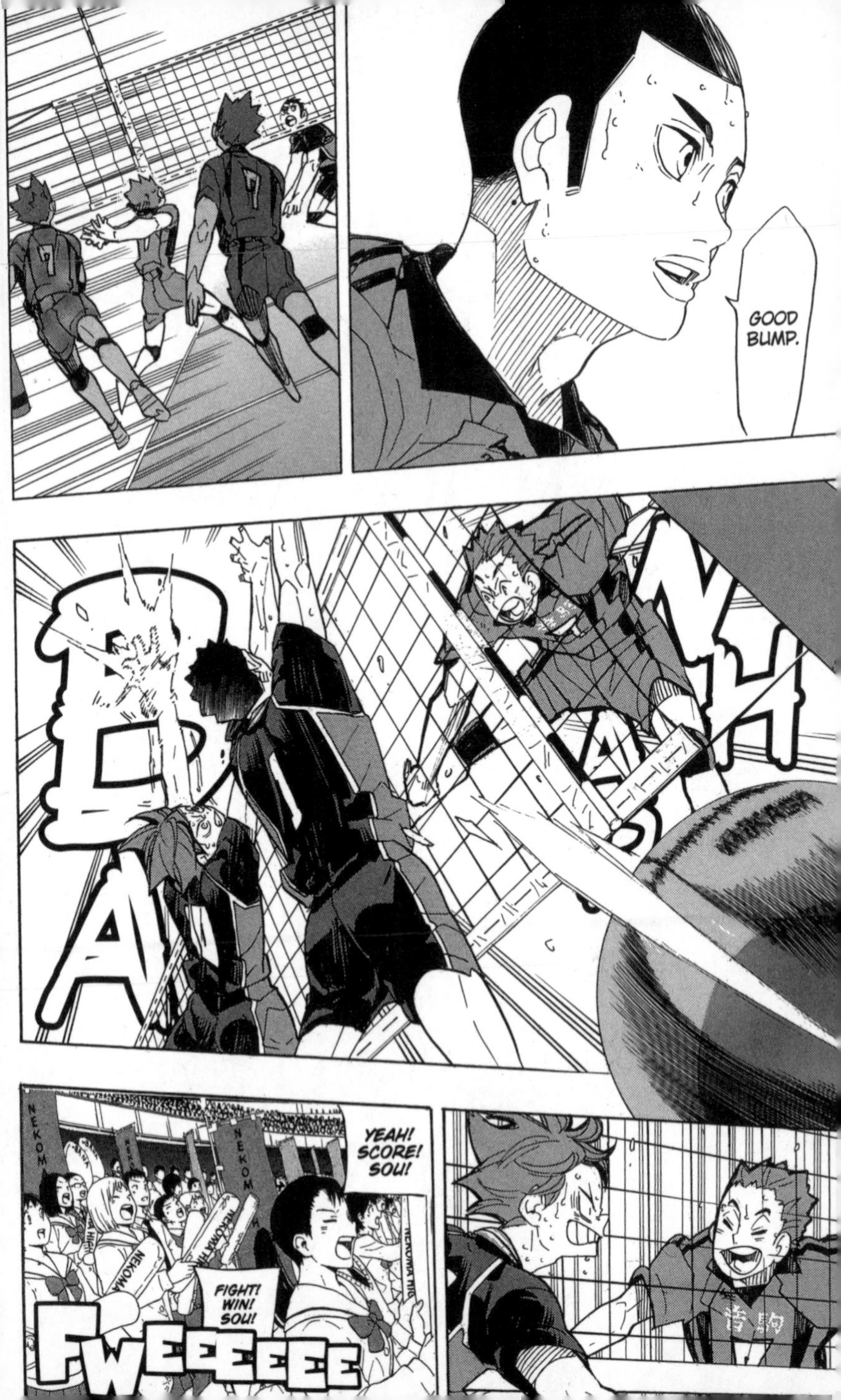
GOOD BUMP.
YEAH! SCORE! SOU!
FIGHT! WIN! SOU!
FWEEEEEE

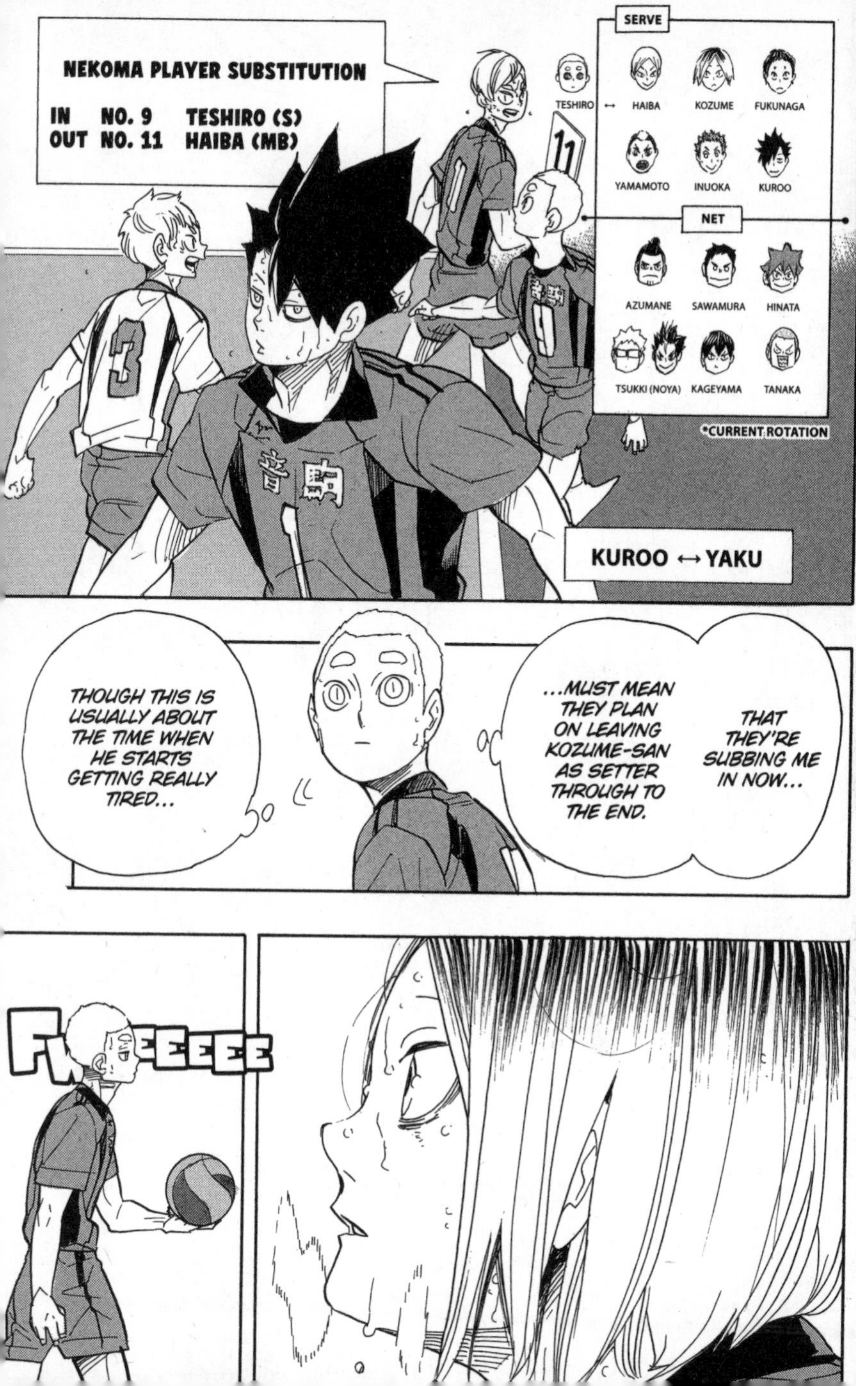
NEKOMA PLAYER SUBSTITUTION
IN NO. 9 TESHIRO (S)
OUT NO. 11 HAIBA (MB)
SERVE
TESHIRO ↔ HAIBA
KOZUME
FUKUNAGA
YAMAMOTO
INUOKA
KUROO
NET
AZUMANE
SAWAMURA
HINATA
TSUKKI (NOYA)
KAGEYAMA
TANAKA
*CURRENT ROTATION
KUROO ↔ YAKU
THAT THEY'RE SUBBING ME IN NOW...
...MUST MEAN THEY PLAN ON LEAVING KOZUME-SAN AS SETTER THROUGH TO THE END.
THOUGH THIS IS USUALLY ABOUT THE TIME WHEN HE STARTS GETTING REALLY TIRED...
FWEEEEE

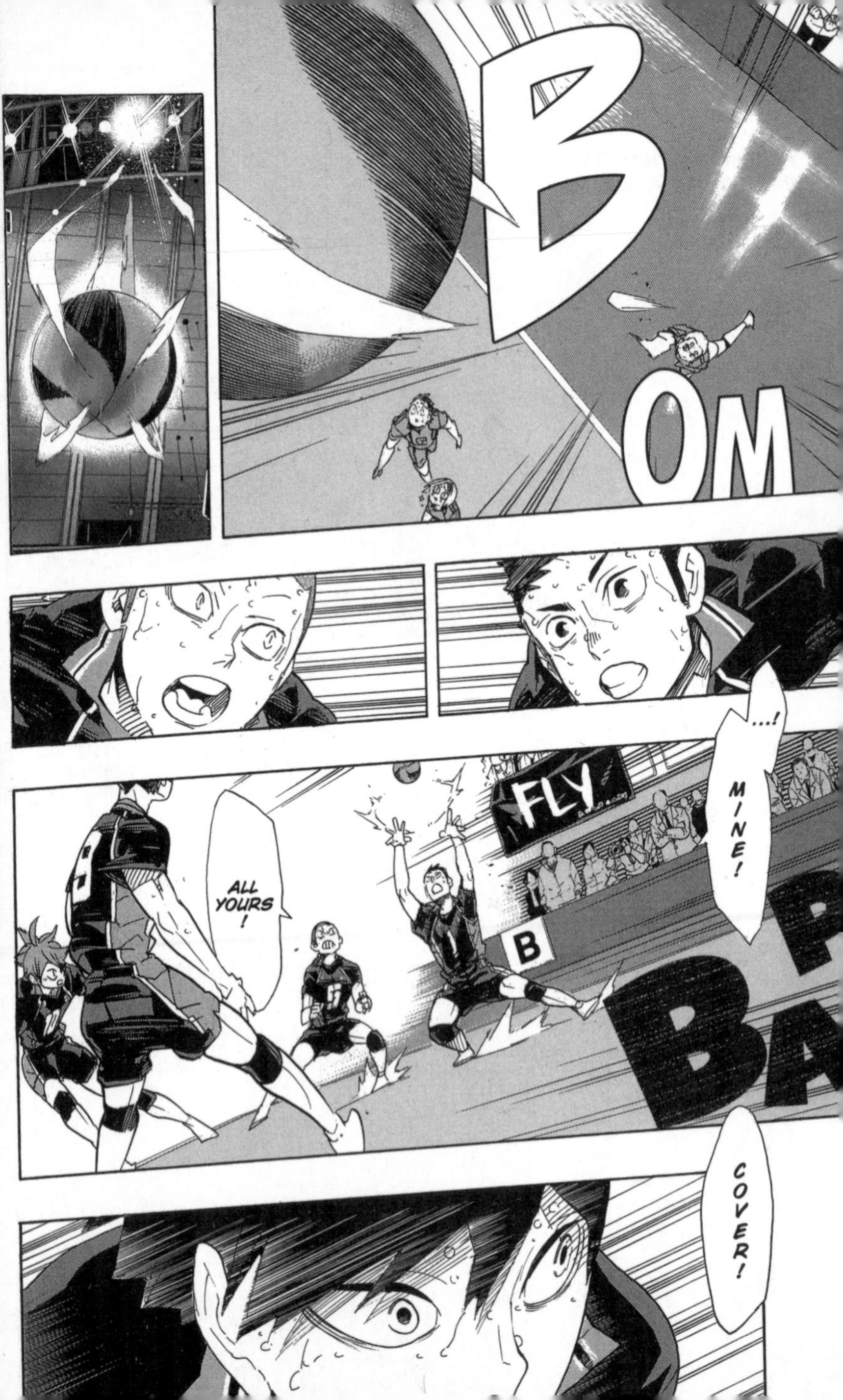

BOOM
...!
MINE!
ALL YOURS!
FLY
B
COVER!

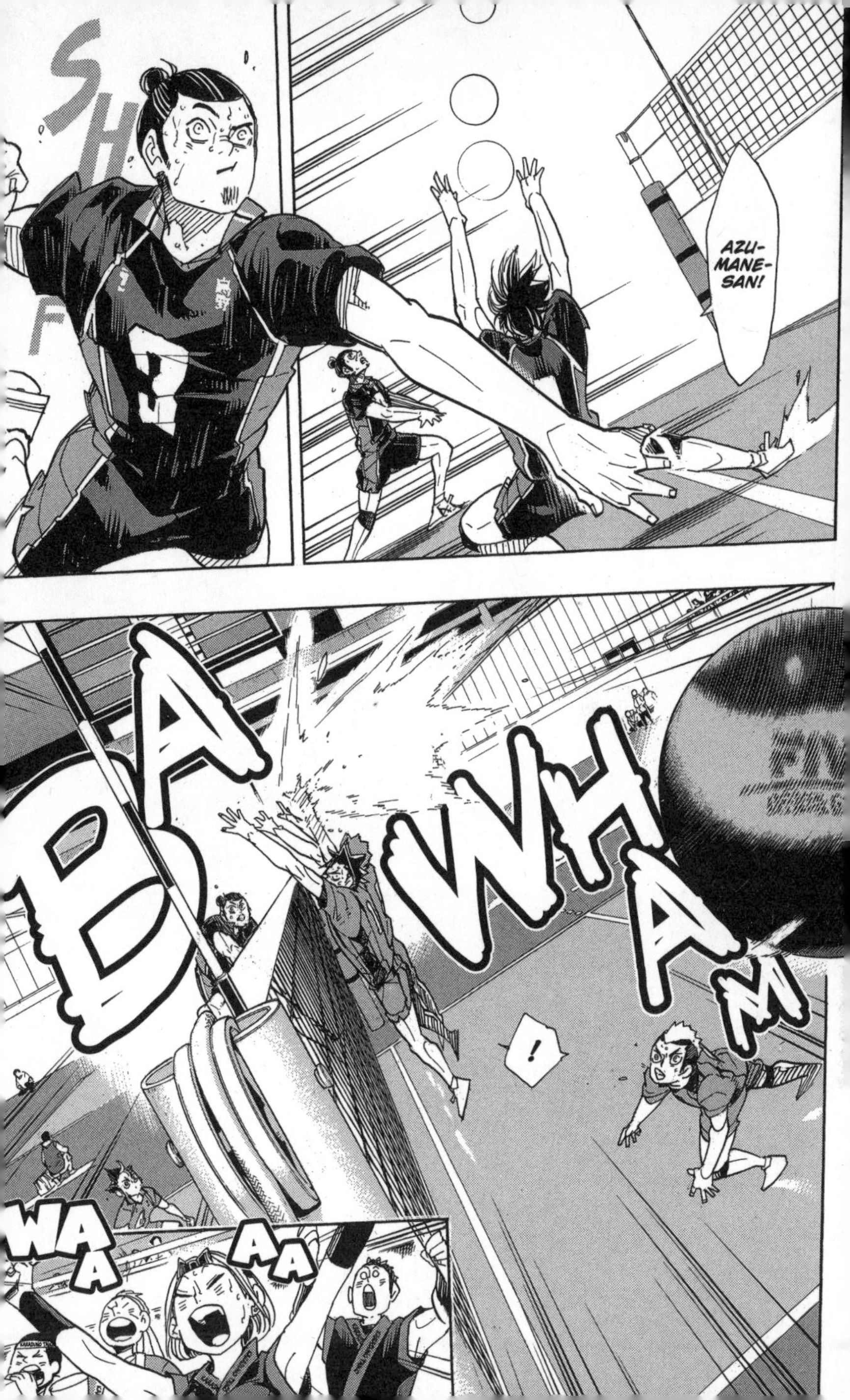

AZU-MANE-SAN!
SHF
BAWHAM
!
WAAA
AA

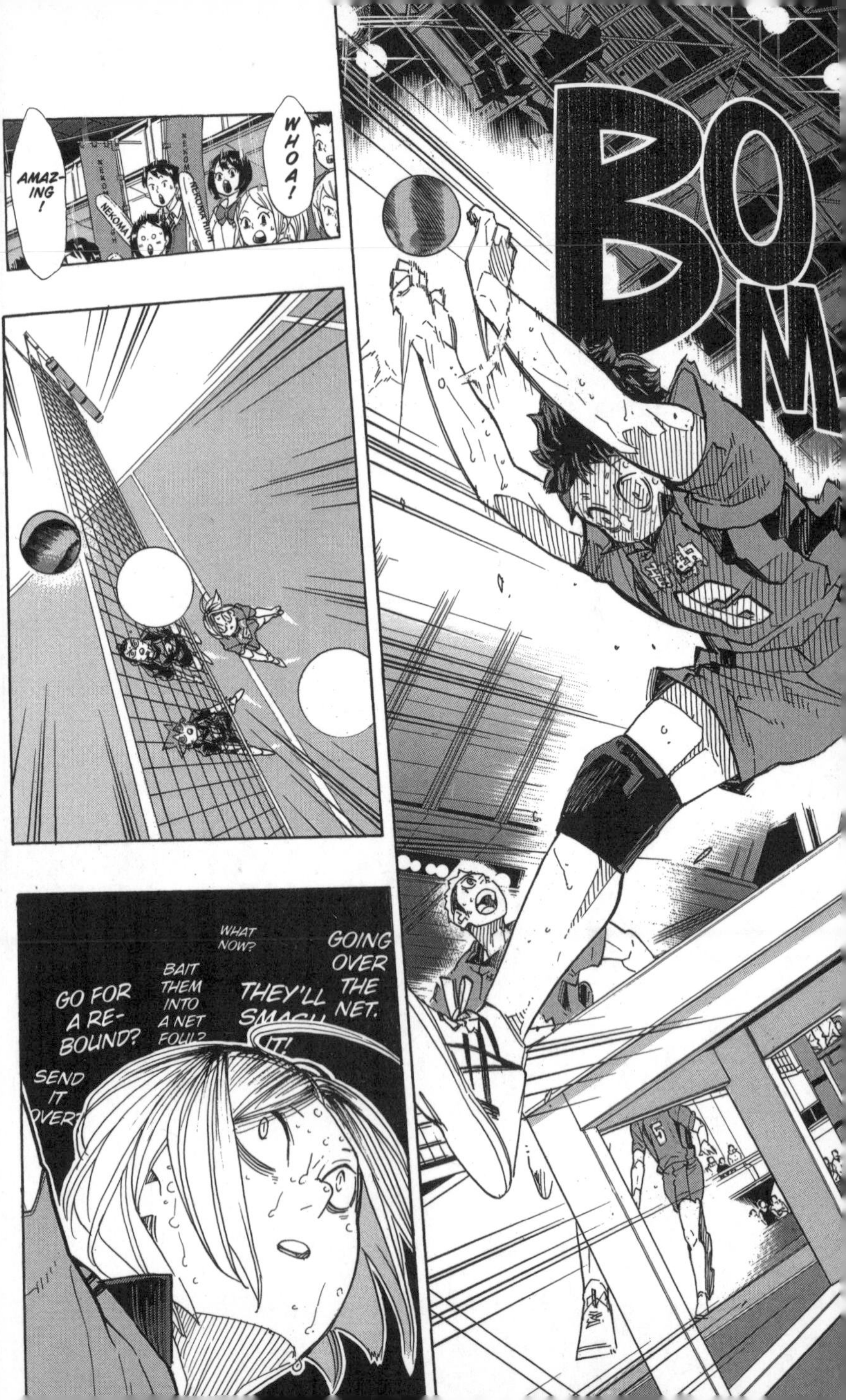

BOOM
WHOA!
AMAZING!
NEKOMA
NEKOMA HIGH
GOING OVER THE NET.
WHAT NOW?
THEY'LL SMASH IT!
BAIT THEM INTO A NET FOUL?
GO FOR A REBOUND?
SEND IT OVER?

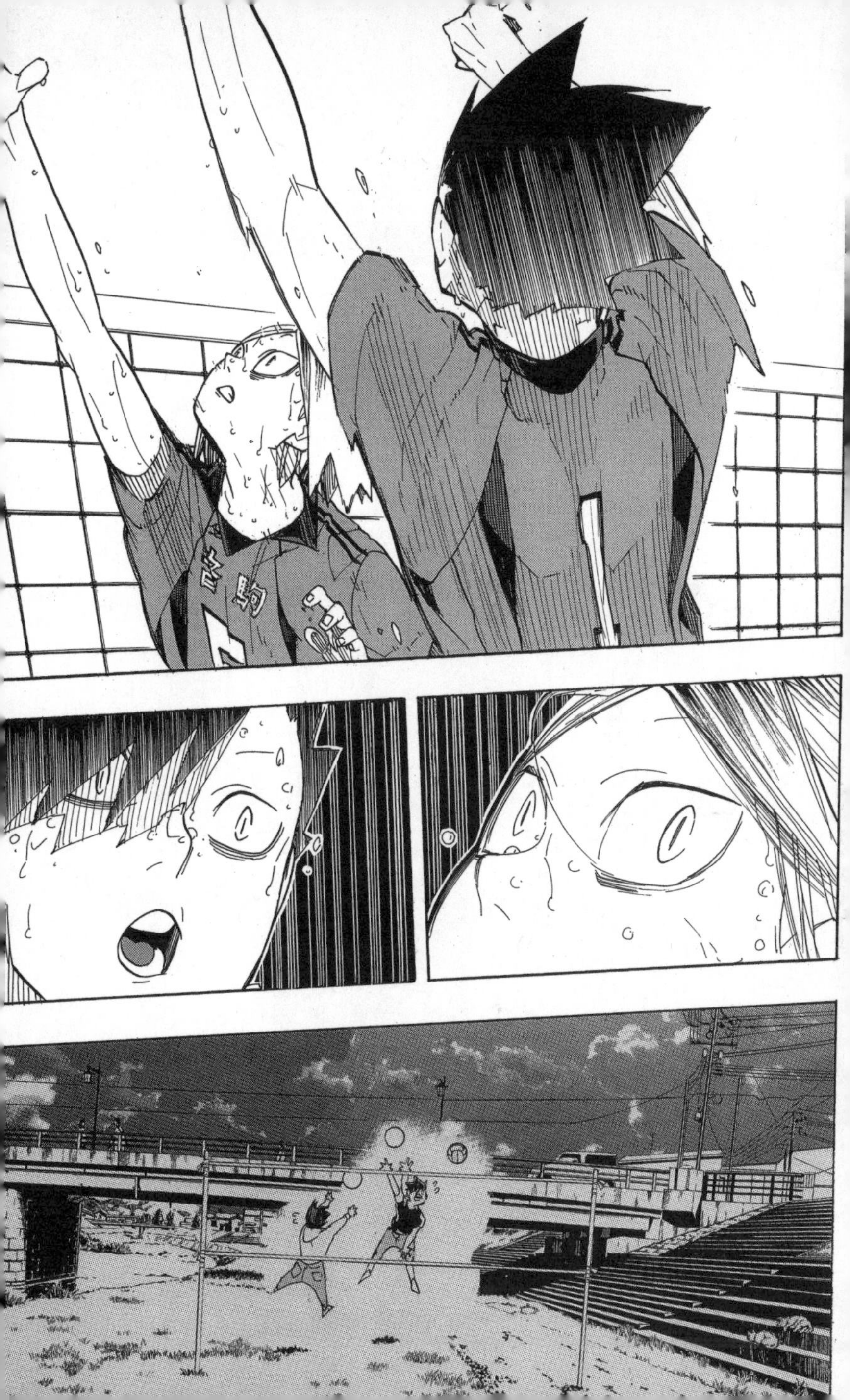

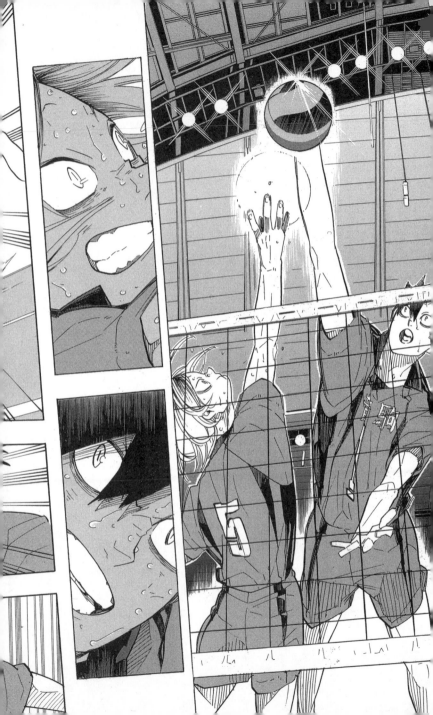

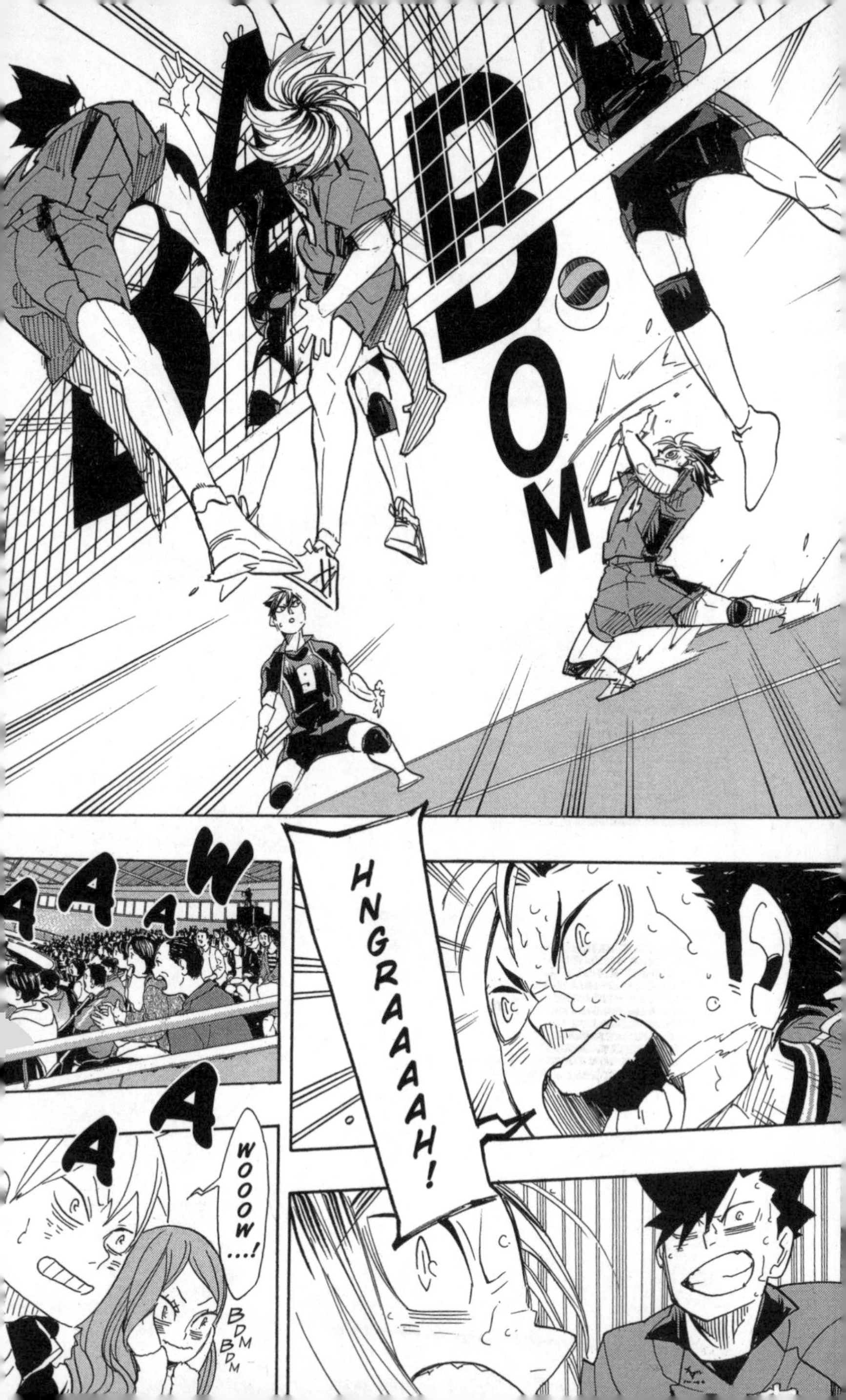
BA
BDOM
HNGRAAAAAH!
WAAAA
AA
WOOOOW...!
BDM
BDM

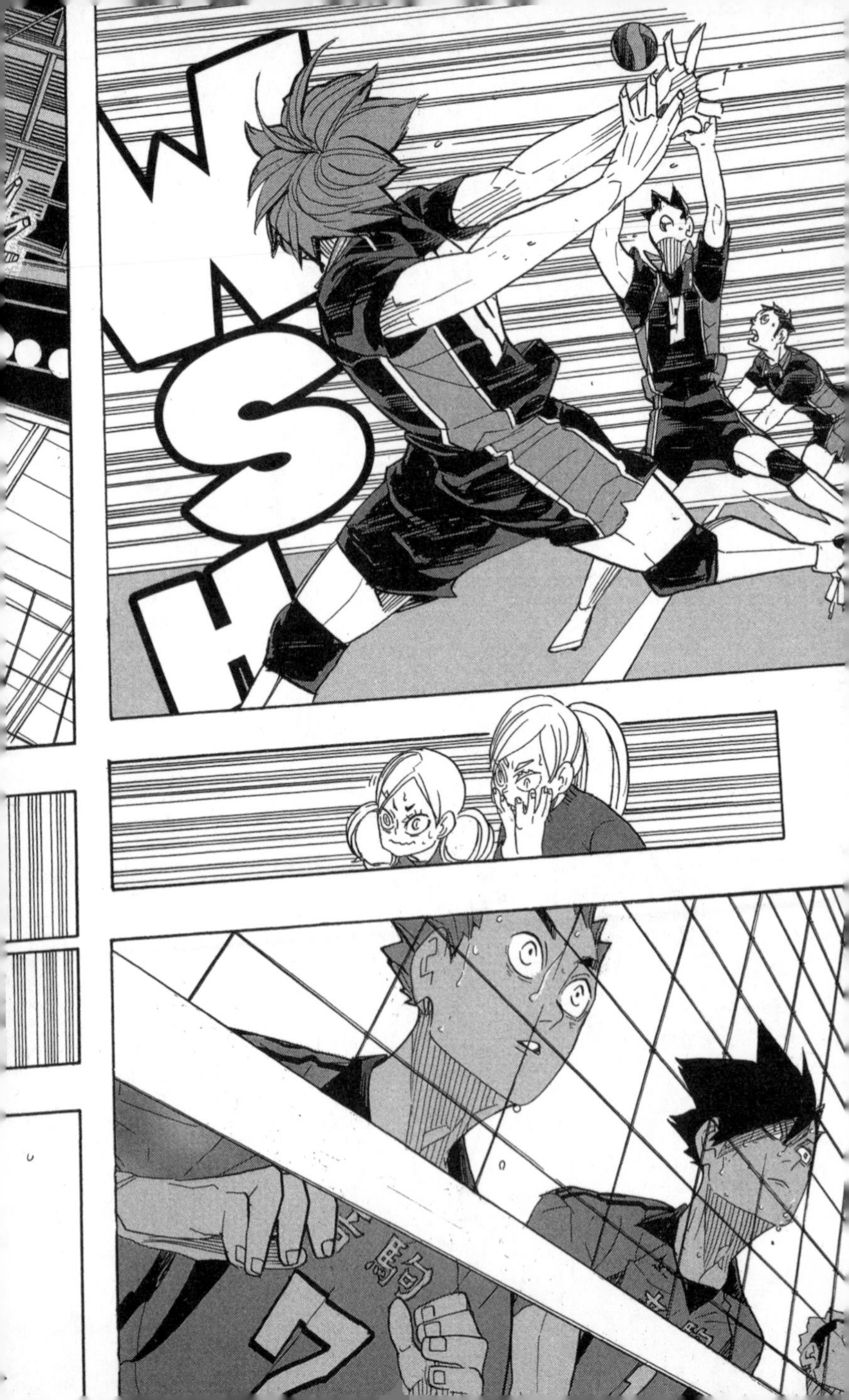

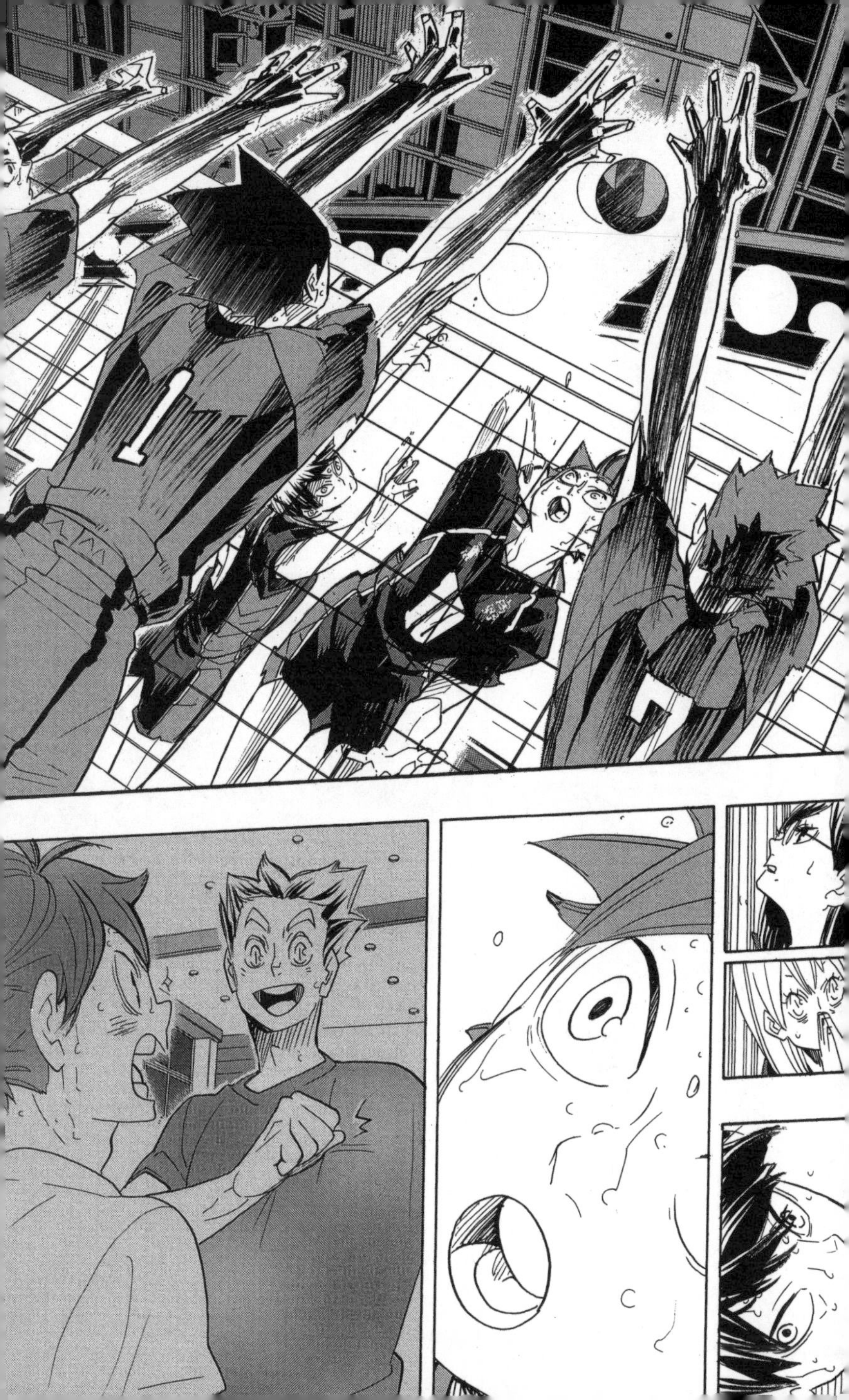

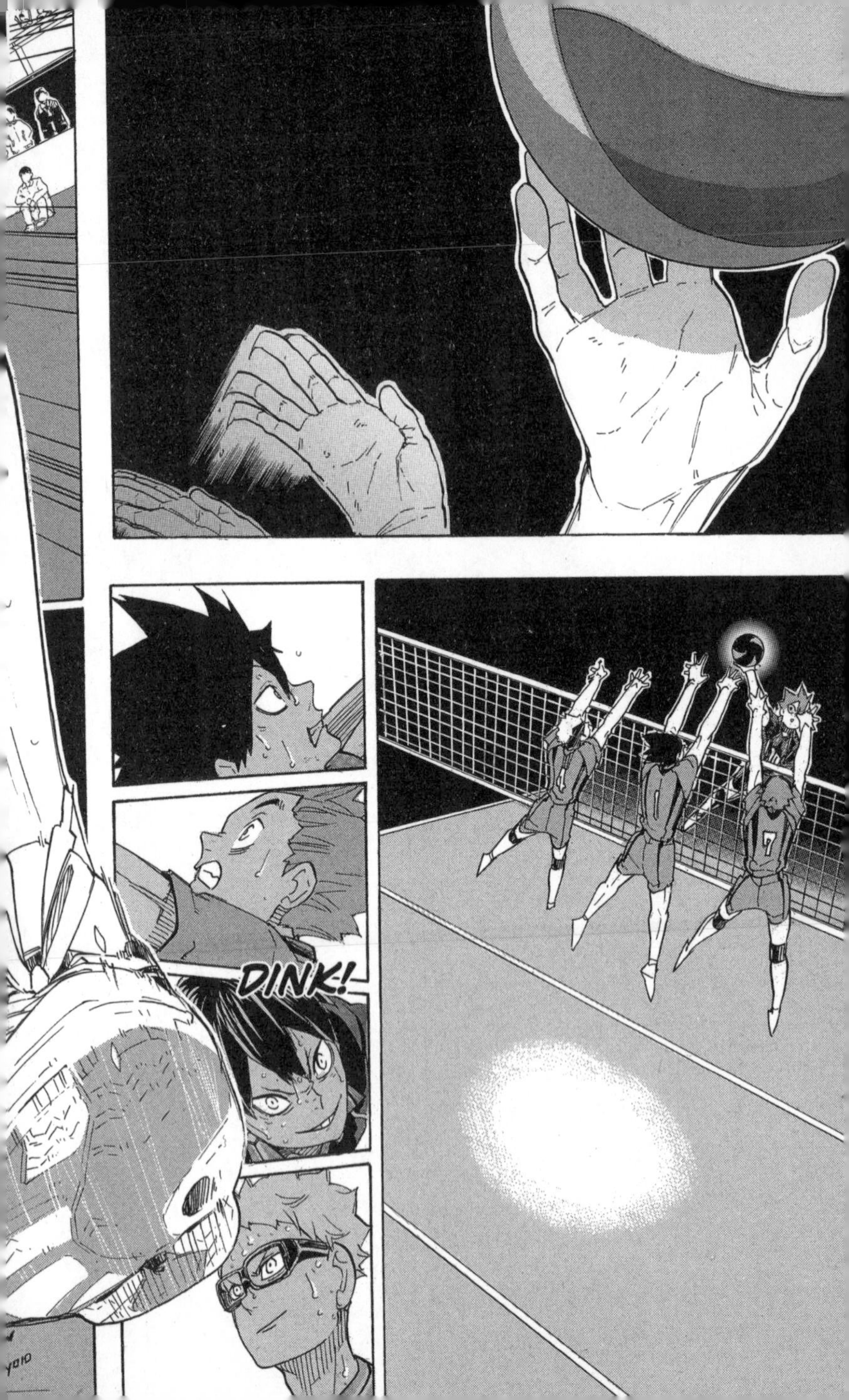
DINK!

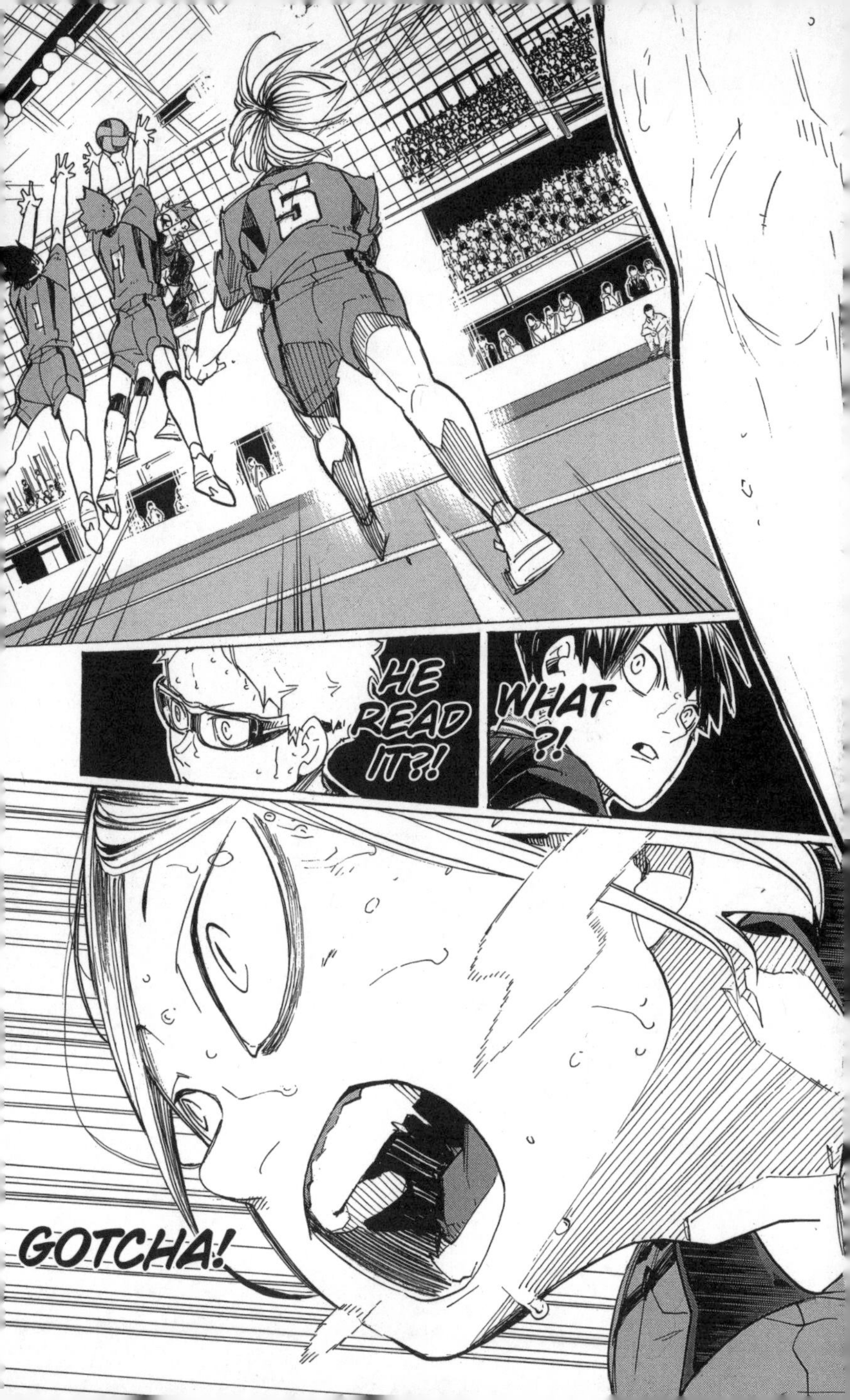
WHAT ?!
HE READ IT?!
GOTCHA!

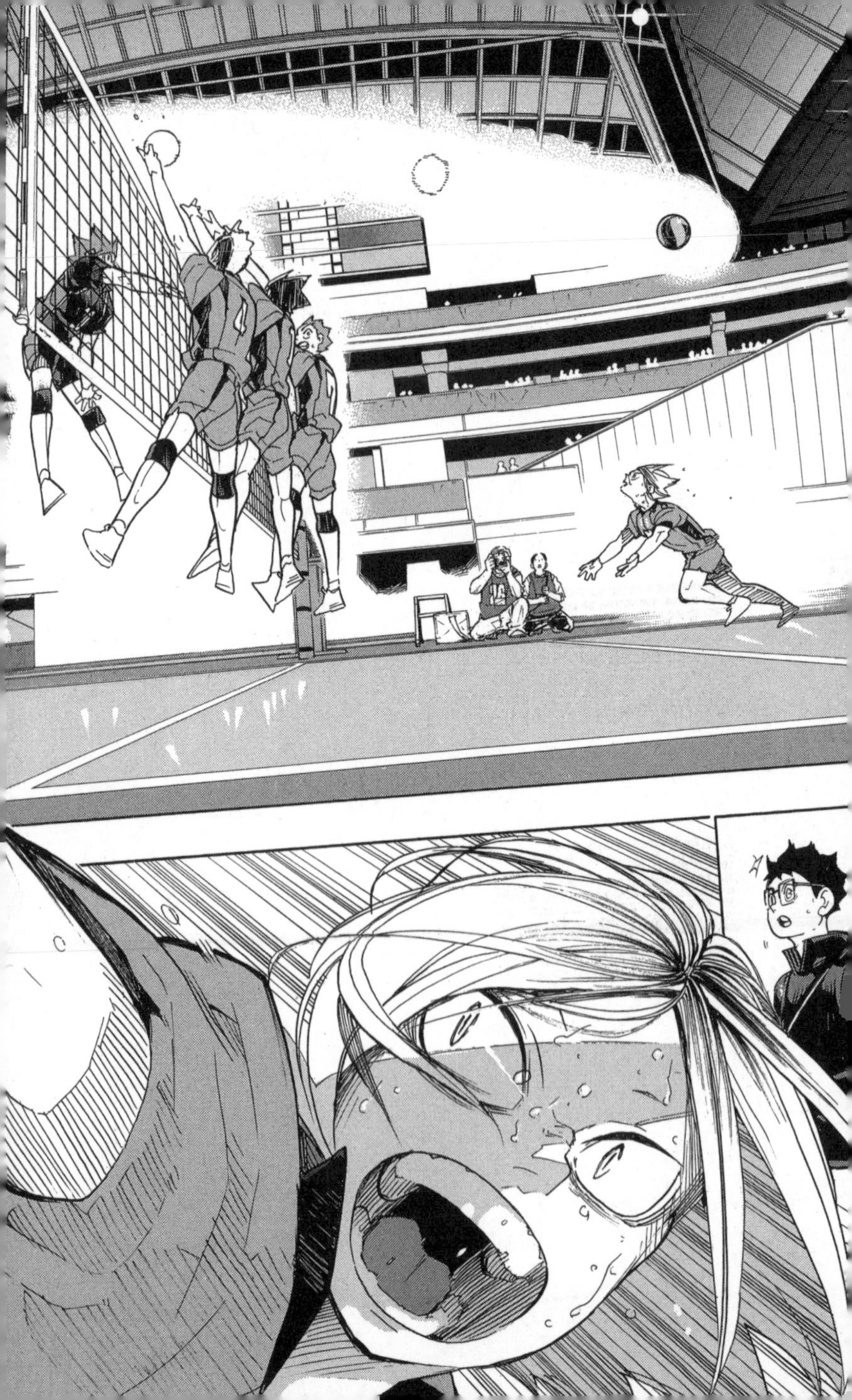

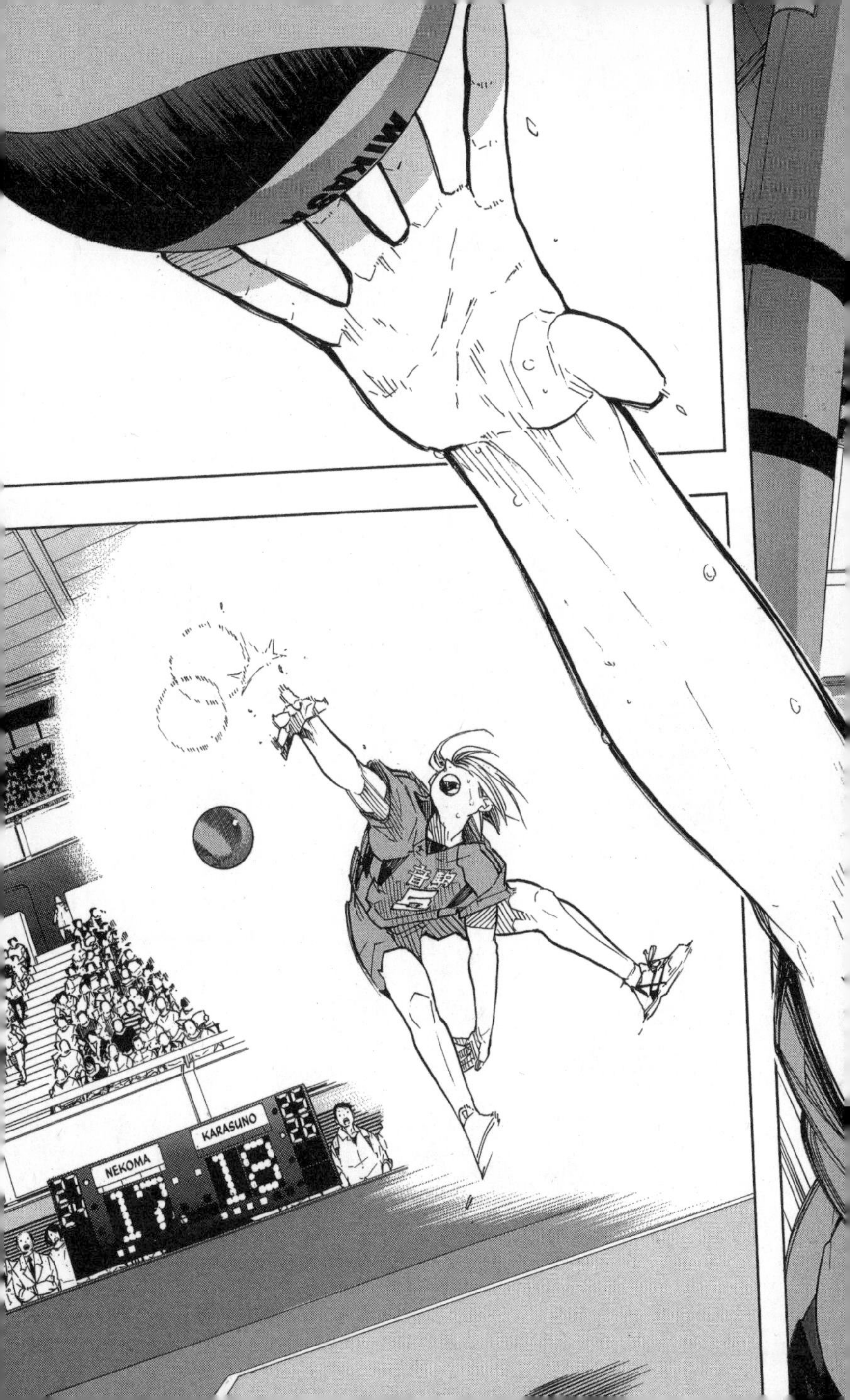
MIKASA
音駒
5
KARASUNO
NEKOMA
17
18

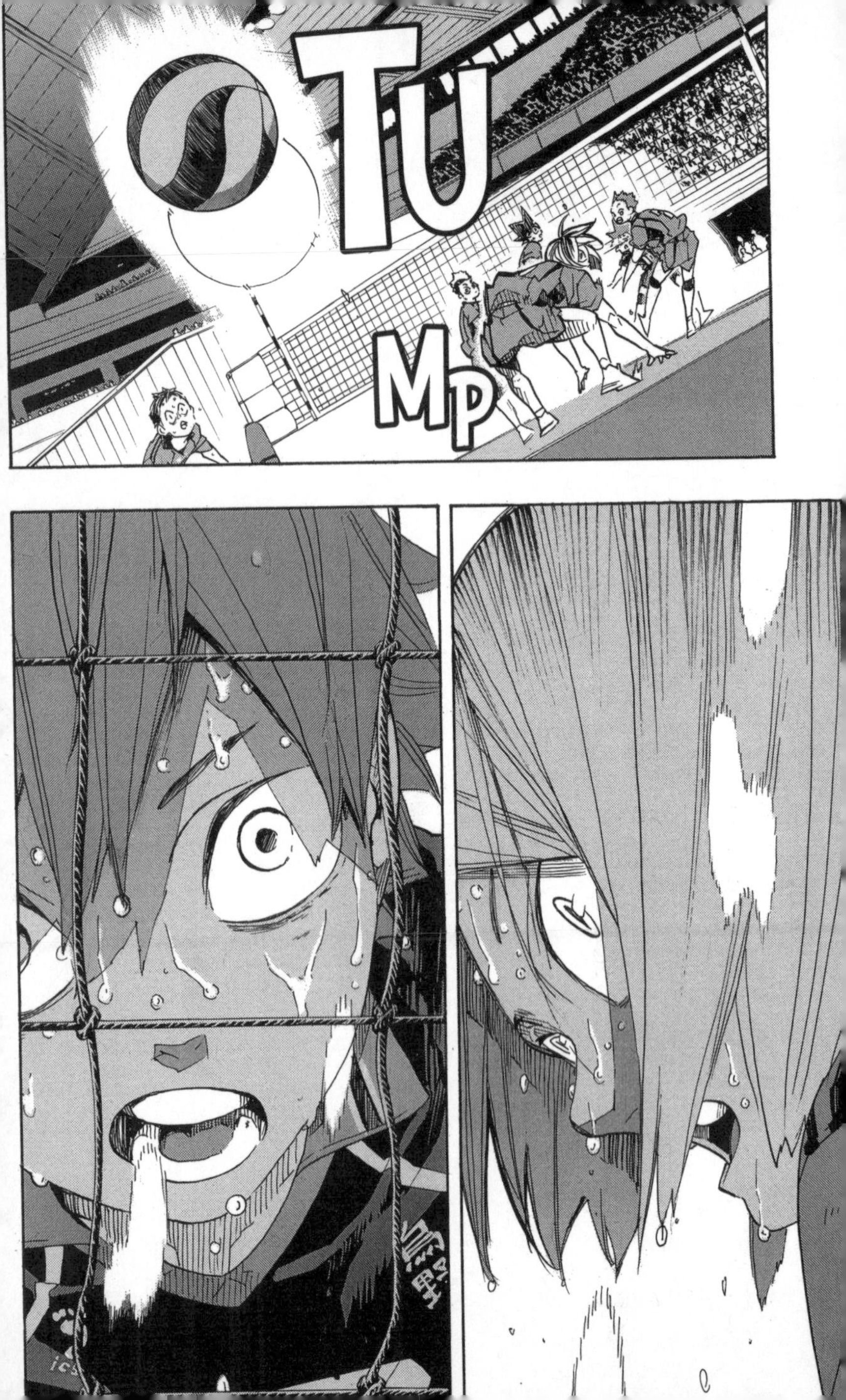
TU
MP

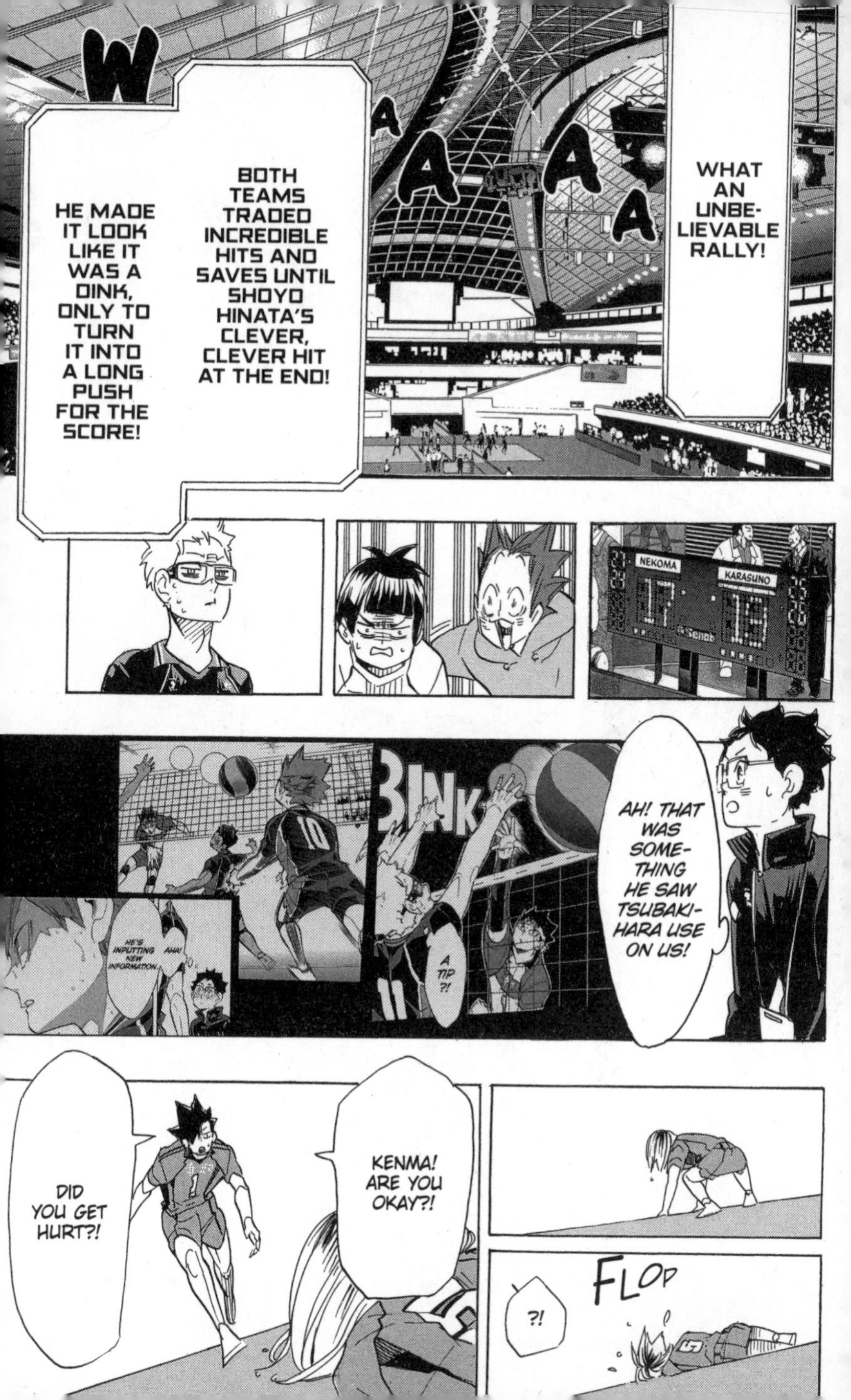
WHAT AN UNBE-LIEVABLE RALLY!
WAAAAA
BOTH TEAMS TRADED INCREDIBLE HITS AND SAVES UNTIL SHOYO HINATA'S CLEVER, CLEVER HIT AT THE END!
HE MADE IT LOOK LIKE IT WAS A DINK, ONLY TO TURN IT INTO A LONG PUSH FOR THE SCORE!
NEKOMA
KARASUNO
AH! THAT WAS SOME-THING HE SAW TSUBAKI-HARA USE ON US!
BINK
A TIP?!
AHA!
HE'S INPUTTING NEW INFORMATION...
FLOP
?!
KENMA! ARE YOU OKAY?!
DID YOU GET HURT?!

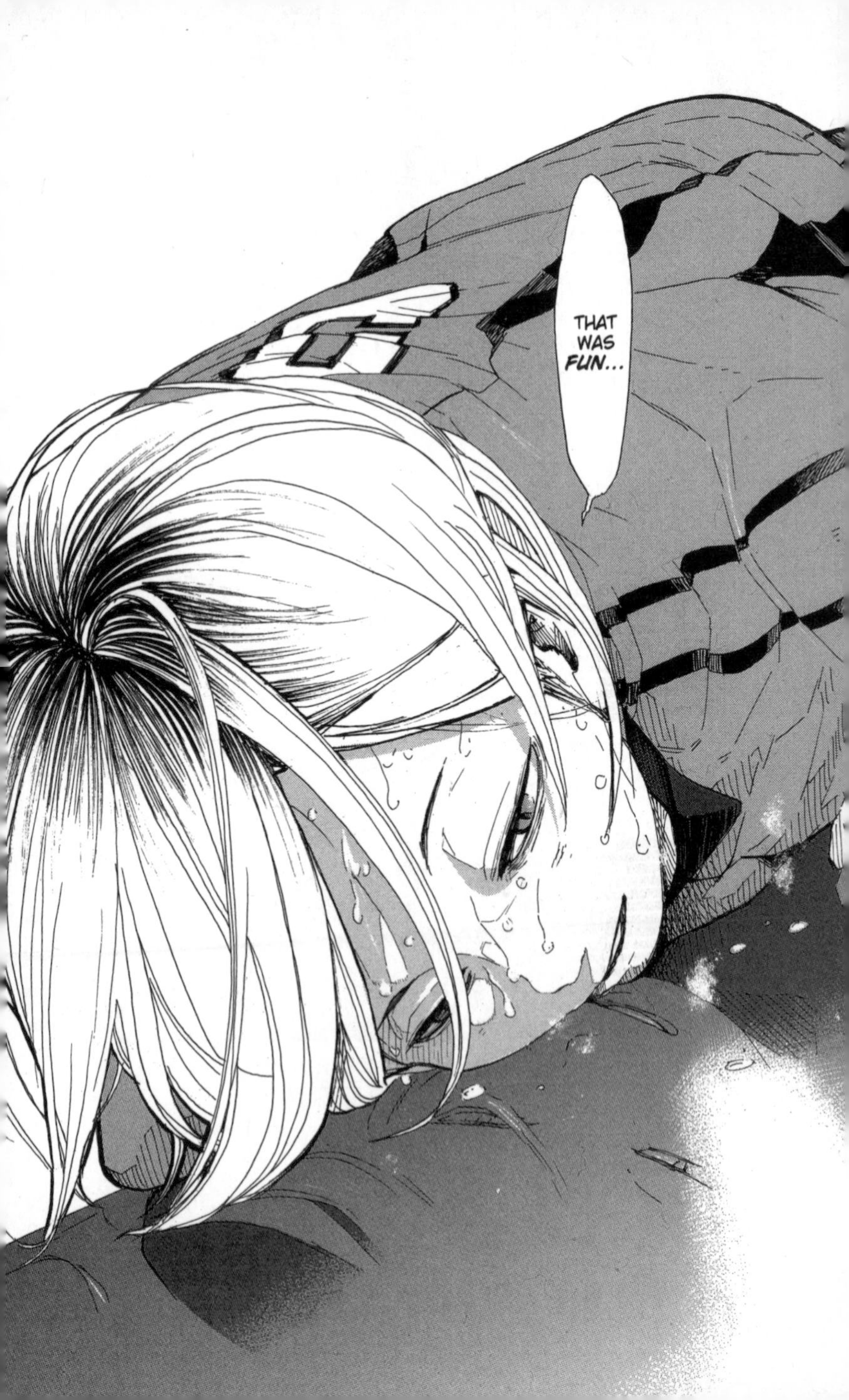
THAT WAS FUN...

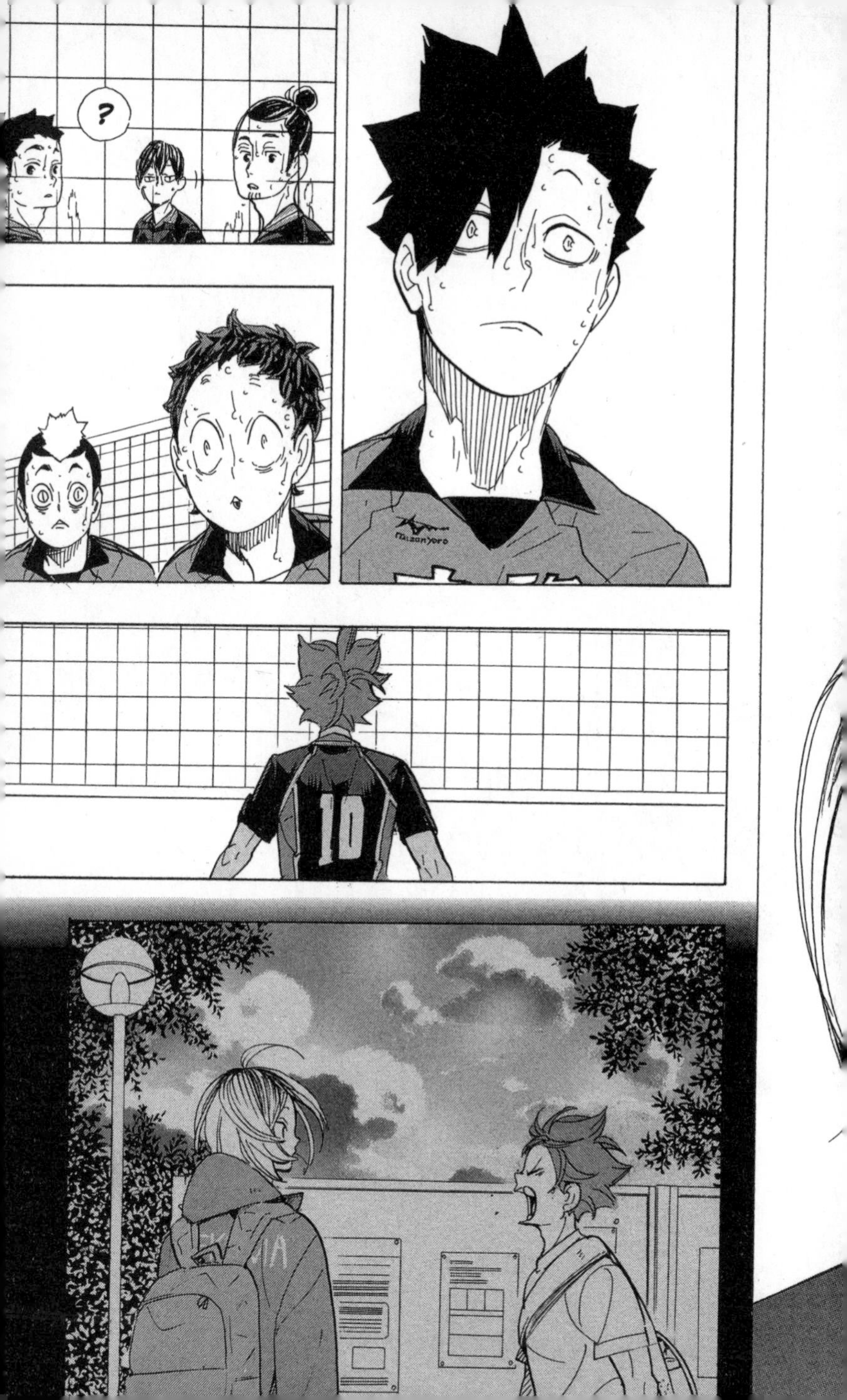
?

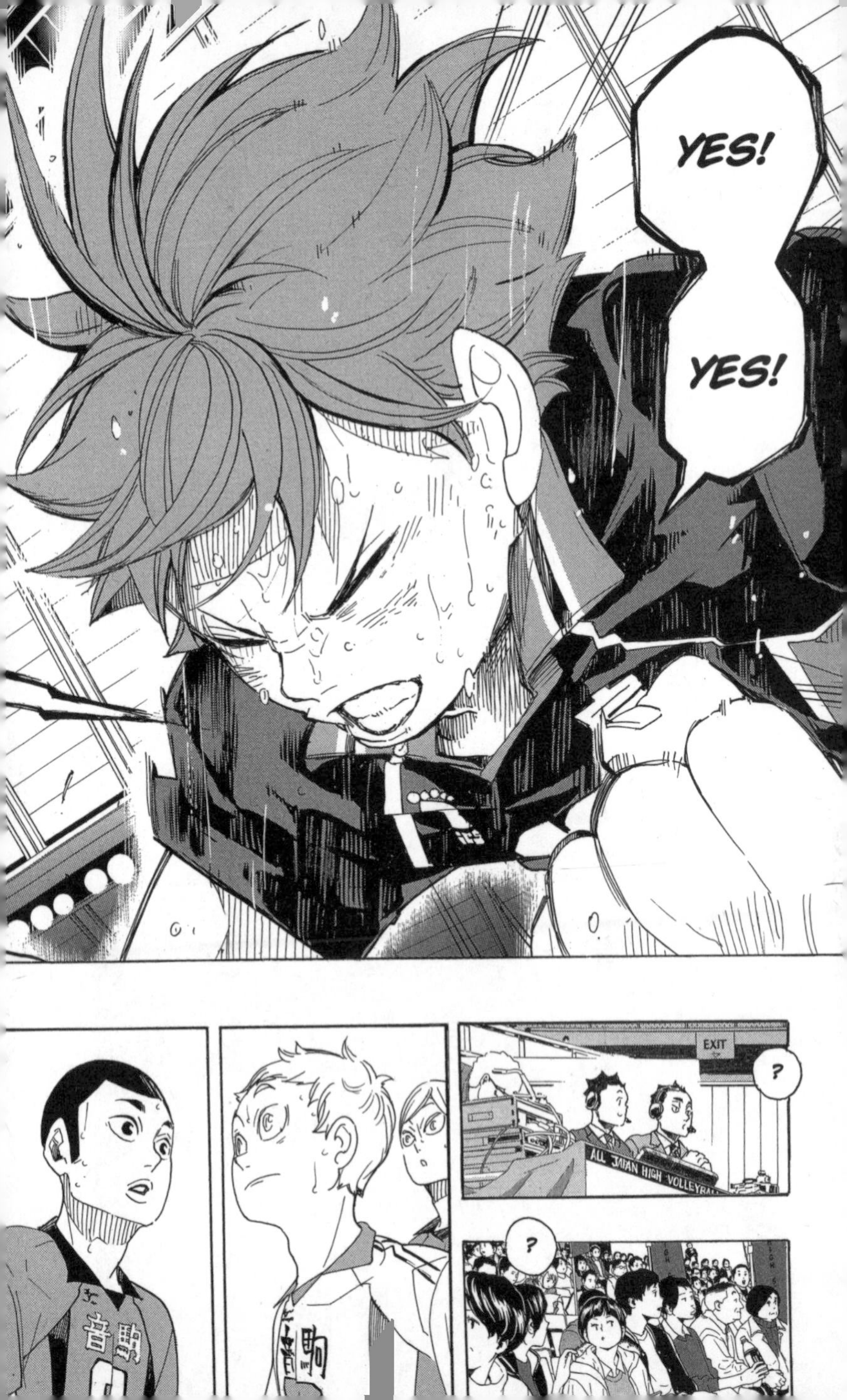
YES!
YES!
EXIT
?
?

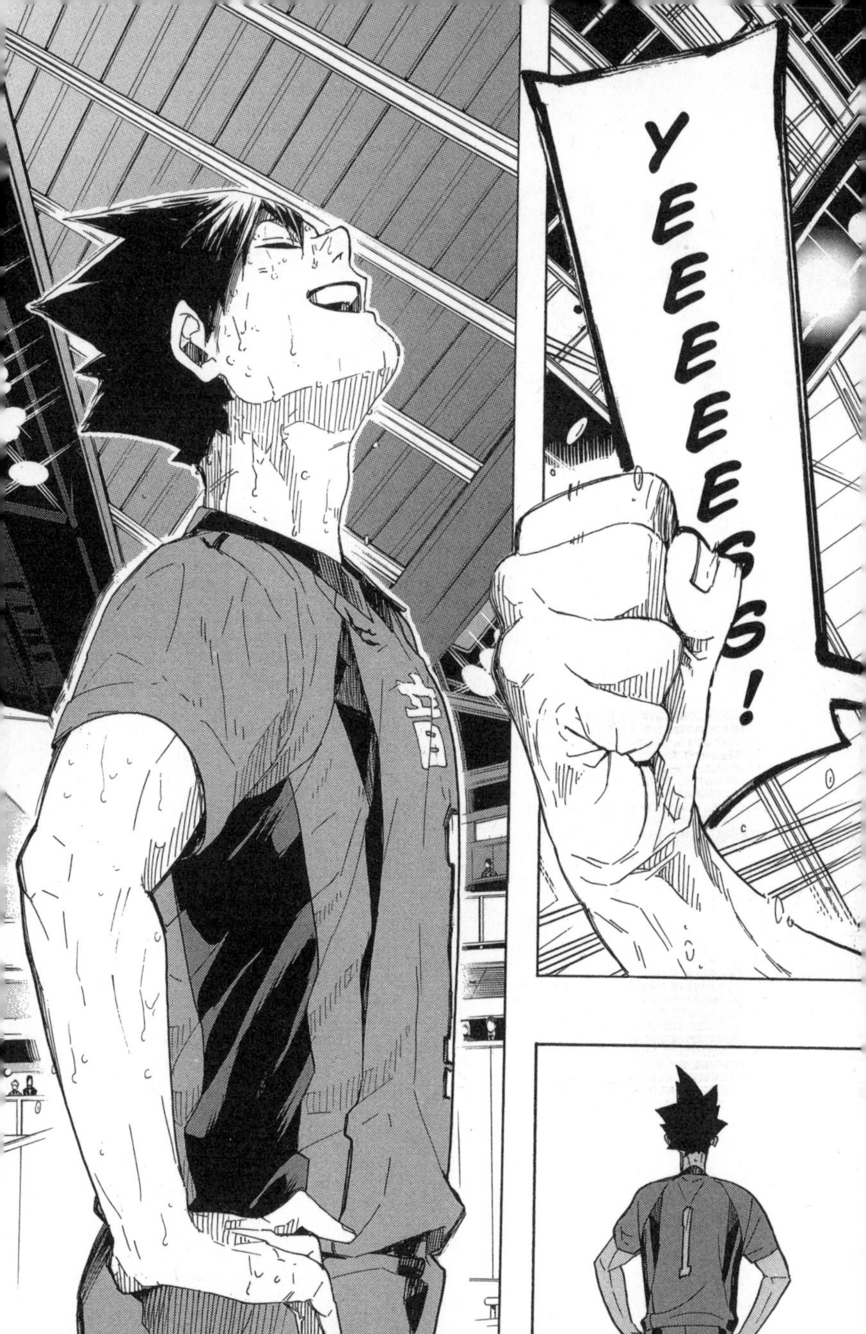
YEEEEESS!

HAIKYU!! VOL 36: I WIN (END)

EDITOR'S NOTES

The English edition of Haikyu!! maintains the honorifics used in the original Japanese version. For those of you who are new to these terms, here's a brief explanation to help with your reading experience!

When saying someone's name in Japanese, a suffix is often attached to indicate how familiar the speaker is with the person. Some are more polite and respectful, while others are endearing.

1 **-kun** is often used for young men or boys, usually someone you are familiar with.

2 **-chan** is used for young children and can be used as a term of endearment.

3 **-san** is used for someone you respect or are not close to, or to be polite.

4 **Senpai** is used for someone who is older than you or in a higher position or grade in school.

5 **Kohai** is used for someone who is younger than you or in a lower position or grade in school.

6 **Sensei** means teacher.

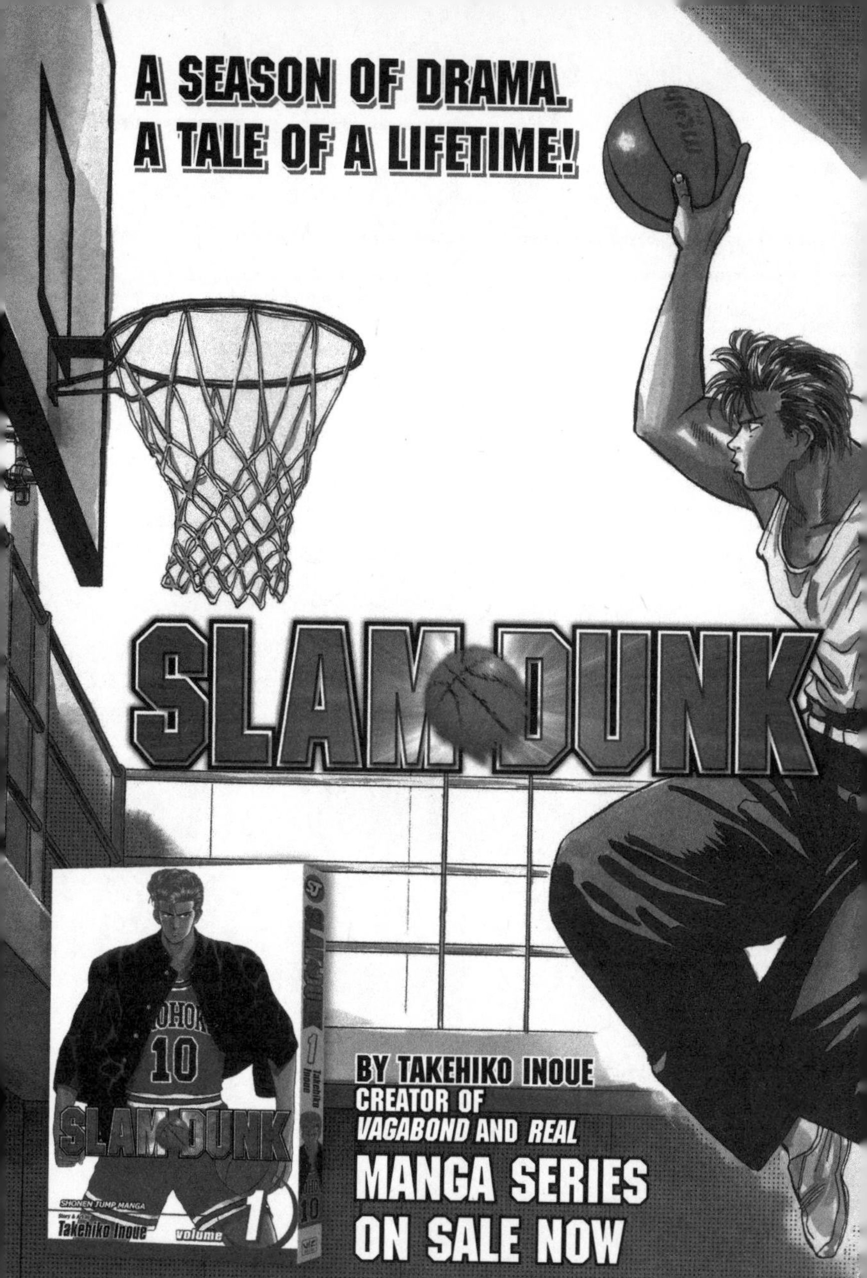
A SEASON OF DRAMA.
A TALE OF A LIFETIME!
SLAM DUNK
SLAM DUNK
SHONEN JUMP MANGA
Takehiko Inoue
volume 1
SLAM DUNK 1 Takehiko Inoue
BY TAKEHIKO INOUE
CREATOR OF
VAGABOND AND *REAL*
MANGA SERIES
ON SALE NOW

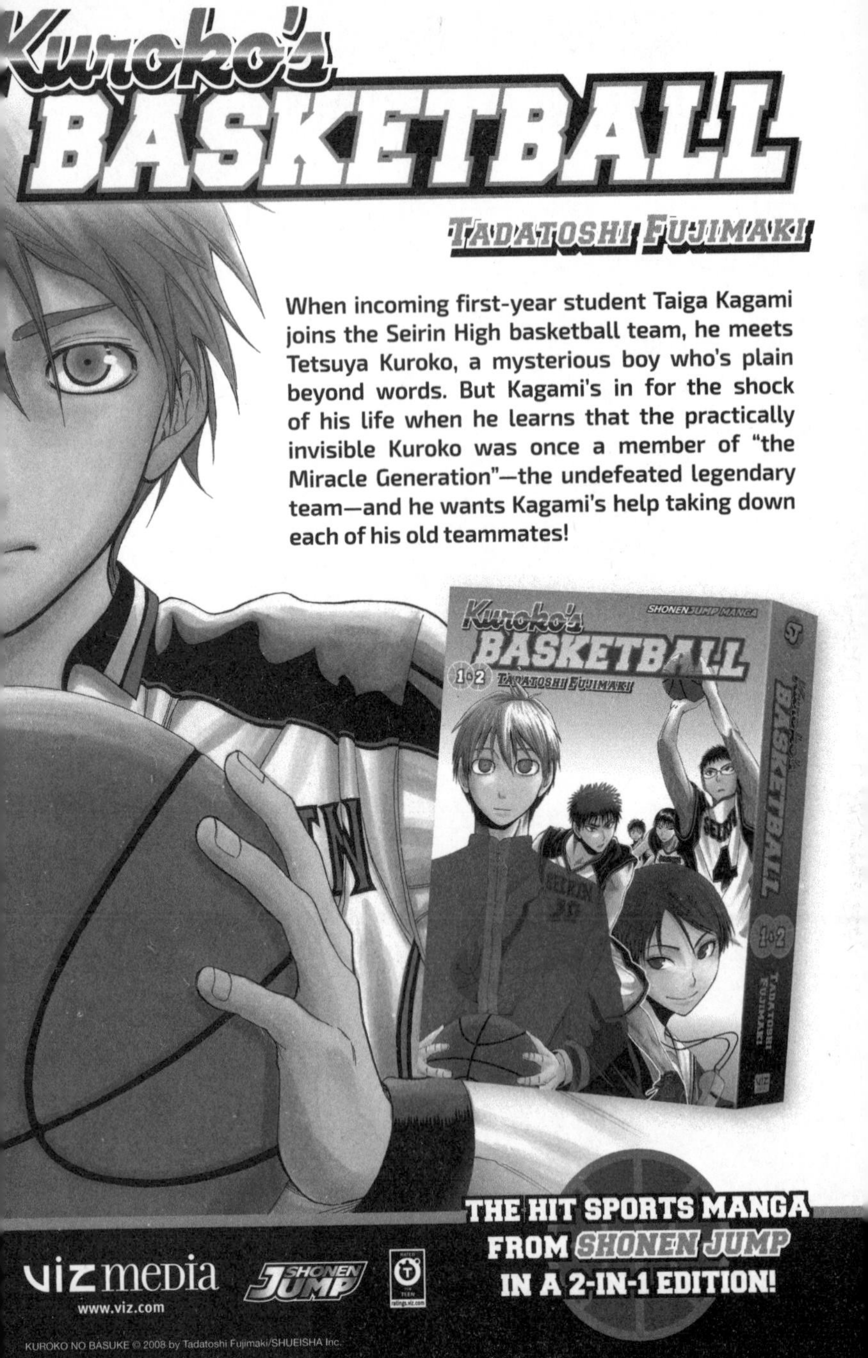
Kuroko's
BASKETBALL
TADATOSHI FUJIMAKI
When incoming first-year student Taiga Kagami joins the Seirin High basketball team, he meets Tetsuya Kuroko, a mysterious boy who's plain beyond words. But Kagami's in for the shock of his life when he learns that the practically invisible Kuroko was once a member of "the Miracle Generation"—the undefeated legendary team—and he wants Kagami's help taking down each of his old teammates!
SHONEN JUMP MANGA
Kuroko's
BASKETBALL
1•2 TADATOSHI FUJIMAKI
THE HIT SPORTS MANGA
FROM SHONEN JUMP
IN A 2-IN-1 EDITION!
viz media
www.viz.com
SHONEN JUMP
KUROKO NO BASUKE © 2008 by Tadatoshi Fujimaki/SHUEISHA Inc.

Four-time consecutive U.S. Junior tournament champ Ryoma Echizen comes to Seishun Academy to further his reign as The Prince of Tennis.

His skill is matched only by his attitude—irking some but impressing all as he leads his team to the Nationals and beyond!

テニスの王子様

THE PRINCE OF TENNIS

STORY AND ART BY **Takeshi Konomi**

IN A SAVAGE WORLD RULED BY THE PURSUIT OF THE MOST DELICIOUS FOODS, IT'S EITHER EAT OR BE EATEN!

"The most bizarrely entertaining manga out there on comic shelves. *Toriko* is a great series. If you're looking for an weirdly fun book or a fighting manga with a bizarre take, this is the story for you to read."

—ComicAttack.com

TORIKO

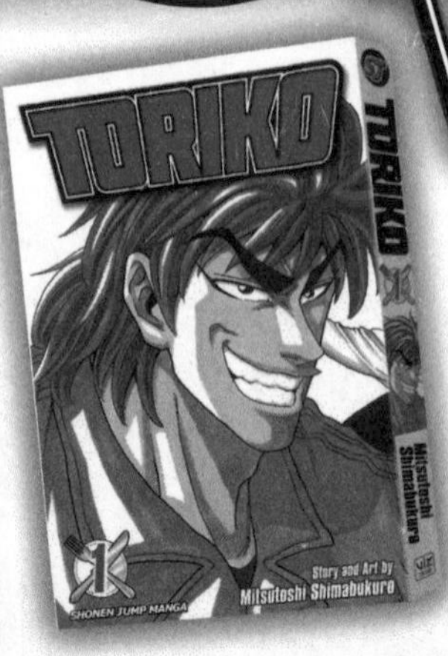

Story and Art by Mitsutoshi Shimabukuro

In an era where the world's gone crazy for increasingly bizarre gourmet foods, only Gourmet Hunter Toriko can hunt down the ferocious ingredients that supply the world's best restaurants. Join Toriko as he tracks and defeats the tastiest and most dangerous animals with his bare hands.

www.shonenjump.com   www.viz.com

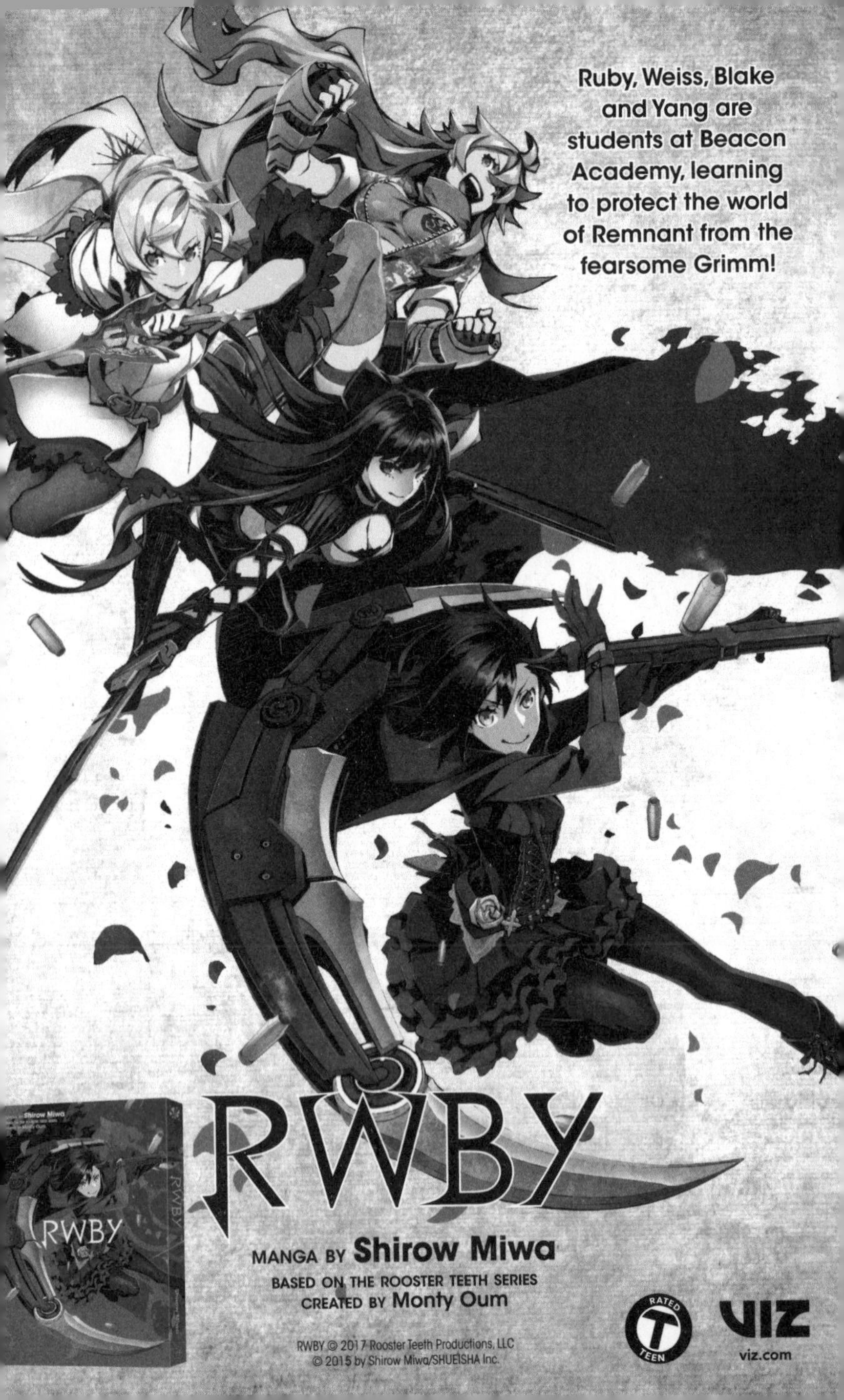
Ruby, Weiss, Blake and Yang are students at Beacon Academy, learning to protect the world of Remnant from the fearsome Grimm!
RWBY
MANGA BY Shirow Miwa
BASED ON THE ROOSTER TEETH SERIES
CREATED BY Monty Oum
RWBY © 2017 Rooster Teeth Productions, LLC
© 2015 by Shirow Miwa/SHUEISHA Inc.
RATED T TEEN
VIZ
viz.com